The Presidency in a Separated System

The Presidency in a Separated System

CHARLES O. JONES

The Brookings Institution
WASHINGTON, D.C.

Copyright © 1994 by
THE BROOKINGS INSTITUTION
1775 Massachusetts Avenue, N.W., Washington, D.C. 20036

Library of Congress Cataloging-in-Publication data:

Jones, Charles O.
 The presidency in a separated system / Charles O. Jones.
  p. cm.
 Includes bibliographical references and index.
 ISBN 0-8157-4710-1 (alk. paper) — ISBN 0-8157-4709-8
(pbk. : alk. paper)
  1. Presidents—United States—History—20th century.
 2. Separation of powers—United States. 3. United States—
Politics and government—20th century. I. Title.
JK516.J66 1994
320.473—dc20   93-51513
                   CIP

9 8 7 6 5 4 3

Set in Times Roman

Composition by Harlowe Typography, Inc.
Cottage City, Maryland

Printed by R.R. Donnelley and Sons Co.
Harrisonburg, Virginia

To
Samuel C. Patterson

Foreword

POPULAR interpretations of American government tend to center on the presidency. Successes and failures are often attributed to presidents themselves. In fact, political analysts typically classify the U.S. system as presidential. But, though the White House does stand as a powerful symbol of government, the United States has a separated system intentionally designed to distribute power, not concentrate it.

Charles O. Jones explains that focusing exclusively on the presidency can lead to a seriously distorted picture of how the national government works. The role of the president varies widely, depending on available resources, advantages, and strategic position. Public and media expectations often far exceed the president's personal, political, institutional, or constitutional capacities for achievement. Jones explores the differences among post–World War II presidents, how they have found their place in the permanent government, and the varying strategies available to them for governing.

The book shows how a separated system of government works under the circumstances created by the Constitution and encouraged by a two-party system. Rejecting the popular presidency-centered, responsible-party perspective, Jones proposes a view of the U.S. system that, among other features, accepts divided government as a legitimate, even productive, form of decisionmaking. He explores the organizational challenges facing presidents, their public standing and what it means, presidential agendas and mandates, and lawmaking (including a detailed examination of twenty-eight important enactments during the postwar era). He concludes with a number of lessons for presidents and advice oriented toward making the separated system work better.

Charles O. Jones is the Douglas Dillon Visiting Fellow at Brookings and is also Glenn B. and Cleone Orr Hawkins Professor of Political Science at the University of Wisconsin–Madison. He wishes to acknowledge the helpful services provided by so many of the Brookings Institution staff during his several visits, particularly Judith L. Chaney, Renuka D. Deonarain, Ingeborg K. Lockwood, Sandra Z. Riegler, Susan A. Stewart, Eloise C. Stinger, and Susan Thompson. Nancy D. Davidson edited the manuscript, providing needed improvements in organization and style. Alison M. Rimsky verified the manuscript for factual accuracy; Susan L. Woollen prepared it for type-setting; and Jean Moody prepared the index.

The author acknowledges with gratitude the financial support for this study. The Florence & John Schumann Foundation provided a grant to the Brookings Institution in support of the project. Jones also relied on the research funds of the Robert Kent Gooch Chair in Government and Foreign Affairs, University of Virginia, and the Glenn B. and Cleone Orr Hawkins Chair in Political Science, University of Wisconsin–Madison, as well as a grant from the University of Wisconsin Graduate School. Funds from the latter two sources were used to support graduate student assistants. Finally, the author is eager to commend the supportive environments of the Brookings Institution; the Department of Political Science, University of Wisconsin–Madison; and North Deer Run Court, Cross Plains, Wisconsin.

The views in this book are solely those of the author and should not be ascribed to the persons or organizations acknowledged above, or to the trustees, officers, or other staff members of the Brookings Institution.

BRUCE K. MACLAURY
President

March 1994
Washington, D.C.

Author's Preface

In mid-July 1985 I was working at the Gerald R. Ford Library in Ann Arbor, Michigan, sorting through documents related to the major reorganization of federal energy agencies before and after the oil embargo by the Organization of Petroleum Exporting Countries. In April 1973 the Nixon administration had proposed the creation of a Federal Energy Administration, an Energy Research and Development Administration (ERDA), and a Department of Energy and Natural Resources. As I tracked the White House memos relating to ERDA that had been written in the summer and fall of 1974, two observations occurred to me: the work on ERDA took place during an institutional crisis of historic proportions, and virtually no trace of this unprecedented crisis appeared in the communications I was reviewing. The creation of ERDA was progressing at a level substantially below that of presidential goings and comings. The relevant participants in the complex energy policy network were hard at work building support for the proposal. The paperwork involved surfaced only occasionally in the Oval Office, as evidenced by presidential initials. While news stories were being written about the virtual collapse of the government, ERDA was approved by Congress and signed into law by President Gerald Ford on October 11, 1974. The presidency, it seems, is not the government.

I vowed at that time to correct what I perceived to be a common misunderstanding about the role of the president in the policy process. I began that endeavor by writing a paper exploring the role of presidents in agenda setting, seeking to identify how presidents varied in their capacities to manage the continuing agenda and to supervise policy alternatives. At a conference at Brown University, the paper played to mixed reviews; in truth, the reactions were more negative than positive and more resistant to an altered interpretation than I had anticipated. For me, however, it was an initial effort in exploring the significant differences among presidents' personal, political, institutional, and policy strengths for governing.

In 1987 I proposed to Paul E. Peterson, then director of the Governmental Studies program at Brookings, that I write a book for Brookings on the role of the president in the policy process. Brookings accepted my proposal. I wrote to Peterson, "I want to understand much better than I do what it is that the White House contributes to policy development and approval. And I want to specify some of the more important conditions associated with what I assume to be variable policy functions and performance." Still motivated by my observations while working with the Ford White House files, I initially planned to study how weak or weakened presidents perform in office. Thus my focus at first was on so-called lame-duck presidents and those, like Ford, who had very limited resources. At this early stage, the study was called "Governing When It's Over." Ultimately I found that it was necessary to compare all presidents in the post–World War II period. It was difficult to define weakness apart from strength. Further, it was apparent that every president faced the problem of "governing when it's over," of seeking a place in the permanent government. This understanding essentially brought me back to where I started: the continuity of governing in a separated system and the variable role of the president.

I do not presume in this book to treat all dimensions of presidential power. I concentrate on those features I know best. In policy terms, that means focusing more on domestic than foreign policy. I expect that a portrayal of post–World War II presidents based primarily on foreign policy would vary somewhat from that produced here (though that portrayal would have to reflect the greater role played by the contemporary Congress in foreign and national security issues). In institutional terms, I focus primarily on presidential-congressional relations. Obviously the president's interactions with the bureaucracy and the courts are of equal interest in a fuller understanding of the role of the president in governing. I would welcome a study of how postwar presidents have oriented themselves to the bureaucracy. If anything, the separateness of the presidential and executive branches is more obscure and misunderstood than that between the president and Congress.

In this book I often challenge the interpretations of analysts who rely on the criteria of a presidency-centered, responsible-party perspective in evaluating the national political system. For the most part, these are persons judged to be substantially more influential than political scientists: journalists, bureau chiefs, editors, political activists and reformers, Washington insiders, even presidents and their staffs. It is not clear why they cling to this perspective in light of the historical fact and daily reminders of separationism as the central feature of our government. I muse about that curiosity in chapter 8. It suffices here to speculate that people commonly reach for simple explanations in the face of complex phenomena. Because the American way of governing is the most intricate ever devised, a perspective that promises code-like explanations is attractive. When political scientists or historians advise that the complex cannot be made simple by proclamation, a common response is that the system should be reformed to make it more "responsible." However, a separated system is a bulwark against major change, as the history of reform efforts demonstrates. Political and institutional reformers are therefore typically frustrated even when they manage to enact change, mostly because their failure to comprehend fully the nature of the system leaves them at a strategic disadvantage in designing and implementing effective reform. Meanwhile, along the way there is adaptation as the separated system surveys and acts on social and political developments. Exactly how that adaptation takes place is worth studying since it would reveal the workings of the American style and form of governing.

I wish to acknowledge my substantial debts in the preparation of this book. They are identified here in no order of importance since all were vital to the design and execution of the research. Several graduate students provided essential research tasks, most notably Katie Dunn Tenpas and John B. Bader. Few scholars have been better served. I am very grateful for their efforts as well as the good humor with which they carried out any number of tedious tasks. Others who assisted at different stages were Joanne Dunkelman, Farhad Malekafzali, and Rickey Vallier.

In the development of the project itself, I conducted a number of conversations and interviews with presidential and congressional scholars, journalists, politicians and former public officials, and various "think tankers" who have had experience in government. These exchanges were of inestimable value in providing context and conceptual direction. Included among the scholars were Bruce Buchanan, Colin Campbell, Louis Fisher, Erwin C. Hargrove, Jr., Anthony King, Paul C. Light, Michael J. Malbin, Richard E. Neustadt, Roger G. Noll, Mark A. Peterson, James P. Pfiffner, Bert A. Rockman, and Stephen G. Wayne. As with all my research efforts, I consulted frequently with my friend of forty-five years, Samuel C. Patterson, to whom the book is dedicated. The journalists included Dom Bonafede, Richard Cohen, Janet Hook, Albert Hunt, Dick Kirschten, Neil MacNeil, Cokie Roberts, Steven Roberts, Gerald Seib, and Juan Williams.

The Brookings Institution more than met my need to talk with scholars with experience in government. I had extensive, recorded conversations with Warren I. Cikins, Stephen Hess, Sidney L. Jones, Lawrence J. Korb, Bradley A. Patterson, Joseph A. Pechman, A. James Reichley, Robert D. Reischauer, Charles L. Schultze, James L. Sundquist, and Joshua M. Wiener. I profited as well from less formal, but frequent, discussions with Robert A. Katzmann, Thomas E. Mann, Pietro S. Nivola, and R. Kent Weaver. Other recorded interviews were held with Robert E. Hunter, Suzanne R. Garment, Norman J. Ornstein, and Isabel V. Sawhill.

Conversations and formal interviews were also conducted with several former and present public officials. The purpose was to explore the variable role of the president in the national policy system with persons known to be reflective on such issues. Included were Charles Brain, Lawrence Eagleburger, Stuart Eizenstat, Bill Frenzel, Steven Hofman, Michael Jackson, Nicholas A. Masters, Philip Odeen, Harold Seidman, Charles Whalen, and Donald Wolfensberger. Some of these talks were tape recorded, and Vera M. Jones transcribed most of the taped interviews. I also had the privilege of attending the seminars for new members of the 101st, 102d, and 103d Congresses in Williamsburg, Virginia, where many of the issues treated in this book were discussed.

Some years ago, Stephen Hess conducted several interviews with public officials on subjects of relevance to this study. He graciously allowed me to listen to these tape-recorded sessions. Mark Rozell also permitted me to read interviews he conducted with officials of the Ford White House. The oral history interviews at the Lyndon Baines Johnson Presidential Library were an immensely useful source for background material on many post–World War II presidencies, and I am grateful for the cooperation of the library staff in making the relevant interviews available for my use.

A number of persons who know a great deal about the subject of this book kindly read and evaluated the manuscript. An initial set of readers included Richard F. Fenno, Jr., Anthony King, and Bert A. Rockman. Their comments were invaluable in the first round of revisions. The second set of readers included Paul C. Light, Richard E. Neustadt, and Nelson W. Polsby. Thomas E. Mann, director of the Governmental Studies program, provided comments along the way and then offered an overview of the critiques as well as suggestions from his own reading of the manuscript. Leon D. Epstein read the manuscript in its final form. I wish to express my appreciation for the efforts of these scholars and friends. Their careful reading resulted in needed improvements in what is written here and how it is presented.

Contents

Figures

The Presidency in a Separated System

CHAPTER ONE

Perspectives on the Presidency

THE PRESIDENT is not the presidency. The presidency is not the government. Ours is not a presidential system.

I begin with these starkly negative themes as partial correctives to the more popular interpretations of the United States government as presidency-centered. Presidents themselves learn these refrains on the job, if they do not know them before. President Lyndon B. Johnson, who had impressive political advantages during the early years of his administration, reflected later on what was required to realize the potentialities of the office:

> Every President has to establish with the various sectors of the country what I call "the right to govern." Just being elected to the office does not guarantee him that right. Every President has to inspire the confidence of the people. Every President has to become a leader, and to be a leader he must attract people who are willing to follow him. Every President has to develop a moral underpinning to his power, or he soon discovers that he has no power at all.[1]

To exercise influence, presidents must learn the setting within which it has bearing. President-elect Bill Clinton recognized the complexities of translating campaign promises into a legislative program during a news conference shortly after his election in 1992:

> It's all very well to say you want an investment tax credit, and quite another thing to make the 15 decisions that have to be made to shape the exact bill you want.
> It's all very well to say . . . that the working poor in this country . . . should be lifted out of poverty by increasing the refundable income tax credit for the working poor, and another thing to answer the five or six questions that define how you get that done.[2]

For presidents, new or experienced, to recognize the limitations of office is commendable. Convincing others to do so is a challenge. Presidents be-

1

come convenient labels for marking historical time: the Johnson years, the Nixon years, the Reagan years. Media coverage naturally focuses more on the president: there is just one at a time, executive organization is oriented in pyramidal fashion toward the Oval Office, Congress is too diffuse an institution to report on as such, and the Supreme Court leads primarily by indirection. Public interest, too, is directed toward the White House as a symbol of the government. As a result, expectations of a president often far exceed the individual's personal, political, institutional, or constitutional capacities for achievement. Performance seldom matches promise. Presidents who understand how it all works resist the inflated image of power born of high-stakes elections and seek to lower expectations. Politically savvy presidents know instinctively that it is precisely at the moment of great achievement that they must prepare themselves for the setback that will surely follow.

Focusing exclusively on the presidency can lead to a seriously distorted picture of how the national government does its work. The plain fact is that the United States does not have a presidential system. It has a *separated* system.[3] It is odd that it is so commonly thought of as otherwise since schoolchildren learn about the separation of powers and checks and balances. As the author of *Federalist* 51 wrote, "Ambition must be made to counteract ambition." No one, least of all presidents, the Founders reasoned, can be entrusted with excessive authority. Human nature, being what it is, requires "auxiliary precautions" in the form of competing legitimacies.

The acceptance that this is a separated, not a presidential, system, prepares one to appraise how politics works, not to be simply reproachful and reformist. Thus, for example, divided (or split-party) government is accepted as a potential or even likely outcome of a separated system, rooted as it is in the separation of elections. Failure to acknowledge the authenticity of the split-party condition leaves one with little to study and much to reform in the post–World War II period, when the government has been divided more than 60 percent of the time.

Simply put, the role of the president in this separated system of governing varies substantially, depending on his resources, advantages, and strategic position.[4] My strong interest is in how presidents place themselves in an ongoing government and are fitted in by other participants, notably those on Capitol Hill. The central purpose of this book is to explore these "fittings." In pursuing this interest, I have found little value in the presidency-centered, party government perspective, as I will explain below. As a substitute, I propose a separationist, diffused-responsibility perspective that I find more suited to the constitutional, institutional, political, and policy conditions associated with the American system of governing. First, however, I offer dramatic cases of how a president's role can change during his term in office, two stories of the highs and lows of serving in the White House.

Landslides and Presidential Power

Surely if any president is to command the government, it will be one who wins so overwhelmingly that no one in Washington can deny his legitimacy for setting and clearing the agenda. Two postwar presidents illustrate that electoral achievement of the highest order is no protection against changing conditions. Lyndon B. Johnson and Richard M. Nixon triumphed at the polls. Both then suffered a dramatic loss in their capacity to lead. Johnson decided not to seek reelection; Nixon resigned in disgrace.

Election does not guarantee power in the American political system. Rather it legitimizes the effort of a president to lead, "to establish . . . the right to govern," in President Johnson's words. Leadership itself depends on opportunity, capability, and resources. By intent, the U.S. government works within a set of limits designed to prevent it from working too well. There is substantial evidence that Americans continue to support the principles of mixed representation, separation of institutions, and distribution of power, with all the checks and balances that follow. These are difficult principles to export or even to explain abroad. It is not certain that Americans understand exactly how a government-in-check works; it is certain that they are consistently critical of government performance.[5] Yet basic constitutional reforms have been few even though institutional adaptation has been substantial.

Lyndon B. Johnson won by a landslide in 1964. His sweeping victory left his conservative opponent, Barry M. Goldwater, with the Dixiecrat states won by Strom Thurmond in 1948 plus a narrow win in his home state of Arizona. On the day following this triumph, a *New York Times* editorial expressed the optimism of most analysts about the victory. Trust had been conveyed, disaster had been averted, and a mandate was declared. It was a "good election" by the criteria of the preferred model of party government.

The American people have given emphatic notice that they want to move forward constructively along the road of international understanding and domestic progress. . . .

Rejected is the thesis that the challenges of an era of dynamic, relentless change in domestic and foreign affairs can be met by dismantling the Federal Government or by shaking a nuclear fist at the rest of the world.

No more decisive rebuke could have been administered to the right-wing extremists whose command of the Republican national machinery plunged that great party into its destructive course. . . .

The strong mandate for flexibility of approach now given to the man in the White House offers some hope, in contrast to the despair that would have been engendered throughout the world—especially among America's allies—by a Goldwater victory.[6]

Johnson's victory was amplified by the gains for congressional Democrats. Already impressive margins in each house increased, producing better than two-to-one majorities. It was a victory akin to those of the Franklin D. Roosevelt era. No one doubted that President Johnson had the right and the responsibility to govern. Yet upon leaving office he pondered that such an election guaranteed only the responsibility; the right had to be established, then continually nurtured.[7]

Conditions changed substantially as a result of the midterm elections of 1966. Republicans realized a net gain of forty-seven House seats (their greatest gain since 1946) and four Senate seats. They also won back several state-houses. This significant showing by Republicans brought rather different editorial comment in the *New York Times*:

There is a widespread dissatisfaction and uneasiness about the course and the prospects of the Vietnam War. . . . There is widespread unhappiness about higher prices. . . . As a result of Tuesday's victories, the Republican Presidential nomination in 1968 now seems very much worth having and the number of potential claimants was increased.[8]

By the final year of the Johnson administration, the commentary could be described as "doleful." David S. Broder of the *Washington Post*, in discussing the 1968 State of the Union message, compared the mood of 1964 with that of 1968. "Above all, the optimistic 'can-do' President of 1964 had been transformed into a sober, slow-talking man who puzzled aloud about the 'restlessness' and 'questioning' in the land."[9] The message from a spent president emphasized crime control legislation.

Johnson himself clearly felt every bit of the burden detected by Broder and others. Here is how he described that last year in his memoirs:

As I look back over the crowded diaries listing the telephone calls and meetings of 1968, as I reread the daily headlines that jumped so steadily and forebodingly from one trouble spot to another, as I review the memos and the intelligence reports, I recall vividly the frustration and genuine anguish I experienced so often during the final year of my administration. I sometimes felt that I was living in a continuous nightmare.[10]

There are few better illustrations of how changes in the political and policy configurations influence the confidence, capacity, dedication, and fever for governing. But there are other interesting cases.

Richard M. Nixon was reelected in 1972 by stunning popular and electoral college margins. His percentage of the popular vote was nearly as great as Johnson's in 1964; his electoral college count was greater (520 to 486). His opponent, George McGovern, won the electoral votes of Massachusetts and the District of Columbia. Editorial comment, however, detected a less significant result than for Johnson in 1964. Why? Primarily because congressional Republicans did not do as well in 1972 as congressional Democrats in 1964, realizing a net gain of twelve House seats and a net loss of two Senate seats and failing to produce majorities in either chamber. Reference was made to the "empty landslide." "What the election appears to say through Congress is: All right, four more years—but only with the continued safeguard of checks and balances in liberal doses."[11] Arthur Krock of the *New York Times* found another reason to declare an "unmandate" in 1972: "Perhaps President Nixon's incredible sweep of virtually all segments of the population may fairly be classified as a 'mandate' for something—the conduct of foreign policy, for example. But in the wide meaning of the term, he has no mandate at all."[12] Krock did not explain why the huge defeat suffered by Goldwater in 1964 gave Johnson a mandate but an equally large loss for McGovern did not produce the same result for Nixon. Still there was grudging acknowledgment by the *New York Times* of an outstanding win for the president and a comment that "we deeply hope that he will succeed."[13]

The whole world knows what happened next: the Watergate scandal. When the president resigned, the reactions were a mixture of pity and relief.

The resignation of Richard M. Nixon . . . comes as a tragic climax to the sordid history of misuse of the Presidential office that has been unfolding before the eyes of a shocked American public for the last two years. . . . What is important is that here was a man who failed his public trust. Never before in American history has there been such a failure at so high a level. This is the sorrow and the tragedy.[14]

The disgraced president returned to California, where he suffered an attack of phlebitis. He had an operation and was in serious condition.

I was a physical wreck; I was emotionally drained; I was mentally burned out. This time, as compared with the other crises I had endured, I could see no reason to live, no cause to fight for. Unless a person has a reason to live for other than himself, he will die—first mentally, then emotionally, then physically.[15]

The Johnson and Nixon cases are particularly dramatic examples of how political and policy conditions can change during a presidential administration. But they are special without being unique. All presidents face ups and downs in their status and influence. There are no exceptions. "And so in the early months of 1935 the New Dealers argued among themselves, while their leader remained unwontedly irresolute and unwontedly reticent. The appearance of presidential weakness naturally stimulated the opposition."[16] And yet Franklin Roosevelt won the greatest election victory of the modern era in 1936; even his opponent, Alfred M. Landon, was bemused by "the completeness of it."[17] But neither the victory nor the huge majorities in Congress ensured that the president would get his way. For example, his plan to increase the membership of the Supreme Court was soundly defeated. By 1939 editorial comment sounded much like that directed to other lame-duck presidents (Roosevelt not having yet announced his intention to run again). The following examples, with a bit of editing, might have been written about, say, Ronald Reagan at the start of his last two years in office. The object of the editorializing was, in fact, Franklin D. Roosevelt as he entered the final years of his second administration.

> The eloquence of which [the President] is master has never been used to better advantage than in his message to Congress yesterday. . . . So far as domestic matters are concerned, it must be admitted that it is disheartening . . . to find the President leaving entirely to Congress all leadership in the matter of putting the fiscal affairs of the Government in better order.
>
> Little by little emphasis on the importance of a balanced budget has been whittled down. Time after time the hope of achieving such a budget has been deferred. . . . There are more economists who disagree with the President than agree with him.[18]

Nowhere in the Constitution is there a guarantee that the power of a president elected by a wide margin will be impervious to change. Likewise, high public approval ratings at one point are no guarantee either of political success at that juncture or of subsequent high ratings. President George Bush can attest to the verity of these observations (see chapter 4). Presidents must be ever attentive to the inconstant nature of their strategic position. Most presidents in the postwar period have hardly needed this advice. Several (Truman, Eisenhower, Nixon, Ford, Reagan, and Bush) served with split-party control between the White House and Congress; others (Truman, Kennedy, Nixon in 1968, Carter, and Clinton) won by narrow margins or less than 50 percent. That leaves just Lyndon Johnson. And he learned that political support can disappear: "A President must always reckon that his mandate will prove short-lived. . . . For me, as for most active Presidents, popularity proved elusive."[19]

Pictures in Our Heads

If the presidency is to be a major source of an understanding of American politics, then it is convenient to have a set of expectations by which to test performance. Richard Rose points out that several "portraits" have been used in recent years—some more idealistic, some more iconoclastic. "The overall effect is confusion rather than understanding; balanced portraits are relatively rare."[20]

At least two types of expectations are frequently relied on by analysts, particularly those in the media who necessarily produce short-term commentary and evaluations. Presidents are tested first by the broader criteria associated with judgments about the role of the presidency in the political system. The specifics may vary from one president to the next, but, in Walter Lippmann's marvelous phrase, we carry "pictures in our heads" that serve as cues for evaluating behavior: "what each man does is based not on direct and certain knowledge, but on pictures made by himself or given to him."[21] Often reactions based on these pictures are not fully or systematically articulated as models of behavior. Rather, they have to be constructed from the judgments made along the way. Sometimes they are traceable to positive evaluations of one president: Franklin D. Roosevelt is a frequent model. Or judgments can be traced to tests drawn from a predecessor of the same political party: Dwight Eisenhower for Richard Nixon, Lyndon Johnson for Jimmy Carter, Ronald Reagan for George Bush.

A second source of evaluation during an administration is a set of judgments about how a particular president ought to behave. This test is based on who the president is (or who everyone thinks he is), what his record has been to that point, and what he has said in gaining office. Mark J. Rozell spotted this second source of judgments in his study of President Carter's press relations.[22] Journalists' conceptions of how Jimmy Carter ought to perform as president were based on what they thought they knew about him; in a sense they were testing him by their understanding of his criteria of performance.

If integrated, these two sources provide the basis for a balanced judgment about presidential performance. Often, however, the two are drawn on sep-

arately and they conflict. For example, President Carter should compromise
in order to get legislation enacted because that is what a president as political
leader should do; yet a compromising Jimmy Carter is out of character and
thus loses credibility. President Ford should restore the leadership of the
White House; yet a vetoing Gerald Ford is out of character with his image
for restoring harmony. President Bush should offer an extensive legislative
program; yet an activist George Bush is out of character with both the man
and his limited mandate.

There also are contrary sets of expectations associated with divided government. There are hopes for reduced partisanship for the good of the country at the same time conditions usually promote partisanship, such as when
one party controls the White House and the other, Congress. These expectations apply to either a Democratic president and Republican Congress (as
in 1947–48) or a Republican president and Democratic Congress. Here, for
example, was editorial analysis following the 1946 elections in which the
Republicans recaptured control of both houses of Congress for the first time
since 1930:

> The greatest danger is that a purely partisan approach to the 1948 Presi-
> dential campaign, now hardly a year and a half off, will stultify the work
> of this Congress. The hope must be that the President and the majority
> and minority leaders will realize that a narrow partisanship will hurt, not
> help, them in 1948.[23]

As it happened, of course, the 80th Congress was highly partisan. Harry
Truman used that fact in the 1948 campaign, he won a surprising victory, the
Democrats recaptured control of Congress, and the *New York Times* then
expressed "gratification . . . in the emergence of a unified National Government."[24]

Likewise, when the Democrats won so overwhelmingly in 1974, increasing
their margins substantially in both houses, President Ford was advised
"to temper partisanship in favor of collaboration with the opposition party."
"A similar spirit of constructive collaboration" was expected "from the
Democrats."[25]

These various impressions or expectations are not models in the systematic
sense of that term. But they do serve similar functions in creating standards
by which presidential performance is tested. Even when presidents exceed
the expectations, there often is a subsequent return to home base, so to
speak. In some cases, as with Carter, those judgments may result in less
credit than is actually due the president; in other cases, as with Reagan, they
may result in more. That is, Carter's penchant for hyperbole led to tests that

were unrealistic; Reagan's capacity for supporting the inevitable led to praise for a positive record with Congress that was in fact questionable.

Behavior or performance that exceeds expectations is treated as just that—exceptional. Thus it is difficult to get an adjusted reading. The notion that a presidency is the composite of accommodations to changing people, politics, and policy issues is, perhaps, too demanding. Yet I will encourage it as the proper context for comparing presidents or evaluating reforms.

The Dominant Perspective

The "pictures in our heads" are impressions, not well thought out theories of governance. The images set forth above, however, are consistent with a dominant and well-developed perspective that has been highly influential in evaluating the American political system. The perspective is that of party government, typically one led by a strong or aggressive president. Those advocating this perspective prefer a system in which political parties are stronger than they normally can be in a system of separated elections. This deficiency naturally encourages a reformist mood so as to overcome what James L. Sundquist refers to as "the constitutional dilemma."[26] Sundquist is concerned, as are many observers of the American political system, that neither conservatives nor liberals can have their way because of the potential roadblocks built into the system.

> A president is expected to lead the Congress, but its two houses are independent institutions and, most of the time of late, one or both are controlled by his political opposition. And when a president fails as leader—whether because the Congress chooses not to follow or because of the many possible forms of personal inadequacy—the system has no safeguard.[27]

Sundquist quotes Douglas Dillon, secretary of the treasury in the Kennedy administration and cochair of the Committee on the Constitutional System (a group committed to reforming the Constitution) in identifying the insufficiencies of the U.S. system:

> Our governmental problems do not lie with the quality or character of our elected representatives. Rather they lie with a system which promotes divisiveness and makes it difficult, if not impossible, to develop truly national policies. . . . No one can place the blame. The President blames the Congress, the Congress blames the President, and the public remains confused and disgusted with government in Washington.[28]

In a direct challenge to Madison's thinking as expressed in *Federalist* 10, Sundquist argues:

> On less partisan issues—foreign policy in particular, but also the many elements of domestic fiscal policy—a national consensus would have to arise that a government able to concert its powers and act decisively will, most of the time, take the right action, that its positive achievements will outnumber its mistakes, that when it speaks with the authority that flows from unity it will speak mostly wisdom and not folly, and that, when it does err, a government capable of decisive action is best able to correct mistakes.[29]

Madison appeared to understand the relative advantages of a majoritarian versus a separated government. He chose the latter. Robert A. Dahl and Charles E. Lindblom described the results of this choice in this way:

> In the United States the structure of government prescribed by the Constitution, court decisions, and traditions vastly increases the amount of bargaining that must take place before policies can be made. . . . The necessity for constant bargaining is . . . built into the very structure of American government.
>
> The strategic consequence of this arrangement, as the Constitutional Convention evidently intended, has been that *no unified, cohesive, acknowledged, and legitimate representative-leaders of the "national majority" exist in the United States.* Often the President claims to represent one national majority, and Congress (or a majority of both houses) another. The convention did its work so well that even when a Congressional majority is nominally of the same party as the President, ordinarily they do not speak with the same voice.[30]

The party government perspective is best summarized in the recommendations made in 1946 by the Committee on Political Parties of the American Political Science Association.

> The party system that is needed must be democratic, responsible and effective. . . .
>
> An effective party system requires, first, that the parties are able to bring forth programs to which they commit themselves and, second, that the parties possess sufficient internal cohesion to carry out these programs. . . .
>
> The fundamental requirement of such accountability is a two-party system in which the opposition party acts as the critic of the party in power, developing, defining, and presenting the policy alternatives which are necessary for a true choice in reaching public decisions.[31]

Note the language in this summary: party in power, opposition party, policy alternatives for choice, accountability, internal cohesion, programs to which parties commit themselves. As a whole, it forms a test that a separated system is bound to fail.

I know of very few contemporary advocates of the two-party responsibility model.[32] But I know many analysts who rely on its criteria when judging the political system. One sees this reliance at work when reviewing how elections are interpreted and presidents are evaluated. By this standard, the good campaign and election have the following characteristics:

—Publicly visible issues that are debated by the candidates during the campaign.

—Clear differences between the candidates on the issues, preferably deriving from ideology.

—A substantial victory for the winning candidate, thus demonstrating public support for one set of issue positions.

—A party win accompanying the victory for the president, notably an increase in the presidential party's share of congressional seats and statehouses so that the president's win can be said to have had an impact on other races (the coattail effect).

—A greater than expected win for the victorious party, preferably at both ends of Pennsylvania Avenue.

—A postelection declaration of support and unity from the congressional leaders of the president's party.

The good president, by this perspective, is one who makes government work, one who has a program and uses his resources to get it enacted. The good president is an activist: he sets the agenda, is attentive to the progress being made, and willingly accepts responsibility for what happens. He can behave in this way because he has demonstrable support.

It is not in the least surprising that the real outcomes of separated elections frustrate those who prefer responsible party government. Even a cursory reading of the Constitution suggests that these demanding tests will be met only by coincidence. Even an election that gives one party control of the White House and both houses of Congress in no way guarantees a unified or responsible party outcome. And even when a president and his congressional party leaders appear to agree on policy priorities, the situation may change dramatically following midterm elections. Understandably, advocates of party government are led to propose constitutional reform. Coincidence is not a reliable basis for ensuring their preferred outcome.

There is no standard formula under present constitutional arrangements for governing from the White House. Presidents must identify their strengths and evaluate their weaknesses in negotiating with Congress or otherwise attempting to lead. They seldom have the advantages desired by the party government advocates. Even in those cases where appearances lead one to expect "responsible party" leadership (for example, in 1932, 1936, and 1964), it is by no means certain either that the appearances are reality or that the advantages can be long sustained. The tests of performance should account for the variations in party splits and in the political and policy advantages available to the president and the Congress.

Variations in Party Splits

Split-party control between the White House and Congress has come to be common in the post–World War II period. It is, of course, a wholly constitutional result in a system of separated elections for three institutions (president, House of Representatives, and Senate). With the establishment of a well-fixed two-party system, there were eight potential combinations of governance: two with one party in command of the three institutions and six split-party arrangements. As it has happened, the voters have frequently exercised their option of producing split-party government. All six split-party combinations have been experienced since the founding of the modern two-party system in 1856. The first case was in 1858, and subsequent cases are shown in table 1-1. Although split-party results were frequent in the nineteenth century, they tended to occur as a result of midterm elections. That is, a president would first be elected with a Congress under the control of his party, which would then lose one or both houses at the midterm. In only three cases (Hayes, 1876; Garfield, 1880; and Cleveland, 1884) did a president begin his administration under split-party conditions, and in each instance the president's party failed to achieve a majority in just one house. These three instances did occur in sequence, however, producing the longest period of split-party government in history—fourteen years (see table 1-2). It was also rare for the president's party to be in the minority in both houses. The two cases (Hayes, 1878; Cleveland, 1894) occurred following the midterm elections (table 1-1).

There are but three instances of split-party control in the early twentieth century: Taft, 1910; Wilson, 1918; and Hoover, 1930 (table 1-1). Only in the case of Wilson did the president's party lose its majority in both houses. These three instances of midterm losses presaged substantial defeats for the president's party in the subsequent presidential election. Perhaps the contemporary presidency-centered, party government perspective derives from analysis of this period, particularly given the expansionist outlooks of Woodrow Wilson and Franklin D. Roosevelt (the quintessential strong president by

Table 1-1. *Split-Party Control, 1858–1994*

President and year	Type of split control		Time split control occurred	
	Both houses	One house	Presidential election	Midterm
Buchanan (D) 1858	. . .	x (H)	. . .	x
Grant (R) 1874	. . .	x (H)	. . .	x
Hayes (R) 1876	. . .	x (H)	x	. . .
Hayes (R) 1878	x	. . .	. . .	x
Garfield (R) 1880	. . .	x (S)[a]	x	. . .
Arthur (R) 1882	. . .	x (H)	. . .	x
Cleveland (D) 1884	. . .	x (S)	x	. . .
Cleveland (D) 1886	. . .	x (S)	. . .	x
Harrison (R) 1890	. . .	x (H)	. . .	x
Cleveland (D) 1894	x	. . .	. . .	x
Taft (R) 1910	. . .	x (H)	. . .	x
Wilson (D) 1918	x	. . .	. . .	x
Hoover (R) 1930	. . .	x (H)[b]	. . .	x
Truman (D) 1946	x	. . .	. . .	x
Eisenhower (R) 1954	x	. . .	. . .	x
Eisenhower (R) 1956	x	. . .	x	. . .
Eisenhower (R) 1958	x	. . .	. . .	x
Nixon (R) 1968	x	. . .	x	. . .
Nixon (R) 1970	x	. . .	. . .	x
Nixon (R) 1972	x	. . .	x	. . .
Ford (R) 1974	x	. . .	. . .	x
Reagan (R) 1980	. . .	x (H)	x	. . .
Reagan (R) 1982	. . .	x (H)	. . .	x
Reagan (R) 1984	. . .	x (H)	x	. . .
Reagan (R) 1986	x	. . .	. . .	x
Bush (R) 1988	x	. . .	x	. . .
Bush (R) 1990	x	. . .	. . .	x

Source: Calculated from data in Harold W. Stanley and Richard G. Niemi, *Vital Statistics on American Politics*, 3d ed. (Washington: CQ Press, 1992), table 3-17.

a. The situation following the 1880 elections was extraordinary. The Senate was split evenly: thirty-seven Democrats, thirty-seven Republicans, two independents. After much maneuvering and two Republican resignations, the Democrats appointed the officers and the Republicans organized the committees.

b. The Republicans, in fact, won a majority of House seats (218–216), but by the time the Congress first met, a sufficient number had died to permit the Democrats to organize the House.

which others are typically measured). It may also be that analysis of this period encourages the view of divided government as a *corruption*—one associated with the failure of party and policy leadership by presidents and therefore a condition that should be corrected.

In the period from 1946 to 1994 there has been split-party government a majority of the time. In contrast to the earlier periods, in this one presidents have typically entered office with their party failing to command majorities

Table 1-2. *Split-Party Control, by Historical Period, 1856–1994*

| Period | Number of splits | | Total years | | Consecutive years of split control |
	Both houses	One house	Number	Percent	
1856–1900 (44 years)	2	8	20	45	14 (1874–88)
1990–1946 (46 years)	1	2	6	13	. . .[a]
1946–1994 (48 years)	11	3	28	58	12 (1980–92)[b]
1856–1994 (138 years)	14	13	54	39	. . .

Source: Calculated from data in table 1-1.
a. There were three Congresses with split control (1911–13, 1919–21, and 1931–33), but no two were consecutive.
b. There were two other lengthy periods of split control: 1954–60 and 1968–76.

in Congress: Eisenhower in his second term, Nixon and Reagan in both terms, and Bush in his single term. Republicans had fourteen opportunities to capture full control of the government; they did so just once (in 1952), though they held Senate majorities for three other Congresses (1980, 1982, and 1984). The longest sequence of divided government in this period (twelve years) does not quite match that in the last century (fourteen years), but, when combined with the eight-year span during the Nixon-Ford administrations, it represents an extraordinarily high percentage for a twenty-four-year period (83 percent).

In summary, it is apparent that split-party control can hardly be labeled an aberration, at least as measured by frequency of occurrence. It has been the result in two out of five elections since 1856 (see table 1-2). Oddly, the period that appears to serve as a model for testing effective government (1900–46) had, in fact, the fewest years of split control. Divided government occurred 52 percent of the time in the other two eras.

Also noteworthy are the differences between the first and third periods. Instead of serving as a corrective check at the midterm, as was so frequently the case in the last century, divided government has been legitimized from the start of an administration in the contemporary period. There must be a point at which an event that is repeated frequently is misdiagnosed as a corruption. In the postwar period, voters have had six opportunities (1948, 1956, 1972, 1976, 1984, and 1992) to make adjustments from an incumbent split-party government to a single-party government. They did so three times, once giving a Democratic president majorities in Congress (1948) and twice giving a Democratic Congress a president (1976, 1992). Interestingly, in each of these three cases the president himself emerged from the election with, at best, an ambiguous charge. And in 1980, the voters chose to go in the opposite direction—from an incumbent single-party government to a split-party government.

Variations in Presidential Advantages

The variation in political advantages and strategic positioning does not end with having identified presidents who had single-party and split-party governments. Presidents in each situation vary substantially in the advantages they have beyond those associated with whether their party has a majority in the House and Senate. These advantages include the election itself and how it is interpreted, the number of House and Senate seats held by the president's party, public and media support, and the nature of the agenda. Thus, for example, there is a substantial difference between Jimmy Carter's single-party government in 1976 and that of Lyndon Johnson in 1964, and, equally, between Richard Nixon's split-party government in 1968 and that of Ronald Reagan in 1980.

These advantages will be identified in subsequent chapters. Suffice it for now to state that sometimes when the president has few resources, the Congress has many (or is led to believe that it does). Thus, for example, the Republicans in the 80th Congress believed that they were on their way back as the majority party and acted accordingly. Similarly, congressional Democrats in the post-Watergate era acted confidently on policy issues and carried this behavior over into the Carter administration. The variations foster distinctions among governments: those that are *presidential* because of extraordinary White House advantages and the wit to use them; those that are *congressional* because of weakness in the White House and leadership capabilities on Capitol Hill; and those that are *balanced*, with advantages more or less evenly distributed at both ends of Pennsylvania Avenue.

Taken together, party splits and differential institutional advantages prepare the analyst for the varied circumstances under which presidents seek to govern. Political parties are simply not strong enough to override these distinctions, to compensate for the limitations experienced by elected officials within the executive and legislature. Nor would one expect them to be so in a separated system. The variations in conditions for governing are clearly consistent with a separation of powers based on independent elections. Richard E. Neustadt observes that this country's version of mixed authority has always meant "separated institutions *sharing* powers."[33] A legitimate inference from the variations above is that these separated institutions often *compete* for shared powers; at least that is a perspective that I want to promote here. The independent sources of power for each institution often lead to different interpretations of the agenda and what is required to cope with the problems on it. As noted above, occasionally one or the other institution is dominant. More typically, however, the White House and Congress must "act in tandem," as Mark A. Peterson correctly asserts. He views the two as a partnership and conjures up the image of a tandem bicycle. "On matters of domestic policy, the president may sit at the 'front' of the process, providing direction by influencing the policy agenda . . . but the choice of direction lacks significance without a synchronized response from the 'rear'."[34] This metaphor is appropriate enough under some conditions, but the variations noted above suggest that the president will not always be riding up front at all times or on all issues. They also suggest that before tandemness there may be competition for who rides up front and, more than likely, for how credits are shared for a race well run.

It is difficult to maintain a distinction between partisan and institutional differences when seeking to understand how this government works. Is it a case of a Republican president versus a Democratic Congress? Or is it simply the president versus the Congress? The puzzlement is a consequence of the constitutional and political structure itself. Dilemmas like this were not resolved in Philadelphia; in fact, they were generated there. To take the case of split-party government, the president obviously cannot appeal solely to his political party under most circumstances (sustaining a veto is an exception). Meanwhile, the majority party in Congress may well appeal to institutional identification in seeking support from members of the president's party. I can promise no more than attentiveness throughout this book to the distinction between conflict that is more strictly partisan and that which is more strictly institutional.

What can be said about responsibility for policy and governing within this system? At least two interpretations are evident: that responsibility is assignable or focused, or that it is nonassignable or diffused. Neither interpretation presumes an empirically demonstrable responsibility, as would suit the criteria of the party government formula. The first simply proposes that under certain conditions (typically single-party government) analysts will be inclined to assign responsibility to the president's party when it has majorities on Capitol Hill, whether it is fair or logical to do so. And the second proposes that under other conditions (typically split-party government) analysts will find it difficult to assign responsibility, though they will often, nonetheless, hold the president accountable.

I make no judgment at this point about a preferred interpretation. The immediate purpose is to encourage the reader to accept both assignable and nonassignable responsibility as legitimate interpretations associated with electoral outcomes and institutional shares of power. Acknowledging the legitimacy of both views is particularly important for the political period under study since the preferred outcome of the party responsibility advocates—single-party control and superior White House advantages—is an *uncommon* occurrence. Analysis limited to presidencies under those conditions has an *N* of one to work with in the postwar period—the presidency of Lyndon Johnson, and then for just two years, 1965–66. Remaining to be explained are the forty-six years of that period when, by a wholly constitutional process, voters produced split-party government or a single-party government with a mixed mandate.

The intention then is to establish a framework that permits analysis of relative presidential and congressional political, institutional, and policy advantages, reserving judgments about the workability of the system for the time being. The party responsibility model provides little or no aid either for describing a significant portion of the politics since 1945 or for predicting policy developments in the period. An alternative perspective is needed: one more suited to the political, institutional, and policy conditions of the time.

An Alternative Perspective

The alternative perspective for understanding American national politics is bound to be anathema to party responsibility advocates. By the rendition promoted here, responsibility is not focused, it is diffused. Representation is not pure and unidirectional; it is mixed, diluted, and multidirectional. Further, the tracking of policy from inception to implementation discourages the most devoted advocate of responsibility theories. In a system of diffused responsibility, credit will be taken and blame will be avoided by both institutions and both parties. For the mature government (one that has achieved substantial involvement in social and economic life), much of the agenda will be self-generating, that is, resulting from programs already on the books. Thus the desire to propose new programs is often frustrated by demands to sustain existing programs, and substantial debt will constrain both.

Additionally there is the matter of who *should* be held accountable for what and when. This is not a novel issue by any means. It is a part of the common rhetoric of split-party government. Are the Democrats responsible for how medicare has worked because it was a part of Lyndon Johnson's Great Society? Or are the Republicans responsible because their presidents accepted, administered, and revised the program? Is President Carter responsible for creating a Department of Energy or President Reagan responsible for failing to abolish it, or both? The partisan rhetoric on deficits continues to blame the Democrats for supporting spending programs and the Republicans for cutting taxes. It is noteworthy that this level of debate fails to treat more fundamental issues, such as the constitutional roadblocks to defining responsibility. In preventing the tyranny of the majority, the founders also made it difficult to specify accountability.

Diffusion of responsibility, then, is not only a likely result of a separated system but may also be a fair outcome. From what was said above, one has to doubt how reasonable it is to hold one institution or one party accountable for a program that has grown incrementally through decades of single- and split-party control. Yet reforming a government program is bound to be an occasion for holding one or the other of the branches accountable for wrongs being righted. If, however, politics allows crossing the partisan threshold to place both parties on the same side, then agreements may be reached that will permit blame avoidance, credit taking, and, potentially, significant policy change. This is not to say that both sides agree from the start about what to do, in a cabal devoted to irresponsibility (though that process is not unknown). Rather it is to suggest that diffusion of responsibility may permit policy reform that would have been much less likely if one party had to absorb all of the criticism for past performance or blame should the reforms fail when implemented.

Institutional competition is an expected outcome of the constitutional arrangements that facilitate mixed representation and variable electoral horizons. In recent decades this competition has been reinforced by Republicans settling into the White House, the Democrats comfortably occupying the House of Representatives, and, in very recent times, both parties hotly contending for majority status in the Senate. Bargains struck under these conditions have the effect of perpetuating split control by denying opposition candidates (Democratic presidential challengers, Republican congressional challengers) both the issues upon which to campaign and the means for defining accountability.

The participants in this system of mixed representation and diffused responsibility naturally accommodate their political surroundings. Put otherwise, congressional Democrats and presidential Republicans learn how to do their work. Not only does each side adjust to its political circumstances, but both may also be expected to provide themselves with the resources to participate meaningfully in policy politics.[35]

Much of the above suggests that the political and policy strategies of presidents in dealing with Congress will depend on the advantages they have available at any one time. One cannot employ a constant model of the activist president leading a party government. Conditions may encourage the president to work at the margins of president-congressional interaction (for example, where he judges that he has an advantage, as with foreign and defense issues). He may allow members of Congress to take policy initiatives, hanging back to see how the issue develops. He may certify an issue as important, propose a program to satisfy certain group demands, but fail to expend the political capital necessary to get the program enacted. The lame-duck president requires clearer explication. The last months and years of a two-term administration may be one of congressional initiative with presidential response.[36] The point is that having been relieved of testing the system for party responsibility, one can proceed to analyze how presidents perform under variable political and policy conditions.

The Politics of Partisan Variations

A main contention so far is that there are several legitimate constitutional patterns of partisan control and policy participation between the White House and Congress (as well as between the two houses of Congress). Further, one-party government with presidential advantages, the arrangement preferred by party government advocates, is an uncommon outcome in the post–World War II period. An alternative perspective should encourage a search for other patterns, including the conditions shaping those patterns and the associated policy product. This approach may even allow for a better understanding of institutional reform by identifying the circumstances under which reform can be effective, given the patterns of partisan interaction that obtain.

I have identified four patterns that will be explored further in the chapters devoted to presidential-congressional interaction on legislation: partisanship,

copartisanship, bipartisanship, and cross partisanship. These categories identify the nature of the coalition building that takes place, directing attention
to who participates in the policy process, how they do so, and at what point.
Most patterns can occur under either split- or single-party government. And
there may be differences between how the president interacts with the House
and the Senate. As will become evident, the patterns may vary within an
administration—either during a particular period or in regard to specific
bills. Much depends on the strategic situation: who initiates the legislation,
the nature of the support, and what additional support is required.

Partisanship

In the partisanship pattern, bargaining and coalition building occur primarily within the president's party, which has majorities in both houses of
Congress. It is this pattern in single-party government that best suits the
conditions of the party government model. Responsibility is presumably focused within the dominant party. The purest example in the postwar period
is that of the first two years of the Johnson administration (1965–66). However, the first two years of the Reagan administration (1981–83) also exhibited
a partisanship pattern. Bargaining and coalition building during those years
generally went from the Republican Senate to the Democratic House, where
there was sufficient solidarity among House Republicans to capitalize on the
predictable southern Democratic defectors. A most interesting case of partisanship under conditions of split-party government developed in the final
eighteen months of the Bush administration (1991–93). Weakness of both
the Republican president and the Democratic Congress seemingly contributed to highly partisan conflict and limited policy product. The two sides lost
a basis for bargaining and compromise because of a serious reduction in
advantages: public confidence in the president declined dramatically following the Persian Gulf War, and Congress experienced a number of humiliating
scandals. The stalemate that many predict for divided government was characteristic of these special circumstances in which partisans in each institution
viewed the others as vulnerable. Thus deadlock was associated not with the
strength but rather the weakness of each set of actors.

Copartisanship

This pattern is among the most interesting in the postwar period. It is
associated with split-party control, typically a Republican president and a

Democratic Congress (though there is one case of the opposite arrangement, 1947–48). Copartisanship is typified by parallel development of proposals at each end of Pennsylvania Avenue or by the two parties in each house of Congress. Often these proposals represent different approaches to the problem, with participants in both institutions having sufficient support and expertise to be credibly involved. The increase in policy analytical capability on Capitol Hill in recent decades has allowed the House and Senate majority parties to be more active players in all phases of the policy process, thus enhancing the copartisan result.

Bargaining and coalition building can and do occur in copartisanship. At some point, the two forces try to reach an agreement. Why try at all? Why not simply "checkmate" and capitalize on the failure of the other side to compromise? Because both sides identify possible political gain in reaching an agreement. Acknowledging that the problem is one requiring attention, as with the mounting deficit and revenue shortfall in 1990, the participants determine that they can claim credit for success while avoiding blame for failure (past, present, or future). The latter point requires more elaboration. The agenda of a government with mature programs often is dominated by reform proposals or adjunct proposals (that is, those further extending particular benefits). As noted earlier, it is difficult to enact reform without partisan recrimination. If, however, the two parties, each in control of an institution, can come to agreement, they can then neutralize the issue for subsequent electoral campaigns yet preserve their right to formulate an initial proposal that reflects partisan concerns. Copartisanship may be expected to work best when there is acknowledged strength in both the White House and Congress, thus creating the bargaining condition. There is less basis for this pattern if one or the other is dominant or if both are weak (as in the Bush case cited above).

Bipartisanship

There is a tendency to think of bipartisanship as characterizing foreign policy. The most frequently cited era of bipartisanship—that following the end of World War II—was primarily characterized by certain congressional leaders, most notably Republican Senator Arthur Vandenberg of Michigan, accepting the president's leadership and convincing other Republicans to do the same. As used here, bipartisanship refers to the active and *cooperative* involvement of Republicans and Democrats in several phases of the policy process, from problem definition through to program approval. Representatives from both parties are involved at the start of policymaking, work together along the way, and eventually form a majority coalition. There would seem to be a public interest orientation in the cases of bipartisan action.

Bipartisanship may occur between the president and Congress or within Congress. The first is likely to be facilitated when the president and congressional leaders from both parties agree on the need for policy action and cooperate along the way to produce a piece of legislation (the Marshall Plan is an example). In the second case, congressional leaders may work together, then convince the president to join them (as in some environmental issues and social security increases), or the issue may be substantially congressional in scope, not requiring presidential involvement (for example, budget reform). There may also be cases of congressional bipartisanship as strategies to counter the president (as with the passage of the War Powers Resolution during the Nixon administration or resistance to the cuts in water control projects recommended by President Carter in the first year of his administration). Such cases illustrate institutional conflict—between the legislative and executive branches—over partisan disagreements.

How does bipartisanship differ from copartisanship? The principal distinction is the stage of policymaking at which the negotiation takes place, as well as the independence of action that is thereby implied. In bipartisanship, the two sides bargain along the way so as to guarantee a winning coalition. In copartisanship, the two sides bargain after independently having prepared proposals. Enactment is not guaranteed in either case—agreements can always break down—but the likelihood of passage is typically greater with bipartisanship. One other difference is that copartisanship frequently results in cross-partisan voting: a substantial portion of one party voting with a sufficient portion of the other party to form a majority. Bipartisanship results in broad voting support from both parties.

Cross Partisanship

In cross partisanship an important segment of one party works with or can be counted on for support by the other party. Typically the initiative comes from one party, which then seeks to win enough support from the other party to form a winning coalition. Often it is the president who needs votes from the other party. The "conservative coalition" illustrates that a cross-party coalition can develop at certain times on some issues. This alliance frequently votes together against legislation, but in 1981 it combined to produce important budget and tax laws.

Cross partisanship differs from copartisanship and bipartisanship in important ways. As noted above, the coalition often forms to stop action, not to initiate it. If there is a proposal, however, it typically comes from the president, who then tries to gain support from a sufficiently large segment of the other party to win. Compromises may have to be accepted, but the process is different from copartisanship, where independent proposals are developed along the way, or bipartisanship, where both parties cooperate from the start (often through their leaders).

Change within Administrations

Research on the presidency is often criticized for being insufficiently comparative, for too often focusing on one president and offering limited capacity for generalizing. That criticism itself is revealing of a common practice in the study of American national politics, dividing political and policy time by presidential administrations. Yet people, politics, and issues also change *during* a presidential administration. For example, the Eisenhower years were considered to be relatively calm, yet the last two years looked very different from the first two. Only three members of Eisenhower's cabinet remained (and Secretary of State John Foster Dulles died early in 1959). The Democrats had nearly two-thirds majorities in both houses of Congress in 1959, after the Republicans had enjoyed majorities in both during Eisenhower's first Congress. The federal budget actually decreased during Eisenhower's first two budget years (1954, 1955), but then increased by a third by his last budget year (1961). The unemployment rate went from 2.9 percent in 1953 to 6.8 percent in 1958.

These changes pale in comparison with what happened to subsequent presidents. There were thirty-one changes in cabinet secretarial positions during the Nixon-Ford presidency, while Eisenhower had ten changes during his eight years (see chapter 3). And, of course, Nixon himself was gone, as was his original vice president, Spiro T. Agnew. Lyndon Johnson's Gallup poll rating went from 80 percent approval in January 1964 to 35 percent approval in August 1968. The Democrats' two-thirds majority in the House shrank to 57 percent, allowing the reemergence of the conservative coalition between Republicans and southern Democrats. And George Bush achieved record public approval in 1991, only to see it soon dissipate. His effectiveness in the Persian Gulf War was long forgotten during the economic recession that persisted through the summer of 1992.

Tracking these changes and their implications for presidential power is not a simple task. And it will not be accomplished here to full satisfaction, to be sure. But this study will emphasize the importance of accounting for change in any effort to locate a president politically, understand how much help he can count on, and estimate what problems he is trying to solve. It is those factors that tend to change and thus produce very different advantages for him in working with the other policymaking institutions in Washington.

There are other, more conceptual reasons for stressing change within as well as between presidential administrations. Developments that carry through from one administration to another can be explored, and the contribution or function of any one presidency is set in the context of the broader national policy process. Thus, for example, analysis of developments in health care costs as a policy problem may elaborate or modify the notion that the president is the agenda setter for Congress. It may show where the president fits within a larger agenda-setting process. Finally, attention to changes within a president's term in office increases the number of presidencies to study. There have been ten post–World War II presidents but, as will be discussed later, these ten have had many more presidencies.

What Is to Follow

This book will emphasize the strategic position of presidents and how it changes. I will rely on the alternative "diffused responsibility" perspective, ever searching for how this nation is governed under the strikingly diverse constitutional arrangements of single- and split-party control. I am interested in the coping and the recouping, the initial efforts to organize and the subsequent adaptations as administrations explore what works best for them, and the variations in the president's role in lawmaking.

There are several expectations stemming from the alternative perspective that help shape the organization of the book from this point forward. Of central interest are those having to do with presidents themselves, White House and cabinet organization, public support, the nature of the agenda, lawmaking, and reform. In a separated system of diffused responsibility, these are the expectations:

—Presidents will enter the White House with variable personal, political, and policy advantages or resources. Presidents are not equally good at comprehending their advantages or identifying how these advantages may work best for purposes of influencing the rest of the government.

—White House and cabinet organization will be quite personal in nature, reflecting the president's assessment of strengths and weaknesses, the challenges the president faces in fitting into the ongoing government, and the political and policy changes that occur during the term of office. There is no formula for organizing the presidency, though certain models can be identified.

—Public support will be an elusive variable in analyzing presidential power. At the very least, its importance for any one president must be considered alongside other advantages. "Going public" does not necessarily carry a special bonus, though presidents with limited advantages otherwise may be forced to rely on this tactic.

—The agenda will be continuous, with many issues derived from programs already being administered. The president surely plays an important role in certifying issues and setting priorities, but Congress and the bureaucracy will also be natural participants. At the very least, therefore, the president will be required to persuade other policy actors that his choices are the right ones. They will do the same with him.

—Lawmaking will vary substantially in terms of initiative, sequence, partisan and institutional interaction, and productivity. The challenge is to comprehend the variable role of the president in a government that is designed for continuity and change.

—Reform will be an especially intricate undertaking since, by constitutional design, the governmental structure is antithetical to efficient goal achievement. Yet many, if not most, reforms seek to achieve efficiency within the basic separated structure. There are not many reforms designed to facilitate the more effective working of split-party government.

I have chosen to organize this book by the set of topics identified in the expectations listed above: who presidents are and how they differ (chapter 2); organization of the White House and the cabinet and how both change during an administration (chapter 3); how public support varies and what it means (chapter 4); the continuing agenda and how presidents manage it (chapter 5); how lawmaking works, where the president fits, and how it varies by issue (chapters 6 and 7); and reform in a separated system of diffused responsibility (chapter 8). I will make comparisons among the postwar presidents, constantly endeavoring to identify the variations in governing that this country has experienced. The chapters on lawmaking focus on specific pieces of legislation. I have, however, selected major bills from each administration and also intend to show how patterns of presidential-congressional interaction vary within one administration.

My main mission is to provide a means for understanding how a separated system of government works under the varying circumstances allowable by the Constitution and a two-party structure. I focus on presidents, but my purpose is broader as I attempt to place them into the continuing process of governing. I am not by nature a reformer. I am, however, eager to see the national government work effectively under all of the conditions sanctioned by the Constitution. Therefore one underlying purpose of this book is to promote a perspective that will encourage analysts to appreciate the unique nature of the American system and to think creatively about how to make it work better.

CHAPTER TWO

Presidents and the Presidency

PRESIDENTS are the people who move into the White House. The presidency is the institution of executive power. As Edward S. Corwin has written, "What the presidency is at any particular moment depends in important measure on who is President. . . . Yet the accumulated tradition of the office is also of vast importance."[1] The way presidents fit into the presidency and affect it is by no means uniform, but their performance may be judged by criteria based on conceptions of what is presidential. These conceptions, in turn, are rooted in "the accumulated tradition of the office." There is, after all, a presidency beyond a president. As Ronald Reagan explained: "Some people become President. I've never thought of it that way. I think the Presidency is an institution over which you have temporary custody and it has to be treated that way. . . . I don't think the Presidency belongs to the individual."[2]

This chapter will explore the different circumstances under which the ten modern presidents (those after World War II) assumed the office. I want to make this simple but immensely important point: Presidents are not created equal, politically or otherwise. Some are well prepared, some are not; some have enormous advantages, others have few; some seek the office, others have it thrust on them. Often, however, expectations of performance are uniform: analysts rely on a generalized conception of the institution in testing each occupant of the office. They seldom make an effort to identify how the person as president is prepared to be fitted into the institution of the presidency. Many, if not most, studies of executive leadership focus on the presidency, not presidents serving variably as leaders. Even those that treat individual presidents often have as their purpose generalizations about the larger institution, thus reinforcing the tendency to verify each performance by an

27

equivalent standard.[3] Alas, that standard draws from an institution-in-the-
making, one to which each president contributes.

The eagerness to rate presidents, so common in biographies and in efforts
to evaluate them comparatively through time, reflects this tendency to derive
expectations from a concept of the office itself rather than from the personal,
political, and policy conditions and experiences associated with a president's
service. Historian Thomas A. Bailey put it this way in commenting on these
ratings: "Judging Presidents is not like judging those who play duplicate
bridge; no two incumbents were ever dealt the same hand." For Bailey,
"Presidential polls are something of a parlor game, and as such should not
be taken too seriously."[4] President John F. Kennedy was more blunt in assessing these rating exercises: "How the hell can you tell? Only the President
himself can know what his real pressures and his real alternatives are. If you
don't know that, how can you judge performance?"[5]

The major purpose, then, of this chapter is to propose what one might
realistically expect of the ten presidents since 1945, possibly inducing a formula for estimating the performance of future presidents. My interest first is
in the accommodation that is likely to occur at the start between person and
position, between the president and the presidency. Later chapters will direct
attention to the extent to which the president influences the presidency as
well as the accumulated experience of exercising power in the same position
over time. Of related interest are the changes that occur over the course of
an administration. What the job looks like upon entry may well change during
time in service. Likewise, those with whom a president must deal normally
profit from learning how that president views his responsibilities and re-
sponds to change.

How They Come to Be There

There are fifteen cases of entering the White House among the ten presidents of the postwar period. They can be classified into five categories.

Elected presidents: Presidents who were initially nominated and elected.
There are six cases: Dwight D. Eisenhower, 1952; John F. Kennedy, 1960;
Richard M. Nixon, 1968; Jimmy Carter, 1976; Ronald Reagan, 1980; and Bill
Clinton, 1992.

Reelected presidents: Presidents who were renominated and reelected.
There are three cases: Eisenhower, 1956; Nixon, 1972; and Reagan, 1984.

Nonelected presidents: Vice presidents who took over for a president due to death or resignation. There are three cases: Harry S. Truman, 1945; Lyndon B. Johnson, 1963; and Gerald R. Ford, 1974.

Elected vice presidents: Vice presidents who were nominated and elected after serving out the term of a president. There are two cases: Truman, 1948, and Johnson, 1964.

Elected heir apparent: A vice president who was nominated and elected after serving with his predecessor. There is one case: George Bush, 1988.

This listing itself evokes assorted expectations of presidential orientations to the office. The first two categories—election and reelection of presidents—isolate those who win the office by virtue of their successful initiatives through a two-stage process of nomination and election. The pledges made along the way are shaped by personal commitments and the campaign experience. There are differences between running initially (more creative) and seeking reelection (more protective), as discussed below. The next three categories—nonelected presidents, elected vice presidents, and elected heir apparent—differ substantially from the first two. Here is a set of persons who either would not try to reach the White House on their own or who tried and failed. They are truly presidents of circumstance. First, note how many there are: six of the fifteen entries in this period. Second, it is vital to appreciate the strikingly different conditions in which they assumed the office, different from those in the first two categories and different within their own sets.

Elected Presidents

Elected presidents endure two related campaigns: one within the party for the nomination, the other to win the office itself. There are important differences in the nominating experience for elected and other presidents (see table 2-1). The most impressive difference came with the increase in the number of presidential primaries following the divisive 1968 Democratic convention. Eisenhower, Kennedy, and Nixon ran in less than half of the few primaries held before 1972. Each established front-runner status in these contests to buttress their efforts inside the party to win the nomination. Eisenhower and Kennedy had to display outside support so as to convince party officials of their credibility as candidates, because both had to run against insider candidates for the nomination (Senator Robert A. Taft for Eisenhower, Senator Lyndon B. Johnson for Kennedy). Nixon was the consummate insider and probably could have been nominated without entering

Table 2-1. *Nomination Experience of Modern Presidents*

President	Run before?	Nomination contested?	Primaries Number	Primaries Entered	Primaries Won	Convention contested?
Elected presidents						
Eisenhower (1952)	No	Yes	13	5	4	Yes
Kennedy (1960)	No	Yes	16	7	7	Yes
Nixon (1968)	Yes	Yes	15	6	6	Yes
Carter (1976)	No	Yes	27	26	17	Token
Reagan (1980)	Yes	Yes	35	33	29	No
Clinton (1992)	No	Yes	37	41	32	Token
Reelected presidents						
Eisenhower (1956)	. . .	No	19	14	14	No
Nixon (1972)	. . .	Minor	20	16	16	No
Reagan (1984)	. . .	No	25	25	25	No
Elected vice presidents						
Truman (1948)	No	No	14	7	7	Yes[a]
Johnson (1964)	Yes	Minor	16	2	2[b]	No
Elected heir apparent						
Bush (1988)	Yes	Yes	38	38	37	No

Sources: Calculated from data in *Congressional Quarterly's Guide to U.S. Elections* (Washington: CQ Press, 1975), pts. 1, 2; *Congressional Quarterly's Guide to 1976 Elections* (Washington: Congressional Quarterly, 1977), pp. 5–30; and *Congressional Quarterly Weekly Report*, various issues, 1980, 1984, 1988, 1992.

a. Many southern Democrats walked out of the convention and formed the Dixiecrat party.

b. Johnson was a write-in candidate in several primaries.

primaries. It had come to be expected, however, that presidential candidates would enter primaries, so Nixon ran and won in six states.

The other interesting characteristic of those first three nominating contests is that closure was not achieved in the preconvention period. Since the primaries were not the only means for garnering delegate votes, it was possible for candidates to remain in the race without engaging other candidates, running alongside the favorite and probable nominee. With the expansion in the number of primaries, however, challengers could be defeated outright and left with no other means for winning delegate support, means that were less engaging and confrontational. Eisenhower was strongly challenged by Taft at the convention in 1952. In fact, he did not receive a majority of the delegates on the first ballot (shifts in delegate votes then provided the margin). Kennedy and Nixon both received just over 50 percent of the delegate support on the first ballot.

A result of nonengagement and the failure to achieve closure before the convention was that the presidential candidate faced a competing organization within the party. Bargaining was then necessary to unite the party for the fall campaign. The contest for the nomination was not diffused by thirty-five or more elections spread geographically and over time. Rather there was a focal activity, a meeting at which the two or more organizations interacted over policy, political, and personnel issues. Negotiations over the platform, the national party structure, selection of the vice president, and future presidential appointments provided executive leadership experience, not unlike that required in the White House for negotiating with Congress.

Essentially the system in place since 1972 requires the presidential candidate, once in office, to compensate for not having had to negotiate with governmental (mostly congressional) leaders in the course of winning the nomination. For example, in 1980, Reagan conducted what I have termed a "trifocal campaign"—one designed to look forward from the preconvention campaign to the convention and on to the general election.[6] His party-oriented campaign showed that a high degree of party unity can be achieved under the new, plebiscitary system. George Bush emulated this approach in 1988, though not to the extent of inviting his chief rival, Robert Dole, to join him on the ticket.

The Democrats have faced a very different problem. The many special interests that are identified with the party often appear reluctant to cooperate with the prospective presidential candidate. Either the challenging candidates are unwilling to withdraw on schedule—as with Edward Kennedy in 1980, Gary Hart in 1984, Jesse Jackson in 1984 and 1988, and Jerry Brown in 1992—or groups demand that their interests be represented in the platform or elsewhere regardless of the consequences for the fall campaign. Further, one of the two successful Democratic candidates in this set, Jimmy Carter, was not predisposed to conduct a party-oriented campaign. He sought from the start to separate himself from the traditional party organization, including that in Congress.[7]

In 1992, Bill Clinton, too, faced challenges from groups within the Democratic party, but he was more inclined than Carter to work with and through the party apparatus. Like Carter, he selected a well-respected senator as a running mate, but he was in a stronger position than previous candidates (Carter in 1980, Mondale in 1984, and Dukakis in 1988) to take charge of the Democratic convention, and he did so. Meanwhile, congressional Democrats were in a substantially weaker political position than in 1976, primarily because of a series of scandals. Thus they were not a presence at the convention and were more likely than in recent years to mesh their reelection campaigns with the Clinton campaign. Even so, this coordination, to the extent that it occurred, was less a Clinton initiative than an interest on the part of anxious Democratic congressional candidates to avoid defeat in the fall elections.

In the general election campaign for elected presidents, there is a less clear pattern or distinction than in the nominating experiences (see table 2-2). I will, however, discuss them in three pairs: Eisenhower and Reagan, Kennedy and Carter, and Nixon and Clinton. The first pair could legitimately claim true victory; in fact, their wins even encouraged talk of party realignment. Eisenhower won handily and, beyond that, his party won majorities in both houses of Congress, making this the first fully Republican government since 1929. What was lacking for the declaration of a true mandate was a clearly defined program, apart from Eisenhower's promise to "go to Korea" and end that conflict.

Reagan's victory was more impressive for three reasons. First, he defeated an incumbent Democratic president, the first time that had happened in this century. His popular vote total was less than Eisenhower's, but there was a third candidate, John Anderson. Reagan's percentage share of the two-party vote was almost exactly the same as Eisenhower's. Second, the increase of thirty-three House seats for the Republicans was the greatest in a presidential election year since 1920, though still insufficient for attaining majority status. In the Senate, Republicans gained twelve additional seats, an absolutely stunning result that gave them majority control of that body. Third, Reagan set forth a clear set of policy priorities during the campaign, which no one doubted that he would try to enact. The 1980 presidential election was perhaps the most policy oriented in recent history.

The Kennedy and Carter elections are alike in many respects. Both presidents won by narrow margins—among the closest in history—in both the popular and electoral college voting. The source of their victories was similar: the Northeast, South, and a few industrial Midwest states. Further, neither could rightfully claim coattails: House and Senate Democrats had net losses in 1960, and there was virtually no change in 1976. Both candidates ran

Table 2-2. *General Election Experience of Modern Presidents*

President	Presidential vote (percent)			Congressional seats by president's party		
	Popular	Two-party	Electoral	House	Senate	Control?
Elected presidents						
Eisenhower (1952)	55	55	83	Gain	Gain	Yes
Kennedy (1960)	50	50	56	Loss	Loss	Yes
Nixon (1968)	43	50	56	Gain	Gain	No
Carter[a] (1976)	50	51	55	No change[b]	No change	Yes
Reagan[a] (1980)	51	55	91	Gain	Gain	Split[c]
Clinton[a] (1992)	43	53	69	Loss	No change	Yes
Reelected presidents						
Eisenhower (1956)	57	58	86	No change[d]	No change	No
Nixon (1972)	61	62	97	Gain	Loss	No
Reagan (1984)	59	59	98	Gain	Loss	Split
Elected vice presidents						
Truman (1948)	50	53	57	Gain	Gain	Yes
Johnson (1964)	61	61	90	Gain	Gain	Yes
Elected heir apparent						
Bush (1988)	53	53	79	No change[d]	No change	No

Sources: Calculated from data in Harold W. Stanley and Richard G. Niemi, *Vital Statistics on American Politics*, 3d ed. (Washington: Congressional Quarterly Press, 1992), tables 3-14; 3-17; and *Congressional Quarterly Weekly Report*, various issues.
a. Defeated an incumbent president.
b. The Democrats did gain one seat.
c. The House remained under Democratic control; the Senate shifted to Republican control.
d. The Republicans did lose two seats.

behind the overwhelming majority of the victorious congressional Democrats. Still, they both could count on sizable Democratic majorities in each house because of landslide midterm victories in 1958 and 1974. It was therefore obvious from the start that Kennedy and Carter would have to work for the support of Congress in spite of the large Democratic majorities in each house.

The last pair has the fewest common features, though there are some. Nixon won narrowly, primarily because of the conflicts raging within the Democratic party. He garnered 43 percent of the popular vote in a three-candidate race (a disaffected Democrat, George Wallace, formed a third party and received 14 percent of the popular vote). After the election, the Republicans successfully sought to attract the Wallace voters, resulting in a winning coalition in presidential elections interrupted only by Carter's win in 1976. Clinton, too, won 43 percent of the popular vote, also in a three-candidate race. The third candidate, Ross Perot, captured 19 percent of the popular vote. Like Nixon's interest in the Wallace voters, Clinton's aim is no doubt to attract Perot supporters in 1996. The most notable difference between the two presidents is that Nixon was the first president in the history of the modern two-party system to enter office in his first term with the opposition party in control of both houses of Congress. Clinton's party won majorities in both houses. The House Republicans experienced a net gain but less than they expected; Clinton's win in certain states, notably California, is credited for saving some Democratic seats. What does seem apparent is that the two presidents entered office needing to strengthen their strategic position. Surely no president with 43 percent of the vote can believe that his legitimacy as leader of the government is secure.

Two tests can be used to summarize the comparison of the six elected presidents: Did the election provide the president with special advantages upon entering the White House? Did the congressional elections complement any advantage gained from the president's election? By these tests only Eisenhower and Reagan, two Republicans, had both advantages (and only Reagan was prepared to use them in the early months of his administration). The other four won narrowly and had to establish credibility as leaders with Congress. For them, being inaugurated was but the start of a process of authenticating their right to lead. I will have more to say about this subject below.

Reelected Presidents

Three presidents have been elected to a second term in office since 1945. All three—Eisenhower, Nixon, and Reagan—are Republicans, and their renominations and reelections had many features in common (see tables 2-1 and 2-2). Not unexpectedly, given the relative success of their first terms, the nomination in each case was essentially a coronation. With virtually no opposition (only Nixon experienced minor opposition from the right), they were free to enter many primaries, thus using the preconvention period to promote their reelection campaign. The convention itself became a rousing kickoff for the general election campaign. Meanwhile, the Democrats experienced growing frustration, given internal disputes that spilled over into the general election campaign. Particularly in 1972 and 1984, the Democratic candidates were unable to concentrate on the Republican opponent because of problems with their vice presidential choices. George McGovern had to choose twice when his first choice, Senator Thomas Eagleton, was discovered to have had undergone electric shock therapy. And Walter Mondale found that his running mate, Representative Geraldine Ferraro, had to respond repeatedly to assertions about her husband's financial dealings. That attention by the media seriously detracted from Mondale's campaign during the crucial first weeks after the convention.

The general election results constituted approval of the whole government, at least by those citizens who bothered to vote. The president in each case was overwhelmingly reelected, the campaign issues were primarily those of continuity and reaffirmation, and there was little or no change in Congress, with Democratic majorities returning in every case but for the Senate in 1984. These elections validated the existing government. They seemingly provided each president with a special personal advantage because of landslide victories, yet advanced no special benefit for negotiating on Capitol Hill. Further, since reelected presidents cannot run again, their strategic position was jeopardized. In spite of the confirmation of their leadership at the polls, they faced the probability of an erosion of status within Washington. Thus reelected Republican presidents (there are no others in the postwar period at this writing) had to sustain and nurture their power every bit as much as those newly elected to the office. It is perhaps not at all surprising that congressional Democrats became particularly active in policymaking during the final years of each of these administrations.

Vice Presidents as Presidents

The three most relevant considerations for comparing the three vice presidents as president are the circumstances under which they assumed the office, the timing of their assumption of office in the presidential term, and the nature of the agenda. Truman and Johnson took over upon the death of the incumbent. But how each incumbent died is relevant for the strategic position of the successor. Roosevelt died of natural causes after having served three full terms as president. He was credited for enacting a domestic New

Deal and directing the nation's war effort. The nation mourned his death, but the shock itself carried only a limited and short-term advantage for Harry Truman. Rather, Truman was compared with the man many consider to be the greatest president of the modern era.

The timing of Roosevelt's death left Truman with nearly a full term—from April 12, 1945, to January 20, 1949. There was no provision for a vice president under these circumstances (the Twenty-fifth Amendment was ratified in 1967). All attention focused on Harry Truman, and the reviews were not typically flattering. He then had to face a midterm election in 1946 as the leader of a party and nation that had not selected him for that purpose. The results of the 1946 election were devastating to the Democrats. House Republicans had a net gain of fifty-six seats and Senate Republicans a net gain of thirteen seats, giving them control of both chambers for the first time since 1929.

Finally, there was a ready-made agenda for Harry Truman when he took office. The war was winding down, and with its end came a predictable, if not readily resolvable, set of issues. Truman had to make a number of important decisions, most notably the dropping of atomic bombs on Hiroshima and Nagasaki. Essentially, however, he was expected to carry on in the shadow of his predecessor, yet he was measured by Roosevelt's example. "His Work Must Go On" was the caption of one cartoonist's dedication to Roosevelt.[8] Because Truman was not well known, his accession to the White House sent analysts scurrying for reassurance, as an editorial in the *New York Times* suggested.

> In one of the great moments of American history there steps into the office of the Presidency of the United States, and into a position of world-wide influence and authority such as no other living American has ever held, a man who is less well known to the people of this country than many other public figures and almost totally unknown abroad. This man is a farmer's son from the Missouri Valley, a veteran of the last war, a self-styled "practical politician," a two-term member of the Senate, a compromise candidate for the comparatively obscure office from which fate, with dramatic suddenness, has now catapulted him to power.[9]

Truman himself expressed it this way in talking to reporters: "Boys, if you ever pray, pray for me now. I don't know whether you fellows ever had a load of hay fall on you, but when they told me yesterday what had happened, I felt like the moon, the stars, and all the planets had fallen on me."[10]

For Lyndon Johnson, the situation was quite different. John F. Kennedy was assassinated in the prime of his life. He had served less than three years and was therefore denied the chance to make his full mark on American politics. His record of success on Capitol Hill was not particularly impressive, yet he had prepared an extensive legislative program. It was therefore left to Johnson, the master legislative leader, to guide the program through Congress. That was the expectation and Johnson's natural inclination.

Johnson did not have to cope with a midterm election, though no doubt the Democrats would have done well, given his positive legislative record during his first year in office. He was free to prepare for the 1964 presidential election by seeking to move as much legislation as possible in the time he had available. He was uniquely equipped to do just that. Most analyses were optimistic about Johnson's capability for serving out the term of the slain young president.

> To these tasks Lyndon Johnson brings experience and qualities of character that should stand him in good stead. He is thoroughly at home in the Congress, which must now share with him the responsibility of steadying the country through the crisis which confronts it. He is well known in all parts of the country, but no one can really know his qualities as leader until he has had a chance to demonstrate them in an assignment more difficult than any other on earth. He is a man of moderate views, with a talent for bringing concord out of disagreement.[11]

This analysis was considerably more hopeful than that for Truman. It was exactly this type of support, along with the desire to honor President Kennedy, that contributed to an outstanding legislative record for Johnson in 1964 and subsequently to his landslide election to a full term.

The third vice president as president entered office with the least advantages of the three, perhaps of any vice president in history. Ford was not elected to the position of vice president; he was nominated under the provisions of the Twenty-fifth Amendment. The elected vice president, Spiro T. Agnew, had resigned in disgrace. Ford was confirmed as vice president by the House (387–35) and the Senate (92–3) and took the oath of office on December 6, 1973. When he assumed the presidency on August 9, 1974, after Nixon's resignation, the Nixon program was stalled because of the Watergate crisis. Nixon had had a relatively successful first term, particularly in foreign policy. His landslide victory in 1972 encouraged a somewhat more audacious approach on the domestic front, particularly in attempting to curb government growth. Like Johnson, Ford was judged to have the qualities to work with Congress and break the stalemate. "Mr. Ford brings to the White House the tremendous advantage of being able to talk constructively with people who had lost all faith in the previous administration and had broken off relations with it."[12]

Thus Ford had an advantage of a stalled but full agenda, his own experience on Capitol Hill, and the hopes of those who found him a welcome successor to Richard Nixon. But, of course, the Nixon legacy included Nixon himself as a possible defendant in a criminal trial. Whatever the burdens of the Roosevelt legacy for Truman or the Kennedy legacy for Johnson, they paled compared to what Nixon left for Ford. A full pardon for Nixon was Ford's solution, and it cost him the few short-run advantages that he had. One editorial placed his action within the context of the Watergate conspiracy.

> This newest use of the powers of the presidency [the pardon] to curtail inquiry and to relieve Mr. Nixon of responsibility for this action will strike you as nothing less than a continuation of a cover-up. We do not believe Mr. Ford intended his action to have that as its primary purpose. But that will be its primary effect.[13]

Finally, the timing of the resignation, then the pardon, could not have been worse for President Ford. Like Truman, Ford had to face a midterm election. Unlike Truman, who had more than eighteen months before the election, Ford had less than three months. Even had he not pardoned Nixon, Ford would have faced the problems of standard midterm losses, possibly amplified by a stagnant economy and the first opportunity for the public to express itself on Nixon and Watergate. As it was, the House Republicans suffered a net loss of forty-three seats and Senate Republicans a net loss of three seats. The Democrats had a two-thirds majority in the House of Representatives in the new Congress.

These cases of vice presidents serving as presidents require special attention throughout this book. However well understood the purpose of having a vice president, few analysts truly consider the likelihood of one serving as president. When it happens, therefore, it will not do to lump them into the other categories. Voters do not elect them as presidents; they did not elect Ford as vice president. No one of these three could conceivably have won nomination as president at the time they became vice president. Their advantages and disadvantages are traceable to the man they succeeded. To create their own presidency they had to work through and around the direct legacy of their predecessor. Two of the three vice presidents as presidents were successful in winning on their own and thus had the opportunity to reduce the effect of the past and create their own White House. The third, Gerald Ford, came astonishingly close to winning. Had he done so, he would have faced a much greater challenge than Truman or Johnson in authenticating his leadership, since the Democrats returned with substantial majorities in both houses of Congress.[14]

Elected Vice Presidents

The nomination and general election politics of the 1948 and 1964 campaigns were very different. Presumably, as the argument has gone here, these differences presaged contrasting administrations. Harry Truman had to fight all the way. Many Democrats opposed him, but none of them could mount a sufficiently strong campaign to prevent him from getting the nomination. And the opposition took the form more of backroom maneuvering than challenging him in the primaries (where he won all that he entered). The 1948 convention offered early signals as to what would happen later within the Democratic party. Some southern Democrats walked out as a result of losing the platform battle on civil rights, leading eventually to the Dixiecrat candidacy of Strom Thurmond of South Carolina (one of two third-party candidates in the postwar period to win electoral votes).

The 1948 general election results were among the most bizarre in history. Congressional Democrats recaptured control of both houses of Congress (see table 2-2). House Democrats' net increase of seventy-five seats ranked it among the largest shifts in this century. And yet it was hard for Truman to take much credit since his margin was among the smallest ever. The fact that he won at all was his primary advantage. He entered office hoping to translate his surprise win into substantive gains in public policy, perhaps by establishing a linkage between the presidential and congressional outcomes that was not apparent on the surface. In his memoirs he points out, making reference to the congressional results: "My long campaign against the Eightieth Congress had convinced the voters that a turnover was necessary, and I was given an overwhelmingly Democratic Congress to replace the one which had blocked the administration's domestic progress for two years."[15] Unfortunately for him, the task of establishing his leadership of Congress was complicated by the fact that he lost four Deep South states to Strom Thurmond. These four states had 8 of the 57 Democrats in the Senate and 30 of the 263 Democrats in the House. The South would not be his friend on many crucial issues in the 81st and 82d Congresses.

Lyndon Johnson swept into office in 1964. In other ways, he, too, was the issue. But the forces were overwhelmingly positive. Since he had no announced opposition, Johnson could ignore the primaries and did so. The convention was like that for presidents seeking reelection, a coronation. The Republicans accommodated Johnson further by nominating Barry Goldwater, who was to the right of center in his own party and therefore could not expect full support even within that minority. Thus, again like that of reelected presidents, the results represented an endorsement of Johnson's style in modifying, expanding, and enacting the Kennedy program. To punctuate this endorsement, voters provided a net increase of thirty-eight House Democrats and two Senate Democrats, bringing the totals in both houses above the two-thirds mark.

President Johnson had extraordinary advantages because of his own election and the results in Congress. His victory and that of Reagan in 1980 come closer to meeting the conditions of the party responsibility model than any other postwar election. President Truman's advantages were less directly translatable into power in office.

Elected Heir Apparent

It is said that a category with an N of 1 is not worth discussing. In this case, I beg to disagree. The election of George Bush in 1988 could be included in the category of elected presidents, but I believe it deserves separate status. Part of the justification is simply the importance of highlighting the special problems for an heir apparent or sitting vice president in establishing his leadership of the government. Additionally, it is worth pointing out that two other heirs apparent—Richard Nixon in 1960 and Hubert Humphrey in 1968—came extremely close to winning the White House.[16] Each would have faced problems similar to those encountered by Bush in following an administration with which they were identified but in which they had limited influence.[17]

The campaign for the nomination in 1988 was a rather short-lived contest. Super Tuesday, the scheduling of several southern primaries on one day, clinched the nomination for Bush. The general election had few major issues. Bush won handily, and there was virtually no change in the number of seats held by each party in Congress. The results look very much like those of the reelected presidents (see table 2-2). In fact, one might make the case that the voters were once again approving the return of the same government, with Bush serving as the representative of a president who could not serve a third term. So conceived, the Bush administration could be expected to encounter the same problems of generating enthusiasm and policy proposals that had been characteristic of the second Reagan term.

Bush was not being reelected, however. He was taking over as a first-term president with the intention of running for a second term. His election did not test well by the two criteria suggested earlier for Eisenhower and Reagan. Given the lack of issues during the campaign, it was difficult to interpret Bush's substantial victory in policy terms. And there was virtually no connection to be made between his victory and congressional results. Thus the heir apparent faced the predicament of separating his administration from that of his popular predecessor and producing an advantage for influencing Congress, given that one was not awarded following the election. As it happened, fashioning his own administration created the risk of alienating members of his own party on Capitol Hill. Few cases can match the Bush experience as illustrations of the varying nature of a president's status in the government.

Different Challenges

This review of how presidents come to serve in the White House identifies a surprising variation in the extent to which the means and nature of succession authenticate the exercise of power. The most striking differences are, of course, between being elected to office and assuming the office upon the death or resignation of the incumbent. Establishing one's independent right to govern as a takeover president is a challenge of a high order. As has been discussed, there are also important differences within the larger set of presidents, vice presidents as presidents, and heirs apparent who are elected, in terms of the special advantages provided by each election.

The optimal conditions for creating presidential advantages once in office would appear to be a contested nomination that is satisfactorily resolved, a landslide victory for the presidential ticket, and substantial gains for the president's party in Congress that can be reasonably attributed to the presidential campaign. As shown, very few of the twelve modern elections meet these conditions, thus reinforcing a point to be reiterated throughout this book: There is nothing automatic about the conferring of power to presidents in a separated system. Eisenhower (1952), Johnson (1964), and Reagan (1980) clearly had the most advantages. Truman (1948), Kennedy (1960), Nixon (1968), Carter (1976), Bush (1988), and Clinton (1992) had many fewer advantages. Eisenhower (1956), Nixon (1972), and Reagan (1984) had to seek advantages in elections that reaffirmed split-party government. In later chapters I will show how these presidents either capitalized on their advantages or sought to compensate for their weaknesses.

Who They Are

I turn next to the personal characteristics of presidents. James David Barber's analysis of presidential character is a significant work, exploring the personal background, attachments, and intellectual development of presidents.[18] He carries that analysis forward to predict how a president will perform in the White House. Such an inventive analysis goes far beyond what will be attempted here. My purpose is to offer a brief biographical sketch that places each president in his time and to pose possible effects of his life experiences on the perspective he brings to the job.

The presidents can be classified into four groups in terms of the eras into which they were born and grew into adulthood. Truman and Eisenhower were between centuries: they are of the World War I generation. The period of Truman's childhood was a difficult one, with many labor disputes and economic woes. His first vote for president was in 1908, in a contest between William Howard Taft and William Jennings Bryan. The period of Eisenhower's childhood also spanned some of the financial troubles of the early part of the century, the rise of the Progressive party as a force, and the resulting split in the Republican party. His first vote was in the three-way race of 1912 between President Taft, former President Theodore Roosevelt, and Woodrow Wilson.

The second group includes Johnson, Nixon, Ford, and Reagan. In their early years they witnessed World War I, the relatively calm period that followed in the 1920s, and the drama of the stock market crash in 1929. They are of the Depression generation. Johnson and Reagan cast their first votes for president in 1932, both for Roosevelt; Nixon and Ford voted first for president in 1936, presumably both for Alfred Landon.

The third group includes Kennedy, Carter, and Bush: the World War II generation. Though Kennedy's death has fixed his youthful image in time, had he lived he would now be the oldest of these three presidents. His first vote was in the 1940 election, when he doubtless cast a vote for the president who had appointed his father ambassador to Great Britain. Carter and Bush voted first in the 1948 election between President Truman and Thomas E. Dewey.

And finally there is Bill Clinton, the first president of the post–World War II generation. The time span from the birth of Truman to Clinton is sixty-two years. Chester Arthur was president when Truman was born, and Truman was president when Clinton was born. Truman was growing into manhood at the time of the Spanish-American War, Clinton at the time of the Cuban missile crisis and the escalation of U.S. involvement in the Vietnam War. Clinton's first vote was in 1968, in what was one of the most troubling and divisive elections ever for the Democratic party.

There are other personal characteristics that are interesting and useful to examine for their potential relevance in distinguishing among presidents. Most had very modest backgrounds. An elitist theory of political recruitment and advancement does not fare well with this set of ten presidents. Only Kennedy and Bush were among the well born, so to speak. The other eight had humble beginnings. Schooling varies somewhat more among the ten, ranging from no college degree for Truman to law degrees for Nixon, Ford, and Clinton. Eisenhower and Carter went to military academies (army and navy, respectively). Kennedy, Bush, and Clinton went to prestigious private institutions (Harvard, Yale, and Georgetown, respectively). Clinton also attended Oxford University as a Rhodes scholar and Yale Law School. Johnson and Reagan attended small colleges lacking in prestige even within their respective states.

Presidents have varied rather substantially in regard to their ages when they first sought elective office and when they entered the White House (see figure 2-1). The age of their first elective political experience ranges from 28 for Johnson to 62 for Eisenhower. The mean is 39, somewhat higher than one might have thought. There is also wide variation in the years of experience (not all of it political) between the first election and entering the White House. For Eisenhower that figure is 0 (although, of course, he had decades of military experience); for Johnson it is 27. The vice presidents who took over (Truman, Johnson, and Ford) had an average of 25 years from their first election to the presidency. Another two vice presidents who won on their own—Nixon and Bush—had nearly the same number of years of experience upon entering the White House (23.5). The rest of the group—Eisenhower, Kennedy, Carter, Reagan, and Clinton—averaged 11.4 years of experience (14.3 excluding Eisenhower).

The limited subnational elective political experience of recent presidents is also shown in figure 2-1. Only one of the ten presidents started at the local level (Truman was the equivalent of a county executive). Carter started as a state senator, then governor; Reagan as a governor; and Clinton as state attorney general, then governor.[19] Eisenhower started right at the top. The other five got into elective office first by running for Congress—the House of Representatives in every case, except for George Bush, who first tried the Senate and was defeated and then was elected to the House.

Figure 2-1. *Age and Political Experience of Modern Presidents*

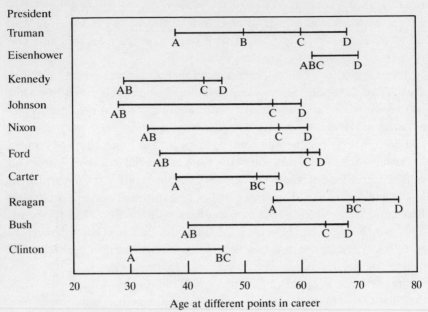

A = First elective political experience
B = First national elective political experience (Congress or president)
C = Enters White House
D = Exits White House

Source: Calculated from data in William A. DeGregorio, *The Complete Book of U.S. Presidents*, 2d ed. (New York: Dembner Books, 1989).

This limited state and local experience is in stark contrast to that of the eight other presidents in this century. All but Herbert Hoover had some elective experience below the national level. Five of the eight were governors, another was a lieutenant governor, four served in the state legislature, and four had local government experience although not always in an elective position. Again by contrast, only two had congressional experience (McKinley in the House, Harding in the Senate). No doubt the differences between the two periods represents judgments by politicians as to what represents potentially valuable experience for winning the presidential nomination and the election. But it may also reflect changes in the agenda, where that agenda is being dealt with, and what best prepares one to manage it. Also reflected are the changes in the political parties and their role in the nominating process. It would have been difficult in the early years of this

Table 2-3. *Legislative Experience of Modern Presidents*
Years

President	State level	Congress	Other	Total
Truman	0	10 (Senate)	Vice president[a]	10+
Eisenhower	0	0	0	0
Kennedy	0	6 (House) 8 (Senate)	0	14
Johnson	0	3 (House staff) 12 (House) 12 (Senate)	2 + (vice president)	29+
Nixon	0	4 (House) 2 (Senate)	8 (vice president)	14
Ford	0	24 (House)	1 (vice president)	25
Carter	4 (Senate) 4 (governor)	0	0	8
Reagan	8 (governor)	0	0	8
Bush	0	4 (House)	8 (vice president)	12
Clinton	12 (governor)	0	0	12

Source: Calculated from data in William A. DeGregorio, *The Complete Book of U.S. Presidents*, 2d ed. (New York: Dembner Books, 1989).

a. Truman served less than three months as vice president.

century to win the nomination outside the political parties. Subsequently the outside route to the nomination became commonplace.

The range of these ten presidents' experience with legislatures (including that gained as a governor or vice president) is from zero to almost thirty years (table 2-3). If one removes the three vice presidents who served as president—Truman, Johnson, and Ford—the average legislative service for the rest drops dramatically, since those three had nearly as much total experience (more than sixty-four years) as the other seven (sixty-eight years). Two others—Nixon and Bush—had brief experiences on the Hill (six and four years, respectively), and it is not absolutely certain that either could have succeeded without having served first as vice president (indeed, Nixon lost on his first try even with that advantage).

That leaves Kennedy as the president with the most congressional experience among those successfully seeking the presidency and the only president of the ten to be elected while serving in Congress. And finally, the last four presidents—Carter, Reagan, Bush, and Clinton—gained most of their pre–White House experience with legislatures outside of Congress, Bush being the only one of the four with service there (four years in the House eighteen years before his election). Clearly presidents are not typically elected from Congress, nor is direct legislative experience a premium qualification for running for the White House. It also follows that several of the modern presidents have had to learn on the job in dealing with Congress.

Very little presidential accession to office takes place by progressive ambition, that is taking advantage of a series of opportunities leading from one office to the next higher office.[20] Only two presidents in this set started at the state level, and they did not then work their way toward Congress. Excluding Eisenhower, all others served in Congress but, again, Truman, Johnson, and Ford were chosen as vice presidents, not a job one necessarily seeks. Nixon too was selected as vice president, although he might have run for president on his own had he stayed in the Senate. Perhaps Kennedy and Bush best fit the theory of progressive ambition. Although he did not serve in the state legislature, Kennedy climbed the ladder nationally from House to Senate to White House. And Bush sought to move from the House to the Senate but was defeated in 1970; he then tried for the presidential nomination in 1980 and lost to Ronald Reagan. But one pure case and one near case do not a theory make. More persuasive is the view that there is no predictable track to the White House. As shown, presidents enter the White House with strikingly varied political experiences. The challenge is in attempting to understand how these various routes help to explain what happens when presidents assume office.

These ten presidents also differ in terms of their experience within their respective political parties (table 2-4). There are some interesting pairings. Truman and Kennedy were in Congress but did not rise to party leadership positions. Truman did, however, serve earlier as a party leader at the county level. Eisenhower obviously had no direct experience with his party. Indeed, he had not declared his party preference before running for president. Some of those wishing to replace Truman as the Democratic nominee in 1948 suggested Eisenhower (and, in fact, he received a few thousand votes in Democratic presidential primaries in that year). Johnson and Ford had lengthy experience as party leaders on Capitol Hill. Neither held state or local party positions, however, nor did they ever work directly for the national party organization.

The other five presidents—Nixon, Carter, Reagan, Bush, and Clinton— had the most diverse party experiences. Nixon and Reagan probably raised more political money than any other leaders in the history of American elections. Both willingly participated in thousands of party and candidate dinners and other organizational events. Bush's association with the party is somewhat different but no less impressive. He is the only one of the presidents to have served as a county chairman (Truman served for only part of a county). He also participated in an endless stream of party activities as vice

Table 2-4. *Political Party Experience of Modern Presidents*

President	Level	Position held
Truman	Local	County leader
Eisenhower	. . .	None
Kennedy	. . .	None
Johnson	Congressional	Senate democratic whip; minority and majority floor leader
Nixon	State, national	Fund raiser; presidential candidate (1960); gubernatorial candidate (1962)
Ford	Congressional	House Republican conference chairman; minority floor leader
Carter	State, national	Governor; Democratic National Committee campaign committee chair
Reagan	State, national	Cochair, California for Goldwater; member, state central committee; governor; Republican Governors' Association chair; fund raiser
Bush	Local, national	County chairman; Republican National Committee chair
Clinton	State, national	Governor; Democratic Leadership Council chair

Source: Compiled from data in DeGregorio, *Complete Book of U.S. Presidents.*

president, and he was the chairman of the Republican National Committee during the difficult Watergate months.

Carter's experience looks good on paper—almost as good as that of the other three just discussed. However, he worked alongside or even against the party as much as for it. He wanted to make change, and it is doubtful that his service as governor encouraged Georgia Democrats to view him as their leader. The posts he held for the Democratic National Committee were more honorary in nature, though they did afford him the chance to travel and make contacts useful to him later in his presidential bid. Clinton was active in the Democratic Leadership Council, serving as chairman for one year.

Presidents naturally seek to compensate for weaknesses. Eisenhower, the president with no party experience, relied on Nixon. Truman worked well at the local level: it may even have won the election for him. Kennedy was on a mission to heal party divisions when he was assassinated. Johnson and Ford were primarily legislative leaders serving in the White House. Carter never blended well with the party apparatus and paid dearly. Reagan worked well with the party apparatus at all levels: he was perhaps the most effective party leader as president. Bush was the only one of the presidents to serve as chairman of his party's national committee. Yet he was never fully accepted by the more conservative wing of the party, a fact that plagued him through-

Table 2-5. *Advantages, Weaknesses, and Strategies of*
Modern Presidents

President	Advantages	Weaknesses	Deduced strategy
Elected presidents			
Eisenhower (1952)	Election by wide margin Congressional majorities Contrast[a]	Lack of Washington experience	Restorative
Kennedy (1960)	Congressional majorities New generation/ contrast[a]	Election by narrow margin No connection[b]	Compensatory
Nixon (1968)	Experience Contrast[a]	Election by narrow margin No congressional majority	Compensatory
Carter (1976)	Congressional majorities Contrast[a]	Election by narrow margin No connection[b] Lack of Washington experience	Compensatory
Reagan (1980)	Election by wide margin Senate majority Connection[b] Contrast[a]	Lack of Washington experience No House majority	Assertive
Clinton (1992)	New generation/ contrast[a] Congressional majorities	Election by narrow margin Limited connection[b] Lack of Washington experience	Compensatory
Reelected presidents			
Eisenhower (1956)	Election by wide margin Experience	No congressional majority Runout[c]	Guardian
Nixon (1972)	Election by wide margin Experience	No congressional majority	Guardian
Reagan (1984)	Election by wide margin Experience Senate majority	No House majority Runout[c]	Guardian

out his presidency and in his campaign for reelection. The mystery case is
that of Nixon. As president he appeared to insulate himself from the party,
essentially going into business for himself in the 1972 presidential campaign.
He, too, paid dearly in the end.

Governing Strategies

To say that presidents are different personally and in how they enter the
White House borders on being trite. To say that these differences are often
ignored in the expectations of performance in office restores interest, however. As a final exercise in this chapter, I will catalog the special advantages

Table 2-5 *(continued)*

President	Advantages	Weaknesses	Deduced strategy
Nonelected presidents			
Truman (1945)	Congressional majorities Congressional experience	Contrast[a] Preparation	Custodial
Johnson (1963)	Congressional majorities Congressional experience Assassination	None	Assertive
Ford (1974)	Contrast[a] Congressional experience	No congressional majority Appointed Watergate legacy	Restorative
Elected vice presidents			
Truman (1948)	Congressional majorities	No connection[b] Party division	Compensatory
Johnson (1964)	Election by wide margin Congressional majorities Connection[b]	None	Assertive
Heir apparent			
Bush (1988)	Experience	No congressional majority Runout[c]	Guardian

a. A favorable or unfavorable comparison with the previous administration.
b. Whether or not the president's win was perceived as related to wins for his party in Congress.
c. The depletion of the agenda, typically associated with reelection.

and weaknesses of the modern presidents upon entering office and speculate about strategies logically associated with each set. Then I will comment on mitigating personal factors that either facilitated or altered the realization of these strategies.

The more outstanding advantages and weaknesses of each of the fifteen assumptions of office for the ten postwar presidents are summarized in table 2-5. The characteristics are drawn from the review provided in this chapter of how presidents came to be in the White House and their personal and political backgrounds. I then deduced governing strategies for each president as reasonably following from the balance of advantages and disadvantages. This exercise produced five strategies:

Assertive: With a strongly positive balance upon entering office, the president is aggressive in promoting policy proposals from the start (three cases: Johnson, 1963 and 1964; Reagan, 1980).

Compensatory: With significant disadvantages, and particularly lacking an electoral edge, the president devises supplementary means for authenticating his leadership (five cases: Truman, 1948; Kennedy, 1960; Nixon, 1968; Carter, 1976; Clinton, 1992).

Custodial: In assuming the office of a strong predecessor, the president takes custody of an agenda already in place (one case: Truman, 1945).

Guardian: Typically associated with reelections; the strongest advantage, a landslide election, is not bolstered by congressional majorities. The president uses his electoral reaffirmation to protect or guard what has been done (four cases: Eisenhower, 1956; Nixon, 1972; Reagan, 1984; Bush, 1988).[21]

Restorative: Due to the stark and positive contrast with his predecessor, the new president at entry adopts a strategy of restoring the status of the office (two cases: Eisenhower, 1952; Ford, 1974).

Are these deductions predictive of the early behavior of these administrations? For the most part the answer is yes. But there are exceptions, seemingly because of the president himself and his determination to ignore the balance of advantages or to believe in a singular interpretation of his mission. The principal exceptions are Truman (1948), Nixon (1972), and Carter (1976). Perhaps buoyed by his surprise win, Truman adopted a more assertive than compensatory strategy. Carter also could claim a surprise win, in capturing the nomination rather than in winning the general election (which he came close to losing). Possibly more important in his greater assertiveness was the fact that he was the first president elected in the post-Watergate period. He believed that he was entrusted by the people to "do the right thing" once in the White House.

Nixon, too, was more assertive than conditions appeared to warrant. Although he won an overwhelming victory in 1972, its size could reasonably be attributed to the weakness of his opponent. In any event, he failed to bring Republican congressional majorities to Washington. Still, Nixon had scores to settle, and a guardianship strategy was not his preference. It is too soon at this writing to make a judgment about Clinton. Early indications are, however, that he is more like Carter than Kennedy, that is, more assertive than compensatory, in part because of his interpretation of the need for change and an almost Johnson-like passion for policy action.

At the very least these incoming strategies alert one to alternative criteria for evaluating performance. If it is correct that presidents enter office with assorted advantages, then it is reasonable to account for the extent to which they match or exceed the performance plausibly associated with one set over another. That evaluation modifies substantially one that is drawn from an idealized concept of a president as presidency, one that judges each occupant by a standard of assertiveness in leading a party government. The alternative tests ask: What can a president reasonably be expected to accomplish? Does he meet those expectations? These tests are not as benign as one might think. Meeting limited expectations may not be at all what is judged to be necessary for the good of the country, either by analysts or by the public. Therefore, one conclusion may well be that a president operating as expected under severe constraints simply cannot do the job. If he is reelected, however, there should be more concern about the viability of the election system than about the performance of the president in question. Reelection under such circumstances suggests either that the voters were not given a choice or that they were uninformed about the president's capacity to lead.

CHAPTER THREE

Organizing to Govern in the Separated System

THE separated system of diffused responsibility, mixed representation, and competing legitimacies presents special problems for presidents. As the focal person for the separated government, they are typically held accountable for policies and events they do not fully control. Unlike most prime ministers, presidents cannot depend on being well acquainted and connected with others in elected and decisionmaking positions. Neither can they assume a standard formula for sharing power with these others: the formula changes within and between presidencies. Further, bureaucrats, legislators, and interest group representatives tend to accommodate to changes at the top by developing continuities below. The triangles of power may not be as cozy as in the past, but the connections among the permanent actors are still a formidable challenge to an incoming president who is expected to take charge of the government. The test can be especially demanding for vice presidents taking over and for elected presidents who have not been part of the national government.

Clearly, then, presidents must become larger than themselves to fulfill their responsibilities and meet performance expectations. Organization is a way they can accomplish these goals. They have a measure of discretion in making appointments and in structuring access to the Oval Office and decisionmaking in the Executive Office. This organization will depend to a considerable extent on the personal, experiential, and political advantages of each president. After all, it is the person as president that must come to life organizationally. If that process is unnatural and forced, it will not work well for achieving the goals of leadership. Of course, the circumstances for organizing will vary. Some presidents, like Eisenhower and Reagan, have the advantages of a fresh start, experience in leading complex organizations, and strong electoral endorsement. Others, like takeover Presidents Johnson and Ford, must manage initially with a structure designed to make someone else larger than life.

This chapter focuses attention on the variations in organizational challenges and experiences of nine post–World War II presidents—Truman through Bush—to determine how presidents take charge and the circumstances in which they do so. I will concentrate primarily on the White House staff and cabinet secretaries as representative of two crucial sets of appointments. The White House staff enlarges the person as president to a group of close advisers and spokespersons for a presidency. The cabinet secretaries extend the president's reach into the permanent bureaucracy. There is substantially more organization and structure to study, but these more public appointments often come to characterize the presidency.

Most of government is already organized and in place when presidents take office. Departments and agencies are at work; a huge proportion of government employees stay at their desks. An immediate task facing the president and his associates is to plug into that permanent government as a prerequisite to establishing a degree of influence or control. Bureaucrats are accustomed to this exercise, and indeed, for the most part, they comply with it. But success for the president in establishing connections to "his" government requires more than moving into the Oval Office and making the necessary appointments. Validating the leadership of the White House and encouraging compliance by the bureaucracy and Congress are not one-time activities. Presidents must shape and reshape their means of governing through a temporary and ever-changing organizational design.

The famed Committee on Administrative Management (the Brownlow committee) rightly concluded in 1937: "The President needs help."[1] Bradley H. Patterson, Jr., who served on the White House staff for three presidents, provides contemporary evidence that the president now needs help more than ever:

> The potential actions of government are now so variegated . . . that coordination among their Cabinet managers is indispensable to permit their full effect. Abroad, the days have vanished when America's national security resources—diplomatic, military intelligence, economic—could be kept in separate compartments. Vanished with them are whatever boundary lines ever existed between domestic policies and foreign affairs, or between politics and policy. The president today acts in a gigantic theater-in-the-round.[2]

Presidents have gotten more assistance, to be sure. But Peri E. Arnold observes: "The plain fact is that no modern president has fully managed the executive branch." He warns that efforts to increase managerial capacities result in setting a "trap" by "offering increased capacity and influence to presidents but creating even greater expectations about presidential performance." Arnold believes that "the president is not so much a manager of administration; he is a tactician using it."[3]

How the president selects and organizes the White House and the cabinet and puts them to work typically depends on his analysis of goals, personal resources, and needs. After all, it is *his* White House, if only *his* government on consignment. The staff represents his effort to find a place within a larger structure that was there when he arrived and will be there after he leaves, albeit influenced in the interim by his presence. In a sense, this staffing process represents an effort to graft a head onto an existing body. No one can imagine that to be a simple exercise. It starts very personally when the president shapes an organization to suit his manner and method of decision-making. It then may be adapted to what the president and his staff find is necessary to get the government to work as they want it to.[4]

It is surely true that presidents seek to organize the White House to serve them and that those appointed intend to achieve that goal if at all possible. But there is an institutional imperative as well, relating to the growth of government and the emergence of a substantial administrative apparatus attached to the presidency, referred to by some as the "presidential branch." Upon entering office, presidents can and do cut back on staff growth, often as a result of a campaign promise and then to compare themselves favorably with a predecessor. These reductions are typically more symbolic than real, however, because of "the recurrent streams of action-forcing questions flowing necessarily to presidents themselves, through regularized procedures."[5] Demands will be made, and the pressure to meet them is substantial. The presidency is increasingly institutionalized, thus placing greater distance between the personal White House staff and the governing departments and agencies.[6] As a consequence of the growth and development of the Executive Office of the President during the postwar period, presidents have found they must manage a nearby government surrounding the White House itself. That management task naturally falls to the White House staff.

The White House Staff

The number of White House and major Executive Office staff at the start of each presidency from 1945 to 1989 are shown in table 3-1. The White

Table 3-1. *Number of White House and Major Executive Office Staff, First Year of Administration, 1945–89*

President	Year	White House staff	Major executive office staff
Truman	1945	64	705[a]
Truman	1949	243	570[b]
Eisenhower	1953	247	473[b]
Eisenhower	1957	399	541[b]
Kennedy	1961	439	544[b]
Johnson	1963	485	663[c]
Johnson	1965	292	689[c]
Nixon	1969	341	793[c]
Nixon	1973	528	839[d]
Ford	1974	560	816[d]
Carter	1977	387	962[e]
Reagan	1981	378	1,172[f]
Reagan	1985	368	1,059[f]
Bush	1989	370	1,064[f]

Source: Compiled from data in Harold W. Stanley and Richard G. Niemi, *Vital Statistics on American Politics*, 3d ed. (Washington: CQ Press, 1992), pp. 265–67.

a. Includes the Bureau of the Budget (BOB).

b. Includes BOB, the Council of Economic Advisers (CEA), and National Security Council (NSC).

c. Includes BOB, CEA, NSC, Office of Science and Technology (OST), and Special Representative for Trade Negotiations (SRTN). Does not include Office of Economic Opportunity (OEO), started in 1965 and located in the Executive Office of the President.

d. Includes BOB (now Office of Management and Budget—OMB), CEA, NSC, SRTN, and Office for Policy Development (OPD).

e. Includes OMB, CEA, NSC, OST, SRTN, and OPD.

f. Includes OMB, CEA, NSC, OST, Office of Administration, SRTN, and OPD.

House staff includes those close aides whose work is oriented around the president's political, policy, social, and constitutional responsibilities (as well as those of his wife). The Executive Office staff include people in units like the Office of Management and Budget, the National Security Council, and the Council of Economic Advisers, which have been created to provide professional advice to the president as well as direction and coordination of the bureaucracy. The White House staff grew to well over 500 during the Nixon administration. Subsequent presidents have sought to work with a leaner staff, seemingly acknowledging that an outer limit had been reached during the Nixon administration, when significant problems of coordination developed.[7]

The Presidential Branch

The Executive Office of the President is now a minigovernment of approximately 1,500 professionals who act as the president's contacts with the bureaucracy, Congress, other governments, the public, the party, and the press.[8] This minigovernment is located in the White House itself, the ornate Old Executive Office Building next door, and a New Executive Office Building one block away. Nelson W. Polsby refers to this solidifying arrangement as "the presidential branch."

> Perhaps the most interesting development of the fifty-year period is the emergence of a presidential branch of government separate and apart from the executive branch. It is the presidential branch that sits across the table from the executive branch at budgetary hearings, and that imperfectly attempts to coordinate both the executive and legislative branches in its own behalf.[9]

The emergence of a presidential branch is bound to threaten the regular departments and agencies. The president is encouraged, if not fully prepared, to go into policy business on his own, without having to depend heavily on advice from the cabinet secretaries and other presidential appointees. Thus the status of cabinet secretaries has declined while that of the president's assistants has increased.[10] These developments have suited those presidents suspicious of the bureaucracy, as most are. Republican presidents particularly welcome an independent source of policy and political advice since they doubt that certain of their proposals are welcome within most departments and agencies.

The White House staff sits atop this branch and is responsible for its management. One may rightly question whether the whole apparatus has resulted in a net gain of influence for the president. Significant numbers of politically ambitious professional people, many with strong policy commitments, spur in-house competition for the president's time. Independent, self-organizing policy entrepreneurs were not exactly what Louis Brownlow had in mind when he concluded that the president needed help. As John Hart describes it:

> Nowadays, senior White House staffers regularly do what Brownlow said they should not do. They quickly become prominent figures in every administration. They do make decisions, issue instructions, and emit public statements. They do interpose themselves between the president and the heads of departments. They do exercise power on their own account, and, on occasions, certain members of the White House staff have not discharged their functions with restraint. In recent years some have clearly lacked the high competence Brownlow thought essential, and few have displayed much passion for anonymity.[11]

Hedrick Smith contends that "presidents developed their own bureaucracy."[12] But the White House staff is not a standard bureaucracy—far from it. Like aggressive staff personnel on Capitol Hill, many are men and women anxious for credentials that will permit them to move elsewhere.[13] They can enhance their résumés substantially with the addition of White House experience, especially if it includes successful encounters with the bureaucracy.

The advent of a presidential branch and an aggressive White House staff is not a cost-free benefit for the president. I have alluded to the "trap" Arnold speaks of: more staff and higher expectations for achieving the unachievable. Adding staff to solve the president's traditional problem of managing and directing the bureaucracy to his own ends can, itself, become a management problem. A former White House staff person who served Eisenhower and Nixon offered a particularly vivid analysis of the consequences of an elaborated staff, as well as how presidents have sought to escape. I quote it at some length here because it so well illustrates both the need for and the costs of such staff.

> The president who understands staff work knows that any staff tries to ensnare its victim. Its victim is its leader. . . . The president moves into the White House . . . and they come trotting into the place with a staff around them that helped them with the election. That staff feels as if the president is a personal possession. . . . And they put this into a hermetically-sealed box and try to keep everyone else away from it.
>
> And so you have the first part of the presidency, the inner circle. . . . Then you have middle season when they have to enlarge it slightly and breach that with a crack or two because they become overworked. And they realize in growing desperation they can't handle all the work and so most grudgingly, they will bring in a newcomer to enlarge their group.
>
> During this season the president gets claustrophobia. He realizes that he's being spoonfed by just this small clique of people, and he wants to break out; he wants to look out the window and see who's out there.
>
> So he uses devices. President Eisenhower used those famous stag dinners . . . to get around his staff. He would call in people from all across the country, . . . and he would sit down to have a very enjoyable dinner and post-dinner conversation. "What's going on in America, boys; tell me what's going on out there?" And they would end up in long discussions and even arguments over the course of America and what's troubling educators, what's troubling businessmen, what's troubling labor. Very valuable to President Eisenhower because he had been on military staffs for many years. He knew precisely what a staff would do to a leader. So he deliberately did that to franchise himself from his own staff.[14]

One need not accept George E. Reedy's admittedly exaggerated image of White House "inner life" as "essentially the life of the barnyard, as set forth so graphically in the study of the pecking order among chickens" to take interest in how the White House is organized and whether it works well.

Reedy's experience in the Johnson White House led him to believe that "below the president is a mass of intrigue, posturing, strutting, cringing, and pious 'commitment' to irrelevant windbaggery." He attributed this tendency to the cloak of power associated with the presidency that invited "intrigue, pomposity, and ambition."[15] In overstating the case, Reedy draws attention to the potential for an unelected staff to act in the name of the president and therefore to the need for control and management by the president and his trusted advisers.

Organizational Models

What are the options in organizing the White House staff? In 1976, President-elect Jimmy Carter asked Stephen Hess, a Brookings Institution senior fellow and former White House staff person, for memorandums on organizing the presidency. In the first edition of his book, *Organizing the Presidency*, which had come to Carter's attention, Hess sensibly stressed the importance of fitting the organization of the White House to the person who is president. Thus, in advising Carter, Hess worked with what he knew about the new president: Carter's stated organizational preferences (for example, that there would be no chief of staff) and his desire to avoid the problems of previous presidents. Hess concluded that "a president need not have a chief of staff— he can divide the duties—but he should not be his own chief of staff. Otherwise he will find that he is spending considerable time on servicing his staff, rather than the other way around."[16]

Hess reviewed two dominant models of organization and proposed a variation that was attentive to preferences Carter had already expressed. According to Hess, the previous models were the circle and the pyramid. The circle was "used by FDR and JFK. The president [is] at the hub with staff impinging on him from all points along the circumference. The model can work well in running small enterprises (such as the White House during the early New Deal), but tends to create undue chaos and confusion in the modern presidency, especially over time as new people are added to the staff who lack established working relationships with each other and the president." The circle is often referred to as the "spokes of the wheel" type of organization with the Oval Office as the hub.

The pyramid was "used by Eisenhower and Nixon. The president [is] at the apex. Extremely orderly; but may tend to screen out creativity and can lead to excessive secrecy. Only advisable for presidents who have long experience with this model (as did Ike in the military)."[17] The pyramid normally requires a chief of staff who acts as the checkpoint for what passes through to the Oval Office. The person who has this position is under tremendous pressure and must have the full confidence of the president. He or she may not be able to withstand this pressure for very long. In fact, in fulfilling the function of protecting the president, such a person may have to resign if there is some crisis, for failure to do so implicates the president in the affair at hand. The rewards for service as chief of staff are not always obvious; Dick Cheney, who served as President Ford's chief of staff, observed: "If there's a dirty deed to be done, it's the chief of staff who's got to do it. The president gets credit for what works, and you get the blame for what doesn't work. That's the nature of the beast."[18]

Instead of either of these models, Hess offered a variation for the Carter White House that he viewed as providing "open efficiency" or "orderly access." It resembled an isosceles trapezoid (a pyramid with its top sawed off). Hess said it "allows wide access to the president in a structured setting. This assumes that you are a highly methodical person who will be ultimately dissatisfied with incomplete staff work or tangled lines of communications, while, at the same time, will wish not to be overly dependent on a small number of aides and as open as possible in your conduct of the presidency."[19]

Others, too, have classified presidential staff management forms as a collegial system or "adhocracy" for the circle and a formalistic or centralized management system for the pyramid. The competitive or multiple advocacy approach of Franklin D. Roosevelt is often added to these core types.[20] The discussion below of individual presidents will show that these forms as ideal types are insufficient to account for the variations found. The spokes are not always the same length, thus producing anything but a circle; pyramids are never that pointed; the trapezoid has not been tried; and multiple advocacy is less a management style than a process of uncovering various policy options. These organizational configurations take too little account of the variables related to the personal and institutional demands of being president.

Cabinet Secretaries: Reaching Within

The terms *government* or *administration* are frequently used to designate the prominent persons who make up the group of presidential appointees.[21] The first—*government*—is particularly susceptible to misunderstanding outside the United States since it is commonly used in parliamentary systems to refer to the prime minister and his or her cabinet. Therefore it conveys the idea of unity as well as a process within the majority party or coalition for developing that unity. The second—*administration*—is somewhat less misleading but it, too, conveys more of a collective sense of purpose than is constitutionally or politically warranted in the American system.

This strength of unity in other systems presumably derives from processes of integration among those who make up the government and also between them and the bureaucracy or the legislature. In many parliamentary systems a measure of integration is achieved at the start through a recruiting process that builds on common experiences, typically drawing cabinet ministers from the parliament. The potential for unity of purpose in this system is highly accommodating to the demands of party government. It facilitates accountability by encouraging policy and administrative integration; indeed, the government may well be judged on that basis.[22]

In the United States, the top appointees thought to be the "government" or "administration" are typically not well integrated through prior policy or political experience. In many instances the prior work or professional association of cabinet secretaries and White House staff is limited or nonexistent. The mix of career ambitions represented by presidential appointees may well bring the outside world to Washington, but there is no guarantee that these officials will cohere into a working government. In fact, there is a high probability that they will not. Thus the president is somewhat in the position of the Olympic basketball coach. He may well have talented players but lack a team.[23]

Proper Tests of Presidencies

If the criteria of a "government" are used to test the strength or weakness of a presidential administration, it will almost always be found wanting. But what is the point in applying those tests? However imperfect by the standards of responsible party government, the separated system persists. Thus other measures of presidential strength or weakness are needed. The tests of presidential effectiveness—if not exactly strength or weakness—may be the extent to which communication is established between the White House and the departments and agencies, the clarity of policy messages that are communicated, and the degree of mutual support that results when the messages are clear. The mixed experience and background of those brought in to manage the permanent government pose a significant communication challenge for the White House. Representing diversity, however admirable on other grounds, may interfere with building unity of purpose. In criticizing the American system, analysts often fail to appreciate what it takes to integrate that which has been so carefully separated.

If a presidency is judged as a communications network, a good cabinet is a set of individuals, each well enough oriented to the White House and informed of its goals to accomplish policy, administrative, and legislative tasks with confidence. The grade given a president properly may be based on how many officials meet this one-on-one test of contact and communication on issues of the moment, not on tests derived from communal decisionmaking.

Viewing the presidency as a set of orientations of cabinet appointees toward the Oval Office (not necessarily toward one another) encourages an analysis of the process by which this happens (or fails to occur), as well as how it may change. It also invites consideration of whether a president is successful in orienting cabinet secretaries to his purposes, and whether the secretaries then represent that orientation in the many individual contacts that they have with other decisionmakers. Dean Rusk, secretary of state for Kennedy and Johnson, illustrated both points in discussing the demands on cabinet secretaries. "President Johnson was always considerate of his Cabinet officers. I think he felt that they were the ones who shared with him the public responsibility and the constitutional and statutory responsibility of office." (This was the result of successful orientation.) "It was the Cabinet officers who had to appear most often before the Congress to defend a program. It was the Cabinet officers who met the press and helped to carry the public explanation of policy, and who had to share the ultimate responsibility."[24] (This was the representation of a successful orientation.)

Cabinet secretaries are, of course, responsible for administering their departments and representing departmental interests within the wider policy process. But, as Rusk states, they are also spokespersons for the administration within their policy areas. Their public responsibility is typically issue-specific. A cabinet secretary speaking for the administration does so regarding the policies proposed by and implemented in his or her department. These policies may be crosscutting, to be sure, but not even a close friend of the president serving as cabinet secretary is likely either to expound on or be listened to in regard to issues outside his departmental jurisdiction. Below the level of the president himself, more general crosscutting discussion or exposition is likely to come from White House staff, possibly the chief of staff or the director of the Office of Management and Budget.

Variations in Appointments

The variable characteristics of presidents should be revealed in the appointments they make, even now, when there is pressure to be more diverse than in the past. Polsby illustrates this point:

> When a new president picks his cabinet, he gives observers the first set of solid clues about the kind of president he intends to be. . . . President Eisenhower's appointment of "nine millionaires and a plumber" gave quite a good forecast of the sort of presidency General Eisenhower wanted to have. When John Kennedy became president he struck a dominant theme of self-consciously moving beyond his own range of personal acquaintance to form a governing coalition. Likewise, his appointment of his brother as attorney general telegraphed a strong desire to keep close control of the civil rights issue.
>
> It is possible to see in Richard Nixon's cabinet appointments a mirror of his emerging view of the role of the president vis-à-vis the rest of the government.[25]

Implicit in these observations is the lack of institutionalization of the cabinet. Jeffrey E. Cohen concludes that each president fashions a role for those who serve in the cabinet, that some of these persons come to have considerable power, and that there may be institutional development within a presidency but not between presidencies. There is little carryover from one president to the next.[26]

It is apparent, then, that cabinets are interesting primarily as they reflect the president's effort to govern within in the separated system. And that is how they will be treated here: as a part of a presidency, not a thing unto themselves. Therefore when cabinet secretaries are successful, they must expect to share that success with the president, and when there is failure, they may expect to be held accountable, perhaps even to resign.

These characteristics do not make the position a highly attractive one. In fact, they help to explain the high turnover among cabinet officials. It is not that one cannot profit from the experience (and there always appear to be takers), but only certain people can make the position work for them. Getting the proper fit between a department's interest and that of the cabinet secretary may only be a happenstance, particularly when there are pressures to represent different groups in the most publicly exposed positions of an administration. If so, it is not in the least surprising that turnover is high. Unconventional demands, the unstructured nature of the job, and the need to satisfy interests not associated with performance in office may contribute to appointees getting in, gaining whatever experience and prestige are allowed, and getting out.

Other features of cabinet life include the following:

—A tendency to identify with the interests and clientele of the department the longer one stays ("going native").

—Variable access to the White House, depending on the agenda and presidential policy interests.

—Greater centralization of decisionmaking in the White House to compensate for the lack of unity or community among the cabinet (amplified even more if a cabinet secretary "goes native").

—Pressure to balance presidential policy positions against congressional support for existing programs (particularly characteristic of divided government between a Republican president and a Democratic Congress).

At the very least, these features prepare one for the variation in the number of cabinet secretarial appointments made by the postwar presidents (see table 3-2). The variation in the total number of appointments is explained in part by the increase in the number of departments. Even accounting for those increases, however, the stability of the Eisenhower years is impressive: just twenty total appointments in eight years. There is greater stability in the first term than in the second term in all but the Truman years. Again, the Eisenhower record is notable: only three cabinet secretaries failed to complete the first term. But the Kennedy-Johnson, Reagan, and Bush first terms are also striking for their relatively low turnover. Truman stabilized his administration following the high turnover of the first term, showing the highest average number of months of service in the second term of the five presidencies spanning eight years.

The variation in turnover among cabinet departments is shown in table 3-3. The Department of Agriculture has held its secretary longer than other departments. Several have served throughout presidential terms. The Departments of State and Interior have also had long-serving secretaries. If one discounts the high turnover in State early in the first Truman term (three secretaries), the average service is more like that of Agriculture. Dean Rusk served a full eight years for Kennedy and Johnson, and John Foster Dulles came close for Eisenhower, as did George Shultz for Reagan.[27]

Hugh Heclo makes the point that "cabinet secretaries may bring with them a cadre of personal acquaintances to fill some of their subordinate political positions, but in general public executives will be strangers with only a fleeting chance to learn how to work together."[28] The same may be said for

Table 3-2. *Number and Length of Service of Cabinet Secretaries, 1945–93*

President	Number of departments	Total number appointed	Average months of service[a]			Number serving full term		
			First term	Second term	Both terms	First term	Second term	Both terms
Roosevelt-Truman (1945–53)	10→9[b]	33	18	29	27	0	6	0
Eisenhower (1953–61)	9→10[c]	20	37	28	48	7	5	2
Kennedy-Johnson (1961–69)	10→12[d]	28	34	23	36	4	4	3
Nixon-Ford (1969–77)	12→11[e]	31	27	19	34	4	1	0
Carter (1977–81)	11→13[f]	21	28	…	…	4	…	…
Reagan (1981–89)	13[g]	32	35	25	36	6	4	1
Bush (1989–93)	14	22	31	…	…	6	…	…

Sources: Calculated from data in Michael Nelson, ed., *Guide to the Presidency* (Washington: Congressional Quarterly, 1989), pp. 1461–63; and William A. Degregorio, *The Complete Book of U.S. Presidents*, 2d ed. (New York: Dembner Books, 1989).

a. The average is calculated by dividing the number of cabinet secretaries into the total number of months of a department's existence in an administration minus the number of months a position was vacant between appointments.

b. The Department of Defense was created in 1947, combining the Departments of War and Navy.

c. The Department of Health, Education, and Welfare was created in 1953.

d. The Department of Housing and Urban Development was created in 1965; the Department of Transportation, in 1966.

e. The Post Office was made into an independent, noncabinet agency in 1970.

f. The Department of Energy was created in 1977; the Department of Education, in 1980.

g. The Department of Veterans Affairs was created in 1988, but the first appointment was made in 1989.

Table 3-3. *Number and Average Length of Service of Cabinet Secretaries, by Department, 1945–93*

Department	Number of secretaries	Average months of service
In existence throughout the period		
State	15	38
Treasury	17	34
Justice	20	29
Interior	15	38
Agriculture	13	44
Commerce	20	34
Labor	18	32
Created in the period		
Defense (1947)	17	33
HEW/HHS (1953/1980)	17	28
HUD (1965)	9	37
Transportation (1966)	11	30
Energy (1977)	6	32
Education (1980)	5	31
Veterans Affairs (1989)	2	24[a]

Sources: Calculated from data in Nelson, *Guide to the Presidency*, pp. 1461–63; DeGregorio, *Complete Book of U.S. Presidents*; Robert Sobel, ed., *Biographical Directory of the United States Executive Branch, 1774–1977* (Westport, Conn.: Greenwood Press, 1977); and *Who's Who in America*.

a. Given that only two persons have served, this average distorts reality. The first person serving in this capacity, Edward Derwinski, served almost the full term.

presidents in regard to cabinet secretaries, except that most are not personal acquaintances of the president, nor are they likely to be there long enough to become so. Some secretaries do stay a long time, not as partners with the president but simply because their work is not of central concern to the president and they are doing a decent job.

Perhaps most striking to foreign observers from parliamentary systems is the extent to which cabinet secretaries, representing the president's reach into the permanent government, are drawn from the private sphere. Cabinet appointments by the elected presidents—that is, excluding those reelected or taking over after serving as vice president—have included far more people drawn from private life or state and local government than from the federal government. Only Bush appointed to his cabinet a sizable proportion of persons with federal executive experience at the time of appointment. Bush was close to being a takeover president, however, and therefore he reappointed several sitting cabinet secretaries. Nixon, Reagan, and Clinton initially appointed no one with federal executive experience immediately before their cabinet service, although several appointees in each case had previous service as federal-level executives. The other elected presidents did little better. Kennedy and Nixon appointed a number of governors; Clinton's cab-

inet secretaries included several with previous state executive experience. Of
course, as administrations mature, they naturally develop more federal executive experience, but presidents, once in office, tend to make new appointments from the executive branch rather than from the private sphere. Thus,
for example, when Nixon made wholesale changes in 1972 and 1973, he drew
much more heavily from those with experience in the federal government.

Cabinet secretaries are, for the most part, intelligent and talented. Yet
the challenge for them in taking charge is considerable, thus contributing to
the delays experienced by new administrations during transitions from one
president to the next.

Organizational Experience of Modern Presidents

However useful as general descriptions or prescriptions for the relationships between a leader and staff, common geometric configurations like the
circle or pyramid fail to describe how modern presidents do their work. I
perceive four organizational patterns of change associated with the presidents
and their terms in office (see figure 3-1):

—Stable: Substantial continuity in organizational structure and personnel
through a term.

—Adjustable: Ordinary organizational adaptation to change through a
term.

—Renewable: Major organizational restructuring during a presidency,
with a substantial number of new appointments.

—Transitional: A transition from an organization in place to one suited
to a new president (associated with takeovers).

White House staff organization differs to exactly the degree one might
expect, based on the nature of its dependency on the president: who he is,
how he got there, and how he sees the job. Differences show up on a number
of dimensions, not just the degree and trail of access to the Oval Office. In
addition, cabinet secretaries appointed by each president reveal the changing
nature of an administration. (See appendix figures A-1 through A-7 for a
detailed presentation of the changes in the cabinets of all the presidents
discussed below.) It is fair to state that each president has more than one
presidency. This variation has implications for the president's strategic position and functioning in the separated system; it affects public standing, influence in agenda setting, and status in the lawmaking process. I will discuss
the organizational experience of each administration in chronological order.

Figure 3-1. *Modern Presidents, by Organizational Pattern, 1945–93*

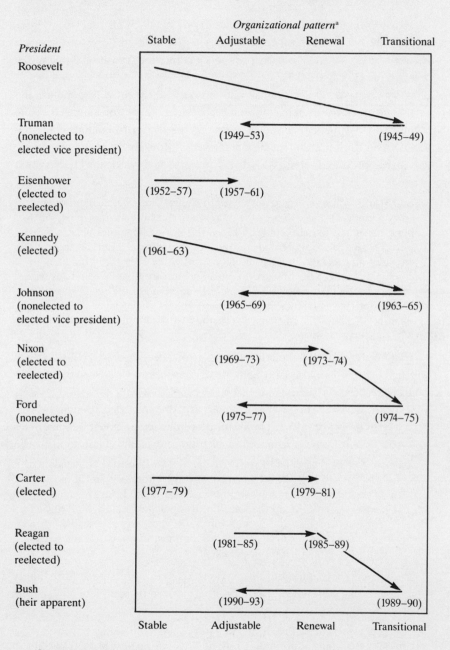

a. See text for explanation of patterns.

Roosevelt to Truman

When Franklin D. Roosevelt died on April 12, 1945, his successor, Harry
S. Truman, had been in office just eighty-two days; thus he served nearly a
full term as president. His early presidency is the first transitional one in the
postwar period (figure 3-1).

WHITE HOUSE STAFF. Truman had virtually no executive experience and
little time as vice president to observe how his predecessor managed. Time
alone was not sufficient, however, either to discern or to emulate the Roosevelt organizational and management style. Roosevelt's techniques were
subtle, complex, and suited to his distinctive personality. Richard E. Neustadt
explains:

> In a White House on Roosevelt's pattern, senior aides were called upon to
> do two things at once: to help their President put his concerns in personal
> perspective and to help him keep his work informed by other perspectives
> also. These two are somewhat contradictory; to manage both a man needs
> empathy and loyalty and self-discipline, all three. For these qualities in
> combination, Roosevelt looked to old associates from politics and govern-
> ment. . . . Truman followed suit as best he could. Lacking at the start
> enough reliable associates, he picked most of his best aides young and grew
> them on the job. . . . In time, this method worked quite well outside the
> national security sphere.[29]

Initially Truman had the advantage of two exceedingly shrewd Roosevelt
advisers, Harry Hopkins and Sam Rosenman. However, Hopkins died in
January 1946, and Rosenman returned to New York City early in that same
year. Clark Clifford replaced Rosenman as Truman's special counsel. Truman's biographer, Robert J. Donovan, describes the personal, if sometimes
awkward and unformed, manner in which the president related to his staff:

> Truman was his own chief of staff. He chaired the morning staff meeting
> in his office, parceled out assignments, gave directions, discussed the con-
> cerns of the different members, and watched the White House budget. . . .
>   He was slow to develop the knack of using a staff well. [John] Snyder
> . . . said afterward that, especially in the hectic early months, Truman
> drew upon the rudimentary principles of administration he had learned at
> reserve army summer camps in the twenties and thirties.[30]

In his memoirs, Clark Clifford stresses Truman's preference for equality
of access among staff aides, a pattern often favored by members of Congress
who become president.

> The manner in which President Truman ran the White House evolved as
> time went on, but at all times it reflected his informality, his accessibility

and openness, and his preference for rapid, intuitive decision making over careful, analytical staff work. His White House could best be visualized as a wheel with spokes: each spoke was one of his key aides, with different (but sometimes overlapping) areas of responsibility. Harry Truman would never have felt comfortable if access to him was controlled by a single person. No organization chart of the Truman White House ever existed.[31]

However equal the access, the infighting between Clifford and Assistant to the President John R. Steelman was well known.[32] Clifford cast the running dispute as that of "liberal versus conservative." Clifford explains: "My other adversary on policy was a member of the White House staff, John Steelman. As time went on, our relationship became increasingly confrontational. To a certain extent, the Presidential staff divided into factions grouped around the two of us." When Clifford left in 1950, he was replaced by Charles Murphy. Well versed in Capitol Hill politics, Murphy became Truman's chief political operative. As Clifford notes, however, "Charlie was comfortable only in the domestic field. . . . Thus for the first time, a clear division between those working on domestic and national security affairs began to emerge in the White House."[33]

Developments during the Truman administration were important for the emergence of the postwar White House staff. Although the organizational pattern was suited to Truman's desire for open access, certain positions and duties were established that would remain in future administrations. Still, the Truman White House staff had a personal, even intimate, quality. It remained relatively inconspicuous to public view. Neither the president nor cabinet officials viewed staff as a barrier to the Oval Office. Indeed, one former aide explained to Stephen J. Wayne that "if any cabinet member had called up and asked for a meeting with the president and been turned off by a staff member, by God that staff member would have been fired within 24 hours by Harry Truman."[34]

CABINET SECRETARIES. The more public extension of the White House during the Truman years was the cabinet. There are three Truman cabinets, as measured by turnover (see appendix figure A-1). The first is essentially the Roosevelt legacy. As G. Calvin Mackenzie put it: "Most Presidents, upon coming to the White House, have to form a government. Harry Truman inherited one."[35] Having served for a long time, several cabinet members resigned soon after Truman took over. Of those who did not, two left under difficult circumstances.[36]

Then there were two waves of Truman appointees. In the first wave of appointments, a government with over twelve years of experience gave Truman the opportunity to select from a sizable pool of subcabinet and ambassadorial talent. Thus, "with little need to 'capture' the government or to redirect it significantly, Truman was able to make a large percentage of his executive nominations from his own circle of acquaintances and from among individuals whose actions and reputations he had been able to observe at close range."[37]

The second wave of appointments, and the third and last Truman cabinet, was the most stable. After Interior Secretary Julius Krug resigned in 1949, there were but three other changes: two in Defense, one in Justice. Managing the new, consolidated defense organization, in particular, proved to be a difficult and demanding task. Apart from Defense and Justice, the average service of this third set of cabinet secretaries was over four years, above the average for service during the last years of a presidency.

In summary, organization during the Truman years was transitional, then adjustable (see figure 3-1). There were many changes in personnel. There was, however, no one point of renewal, of recreating a Truman presidency after the initial resignations of Roosevelt appointees. The transition itself was relatively swift due to the age, perhaps the weariness, of the Roosevelt government. The comparison with the Johnson and Ford presidencies is striking in this regard. There was a substantial foreign and domestic policy legacy. The new president could pick and choose among experienced people in coping with this large agenda. The organization that resulted was, as described by Stephen Hess, "a blending of stunningly capable patricians, unimaginative professionals, and incompetent cronies."[38] Fortunately for the country, Truman often chose the best people for the biggest jobs. Unfortunately for his presidency, his poor choices and inelegant style detracted from his contributions, substantially delaying the credit due him for certain courageous decisions.

Eisenhower

There are two presidencies in the postwar period that do not involve transitions, or a carryover of one president's cabinet to the next. The first is that of Dwight D. Eisenhower, the second that of Jimmy Carter. As shown in figure 3-1, the eight-year Eisenhower administration moved from a stable organization to one that experienced normal adjustments.

WHITE HOUSE STAFF. No modern president has entered the White House with as much organizational experience as Dwight D. Eisenhower. Nor has any other president written so clearly and so directly on the subject. According to one account, he had "a passion for organization."[39] Andrew Good-paster, staff secretary to Eisenhower, explained: "We had a president who was, if I may say so, the most skillful man when it came to organizing, to performing functions well, with the deepest understanding of the role of organization, of how to use staff, of subordination and decentralization . . . of anyone I've ever known or known of."[40]

Eisenhower's own discussion of the topic reveals more than his preferences. It offers evidence of a well-developed conceptual approach to the topic.

> For years I had been in frequent contact with the Executive Office of the White House and I had certain ideas about the system, or lack of system, under which it operated. With my training in problems involving organization it was inconceivable to me that the work of the White House could not be better systemized than had been the case during the years I observed it.[41]

Eisenhower then outlined the major functions of a White House staff, stressing the need for coordination, which led him to justify appointing a "responsible head." He "sought a competent administrator and a good friend" for this post, but judged that "it would create in many quarters a suspicion of excessive military influence" to select one of his military friends. After considering former Senator Henry Cabot Lodge of Massachusetts and Sherman Adams, former governor of New Hampshire, Eisenhower selected the latter.

Eisenhower had no intention of serving as his own chief of staff. Yet he fully understood the role to be played by such a person. A chief of staff worked for the president, not the other way around. Eisenhower also had a clear conception of how the operating staff (which he thought should be called the "president's staff" to avoid confusion with the Executive Office of the President) should organize and work. According to Fred I. Greenstein, Eisenhower's use of Adams was that of a top assistant for coordination and communication but also as a deputy. "In this status, an aide was supposed to be fully aware of his superior's policies or be able immediately to get clarification and further instructions." The chief of staff as deputy was a conception developed by Eisenhower as military commander and was designed "to extend [the] superior's impact, making decisions of his own."[42]

The president's concept of and reliance on a chief of staff as deputy was the subject of strong criticism. Beyond the charges that Adams acted arrogantly was the conclusion by Louis Koenig that "Adams suffered from, and eventually succumbed to, the hazards of unreviewed judgment."[43] Eisenhower depended too heavily on Adams, thus failing to provide a sufficient check on the chief of staff's exercise of power and creating a system that depended too heavily on one person.[44] Adams was forced to resign when he appeared to have intervened with regulatory commissions for a friend, Bernard Goldfine. He was succeeded by General Wilton Persons, whose "health was frail and his age—sixty-two—advanced for the grueling pace."[45] Thus Eisenhower was denied Adams's strong administrative direction during the last two years of his second term.

A number of Eisenhower staff innovations remained as part of the developing presidential branch. They included a special assistant for national security affairs, a congressional relations office, staff secretaries to coordinate the paperwork coming into the White House (with a special secretary for the cabinet), and several special assistants as a way of bringing in prominent outsiders. The presidential branch was first institutionalized during the Eisenhower administration. As with the cabinet, there was substantial continuity in the White House staff. The most serious break came with the resignation of Sherman Adams in 1958. There was, however, relatively little change in Eisenhower's preferences for governing with the use of staff. General Persons was a much softer personality than Governor Adams, but he managed a system of controlled and coordinated access.

CABINET SECRETARIES. Possibly because he was new to the politics of governing, President Eisenhower liked the idea of a cabinet as a functioning body. He found it useful as an orienting instrument. "I not only found a spirit of teamwork and friendship in the Cabinet, but I also found its deliberations and debates enlightening as I faced important decisions." He established a cabinet secretariat to "work up agendas for the discussions and see that all my decisions respecting them were properly reported and communicated to interested parties."[46] A former Eisenhower aide who helped develop the secretariat explained that it "acted as a radar set, constantly scanning what was going on among its staff colleagues, at the departments, in the press, the Congress, the states."[47] Clearly the president believed that if it were organized properly, the cabinet could perform advisory and coordinating functions.

Eisenhower identified the important orienting function straightforwardly at the first cabinet meeting: "I wanted this fine group of men who had signaled their willingness to serve their country, and to help me, *to understand the job as I saw it*." He expected "this fine group of men" to contribute to a presidency that he well understood to be his. To this end, he anticipated that they would express themselves on issues beyond those of their immediate cabinet responsibility. "No one was relieved of his responsibility or the opportunity to think broadly and to make suggestions."[48]

Continuity of personnel was a highly desirable feature of a cabinet used in this way. The continuity in the Eisenhower cabinet was extraordinary for postwar presidents (see table 3-2). By definition, frequent turnover would adversely affect the president's confidence in the cabinet and also how others viewed the administration. Unity and clarity of purpose are important features of a military organization. Eisenhower meant to achieve both in his government.

There were two Eisenhower cabinets, with substantial overlap between them. There were but three changes in the cabinet during the first term in office, only one in the first two years (see appendix figure A-2). By contrast, the Kennedy-Johnson first term had four changes, Nixon and Carter both had eight, Reagan had five, and Bush had eight. Two cabinet secretaries, Ezra Taft Benson in Agriculture and Arthur Summerfield as postmaster general, served the full eight years. Three others—Sinclair Weeks in Commerce, James Mitchell in Labor, and John Foster Dulles in State—served for six years. Of the ten total changes among cabinet secretaries, seven occurred in the second term (one was the result of the Senate's failure to confirm Lewis Strauss as secretary of commerce).

Perhaps the most striking feature of the Eisenhower cabinet was simply how much each secretary looked like the other. Compared with how cabinets look today, this one was virtually interchangeable. Eight of the original ten were within ten years of Eisenhower's age, six within four years. The secretaries tended to be Protestants and from business, banking, and the legal profession. With the exception of Martin Durkin, the secretary of labor who left first and quickly, it was very much a "gray suit" set of government officials.

In one sense the Eisenhower cabinet was like that of the other presidents of this era: it was selected and it functioned to serve the president's orientation to governing. It would be inconceivable today, however, that a president's orientation would lead him to appoint such a homogeneous cabinet. The contemporary appointment of cabinet secretaries must meet a test of representational diversity. That standard of diversity, in turn, modifies the extent to which the president is free to determine how the group will contribute to governing. Cabinet secretaries are presumably at least partially responsive to the clienteles they represent.

Kennedy to Johnson

The shocking assassination of John F. Kennedy created the second postwar transitional presidency (see figure 3-1). Circumstances were very different from those characterizing the Roosevelt-to-Truman transition. The Kennedy government was new, not old; vigorous, not weary; anxious to start, not finish. The organizational consequences were therefore very different.

WHITE HOUSE STAFF. In organizing the White House, President Kennedy "purposively reverted to the Roosevelt model, but with modifications."[49] The highly structured, hierarchical Eisenhower staff was scrapped in favor of a much less structured "buddy" system. Kennedy asked Professor Richard E. Neustadt and former White House Special Counsel Clark Clifford for independent memos on the transition, with recommendations for organizing the new White House. Neustadt cautioned against blind acceptance of the Roosevelt model but proposed committing to "the *spirit* of his [Roosevelt's] presidential operation." Clifford favored "a lean and fast-moving White House," concluding that "a vigorous President in the Democratic tradition of the Presidency will probably find it best to act as his own chief of staff, and to have no highly visible majordomo standing between him and his staff (and, incidentally, between him and the public)."[50] Theodore Sorenson, who served as Kennedy's Clark Clifford, approved of this arrangement in reflections many years later: "We had a modified system under which one person on policy and program, one person on national security operations, one person on press, and one person on congressional relations each had equal access to the president. We kept in touch with each other, and I think it worked reasonably well without a chief of staff."[51]

As with Roosevelt and Truman, Kennedy worked one-on-one with many of his staff aides. Many of the closest aides had served with Kennedy in the Senate and worked with him through the campaign for president. They looked like a composite of the president—young, quick, aggressive, and ambitious. Therefore, "he was infinitely accessible to the Special Assistants" who were his friends, virtually his clones.

> He liked to regard his staff as generalists rather than specialists and had a distressing tendency to take up whatever happened to be on his desk and hand it to whoever happened to be in the room. But a measure of specialization was inevitable, and the staff on the whole contrived its own clandestine structure, taking care to pass on a presidential directive to the person in whose area it lay.[52]

As Sorenson describes it, Kennedy wished to use his staff as an extension of himself, "one that represented *his* personal ways, means and purposes."[53] If the staff were truly socialized to his interests and needs, then he could multiply many times his own capacity to hear, read, and understand what was going on in government.

This approach to organizing the White House was as suited to Kennedy's experience and personal preferences as the more structured version was to Eisenhower's. Kennedy had not previously managed a large organization: the 1960 presidential campaign was his first real such experience. This lack of executive training contributed to a system that was ad hoc and eclectic in its staffing and its style of service. The president preferred that the staff be small ("to keep it more personal than institutional"), fluid, and organizationally flat.[54]

The untimely death of President Kennedy made it impossible to evaluate the full effectiveness of the White House staff operation or to know how stable it may have been over an extended period. Perhaps to an even greater extent than in the case of Truman's takeover in 1945, Vice President Lyndon B. Johnson was faced with having to demonstrate continuity. Johnson inherited a substantial agenda and a staff anxious to complete its work as a part of the legacy of the dead president. The new president himself explained in his memoirs that he considered himself "the caretaker of both his people and his policies."[55]

Although Johnson shared many of Kennedy's unmet goals, his style was very different from that of his predecessor. Thus he faced all the problems normally attendant to taking over, yet had the challenge of adapting himself to the Kennedy staff as symbolic recognition of the legacy. All of Kennedy's principal staff aides stayed on for an interim period; National Security Adviser McGeorge Bundy stayed until 1966. Meanwhile Johnson appointed other aides who were given "ad hoc assignments conditioned largely by the immediate needs of the president."[56] In a sense, then, to a greater extent than was the case under Truman, there was a dual staff operation: the Kennedy holdovers and the new Johnson ad hoc appointments.

Harry McPherson, special counsel to Johnson, notes that "the potential for savage internecine warfare was very high."[57] And, inevitably, Johnson worried about the loyalty of the Kennedy staff. As Doris Kearns points out, there was a mutuality of need: Johnson profited from their talent and they ensured that there would be a "martyr's cause."[58] But it was hard to sustain the dual arrangement. Among other developments, Johnson himself became suspicious, perhaps even a bit paranoid, about the Kennedys and their supporters.

Those requiring geometric images (triangles, circles, trapezoids) in order to understand organizational relationships are bound to be frustrated by the Johnson White House. In the initial phase one must picture two circles or wheels, with a set of connectors. Johnson's overwhelming victory in 1964 permitted him to become his own president, though he was not moved, nor was it politically wise, to define his administration by making a clean break from the Kennedy legacy. Those Kennedy men who stayed on melded into one circle of advisers: the classic spokes-of-the-wheel organization, with one important caveat. Perhaps more than with other presidents employing this structure, not all of the spokes on Johnson's wheel were the same length. Further, one's spoke could be lengthened quickly should the president become displeased.

Given what is thought to be known about Kennedy and Johnson, there was remarkably little reforming of the White House following the assassination. Even accounting for Johnson's determination to be the "executor of [Kennedy's] will", the continuity-in-change was extraordinary.[59] The reformation had to, and did, occur within a context of a reassuring constancy. That it was accomplished encourages an analysis of qualities not typically attributed to Johnson, such as sensitivity, patience, and commitment. Unfortunately for his own legacy, Johnson was not able to match his domestic policy record with one in foreign policy. By 1968 his policies in Vietnam had virtually made him a prisoner in the White House. "In the end, Lyndon Johnson had turned the presidency into a bunker. Then he handed it over to Richard Nixon."[60]

CABINET SECRETARIES. Though well connected to governing elites through political service and family ties, Kennedy was reportedly awed by the task of creating a government. The Democrats had been out of the White House for eight years. Therefore the pool of available talent was limited. Neustadt recalls the president exclaiming after the election: "People, people, people! I don't know any people. I only know voters. How am I going to fill these 1200 jobs?"[61]

However many close friends one has, they become few when faced with the challenge of taking charge of the federal government. Further, friendships may make a limited contribution to meeting this challenge. The quest is for a workable government, as defined by the president and as directed by an organization orienting itself to his style and policy goals. Therefore it is more important in making appointments to determine how this or that person will serve those ends than it is to ensure good companionship.

Kennedy achieved impressive continuity among his cabinet secretaries during his short term in office (see appendix figure A-3). The initial group was carefully selected, with a number of major appointments going to persons with whom the president was not well acquainted. The big three—State, Defense, and Treasury—were filled with surprising choices. Dean Rusk (State) had experience in foreign affairs but was unknown to Kennedy. Robert Lovett, former secretary of defense for Truman, recommended Robert McNamara (Defense) for either Treasury or Defense. He, too, was unknown to the president. Douglas Dillon (Treasury) was known to the Kennedys, including the president, but he had just served the Eisenhower administration as under secretary of state for economic affairs. Seemingly, each of these appointments was special and unexpected enough to represent genuine interest in serving on the part of the designee.[62] And by the Polsby test, the cabinet secretaries taken as a whole came to reflect the president's interests and style.

The pattern among cabinet secretaries for the full eight years of the Kennedy-Johnson period is very different from that of the Roosevelt-Truman experience. The longevity within certain departments is impressive. Three secretaries—Orville Freeman in Agriculture, Stewart Udall in Interior, and Rusk in State—served the full eight years. The average length of service in State, Defense, and Treasury was greater even than that during the Eisenhower administration. Of the thirteen changes during the eight years, nine occurred within three departments: three each in Commerce, Health, Education, and Welfare, and the Post Office. Thus remarkable stability was achieved during a period of substantial upheaval (the assassination, conflict over civil rights, and the Vietnam War) and change (the enactment of the Great Society).

It is fair to say that Johnson never did exercise the option of putting a strong stamp of his own on the Kennedy government through cabinet secretarial appointments. This was due in part to Johnson's vision of himself as fulfilling the Kennedy legacy. But it was also due to Johnson's belief that many in the cabinet were good at their jobs. Eric F. Goldman explains that Johnson made a distinction in judging the cabinet: "There were the JFK men, whom he considered for the most part able, dedicated to public service and quite capable of serving another President loyally. Then there were the RFK men; whether able or not, they were 'sonsofbitches, plotting inside my own house.'" Rusk, McNamara, Udall, Freeman, and Willard Wirtz (Labor) were among the JFK men; of the others, Johnson proceeded to replace them "at a leisurely pace and in ways that expressed his debts, needs and enthusiasms."[63]

Did Lyndon Johnson have a concept of the cabinet within his presidency? Doris Kearns quotes the president as saying that he expected loyalty but worried that "all too often they [department heads] responded to their constituencies instead of mine." Johnson explained that he "was determined to turn those lordly men into good soldiers." Kearns viewed this statement as a familiar Johnson formula for the exercise of power: a "one-sided dependence."[64] Had he originally been elected on his own, Johnson might have had the opportunity to create this dependence. As it was, however, he was put in charge of another president's White House.

In fact, where Johnson did have the option to make changes, he did not alter things very much. Thus, although it is possible to identify two cabinets for these eight years—the initial Kennedy group adjusted to the eventual Johnson group—the most outstanding characteristic of the period is stability (figure 3-1). Like the Eisenhower years, the initial appointments from the outside were followed by the elevation of several subcabinet personnel to cabinet secretarial status. Johnson appointed the largest number of such persons of any postwar president (although three served for short periods at the end of the administration).

Nixon to Ford

The third transitional presidency in the postwar period is the least conventional in history (figure 3-1). Never before had a president resigned, nor had a vice president ever taken over who was not himself a part of the elected ticket. The organizational patterns were unusual, to say the least.

WHITE HOUSE STAFF. Stephen Hess describes Richard Nixon as a "management-conscious president" who was constantly tinkering with White House organization.[65] His interest in management was seemingly driven by a concern for order and control, as well as the usual desire to create a structure that would sustain him and his presidency. The president lacked the experience of directing large organizations and thus was never certain what would work best or, indeed, whether organization and management could serve the purposes he had in mind.

Nixon, like Eisenhower, expected a lot from formal organization. Organizational charts were back after an eight-year absence. But Nixon also liked "an adversarial proceeding within the staff," according to his chief of staff,

H. R. Haldeman.[66] So although he structured his staff like Eisenhower's, from the start Nixon wished to use it in ways that were not necessarily facilitated by a hierarchy. He said he wanted a "dispersal of power" and "multiple advocacy" of policy positions.[67] Yet, in contrast to Roosevelt, he was anxious not to have conflicts in these positions left unresolved on his doorstep. As Haldeman explained:

> Nixon wanted these officials to submit their problems in writing or to deal with someone on the staff better able to handle their concerns than the President *before* they were granted precious Presidential time. And this infuriated them, because the man who said "no" to them was a staffer, me. . . . They vented their fury on me, but every White House insider knew that I was doing this at the President's direct order. And so did most of the outsiders.[68]

An aide who served both Eisenhower and Nixon explained that the Nixon administration became "oddly far more structured" than the Eisenhower administration.

> It was not that way in the beginning. It evolved into a very tight control and it got tighter . . . as time went on. Ordinarily White House staffs start out very tight, very closed in, with a small band of people around the president allowing very few others into that inner circle. As the time moves they find out they can't handle all that business themselves, and the president has claustrophobia, so the band starts to expand and ordinarily by his third year or fourth year, the presidency has been opened up. But in the Nixon instance it went the other way.[69]

The organization of the Nixon White House was every bit as complex as the person it served. With other presidents the staff operations represented an extension of the strengths and weaknesses of the president. With Nixon it seemed that the structure was a blend of what he truly wanted and what he thought he should have, based on an unarticulated concept of what was right for the "good" president. While this blend reflected his complex personality, it did not always make it easy to predict either his behavior or the consequences of mixing staff in this way.

Haldeman was clearly in charge as chief of staff, and that was the role Nixon wanted him to play, according to Haldeman himself: "Instead of having to figure out who to contact on each particular item, he could simply call me in and cover everything on his mind, leaving it to me to follow up with the appropriate people."[70] One staff aide estimated that "Nixon spent over 70 percent of his staff time with Haldeman alone." John Ehrlichman wrote: "The two became complementary, and by 1968 it was hard to tell where Richard Nixon left off and H. R. Haldeman began."[71]

The other principal close advisers were John Ehrlichman and Henry Kissinger. Both had sources of strength independent of Haldeman that ensured their direct contact with the president. Ehrlichman began as White House counsel but then took over responsibility for domestic policy. Ehrlichman was very close to Haldeman (they had known each other in college and worked for Nixon in the 1960 campaign). He would occasionally fill in on the rare occasions when Haldeman was on vacation. As national security adviser, Kissinger had direct access to the president, though Haldeman typically sat in when foreign policy issues were presented (offering political, not substantive, comments).[72]

Ehrlichman once observed that it took six years for Nixon to settle on how he wanted to organize his government.[73] Hess points out: "In each year of the Nixon presidency the White House looked different from the year before."[74] As Hess observes, most presidents make changes, but Nixon appeared to be engaged in continual experimentation to have organization to work for him, not necessarily with him.

One other more or less independent operation developed. Charles Colson was a sort of "wild card," formally responsible for public liaison. The open-ended nature of his assignment, along with his access to Nixon, meant that he often operated in others' substantive areas (usually at the president's behest). Haldeman believed that

Colson encouraged the dark impulses in Nixon's mind. . . . By 1971 Nixon was using three subordinates—Haldeman, Ehrlichman, and Colson—for three different approaches to some projects. I was the man for the straight, hit-them-over-the-head strategy. Ehrlichman, who loved intrigue, was given the more devious approach. And Colson was assigned the real underground routes.[75]

Following the 1972 election, two developments led to a substantially restructured White House (the renewable pattern, as shown in figure 3-1). First was the aforementioned perpetual search for the best organization. The reelected president announced wholesale resignations and reassignments of both staff and cabinet members before his second inauguration (see below). Second was the Watergate incident that led to the resignations of Haldeman, Ehrlichman, and Colson, all three of whom later served prison terms. The new group of staff aides was not close to Nixon, nor did he want them to be. And in any event, they had barely gotten accustomed to their jobs when the president resigned.

The Nixon legacy for Gerald R. Ford was very different again from those of Roosevelt for Truman and Kennedy for Johnson. Truman and Johnson were expected to fulfill the goals of their predecessors; Ford was expected to restore honor to the White House. Ford was under substantial pressure to get rid of Nixon's staff, including strong advice to do so from his long-time aide, Robert Hartmann. He resisted a "Stalin-like purge," feeling that "there were people on the White House staff who had nothing to do with Watergate. For me to have fired them all would have tarred them with the Nixon brush. . . . I made the decision to proceed gradually."[76]

Ford paid a price with the press for this decision. "The press demanded a wholesale cleansing of the White House of all Nixon 'holdovers' and criticized Ford for failing resolutely to take such action."[77] Ford's first press secretary, Jerald R. terHorst, doubted that the president could escape criticism; there had to be some continuity and finding a totally new "clean" team was difficult. Unbeknownst to Ford, a group headed by Philip Buchen, a long-time friend of Ford from Michigan, had begun to meet in anticipation of Nixon's resignation so as to provide the new president with advice.[78] Among their recommendations was that "there should be no Chief of Staff, especially at the outset." This was the standard reaction to avoid what was judged to be a core organizational problem of one's predecessor, in this case the "Haldeman" problem. Yet the group believed that it was important to have a manager or coordinator of the new staff who would not be interested in serving as a chief of staff. Ford selected Donald Rumsfeld, then serving as ambassador to NATO, for this job.

Upon taking over, Ford's conception of his White House staff operation borrowed from his congressional experience of managing a relatively small office in which staff aides typically have access to the boss. He endorsed the spokes-of-the-wheel concept, with himself as the hub, serving as his own chief of staff. Rumsfeld and others argued for a more hierarchical structure, "but the president had to go through his period where he got that out of his system."[79]

The initial period of Ford's presidency featured a great deal of staff in-fighting, due in large measure to conflicts between those who were already close to Ford and those who had served Nixon. Particularly bitter was the running dispute between Robert Hartmann and Haldeman's replacement, General Alexander Haig (who stayed on as staff coordinator). Ford's eventual solution was to give Haig another assignment and convince Rumsfeld to take Haig's post. In his meeting with the president, Rumsfeld apparently explained the drawbacks of the spokes-of-the-wheel organization, clearly communicating that he would not take Haig's job unless it were more of a chief-of-staff position. Ford agreed that the system was not working well and made Rumsfeld the chief of staff.

The confusion and uncertainty that characterized staff operations on the domestic side were not repeated on foreign and defense matters, though there were problems. Henry Kissinger carried over into the Ford administration, initially holding the key posts of secretary of state and national security adviser. He himself conceded the awkwardness of this arrangement. He was both in charge of the Department of State and in a position to coordinate that department's recommendations with those from other departments, notably Defense.[80]

The circumstances of Ford's accession to the White House seemingly offered significant advantages over that of Truman and Johnson in organizational and staff matters. After all, he was not charged with being the executor of the Nixon will—quite the opposite. Yet he was not able to realize the full benefits of the expectations of change because of his own lack of executive experience, the lack of available talent, the need for some continuity, and, perhaps most important, his decision to pardon Nixon. As a result, a Ford White House was established too late for the president to ever gain the offensive in governing.

CABINET SECRETARIES. In his candid account of life in the Nixon administration, John Ehrlichman reflected on the difficulties between the White House and the cabinet:

> What went wrong with the Nixon Cabinet? Surely something did. Most of the Cabinet members were discontented most of the time, and many of them failed to manage their departments well. . . . The President, from 1970 on, spent a significant percentage of time worrying about the Cabinet and tinkering with it. And so did some of us on his staff.
>
> At root were the President's own shifting and variable concepts of the Cabinet—of what it should be and do—and what the President expected from it.[81]

In his memoirs, Nixon explains that he "had strong opinions . . . about the way a President should work," developed during his time as vice president. Eisenhower's staff "had too often cluttered his schedule with unimportant events and bothered him with minor problems." Nixon believed that he could accomplish far more by reading memos than by meeting with cabinet secretaries.[82]

In relating to the department heads, at times Nixon seemed almost suspended between his own strong convictions regarding loyalty and his sensitivity to how his presidency would be viewed by others. Nixon wanted "good managers" who would serve on the "team." "I had . . . seen the hazards of appointing Cabinet members who were too strong-willed to act as part of a team. I wanted people who would fight to the finish in private for what they thought was right but would support my decision once it was made."[83] The private battle had to take place on paper, however, since Nixon did not like face-to-face confrontations. It was little wonder that the cabinet secretaries became confused as to what signals were being sent. Ehrlichman reports:

> The Cabinet men undoubtedly began their jobs with the euphoric and erroneous idea that Nixon reposed great, almost unbounded confidence in each of them. At the time Nixon probably *believed* that he did, but essentially he didn't. He wanted to be reelected and he wanted a place in history as a great President. Because he wanted these things he couldn't possibly give the Cabinet free rein.[84]

Thus it did not take long for dissension to arise between the White House and the cabinet departments. Nixon's failure to communicate his expectations clearly at the start was then compounded by his indirectness in conveying how these privately held expectations were modified along the way. Consequently all a cabinet secretary could do was to guess how his actions would be interpreted within the White House, and several were not very good at making those estimates.

This same pattern of undelivered yet strong opinions about cabinet members; avoidance of face-to-face meetings; and searches for a publicly acceptable rationale to make changes was to be repeated several times.[85] The first wave of five changes came in 1970. The next round of changes was breathtaking in scope (see appendix figure A-4). It started in late 1971, when Earl Butz replaced Clifford Hardin as secretary of agriculture, followed by three other changes in 1972. To that point the changes were rational, ordinary adjustments, not very different in purpose from those of other administrations. Following his landslide reelection, however, the president was determined to clean house, to deal more directly and confidently with those "crybabies" in the cabinet, as Nixon was wont to refer to them.[86]

> He got started the day after the election. At 11 a.m. he met with the White House staff. . . . To his National Security Adviser, Henry Kissinger, he appeared withdrawn, "grim and remote." Kissinger sensed his mood accurately: "It was as if victory was not an occasion for reconciliation but an opportunity to settle the scores of a lifetime." Nixon gave perfunctory thanks to the staff, before announcing that the first order of business was to reorganize. "There are no sacred cows," he declared, then changed the metaphor: "We will tear up the pea patch."[87]

Nixon soon left the meeting. Haldeman then asked everyone to submit a resignation immediately and fill out a form declaring the documents in their possession. According to Kissinger, "The audience was stunned. It was the morning after a triumph and they were being, in effect, fired." One hour later the same "wounding and humiliating" procedure was repeated before the cabinet. "It made removal from office appear to be not the result of Presidential reflection about the future but a grudge from the past."[88]

Only three departments—Treasury, Interior, and Agriculture—were left unchanged. Six resignations were immediately accepted; two others followed some months later. There were ten total changes within the year. The Watergate scandal that occurred during this period does not account for all these changes. In fact, it really accounts only for the resignations of Richard Kleindeinst and Elliot Richardson as attorneys general. More important as an explanation was Nixon's own intention upon reelection to renew his government. Possibly he believed that tearing up the "pea patch" at the moment of triumph itself conveyed to the new appointees how it was he wanted them to serve.

Gerald R. Ford was sworn in as the thirty-eighth president on August 9, 1974, just minutes after President Nixon resigned. The new president well understood his precarious political situation: "Most Vice Presidents who become President have buried their predecessors and then gone on to reassure the people by wrapping themselves in the mantle of the men they followed. . . . At the time of *his* departure, Nixon had no mantle left." He also perceived correctly that reporters "harbored a natural skepticism about my talents and skills" and that "I had no mandate from the people, and the Congress understood that."[89] On the other hand, Ford had one substantial advantage: he was *not* Richard Nixon. That fact helped establish his legitimacy with the American people, but it was also important in restoring the credibility of the executive branch, internally and externally.

Ford's assumption of the White House did represent a stylistic sea change. And the circumstances of the takeover invited greater than usual reflections on White House management of the executive and of congressional relations. Organization may not be the key variable to governing if the president has the advantages of a large electoral victory. But President Ford and his associates had to judge how best to reconnect the White House to a government that had learned to operate in its absence. However, Ford was not the best person to figure this all out. As his close friend and counsel, Philip Buchen, explained, "He was weak as an administrator and a planner." And yet "he was always ready to receive advice."[90]

Since the departments and agencies had had to manage on their own, "it was a little difficult to persuade [them] to coordinate their efforts with the White House."[91] One method was to hold meetings, if for no other reason than to get better acquainted and to reinforce the stylistic change that had occurred. Chief of Staff Richard Cheney explains: "We started like all administrations do, with a Cabinet meeting every week. Of course, by the end of the term we probably had one a month, because cabinet meetings are basically irrelevant to the function of the government."[92] Meetings were held in connection with specific policy areas, however, and Ford's style was as one would expect: basically consultative.

Just two of Nixon's appointees—Secretary of State Kissinger and Secretary of the Treasury William Simon—stayed through Ford's term (appendix figure A-4). There were a significant number of changes for so short a period of time—twelve in all, with two each in Interior, Commerce, and Labor. The numerous changes are explained more as Ford's attempt to create his own team than as typical for the ending of a term. After all, the president was seeking election in 1976, and prospects were that the new appointees would remain in the administration. In making his replacements, Ford drew heavily from those with federal executive experience. Of the twelve appointees, just three came from outside the beltway.

Although conservatives may be thought of as status quo oriented, the Nixon-Ford government was anything but unchanging. Seven of the eleven departments had four or more changes during the eight years, including such blue-chip agencies as Treasury, Defense, and Justice. Here was an administration that never truly hardened. It would be difficult to argue that it experienced an increasing cycle of effectiveness. And yet it was a time in which a great deal of major legislation was enacted and a number of foreign policy breakthroughs occurred.[93] At the very least this remarkable period should arouse curiosity about the role of the presidency in governing. This third transitional presidency displays further variations in the organizational patterns by which presidents seek to work within the separated system (figure 3-1).

Carter

The one-term administration of Jimmy Carter is the second self-contained presidency in the postwar period. In contrast with the stability of Eisenhower's first term, however, the Carter administration accomplished a renewal shortly after midterm (see figure 3-1).

WHITE HOUSE STAFF. James P. Pfiffner relates this story, learned in an interview with Richard Cheney:

At a White House staff party Cheney was presented with a bicycle wheel mounted on a large board with all of the spokes of the wheel mangled and tangled except for one that was all that held the structure together. A plaque mounted on the board read: "The spokes of the wheel: a rare form of management artistry as conceived by Don Rumsfeld and modified by Dick Cheney." When the Ford administration left office on January 20, 1977 Cheney left the present on his desk and appended a note reading "Dear Ham [Jordan], beware the spokes of the wheel."[94]

Presidents are amazingly unwilling to accept good organizational advice and anxious to avoid what they judge to be the organizational failures of a previous administration. In Carter's case, Cheney's advice was supplemented by that of Jack Watson, who served as head of Carter's transition team, and Stephen Hess, whom Carter asked to provide recommendations. Watson warned the new president in a private memorandum that one of his strengths—an interest in "the pros and the cons and the ins and the outs of every issue"—could become a weakness. It could result in "overinvolvement," of "pulling too many things into the White House." This strength as weakness, along with a determination to avoid a Haldeman-style staff system, naturally led Carter away from a chief-of-staff, funnel type of organization and toward the spokes of the wheel, with the president at the hub. Later Watson reflected that this was a "fatal mistake."[95]

By the time Hess was asked for advice, a decision had already been made against having a chief of staff. Hess proposed a model that permitted "wide access . . . in a structured setting," thus allowing more screening than is typical of the spokes of the wheel.[96] It was not altogether clear how the Hess "isosceles trapezoid" would function in practice. He was merely suggesting a middle ground between the other models, possibly not unlike that developed in the first Reagan administration. And the clear implication was that while a president need not necessarily have a chief of staff, he should also avoid giving open access to all his assistants.

Jimmy Carter was a true outsider to the Washington political scene. It was, in his judgment, due to this fact that he won the presidency. More than most, therefore, he was likely to bring a trusted team of advisers who, like him, were new to national politics and policymaking. In his memoirs, Carter acknowledges the criticism other presidents had received "for installing their 'cronies' in the White House." At the same time, however, he was wary "about bringing new people into our most intimate circle." That intimacy itself made it difficult to opt for a hierarchical organization. The obvious choice for a chief of staff, if there was to be one, was Hamilton Jordan, who had "devised and managed" the presidential campaign. But Jordan himself resisted being put in charge of his friends, although Carter turned to him later when he finally "acquiesced to the requests of other staff members" in appointing a chief of staff.[97]

Carter's concern about not "bringing new people into our most intimate circle" resulted in an extraordinarily parochial group of close advisers. Among his top aides, only the national security adviser, Zbigniew Brzezinski, was not a Georgian. The new president was heavily criticized for essentially bringing his campaign staff and former gubernatorial appointees into the White House. Yet these appointments reflected the very essence of Carter's campaign and approach. He was anxious to establish the outside nature of his presidency, particularly in a post-Watergate period.

One of the more successful organizational features of the Carter White House was the use of Vice President Walter Mondale. The two staffs worked well together during the campaign and meshed well in the White House. Carter insisted that Mondale be kept informed on major policy matters. And in a White House that was heavily criticized for proposing too much and lacking priorities, Mondale came to head a group that helped "the president unclog a glut of issues that could otherwise immobilize the White House."[98]

More than most recent presidents, and somewhat akin to Eisenhower, Carter had an integrated view of his government, in which the president managed and worked with the departments and agencies to carry out policy and White House aides assisted in that large task. This conception challenged the idea that a separate presidential branch was needed, a reasonable enough reaction if, in fact, the creation of an independent White House policy capability was due mostly to Republican presidents' suspicions about an entrenched bureaucracy working closely with a Democratic Congress. But this reason for integrating the cabinet with the White House in policy matters was apparently not central to Carter's organizational preferences. For example, Erwin C. Hargrove sees three major influences that seemed to have guided Carter's thinking about how to organize his presidency. First was his "experience as governor of Georgia." Carter used his personal assistants to "work with the legislature and the public" and his department heads to "develop programs and administer them." Second was Carter's negative reaction to the centralization in the Nixon White House. "During the campaign he promised that no White House staff person would ever be permitted to come between him and the cabinet officers, who were to be his principal advisers." Third was his preference for getting involved in selected policy issues and a low tolerance for "layering of advisory levels between himself and any of his key associates."[99]

Hargrove notes that Carter stressed a decisionmaking process that was "collegial rather than competitive, with the president at the center."[100] The system would definitely include the cabinet, as the president explained in a meeting with members of Congress. "He was going to use [the cabinet] as a collegial body and had asked them to contact the appropriate congressional committee leaders to work directly in the drafting of legislation. That's the way he had operated in Georgia, he said."[101]

This system of "centralized collegiality," as Hargrove refers to it, worked best in foreign policy, not as well in economic policy, and poorly in domestic policy. In fact, Carter relied heavily on Stuart Eizenstat, head of the Domestic Policy Staff, as a kind of chief of staff for coordinating domestic policy.

In a study of Carter's White House staff operations, John H. Kessel's findings complement those of Hargrove. Kessel found a lack of congruence among the various staff structures, not untypical of the spokes-of-the-wheel organization. Like the Kennedy organization, much depended on the president's own "intellectual capacity to absorb and structure all the information that is available to him."[102] No one questioned Carter's capacity to absorb and even integrate independent streams of information. However, integration in the Oval Office did not automatically encourage coordination among the various units.

One more very important preference perhaps influenced how Carter organized his administration: he wished to be viewed as governing in the public interest, doing the right thing. He was viewed as antipolitical, even apolitical, by many analysts and some of his closest associates. Closer examination suggests that he simply preferred a different type of politics to that which was dominant in Washington. As I have written elsewhere: "'Doing what's right, not what's political' is . . . *doing the political in the right way*, based on the president's estimate of his personal advantages and how they contribute to his being in the White House."[103] This basic approach meant that "Carter wanted policy objectives to drive politics. The higher the objective the better the quality of the politics; he hoped to evoke the best in his lieutenants and in the public."[104]

In July 1979, President Carter led what surely stands as one of the most unusual and introspective exercises in White House history. After returning from Japan and seeing that the nation faced further gasoline shortages, Carter decided to cancel a major energy speech. He was at Camp David over the Fourth of July and decided not to return to Washington but rather "have some people come in whom we trusted to give me advice on where we should go from here."[105]

One of the most "extensive and helpful sessions" was with a group of political advisers. By the president's own account, much of the talk was about organizational and personal decisionmaking style. The cabinet was reviewed person by person, with recommendations that some resign. The group judged the White House staff to be "competent, but . . . most . . . had an air of immaturity about them." The "strong advice" was that the staff be strengthened. The discussion then turned to the president himself. I give many illustrations in this book of how organizational issues are traceable to presidential characteristics, preferences, and style. Seldom, however, is there a president's own summary.

> Their criticisms of me were the most severe, questioning my ability to deal with the existing problems of the nation without bringing about some change in public perceptions. They told me that I seemed bogged down in the details of administration, and that the public was disillusioned in having to face intractable problems like energy shortages and growing inflation. . . . On the one hand, I was involved in too many things simultaneously, but, in some cases, I had delegated too much authority to my Cabinet members. The consensus was that the public acknowledged my intelligence and integrity, my ability to articulate problems and to devise good solutions to them, but doubted my capacity to follow through with a strong enough thrust to succeed.[106]

One can appreciate why those working in the Carter government as well as those observing it from the outside were often perplexed by the president's methods. There did not appear to be a formula for separating that which was presidential from that which was to be delegated. Therefore a Sherman Adams-as-deputy-president model would have failed. Carter would not have tolerated such an arrangement, and no one except the president himself could play that role.

Two types of action followed the ten-day Camp David retreat. Both had organizational overtones. The first was a speech by the president on what he had learned; the second was reorganization of the cabinet and the White House staff. The debate over what was to be included in the speech triggered a conflict within the Carter White House staff and between his staff and that of Vice President Mondale. The personnel changes resulted in a major shakeup in the cabinet. Carter accepted the resignations of six cabinet secretaries. He also asked that the cabinet secretaries fill out personnel evaluation forms on each of the key departmental staff members so that the president could make judgments about competence and loyalty. According to Joseph A. Califano, the meeting evidenced considerable tension between cabinet members and White House staff.[107]

Within the White House staff, Carter decided at long last to appoint Hamilton Jordan as chief of staff. He announced his decision during the cabinet meeting at which he asked for the resignations of his cabinet. The president was seeking a correction in the organizational course set earlier that gave cabinet departments and many on his own staff greater autonomy. Jordan later left the White House to head up the 1980 reelection campaign, and Jack Watson took over as chief of staff.[108]

Jimmy Carter was his own close adviser. He was actively involved in the large agenda he set for himself. He had wide interests in both domestic and foreign policy issues, if limited experience and expertise in the latter. He had confidence in his capacity to remain centrally involved in many policy areas and to make the right choices among the options provided by a working cabinet and a supportive staff. Thus an organization permitting substantial access to the Oval Office suited him well even if it had unfortunate effects on his image as a leader outside the White House. "Doing the right thing" is generally instructive once priorities are set; it is not, itself, a priority-setting process. As Kessel explains: "Given . . . the staff disagreement about issues and President Carter's own cognitive style—it was all but inevitable that the Carter White House would not be seen as standing for clear political goals."[109]

CABINET SECRETARIES. Jimmy Carter's relationship to the cabinet was clear in his own mind, growing out of his more general conception of a working government.

> He had a broad conception of what he loosely called cabinet government, by which he meant policy development in the departments, rather than in the White House. White House staffs were to assist him in making decisions, but beyond that he did not have in mind a well-developed model for the relation of these staffs to the departments should the need for central coordination of policy development appear.[110]

Disagreements within the cabinet and between the cabinet and White House staff did not bother Carter since he had confidence in his ability to profit from the varying points of view. In this process of "centralized collegiality," Carter assumed good will on the part of those upon whom he relied for advice and expressed personal confidence that he could "balance competing demands."[111]

Carter records that "at the beginning, I decided to meet frequently with my entire Cabinet, and scheduled two-hour sessions every Monday morning."[112] These "get-acquainted" meetings also served the purpose of clarifying jurisdictions and responsibilities. There were thirty-six such meetings in the first year, twenty-three in the second year, nine in the third year, and just six in the fourth and final year.

Like Nixon, and, indeed, all other presidents, Carter expected loyalty. But Carter's brand of loyalty was very different from that of Nixon. It was influenced by a collegialism that provided opportunities for face-to-face communication, even appeals. In Carter's view, his highly disciplined style begged to be emulated. Loyalty, then, included a devotion to excellence and hard work on the part of department heads. Communication was also serious business for the president since it involved time commitments on his part.

Making cabinet appointments was a very deliberative process for Carter; he perhaps discovered that it was not as possible as he might have thought to bring new leaders to Washington. It is true, as Hess points out, that "those filling the top slots would likely have been included in any Democrat's administration," and that "most of the heavyweights were best known for their accomplishments in Washington."[113] Still, at the time of appointment the cabinet secretaries were drawn mostly from the private sphere, making Carter's cabinet look much like Kennedy's.[114]

Although he was a one-term president, there were two Carter governments, more or less by design (see appendix figure A-5). When he first entered office, as the first elected post-Watergate president, Carter was determined to distinguish his government from that of Nixon. Yet one result of his unprecedented exercise in self-examination in early July 1979 was to ask, Nixon style, for the resignations of his cabinet. Carter quite startled his own government with this action. Health, Education and Welfare Secretary Joseph Califano's recounting of the cabinet meeting in which the action took place is reminiscent of that by Henry Kissinger of the Nixon firings.

> The President began softly. "I have deliberately excluded most of you from my life for the past couple of weeks." He said he had "wanted to get away from you and from Washington." He felt an obligation to reassess his presidency. . . . His words were pessimistic, his voice somber. It was as close to quiet desperation as I had ever seen him.

By Califano's report, Carter then explained what he had been told about his administration by his many visitors to Camp David: that "the people had lost confidence . . . that there was disloyalty 'among some Cabinet members,' and that many had been the source of leaks that had hurt him."

Scanning the table, he added, "I want each of you to assess your subordinates, their loyalty to us, whether they are team players, whether they will

speak with one voice. . . ." Then he said that he wanted us all to submit
"pro forma resignations" [in writing]. He was evaluating each of us and he
would decide whether to accept the resignations or not. . . .

[Secretary of State Cyrus] Vance immediately opposed the idea, and
was supported by [Secretary of Defense Harold] Brown, and then most of
the Cabinet. It would be "too much like Nixon in 1972," we said like a
Greek chorus.[115]

It was no doubt perplexing to the cabinet to be brought to heel on the
criterion of the Nixon brand of loyalty when that concept had not previously
been set forth as central to the management of the Carter administration and
a premium had been placed on independent thought by the president himself.

In the end, the president did not insist on written resignations, nor did he
fire the whole cabinet. But there were a number of changes: six new secretaries were appointed (one shifting from one department to another). Two
other changes were made later when Juanita Kreps resigned for personal
reasons and Cyrus Vance resigned in protest over the Iran hostage crisis.
Also, a thirteenth cabinet department was created, and Shirley Hufstedler
was appointed the first secretary of education. In replacing cabinet secretaries, Carter drew less from those inside the government than did other
presidents in making replacements.

It is likely that Carter did achieve more control over the government with
the moves that he made in 1979, perhaps for some of the same reasons and
to achieve the same goals as Richard Nixon. The changes also reflected
revisions in Carter's concept of his place in the government, resulting from
the extraordinary retreat at Camp David. But they were done so clumsily
that they were not likely to enhance Carter's standing as a leader—the very
goal he was seeking to achieve. Carter is the only president to renew his
organization substantially in the first term, a change made even more dramatic because of the stability that characterized the early months of the
administration (see figure 3-1).

Reagan to Bush

The final postwar transitional presidency also has special markings. A vice
president assumed the office, as with the other three during this period, but
he was elected on his own. Still there was a transitional character: the successor, George Bush, had to accommodate expectations borne from the
legacy of Ronald Reagan (see figure 3-1).

REAGAN WHITE HOUSE STAFF. Of the presidents reviewed here, Reagan
was least directly interested in White House organization. He had strong and

clearly articulated, if quite general, policy ideas about what his administration should accomplish. Further, he expected these goals to be achieved, as did others. But he did not come to the White House with well-formed notions about how an organization might be set up to reach these goals. According to Neustadt, the Reagan management style, if it can be called that, was to "choose targets and men, leave the details to them—except that he was evidently careless in his choice of words and distinctly casual in his choice of men."[116] It was a loose style, to say the least, but, again, by the Polsby test, one revealing of the person for whom it was designed to work.

Whereas most presidents discuss organizational matters in their memoirs—particularly those affecting the White House and cabinet—Reagan has virtually nothing to say in his. In fact, one chapter ends with his having gotten out of the shower to receive the concession call from Jimmy Carter; the next chapter begins with his inauguration as president.[117] There is no mention of the eleven-week interim period in which the foundations of an administration must be laid.

The lack of strong direction from the president in regard to organization naturally left it to others to frame the Reagan government. The responsibility lay primarily with an unusual "troika" of James Baker, Michael Deaver, and Edwin Meese, all active in the Reagan campaign. According to Lou Cannon's biography, an understanding of the Reagan organizational team and strategy begins with the removal of John Sears as campaign manager early in the 1980 campaign. William Casey was then made campaign manager and Edwin Meese chief of staff (a position he held with Governor Reagan). Their lack of experience in managing a national campaign worried Nancy Reagan, among others, so a rival team was created: Stuart Spencer, an experienced political consultant, and Michael Deaver, a long-time Reagan loyalist. "The rival teams managed to work together in uneasy coexistence."[118]

Spencer and Deaver looked ahead to organizing the White House and were determined that James Baker, not Meese, should be the chief of staff. Given that Baker was not a Californian and that he had managed Bush's nomination campaign, the proposal had to be presented tactfully to Reagan. However, Reagan reportedly realized that Meese was not organized enough for the job, and he readily accepted the idea of appointing Baker.[119] Even so, it was inconceivable that Baker could perform the chief-of-staff role in the manner of Sherman Adams or Bob Haldeman. Thus the troika was created with Meese serving as counselor and Deaver as deputy chief of staff. All three had equal access to the president. Colin Campbell labeled this a "modified spokes-in-a-wheel format" that was "a middle ground between a hierarchical

White House and one attempting to offer equal access for all senior assistants."[120] The principal difference between the Reagan operation and other multiple-access systems was that it emerged more from the preferences and positioning of his aides than those of the president. When a hierarchical system was set in place later, it too was less Reagan's choice than that of his aides.

Reagan had one chief of staff, James Baker, during the first four years and three during his second four years: Donald Regan, Howard Baker, and Kenneth Duberstein. A review of the changes in that position is revealing of how the president related to his staff. The first change was a consequence of an independent decision by Secretary of the Treasury Donald Regan and Baker to switch jobs. According to Regan, the idea was born out of a confrontation between the two that resulted in a "chat."

Baker and Regan then met with the president, with Deaver also present. Deaver had been let in on the proposal and had first gotten Nancy Reagan's approval. Reagan had been briefed by his wife and "listened without any sign of surprise" to the planned switch. Regan wrote: "He seemed equable, relaxed—almost incurious. This seemed odd under the circumstances."[121] Yet the president had confidence in both men and no strong preference as to their respective positions, only that they serve (both having thought about leaving).

Regan's assumption of the chief-of-staff post led to important changes in White House staff organization. The multiple-access troika was no more. Baker went to Treasury, Meese was appointed attorney general, and Deaver returned to private life. Regan assumed a role much more like that of Sherman Adams and Bob Haldeman (minus the close, personal association with a president aware of why he wanted a functioning chief of staff). Cannon concludes correctly that no modern presidency "has ever undergone such a thoroughgoing transformation in management style as Reagan's did under his new chief of staff." Most postwar presidencies experienced an adaptive or evolutionary staff development. The Baker-Regan shift was breathtakingly abrupt. As Cannon observes: "Because of Reagan's passivity, his presidency easily assumed the coloration of whoever was running the White House."[122]

In the classic hierarchical, chief-of-staff system, responsibility is clearly set. Thus, when there was a search for who was in charge of the White House following the Iran-contra revelations, Donald Regan was naturally at the top of the list. The report of the President's Special Review Board (the Tower board) concluded: "More than any other Chief of Staff in recent memory, [Regan] asserted personal control over the White House staff and sought to extend this control to the National Security Advisor. . . . He must bear primary responsibility for the chaos that descended upon the White

House. . . ."[123] Regan strongly rejected this assessment; as he saw it, he did not have personal control over the national security adviser. Whether he had control or not, Regan was bound to be held responsible for the reasons cited in the report, and he was removed.

President Reagan has written that "Iran-contra had nothing to do with his [Regan's] replacement." His analysis of this case reveals something of the president's style in regard to organizational matters, as well as his reliance on his wife for advice.

> I learned from Nancy and then from others that many people—staff members, cabinet members, and congressional leaders—felt that Don had an oversized ego that made him difficult to deal with. . . . According to some, Don thought of himself as a kind of "deputy president" empowered to make important decisions involving the administration. . . . In short, he wanted to be the *only* conduit to the Oval Office, in effect making that presidential isolation I just complained about even more complete.[124]

Reagan's description of Regan's role as deputy president is not unlike others' conception of a chief-of-staff position. But to be effective, such a relationship has to be based on mutual understanding and communication— not delegation by inadvertence. It also requires self-effacement, sensitivity to and appreciation of politics, an understanding of who else is close to the president and why, and a staff to assist in realizing the first three goals. According to Cannon, and as corroborated by the president's own final assessment, Regan lacked all four requisites.[125]

Reagan's choice for a new chief of staff was former Senator Paul Laxalt of Nevada, but he declined. Laxalt's suggestion was former Senator Howard W. Baker of Tennessee. Baker accepted, the news was leaked before Regan had been told (though Regan had informed the president that he would resign), and the Reagan-Regan parting was quite bitter.

Once more there was an abrupt change in White House staff organizational style. With the change in chief of staff, there was also a new team at the National Security Council: Frank Carlucci and Lieutenant General Colin Powell. When Carlucci later became secretary of defense, General Powell was appointed national security adviser. Wholesale changes occurred in other vital White House staff positions as well. The whole atmosphere changed dramatically, primarily because of Baker's experience and personal style. "The low-profile Baker, skilled at accommodating Congress, pursued no agenda of his own; rather, he returned the chief of staff's role to that of mediator, while opening access to the president and broadening the decision-making process."[126]

The new style could not prevent organizational problems, as Hess and others point out. The administration was winding down, completing its last two years. And the Iran-contra scandal was unfolding as a possible fatal threat to the Reagan White House. Under the circumstances, however, Baker gets credit for restoring a workable system.

Among those Baker brought to the White House was the former director of congressional liaison, Kenneth Duberstein, a knowledgeable and professional staff person. "At Baker's behest, Duberstein accepted the responsibility of dealing with Nancy Reagan, who was once more openly welcomed as a political adviser."[127] When Baker stepped down as chief of staff in 1988, Duberstein took over—a change that barely produced a ripple in White House staff operations.

BUSH WHITE HOUSE STAFF. Like other takeover presidents in this group, it was unlikely that George Bush could have won the presidency on his own. He tried and failed in 1980, winning primaries in only four states and the District of Columbia. Bush's advantage in 1988 was clearly that he was a sitting vice president for a popular president. He was the heir apparent, or as Walter Dean Burnham labels him, a third-term understudy selected as a "promising conservator of the 'revolution' carried out by others."[128]

One might reasonably question whether Bush was an understudy of Reagan as president or of the presidency more generally. His career represented a model of what many think is required for the White House: service in the House of Representatives, in several executive posts, and as national party chairman. This vast governmental experience even before Reagan chose him as vice president, as well as his opportunity to observe White House organization closely, meant that Bush arrived at the Oval Office with definite ideas as to how to structure his presidency. And, in fact, it was a relatively stable administration as reflected in the White House and departmental organization.

One special feature of the Bush presidency that had important organizational connotations was his close, long-term friendship with James Baker, his campaign manager and secretary of state. The association between the two men sent signals as to how the White House would likely be organized. After all, Baker himself served as chief of staff for Reagan and thus was familiar with the problems of internal staff structure. No member of the White House staff could ever expect to be as close to the president as was Baker.

It was a foregone conclusion that Bush would opt for a chief of staff. He had used such a position when serving as vice president. But many were surprised when Bush chose John Sununu, the acerbic governor of New Hampshire who had strongly supported him in his crucial battle with Robert Dole in that state's primary. The reasons for this choice reveal yet another variation in structuring the White House, again reflecting the personal preferences, strengths, and weaknesses of the president.

Sununu was not part of the Bush inner circle. He had not previously served in Washington. He was an engineer, educator, and businessman with a reputation for offending those who disagreed with him. The most popular explanation for his choice was that Sununu was willing to be the person Bush did not want to be but judged he needed. Since he had selected so many staff aides with White House experience, Sununu was needed "to kick the administration out of its almost certain 'we know best' complacency," and to run the White House "with an iron fist."[129]

The strong role for Sununu as the White House "bully" did not prevent others from gaining access to the president. In fact, Bush was unwilling to be isolated from the many close associates he had come to know in his many years of service in the national government. Thus geometric models once again failed as symbols of White House organization. The aforementioned relationship with Baker cut across and through any pyramid that might have been imposed. Within the White House itself, Bush's long association with Brent Scowcroft, the national security adviser; C. Boyden Gray, counsel to the president; and Richard G. Darman, director of the Office of Management and Budget, among others, was unlikely to be altered or interrupted by a chief of staff.[130]

Sununu met his downfall when it was revealed that he had taken many personal and political trips on Air Force jets at taxpayer expense and he refused to apologize for his behavior. Since any chief of staff who is headline news has lost effectiveness, Sununu resigned in early December 1991. The new chief of staff was Samuel Skinner, then serving as secretary of transportation. Skinner reorganized the White House staff, bringing in new people and attempting to prepare for the ensuing campaign. No reorganization was likely to have a measurable impact on two crippling developments: the steady decline in the president's approval ratings, and the increase in conflicts with congressional Democrats.

In the end, Bush turned to his close friend, James Baker, to take charge of his campaign and his White House in August 1992. (Skinner was moved to the Republican National Committee.) There was, at this point, very little to manage in the White House itself, and, as it happened, Baker's arrival was too late to help his friend's campaign very much. Baker's steady hand did assist in the transition to a new president, however.

REAGAN-BUSH CABINET SECRETARIES. Lou Cannon explains that Reagan had been devoted "to the grail of cabinet government" as governor of California. However, cabinet meetings were less "instruments of decision-making" than "convenient forums for keeping 'citizen-governor' Reagan roughly familiar with issues and for ratifying decisions that had been made before the cabinet assembled." Cannon observed that the symbolic value of the cabinet-as-government was not lost on the president. "Reagan hugely enjoyed the spectacle of cabinet meetings, even if he did not always stay awake at them."[131]

However, Reagan was quite disengaged from the task of building his presidential cabinet. He had set the course; now it was the job of others to form a government that would reach his goals. This detachment apparently led to an effort by Reagan's staff to organize themselves so as to achieve the president's stated goals. In their study of the Reagan transition period, William E. Walker and Michael R. Reopel conclude that "the Reagan transition was the most carefully planned and effective in American political history."[132] Clearly the concept of Ronald Reagan as leader had sufficient meaning in and of itself as to be a force for organization.

Reagan's domestic policy chief, Martin Anderson, outlined the complex tasks involved in ensuring that the message was conveyed to those appointees who were not a part of the campaign. Cabinet members often were persons of stature, unlikely to have been a part of the "hurly-burly" of campaigning. "The problem every winning campaign faces is how to ensure that those with more distinguished public reputations who will be chosen for the cabinet posts do not betray the policies the campaign was fought on. . . . The president-elect placed Ed Meese in charge of all transition activities . . . ." Meese developed an "indoctrination course for cabinet members . . . [on] ideas and people." Cabinet secretaries were consulted in making subcabinet appointments, but they were also informed "that they could not freely choose the people who would work for them."[133]

The Reagan team wished to avoid the mistake made by Nixon and Carter of allowing cabinet secretaries to appoint their subordinates.[134] Therefore, months before the election, Meese enlisted the help of E. Pendleton James, a corporate headhunter, to create a personnel selection system that would guarantee fidelity to the political and policy aims of the new president. By all accounts, James was notably successful.

No administration before had attempted such an elaborate clearance system. "Each nomination had to run a formidable gauntlet running from the cabinet secretary and the personnel office to Lyn Nofziger (political clearance), to White House counsel Fred Fielding (conflict of interest), to either Martin Anderson (domestic) or Richard Allen (national security), to the triad (James Baker, Michael Deaver, Edwin Meese), to the congressional liaison office and finally to the president himself."[135]

This elaborate process took time, and the administration was criticized for the delay in filling certain positions. This criticism did not appear to bother Reagan, who was not greatly involved, and he certainly agreed with the results. For while "publicly extolling the virtues of cabinet government, steps were being taken to ensure that ultimate control over subcabinet appointments—indeed, over *all* lower-level political appointments—would remain firmly in the hands of the White House."[136] Further, as John Kessel has shown, the structure resulted in substantial issue agreement among staff, as well as a clear sense as to who was in charge.[137]

Control through personnel appointments could work only if there was clear policy direction and a system for implementing it. The Reagan administration developed a network of cabinet councils, cross-departmental units to control and coordinate policy. These councils met at the White House, close to the Oval Office. This meant that the president could attend (he chaired approximately one-fifth of the meetings in the first year). Just as important, however, was the fact that departmental secretaries or their representatives were brought to the White House for policy discussion. It was an excellent counterforce to the tendency to "go native" within the departments. Anderson explains:

> Just the act of having to leave their fiefdoms, get into a car, and be driven to the White House was a powerful reminder to every member of the cabinet that it was the president's business they were about, not theirs or their department's constituents. . . . It simply is easier to elevate the national interest above special interests in that building. It does not always happen, but it is easier.[138]

There were three identifiable cabinets during the Reagan years: the initial group with several early changes, a second-term cabinet that included a number of holdovers, and a most interesting third group that acted almost as a transition cabinet for George Bush (see appendix figures A-6 and A-7). In the initial set of appointments, Reagan followed the standard pattern of drawing primarily from outside Washington. Still, he included as many or more with executive and congressional or court experience as had other presidents, and substantially more than his Republican predecessors.

The second cabinet was one of the more seasoned in federal government experience of those treated here. The combination of carryover appointments and new appointments drawn from within the government meant that all cabinet secretaries had executive experience. There was no mass firing following the 1984 reelection, yet such a break offered a natural point for turnover and renewal. There were five changes among the cabinet secretaries; one involved a switch in departments, and two involved moving White House staff to cabinet departments.

It is not uncommon to have high turnover in the cabinet toward the end of an administration. Often cabinet secretaries resign and a deputy or under secretary assumes the position for the last few months. In the last months of the Reagan administration, however, the appointments appeared to be more than temporary and terminal replacements. Three members of the third cabinet carried over to the new Bush government. In addition, Bush appointed two other persons who had served earlier in Reagan cabinets.

Bush's cabinet secretarial appointments "were widely praised for their experience and competence."[139] One appointee, former Senator John Tower of Texas, was rejected for secretary of defense by a majority of his former colleagues, which was an embarrassment for the new administration. But this position was then filled by Representative Richard Cheney of Wyoming, who served with distinction. It was a "friends and neighbors" kind of cabinet: many of Bush's long-time associates, most of whom had impressive political and administrative experience. Given this acquaintance, the president was comfortable with providing a fair amount of discretion. Still, this characteristic has to be evaluated in the context of the lack of strong programmatic direction from the White House.

Following the transition, there were relatively few adjustments and no wholesale firings in the Bush cabinet. A high proportion of the secretaries— six of fourteen—served through the four years, and four of those who left did so to take other jobs in the administration. The president hinted during the 1992 campaign that he might make changes if he were to be reelected, but this announcement appeared to be motivated more by a desire to show that a second term would differ from a first than by dissatisfaction with specific individuals or an announcement of a new policy direction.

In summary, the Reagan-to-Bush transition was the least dramatic of those examined in this chapter. George Bush was the inheritor of the Reagan legacy, and there was no reason to make major organizational changes. The difference was in the person now occupying the Oval Office. Whereas Reagan set a general policy direction and expected his aides and secretaries to move the government in that way, Bush actively presided over an organization designed primarily to carry on.

Organizing and Adapting

Presidents face the distinctive problem in a separated system of developing an organization that will suit their personal style, policy goals, and temporary custody of a continuous government. There is no one formula for accomplishing these ends, and even if there were, most presidents are not trained to make such a formula work well for them. Much of what has been described here appears to be trial-and-error experimentation in which presidents often appoint large numbers of persons with little or no background or training in the organization and management of the federal government. A White House staff of close advisers and a presidential branch have emerged over the postwar period to enhance the president's control, but these developments have created as many organizational problems as they have solved.

I have concentrated on two features of a president's effort to attach himself to the government for which he will be held responsible: the White House staff and the cabinet secretaries. There are three conclusions with special merit from this discussion: Some presidents (four of the nine in the postwar period) have a limited opportunity in the crucial early stages of their administration to fashion an organization suited to their style and goals; the standard models for White House organization do not adequately account for the variations in how presidents structure their staffs; and likewise, there is no formula for appointing and interacting with cabinet secretaries.

I have little to add to the first conclusion, except to remind the reader that some presidents are faced with the even more formidable task of restructuring an organization already in place while determining the goals for guiding change. Their degrees of latitude in reshaping the administration will vary, circumscribed by their predecessor's legacy.

Regarding the second conclusion, the review of White House staffs indicates that the dominant models—the hierarchy or chief of staff and the circle or spokes of the wheel—vastly oversimplify the many differences among presidents' interactions with staff.

Several dimensions of White House organization are shown in table 3-4, noting the variation for each president in the postwar period. The principal finding is that no two staff organizations look exactly alike for the very good reason that, as Clark Clifford observed, "no single structure is right for every

Table 3-4. *Characteristics of White House Staff Organization, Truman–Bush*

	All presidents					Takeover presidents only	
President	Access	President's concept	President's interaction	Change	Staff relations	Transition	Interim arrangements
Truman	Multiple	Unformed	Occasional	High	Conflictual	Continuance	Cordial
Eisenhower	Controlled	Well formed	Occasional	Low	Harmonious	...	...
Kennedy	Open	Well formed	Frequent	Low	Harmonious	...	...
Johnson	Multiple	Unformed	Frequent	Moderate	Conflictual	Continuance	Conflictual
Nixon	Controlled	Changeable	Occasional	High	Conflictual	...	...
Ford	Open to controlled	Changeable	Frequent	High	Conflictual	Change	Conflictual
Carter	Open to multiple	Well formed	Frequent	Moderate	Variable	...	...
Reagan	Multiple to controlled to multiple	Unformed	Passive	High	Variable	...	...
Bush	Multiple	Well formed	Frequent	Moderate	Variable	Change	Cordial

President." However, even where a concept from the top is lacking, the staff will try to form one that suits their understanding of what works best in the Oval Office. Sometimes that is very frustrating work, as can be attested to by the staffs of Carter, Reagan, and Bush.

A second pattern is the significant amount of change that occurs in how presidents organize the White House. The process of designing a presidency at the top is allowed to be quite personal, suited to the perception of needs and responsibilities of the occupant. As a consequence, there is an astonishing lack of accepted wisdom as to how it should be done. It is true, of course, that there have been developments within each presidency that have then been carried over to form a predictable set of organizational units labeled now as the "presidential branch." I am referring, rather, to how the people within those units work with each other and with the president. Presidents and their aides often rely on quaint maxims such as "Don't do it like your predecessor" or "Don't trust those in Washington to know how to manage." And so the variation shown in table 3-4 may be expected to characterize future presidencies as well.

My third conclusion directs attention to the president's relationship with the cabinet secretaries. These appointments receive the most media and public attention, particularly in the recent monitoring of representativeness. I have stressed that cabinet secretaries are unlikely to form a policymaking unit, although presidents often enter office believing that the group can perform that role. They serve primarily as emissaries to the departments and variably as policy advisers to the president singly or as teams for related issues. Those types of interactions are consistent with the nature of a separated system, which lacks a structure or motivation for appointing persons with similar political backgrounds.

All postwar presidents except Kennedy had more than one distinct cabinet, as measured by turnover. Often these changes were a result of the transition from an elected president to a vice president taking over, or the expected adjustments during an administration. There were, however, three cases of renewal: Nixon, Carter, and Reagan. Given these patterns of change (see figure 3-1), the process of connecting presidents with the departments through cabinet secretaries is constant. Secretaries' tenure rarely matches that of the relatively short term of the president himself. Only six secretaries served through two full terms—for eight years—in the postwar period. Many others served at least through one term with a president (see table 3-2), but just twenty-six served as long as the president, and nineteen of these were with presidents who were in office four or fewer years.

It is difficult to imagine how a cabinet secretary can be an effective emissary with this amount of turnover. Accordingly, evaluating a presidency by a collective one-on-one test—that is, as a composite of the president interacting with individual cabinet secretaries—will prove challenging. There are cases—the first Eisenhower administration or the first years of the Kennedy, Carter, and Bush administrations—that would permit development of such a composite. But for most presidencies, a portrayal just completed would have to be redrawn, then redrawn again. Such an undertaking is to be recommended, but it does not surprise me that it has not been done.

The U.S. executive branch is managed by people hardly in place long enough to learn their immediate responsibilities, let alone the intricacies of participating meaningfully in the policymaking and politics of a separated system. It is understandable that representativeness has come to be an important criterion for appointment, but the transient quality of departmental leadership suggests that allegiance to an administration over time is equally, if not more, important. The permanent government has enough reasons to be reluctant to conform to an impermanent leadership.

There are a number of potential effects of meeting the organizational demands of the presidency. Those presidents who are successful in establishing a compatible organization are likely to enjoy more positive public standing, a greater capacity for designating priorities, and more active participation in lawmaking. In fact, one can imagine a continuum from the presidencies with clearly etched organizational images (Eisenhower, Kennedy, and Reagan) to those substantially less fixed (Ford and Carter). In some cases that imagery changed significantly during the president's term in office (most notably in the case of Nixon). Organization cannot save a presidency from failure, but it can surely aid in preventing disaster in the first place.

Figure A-1. *Cabinet Changes, Truman Administration, 1945–53*

Department	First appointee[a]	1945	1946	1947	1948	1949	1950	1951	1952
State	Edward Stettinius	├ James Byrnes	┼ George Marshall			┼ Dean Acheson ──────────────────────────			
Treasury	Henry Morganthau	├ Fred Vinson ┼ John Snyder ──							
War	Henry Stimson	├ Robert Patterson ─────── Kenneth Royal (Department reorganization)							
Navy	James Forrestal	─────────────── [Department reorganization]							
Defense[b]				James Forrestal ┼ Louis Johnson ┼ George Marshall ┼ Robert Lovett					
Justice	Francis Biddle	├ Tom Clark ───────────────────────────── ┼ J. Howard McGrath ─┼●┼ James McGranery							
Post Office	Frank Walker	├ Robert Hannegan ──────────── ┼ Jesse Donaldson ────────────────────────							
Interior	Harold Ickes	├●┼ Julius Krug ────────────────────────────── ┼ Oscar Chapman ────────────							
Agriculture	Claude Wickard	├ Clinton Anderson ───────────── ●┼ Charles Brannan ────────────────────────							
Commerce	Henry Wallace	├ Averill Harriman ┼ Charles Sawyer ────────────							
Labor	Lewis Schwellenbach	├ Maurice Tobin ●┼ ───────────────────────							

Cabinets	First	Second		Third
			(Election)	

Sources: Created from data in Michael Nelson, ed., *Guide to the Presidency* (Washington: Congressional Quarterly, 1989), pp. 1461–63; William A. DeGregorio, *The Complete Book of U.S. Presidents*, 2d ed. (New York: Dembner Books, 1989); Robert Sobel, ed., *Biographical Directory of the United States Executive Branch, 1774–1977* (Westport, Conn.: Greenwood Press, 1977); and *Who's Who in America*.

● Vacancy.

a. Initial Truman cabinet originally appointed by Roosevelt.

b. The Department of Defense began operations in 1947. James Forrestal, who was serving as secretary of the navy, was the first secretary.

Figure A-2. *Cabinet Changes, Eisenhower Administration, 1953–61*

Department	First appointee								
		1953	1954	1955	1956	1957	1958	1959	1960
State	John Foster Dulles						┼Christian Herter		
Treasury	George Humphrey					┼Robert Anderson			
Defense	Charles Wilson					┼Neil McElroy		┼Thomas Gates	
Justice	Herbert Brownell					┼William Rogers			
Post Office	Arthur Summerfield								
Interior	Douglas McKay			●┼Fred Seaton					
Agriculture	Ezra Benson								
Commerce	Sinclair Weeks						●┼Frederick Mueller		
Labor	Martin Durkin	┼James Mitchell							
HEW[b]	Oveta Culp Hobby		┼Marion Folsom				┼Arthur Flemming		

First   (Reelection)   Second

Cabinets

Sources: See figure A-1.
● Vacancy.
a. Lewis Strauss was appointed secretary of commerce but failed to be confirmed by the Senate.
b. The Department of Health, Education, and Welfare began operations in 1953. Oveta Culp Hobby was the first secretary.

Figure A-3. *Cabinet Changes, Kennedy-Johnson Administration, 1961–69*

Department	First appointee
State	Dean Rusk
Treasury	Douglas Dillon — Henry Fowler — Joseph Barr[a]
Defense	Robert McNamara — Clark Clifford
Justice	Robert Kennedy — Nicholas Katzenbach — Ramsey Clark
Post Office	J. Edward Day — John Gronouski — Lawrence O'Brien — W. Marvin Watson
Interior	Stewart Udall
Agriculture	Orville Freeman
Commerce	Luther Hodges — John Connor — Alexander Trowbridge — Cyrus Smith
Labor	Arthur Goldberg — Willard Wirtz
HEW	Abraham Ribicoff — Anthony Celebrezze — John Gardner — Wilbur Cohen
HUD[b]	Robert Weaver[c]
Transportation[d]	Alan Boyd

Timeline years: 1961 · 1962 · 1963 (Assassination) · 1964 (Election) · 1965 · 1966 · 1967 · 1968

Cabinets: First (Kennedy-Johnson) · Second (Johnson)

Sources: See figure A-1.

● Vacancy.

a. Joseph Barr served as secretary of the treasury for one month at the end of the Johnson administration.
b. The Department of Housing and Urban Development began operations in 1966. Robert Weaver was the first secretary.
c. Robert Wood served as secretary of HUD for less than a month at the end of the Johnson administration.
d. The Department of Transportation began operations in 1967. Alan Boyd was the first secretary.

Figure A-4. Cabinet Changes, Nixon-Ford Administration, 1969–77

Department	First appointee
State	William Rogers ●├ Henry Kissinger
Treasury	David Kennedy ┼ John Connally ┼ George Shultz ┼ William Simon
Defense	Melvin Laird ├ James Schlesinger[a] ┼ Donald Rumsfeld
Justice	John Mitchell ┼ Richard Kleindeinst[b] ┤ ● ├ William Saxbe ┼ Edward Levi
Post Office	Winton Blount[c]
Interior	Walter Hickel ● ├ Rogers Morton ┤ ● ├[d] ├ Thomas Kleppe ● ├[e]
Agriculture	Clifford Hardin ● ├ Earl Butz
Commerce	Maurice Stans ┼ Peter Peterson ┼ Frederick Dent ● ├ Rogers Morton ┼ Elliot Richardson
Labor	George Shultz ┼ James Hodgson ┼ Peter Brennan ┼ John Dunlop ┼ W. J. Usery
HEW	Robert Finch ┼ Elliot Richardson ┼ Caspar Weinberger ┼ David Mathews
HUD	George Romney ● ├ James Lynn ● ├ Carla Hills
Transportation	John Volpe ┼ Claude Brinegar ┼ William Coleman

	1969	1970	1971	1972	1973	1974	1975	1976
Cabinets	First		Second		Third		Fourth	
				(Reelection)		(Resignation)		

Sources: See figure A-1.
● Vacancy.
a. Elliot Richardson served as secretary of defense for three months in 1973.
b. Elliot Richardson served as attorney general for five months in 1973.
c. The Post Office lost cabinet status in 1970.
d. Stanley Hathaway served as secretary of the interior for four months in 1975.
e. John Knebel served as secretary of agriculture for two months at the end of the Ford administration.

Figure A-5. *Cabinet Changes, Carter Administration, 1977–81*

Department	First appointee		
State	Cyrus Vance		Edmund Muskie
Treasury	Michael Blumenthal	G. William Miller	
Defense	Harold Brown		
Justice	Griffin Bell	Benjamin Civiletti	
Interior	Cecil Andrus		
Agriculture	Robert Bergland		
Commerce	Juanita Kreps	Philip Klutznick	
Labor	Ray Marshall		
HEW/HHS[a]	Joseph Califano	Patricia Harris	
HUD	Patricia Harris	Moon Landrieu	
Transportation	Brock Adams	Neil Goldschmidt	
Energy[b]	James Schlesinger	Charles Duncan	
Education[c]			Shirley Hufstedler
	1977	1978	1979	1980
Cabinets	First		Second

Sources: See figure A-1.
a. With the creation of the Department of Education in 1980, HEW was changed to the Department of Health and Human Services (HHS).
b. The Department of Energy began operations in 1977. James Schlesinger was the first secretary.
c. The Department of Education began operations in 1980. Shirley Hufstedler was the first secretary.

Figure A-6. *Cabinet Changes, Reagan Administration, 1981–89*

Department	First appointee	1981	1982	1983	1984	1985	1986	1987	1988
State	Alexander Haig		┼George Shultz						
Treasury	Donald Regan				┼James Baker			●┼Nicholas Brady	
Defense	Caspar Weinberger							┼Frank Carlucci	
Justice	William Smith				┼Edwin Meese			┼Richard Thornburgh	
Interior	James Watt			●┼William Clark		┼Donald Hodel			
Agriculture	John Block					●┼Richard Lyng			
Commerce	Malcolm Baldridge						●	┼William Verity	
Labor	Raymond Donovan					●┼William Brock		●┼Ann McLaughlin	
HHS	Richard Schweiker			●┼Margaret Heckler		┼Otis Bowen			
HUD	Samuel Pierce								
Transportation	Andrew Lewis		┼Elizabeth Dole					●┼James Burnley	
Energy	James Edwards		●┼Donald Hodel			┼John Herrington			
Education	Terrel Bell				●┼William Bennett			┼Lauro Cavasos	

		1981	1982	1983	1984	1985	1986	1987	1988
		First			(Reelection) Second			Third	

Cabinets

Sources: See figure A-1.
● Vacancy.

Figure A-7. *Cabinet Changes, Bush Administration, 1989–93*

Department	First appointee
State	James Baker — Lawrence Eagleburger
Treasury	Nicholas Brady
Defense	Richard Cheney
Justice	Richard Thornburgh — William Barr
Interior	Manuel Lujan
Agriculture	Clayton Yeutter — Edward Madigan
Commerce	Robert Mosbacher — Barbara Franklin
Labor	Elizabeth Dole — Lynn Martin
HHS	Louis Sullivan
HUD	Jack Kemp
Transportation	Samuel Skinner — Andrew Card
Energy	James Watkins
Education	Lauro Cavazos — Lamar Alexander
Veterans Affairs	Edward Derwinski — Anthony Principi

1989   1990   1991   1992

First   Second

Cabinets

Sources: See figure A-1.

CHAPTER FOUR

Public Standing of the President

ONCE in office and organized to govern, presidents are watched carefully and evaluated frequently. Analysts are not content to await the next presidential election as a test of public approval of presidential performance. Nor need they do so. Americans are polled regularly on the subject, and the results are treated as news. This news, in turn, is used as a basis for evaluating a president's record and advising him on governing. High ratings represent power, which should be used to enact programs; low ratings suggest failure, which should encourage a president to reorient his leadership practices.

I will propose here that presidents pay little heed to counsel of this type. They should not ignore public approval ratings, but neither should such ratings be the sole basis for judgment. Rather, they should be considered in the context of the president's overall status in the separated system. The same ratings simply cannot be interpreted in the same way for every president. The work of evaluating presidential performance is not made less taxing by the periodic creation of numbers; and public approval ratings, as distinct from votes in an election, are generated numbers. To clarify, I begin with the tale of George Bush, who was at one point, by these generated numbers, the most popular president of modern times.

The Most Popular President

Often the polls differ regarding presidential approval. But after the successful conduct and conclusion of the Persian Gulf War, it did not matter much which poll one selected: they all showed record levels of approval for

President George Bush. Only once before in the post–World War II period had a president exceeded 85 percent approval. Harry Truman had an 87 percent rating shortly after having assumed office upon Roosevelt's death. Bush reached a high point of 89 percent approval at the end of February 1991.[1] As one would expect with such a high rating, the support was impressive among all groups. In the *Wall Street Journal*/NBC News poll, approval varied from 66 percent among blacks to 96 percent among Republicans, and even 76 percent of the Democrats in the sample approved of the president's job performance.[2]

These results were all the more remarkable considering that prognostications following Bush's election were not encouraging. Editorial writers for *The Economist* were certain that Bush could never match Ronald Reagan's popular approval. "After eight years in the shadows, he has his own presidency. But George Bush will never enjoy the popularity of Ronald Reagan . . . nor will he have the same opportunity to shine."[3]

In fact, Bush and Reagan had exactly the same Gallup poll approval ratings during the month each assumed office, 51 percent. After twelve months, Bush's rating was at 80 percent, Reagan's at 47 percent. After twenty-three months, Bush's rating was at 63 percent, Reagan's at 41 percent. Two months later the difference between the two was 49 points: Bush at 89 percent, Reagan at 40 percent. At no time in his eight-year presidency did Ronald Reagan reach 70 percent approval, but Bush did so for ten of his first twenty-four months in office.[4]

Bush's extraordinarily high ratings in the early months of 1991 were naturally attributed to the successful conduct of the Persian Gulf War.[5] With the end of the war, attention turned to how President Bush would use this high rating. Presidential job approval is assumed to be translatable into influence on Capitol Hill. Furthermore, the ultimate judgment about effectiveness seemingly is whether the president uses this source of influence to enact programs favored by the evaluators. At the conclusion of the Gulf War, *Washington Post* columnist Haynes Johnson wrote: "Bush now has an opportunity to take advantage of the public glow and summon the nation to tackle unfinished agendas at home. If he does, Americans will have far more sound reason to cheer."[6] Both the tone and substance of Johnson's comment suggested that the true test is not the approval itself but whether it is then used for specific policy purposes.

Johnson was not unique in his appraisal. A *Wall Street Journal* headline read: "Bush's Surging Across-the-Board Popularity May Translate into Greater 'Clout' in Congress."[7] These appraisals suit what Mark J. Rozell refers to as the "activist-visionary leadership model" that is relied on to test the president.

Journalists view as "successful" those presidents who articulate a leadership "vision" and a set of broad-ranging government policies to achieve the public good. The press view of presidential leadership entails an activist policy agenda framed by the White House. The president is expected to use the White House "bully pulpit" to "sell" his proposals to the public and Congress.[8]

Expectations of presidential activism are not limited to the press. Republican Senator Trent Lott (Mississippi) was quoted as saying, "This is a golden opportunity. It's a matter now of focusing on some of these domestic issues and pushing them through."[9] Congressional Democrats, too, joined in this call for domestic policy action. Senate Majority Leader George Mitchell (Maine) did not disappoint: "In the wake of the war, the President says he seeks a new world order. We say, Join us in putting our own house in order. Our first priority must be the American people and economic growth and jobs in the United States."[10]

The logic of using increases in approval ratings to get Congress to act when it would not do so otherwise is somewhat unclear. The reasoning seems to derive from an activist, presidency-centered model in which the system awaits presidential action. An alternative view, however, imagines a government working continuously on a relatively stable agenda that carries over from one year to the next. In such a system, a president would judge, on a regular basis, when, where, and how his popularity might be a factor in regard to a specific policy. High ratings would not be deemed automatically translatable into legislative breakthroughs. In fact, the president might be moved in some cases to rely on that popularity as a potential source of power to thwart action as well as to promote it.

In the case of Bush, he had reasons to doubt that success in Congress was in any way related to high approval ratings. He had the highest approval rating of any postwar president at the end of his first year in office and the lowest presidential support score in Congress, eleven points below that of Richard Nixon in 1969.[11] While these records would not in themselves dissuade any president from seeking congressional approval of important legislative proposals, neither would they encourage extraordinary efforts to clear the domestic agenda at the point of high approval.

There are other reasons why President Bush might not have interpreted his high approval rating in the early months of 1991 as bearing policy instructions for Capitol Hill. Most obvious, perhaps, was the fact that Democratic congressional leaders did not even support his decision on the action that appeared to contribute to his popularity, the use of military force to make Iraq withdraw from Kuwait. Further, he asked in a speech marking the end of the Persian Gulf War that Congress "move forward aggressively" on the domestic front.[12] He requested that transportation and crime legislation be passed in one hundred days. It did not happen. On the day after his speech, the House rejected funding for a housing program favored by the president. In a strongly partisan vote, the House said "no," 177–240.[13]

Finally, one must question what the strategic advantage is at the point of maximum popularity, particularly if it is attributed to a single act. Surely the likelihood that the advantage will decrease is greater as approval approaches 100 percent. And with the event itself having ended, the probability of decline in approval is extremely high. Scholars at the time agreed. Paul C. Light observed: "I don't think it's going to translate quickly into an enormously successful Congress for him. Even Norman Schwarzkopf would have difficulty negotiating a bill through the bunkers and minefields on Capitol Hill."[14] Jon R. Bond explained that he and his coauthor, Richard Fleisher, had "analyzed popularity and success every way you can think of, and, basically, popular presidents don't win that much more than unpopular presidents."[15]

I begin this chapter with the story of President Bush and the Gulf War to illustrate the common misconceptions associated with translating popularity into policy success as well as misunderstandings about how the American system works. Popular approval is sometimes a recognition or reward for an action deemed successful or an acknowledgement that things are going well. George Bush's highest approval rating, in early March 1991, was more than halved by March 1992. With the Gulf War long forgotten and a stubborn economic recession at hand, many viewed the president as lacking the leadership required for making things better.

Approval Ratings and the Diffusion of Responsibility

In a system of separated elections, the elections themselves do not fully convey legitimacy. This is particularly true when voters send mixed signals by producing divided government. According to Gary C. Jacobson, "Democratic congresses and Republican presidencies reinforce one another. . . . Democratic majorities in Congress make a Republican presidential candidate's promise of 'no new taxes' more appealing; at the same time, people may feel more comfortable voting for a Republican president knowing that the Democratic Congress will keep him from gutting their favorite programs or invading Nicaragua."[16] Even when a Republican president is declared to have a mandate, such as Reagan in 1980, there is sufficient doubt in the minds of postelection analysts that further tests are invited. After all, Reagan's 91 percent "landslide" electoral college win (doubling Ford's electoral college percentage) was gained with less than 51 percent of the popular vote (just 2.7 percent greater than that received by Ford). Further, the dramatic results in the Senate in 1980 were the consequence of Republicans winning most of the close races: fifteen won by 54 percent or less, nine by 51 percent or less.[17] The Democrats actually garnered a majority of the two-party Senate vote in 1980, even though they lost twelve seats (and control of the Senate).[18]

It is reasonable to expect more polls, more analysis, and frequent revisiting of presidential power and the ends to which it should be put. Public standing has always been of interest because of the inherent limitations of the president's formal powers. Every White House is organized to seek and maintain power. There will be even more intense searches when there is divided government or when analysis casts doubt on whether a mandate should have been declared in the first place (as in 1964 and 1980).

Polls increase the number of data points for testing public acceptance of the president. Thus analysts will pay them greater attention even though polls do not change the basic structure by which presidents govern. Increasing the number of approval ratings from one to a dozen does not greatly alter the capacity of the president to translate those numbers into legislation or other governmental actions. In a system of separated institutions, participants in each unit (congressional committees, bureaucratic agencies) typically are cognizant of the function and role of the other units yet retain a substantial degree of autonomy and self-purpose. Popular approval may improve a president's capacity to bargain if he is resourceful enough to know how to use it to that end. But even then its effect will likely be marginal, that is, in the context of other advantages and dependent on the commitments already made by him and other crucial participants. No one president can expect the ongoing policy process for an issue to be held in place to absorb an increment in his popularity. Any increase in approval will be fitted in to the extent that it improves the president's power of persuasion or other participants judge the ratings to be relevant.

James W. Ceaser points out that presidents are wrong to build their presidencies around approval ratings. Presumably most are shrewd enough not to try to do so.

It is worth emphasizing how little approval ratings have to do with any lasting judgment of presidential performance. A President's legacy derives from his accomplishments or failures, and no President will be long remembered for having an average approval rating of more than 60 percent, nor quickly forgotten for having an average lower than 45 percent. As an instrument of presidential power, a high approval rating has some value as a reminder to others of the potential "cost" they might have to pay in opposing a popular President. Yet it is important to remember that an approval rating is a lag, rather than a lead, indicator. What determines the score will be the public's assessment of conditions, performance, and persona. An astute President should accordingly be prepared in most cases to sacrifice his standing today, if by doing so he can affect positively the future assessment of these factors.[19]

Thus it is curious that there is a fascination, almost fixation, with approval ratings. This obsession is partially due, I argue, to a devotion to the dominant perspective of party government and the disappointment that it seldom, if ever, exists. Given the failure of elections to clearly define and entrust a government, approval ratings become periodic tests of public support. Richard A. Brody explains it this way:

> In a nation as large and politically complex as the United States, opinion polls become the only practicable means for one leader to find out how another leader is viewed by the public. The president is the figure about whom other national leaders regularly need information, and the polls on the division of opinion in the public, on the way the president is doing his job, regularly provide this information.[20]

White House Efforts to Improve Ratings

Knowing of the media's interest in approval ratings, presidents naturally try to project the most favorable image of their performance. Few White House organizational units have grown as much as those of the Office of Communication and the Office of the Press Secretary. In the Bush White House, the Office of Communication was organized into five subunits: speechwriting, research, media relations, public affairs, and public liaison, with a total staff of forty-one (approximately the entire staff of Franklin Roosevelt's White House). In the Office of Public Liaison alone there were eight persons with the title of assistant director.

Although all presidents are concerned to maintain a favorable public standing, Republicans have a special incentive because they typically face Democratic majorities in Congress. Therefore they are moved to secure high approval ratings as a potential source of influence. Republican presidents serving in split-party governments cannot be choosy. They will accept any advantage, understanding that a gain in approval may not mean much but a loss weakens them even more.

The extent to which White House staff can improve public standing is uncertain, in spite of the efforts made to do so. According to Ron Nessen, former press secretary to President Ford,

> The ability of the White House to manage the image of a president, to manipulate the press, is wildly exaggerated. . . . A President who is doing the right things in a substantive way and is popular because of what he is doing or for what he stands for is not going to have to worry about his image in the press. A president who is doing things that are unpopular, or the economy is bad, or his views are not fully accepted—he's going to have problems with the press. There's only a marginal, small impact that any sort of media management or image making can have on this relationship.[21]

Richard A. Brody and Benjamin I. Page provide evidence in support of Nessen's conclusions. In studying the effect of events on presidential popularity, they conclude: "In general, people seem to cast a broad net of responsibility, blaming the President (or giving him credit) for bad or good news even in matters we might consider beyond his control. . . . If the news was good, the President's popularity rose; if bad, it fell. . . . A popularity-maximizing President, then, would do well to produce good results."[22]

These conclusions intimate that the common question asked to elicit public evaluation of the president ("Do you approve or disapprove of the way [name of the president] is handling his job as president?") may be heard as asking "How are things going?" A composite answer to this question may obscure respondents' distinctions between types of issues or the importance they assign to one over another at any one time. For example, at the height of his approval for conducting the war, President Bush had relatively low ratings for his handling of the economy. For the time being, respondents judged the performance on the war to be of primary importance, producing the high rating. John E. Mueller refers to a "rally round the flag effect" that can provide an edge for a president during a national security crisis.[23] Without such a crisis, a serious economic recession can have a negative effect even on a president said to have been protected by a Teflon coating. Reagan's approval rating slipped to 35 percent at the height of the 1982 recession. And Bush's rating fell dramatically once the economy superseded the war as the major issue.

In his analysis of what can be done to improve a president's public standing, Rozell concludes that the White House staff has little choice but to work at the problem and try to have some effect, although it cannot guarantee success.[24] Equally, the staff cannot ignore how the president is being perceived, whether or not it is in a position to shape those perceptions. The situation is not unlike that for election campaigning. Although no one knows precisely what makes a difference, everyone assumes that everything possible must be done, while fully realizing that even with the best of efforts the candidate may lose.

Some scholars, however, have evidence that "public support is amenable to presidential management and influence." Charles W. Ostrom, Jr., and Dennis M. Simon draw this conclusion as a result of identifying the factors that contribute to approval ratings. High approval may be a response to how things are going, but the president is a part of these events and can therefore try to influence them.[25]

Congressional Calculations

Ostrom and Simon find that how well a president does with Congress contributes to evaluations of performance by the public. Much less clear, however, is the extent to which high approval ratings help a president to buy influence with Congress. If a high approval rating is the result of things going well in the country, why should this cause a member of Congress to follow the lead of the president? A member might logically be cautious in opposing the president on an issue of major importance and yet not be prepared to support him on all issues, especially those of direct interest to the constituency. "When [a member is] confronted by a choice between supporting a popular president and the clear interests of his constituents, the president's public prestige is a poor match for his or her constituents' interests."[26]

Ceaser's observation would seem to be the correct one: that a high approval rating is a reminder of the potential costs in opposing the president. Members of Congress will vary considerably in their individual calculation of the costs within their own states and districts of opposing a popular president. Further, approval is "an important background resource for leadership" that helps a president determine "whether or not an opportunity for change exists" and makes "other resources more efficacious."[27] Thus presidents will also vary in the availability of this resource and their individual capacities to use it effectively. In brief, the president's prestige may be important on issues for which members of Congress sense they share a "common fate" among themselves and with the president.[28]

This is not to say that members of Congress ignore a high approval rating for a president. Members naturally interpret the meaning of these numbers for their states or districts. A former House Republican member explains:

> Among Republicans, there is a greater willingness to support the president . . . if, by golly, the president is so popular that I'd be nuts not to support him. Democrats tend to move the same way, but less markedly. We are talking about more moderate and centrist Democrats who tend to vote with the president if they think he is powerful. That won't necessarily help them but it could hurt them.
>
> I don't think you have to say that the president is at 90 percent. Everybody has noticed it and calculated whatever odds one's places on one's own conduct. How much of a political risk is it for me to oppose President Bush given where he is? For instance, [suppose] I decided not to give him the right to risk the lives of my sons and daughters in the Persian Gulf. Do I have the guts to turn around and not let him sit down and negotiate with our partners on this vote on the extension of negotiating for the Uruguay Round [trade talks], when he is so popular. Maybe I can get away with voting against him once, but with two, I'm dead meat.[29]

This discussion provides an example of how an individual member might calculate the costs of voting against a popular president. It also illustrates the often personal nature of the calculation, which will unquestionably take the constituency into account. This is not surprising, given the representational nature of Congress.

Harvey G. Zeidenstein has sought to identify the effect of approval ratings at the aggregated level of congressional roll call votes on key issues. He found a strong relationship between popularity (as measured by the approval question) and doing well on congressional roll call votes in three-fourths of the correlations. In nearly half of these cases, however, the relationships were inverse: high popularity was correlated with low legislative success and vice versa.[30] Zeidenstein then reversed the analysis to determine whether high legislative success might explain increases in presidential popularity. He discovered differences among policy areas but concluded that "whether a president is an able legislative leader does not directly affect his popularity."[31]

Perhaps the most telling comment on studies that correlate approval ratings with key votes in Congress is that they are "theoretically irrelevant." According to George C. Edwards III, "There is no theoretical reason to expect such close associations. The impact of public approval is at once broader and more subtle."[32] Jon R. Bond and Richard Fleisher agree:

> The proposition that the president's popularity *systematically* alters congressional support is based on a rather naive theory of democracy and

representation that assumes levels of citizen knowledge and interest that rarely exist. Most members of Congress know that very few voters are likely to have information about their votes on specific roll calls or about their support for the president. . . . Incumbents seldom lose because they support a popular president too little or support an unpopular president too much; they are more likely to lose because they are too liberal or conservative for their constituencies.[33]

Exactly so. This conclusion follows from what has been learned about why approval ratings rise and fall, as well as the logic of how individual members of Congress are likely to interpret the effects of the ratings for themselves and their constituencies. Some members of Congress will make individual judgments about the effects of going against a popular president, whether or not those judgments can be empirically demonstrated to be sound. And in some cases, a member may simply wish to be identified with a president who is loved by the public or feel sympathy for one who is not. It is because of such cases that Bond and Fleisher include the qualifier "systematically."

The Larger Context

Put together, these studies and observations advise one to pay attention to presidential approval but to set it in the context of what else is happening in the policy and political life of the president and Congress. This book is about the president's role in the national policy process of a separated system. It is a process that has life before and after any one president and also before and after any one president's approval scores. Legislation for certain pressing issues will get passed in some form no matter who is in the Oval Office. This is not to suggest that presidents are unimportant; rather, they are part of a large and complex working government.

 Going Public

Samuel Kernell draws attention to the growing tendency "whereby a president promotes himself and his policies in Washington by appealing to the American public for support." While acknowledging that such a strategy is not new, Kernell argues that it has increased substantially. He points out that presidents give more public speeches, travel more, appear on television, and have expanded their press operations. These developments have coincided with "the continuous technological advances in transportation and mass communications during the past half century."[34] It would be odd in the extreme if, in the face of these developments, presidents were to "hunker down" in the White House. Surely such behavior would gain the critical attention of the press (as, for example, when President Carter decided against campaigning until the American hostages held in Iran were released).

Thus the fact that presidents are heard more and seen more is not in the least surprising. It has been documented and commented on by many others.[35] What is of particular interest here is Kernell's argument that "going public violates" and threatens "to displace" bargaining. Instead of "benefits for compliance," the strategy of going public "imposes costs for noncompliance." It also involves "public posturing" and may undermine "the legitimacy of other politicians." Kernell seems not to like this development, and yet he acknowledges that a president has a strong incentive to go public because of important changes that have occurred in Washington politics. "Individualized pluralism" (a sort of atomistic politics) has replaced "institutionalized pluralism" (characterized by bargaining among large coalitions). "As Washington comes to depend on looser, more individualistic political relations, presidents searching for strategies that work will increasingly go public."[36]

It is important for the purposes of this book to clarify the developments Kernell has identified. He believes that the stimulus to go public in response to the new politics in Washington creates a different politics from that of bargaining. Another interpretation, however, might be simply that bargaining conditions have changed because of the many developments Kernell cites. I add yet another development: the frequent election of Republican presidents and Democratic congresses. It may well be that the only option available to a Republican president for improving his position at the bargaining table is to go public. It then is less a case of freely imposing "costs for noncompliance" than, in Ceaser's words, a reminder of the potential costs of opposing the president. Bargaining as a process does not disappear in a system of diffused responsibility and copartisan politics. But it may well look very different from that in a system of focused responsibility and partisan politics.

In a system of diffused responsibility a president may also go public to prevent legislation from passing. He may not wish to bargain at all but to prevent enactment of a law. Although technological developments may make going public a more rational strategy to achieve this goal than in the past, the goal itself is common enough throughout history. And, in fact, the veto power is there precisely to permit the president to stop a bill from becoming law either because he failed to win through bargaining or he refused to participate in bargaining from the start. Ford and Bush, in particular, employed a veto strategy, sometimes going public with their objections to provide a rationale for congressional Republicans to sustain the veto. Each president had serious weaknesses for classic bargaining: Ford had not been elected even as a vice president, and Bush had a smaller proportion of his party in the House of Representatives than any newly elected president in this century.

Kernell's book helps to place the politics of divided government in sharper relief. The juxtaposition of going public and bargaining suits the party responsibility perspective quite well. Lyndon Johnson, who had huge Democratic majorities in Congress, explained that he "preferred to work from within, knowing that good legislation is the product not of public rhetoric but of private negotiations and compromise." He was not anxious to go to the public because to do so typically involved picking "a fight with the Congress" in order to satisfy the press.[37] Johnson was not anxious to pick a fight with his Democratic Congress, nor did he have any illusions that he would always win. His successors were less reticent in taking this route, in part because they had many fewer resources. This "new breed of presidents," as Kernell refers to them, not only lacked the two-thirds majorities Johnson enjoyed, most did not even have simple majorities. These political realities reinforce the viability of the diffused-responsibility perspective by directing attention to the variation in political resources and strategic advantages.

The Public Standing of Modern Presidents

There is a substantial literature dealing with the public approval of presidents as measured by various polls. Much of this work concentrates on why approval ratings change over a presidential term. Typically the overall trend is down, with numerous upticks or spikes along the way. Various explanations are given for both the overall trend and the jagged nature of the downhill slide. Mueller attributes the decline to a "coalition of minorities," that is, a growing number of interests displeased with presidential decisions. Short-term boosts can be realized by a "rally round the flag" effect in international crises.[38] Kernell finds that changes in the president's popularity are related to events and government actions for which he is held accountable. "Fluctuations in his prestige can be located in observable events and conditions. . . . His decisions on policy do not affect his popularity so much as their results."[39] He may be held as responsible for inaction as for action. Barbara Hinckley and Lyn Ragsdale find that presidential speechmaking can improve approval ratings.[40] In the case of some presidents, the principal loss of support seems to be among the other party: Eisenhower, Nixon, and Reagan lost among Democrats, Kennedy among Republicans. Each of these presidents retained steady support within his own party (except Nixon in his final year in office).[41]

In his review and summation of much of this literature, Dean Keith Simonton observes that "a president's approval rating seems to be a partial consequence of an early term effect. A honeymoon occurs at the onset of a presidential term in which the president receives high, and usually his highest, ratings."[42] The initial measure is apparently less one of approval than of public willingness to encourage a new president. If so, that point may not be the best one from which to measure subsequent standing.

My purpose here, however, is to consider what difference these changes in approval of presidential performance make. Do presidents care? Should they? A check of presidential memoirs revealed that before Nixon, only Truman had much to say about public opinion polls—understandably, since the polls were wrong in predicting the outcome of the 1948 election. In classic Truman prose style, he explained: "A man who is influenced by the polls or is afraid to make decisions which may make him unpopular is not a man to represent the welfare of the country."[43] Eisenhower and Johnson make only brief mention of polls. Nixon, Ford, and Carter comment frequently, noting their approval ratings as associated with particular decisions. Reagan makes no reference to polls in his memoirs.

Is there reason to nurture public approval ratings in order to establish one's place in history? The average Gallup Poll public approval ratings for presidents for their full service and for the last quarter of their presidency, as well as how the public ranked the presidents historically, are shown in table 4-1.

There are several interesting juxtapositions in table 4-1. Kennedy's high ratings throughout are noteworthy, but it is difficult to draw any definitive conclusions, given his limited tenure. Eisenhower's outstanding approval ratings at the time of his presidency did not carry over to later comparative public judgments (though he did gain an "above average" ranking from the historians). Johnson's ratings plummeted during his presidency, but because he started at a very high point his average was substantial. His subsequent public ratings were low, however, and at odds with those of the historians, who rated him "above average." The public ratings for Johnson may improve over time. Public rankings of Reagan remain relatively high, perhaps because of the recency of his presidency and the myth that he was the most popular president at the time of his service. The historians have not yet ranked

Table 4-1. *Public Approval and Historical Rankings of Presidents, Truman–Reagan*

President	Rankings by average approval for administration[a]	Ranking by average in last quarter of administration[a]	Harris poll ranking[b]	Gallup poll ranking[c]	Historians' rating[d]
Kennedy	1	2	1	1	Above average
Eisenhower	2	1	4	4	Above average
Johnson	3	5	7	7	Above average
Reagan	4	3	2	3	Not rated
Nixon	5	8	5	5	Failure
Carter	6	6	6	6	Average
Ford	7	4	8	Not ranked	Average
Truman	8	7	3	2	Near great

a. Calculated from *Gallup Report*, various issues.

b. Harris poll rankings in 1987, as reported in Michael Nelson, ed., *Guide to the Presidency* (Congressional Quarterly Press, 1989), pp. 146–47.

c. Gallup poll rankings in 1989, as reported in Nelson, ed., *Guide to the Presidency*. The poll asked which *three* presidents were best.

d. Results of a survey of historians by Robert K. Murray and Tim H. Blessing, "The Presidential Performance Study: A Progress Report," *Journal of American History*, vol. 70 (December 1983), pp. 535–55, as reported in Nelson, ed., *Guide to the Presidency*.

Reagan, but they are unlikely to rank him as high as the public does. It may also be too soon for a reliable comparative judgment on Nixon, Carter, and Ford. Each may do better with the passage of time. Nixon and Carter's postpresidency activities may improve their rankings. And the judgment by historians that Nixon was a "failure" will at least have to accommodate the legislative product of his years in the White House as well as the standard view that his foreign policy record was admirable. Finally, there is the remarkable transformation of Harry Truman from the lowest average approval rating to a high subsequent public ranking and the historians' highest rating for this group.

In Brody's analysis of presidential popularity, commenting specifically on the so-called honeymoon period, he emphasizes the policy outcomes of an administration as important even at the time. "In the end, opinion on President Reagan . . . depends less upon the public's response to him as a person than on the success or failure of his policies to achieve the outcomes he has led the American people to expect. After the honeymoon is over, it is by this standard that the president will be judged."[44] Brody's standard is also relevant after the presidency is over. In other words, a presidency is ultimately judged more by its legacy than by how respondents in a survey react to events at the time and associate those events with the person in the White House. Ceaser's admonition (see above) might well be recast to state that "an astute President should . . . be prepared in most cases to sacrifice his standing today, if by doing so he can affect positively the future assessment *of his presidency*." If it is correct that the ultimate historical judgment, like that of the posthoneymoon period, is based on the policy outcomes, then a preoccupation with public approval ratings is both wrong and self-defeating.

Contrary to this advice, the White House has been increasingly attentive to approval ratings and other relevant polls. No doubt this reaction is due in part to media interest in these ratings. The number of organizations now measuring presidential popularity is substantially greater than before. *The American Enterprise* included nine measures of presidential approval in a recent public opinion report. The three major networks have teamed up with the three major national newspapers—*Washington Post* (ABC), *New York Times* (CBS), and *Wall Street Journal* (NBC)—to sponsor polls. And several other newspapers and news magazines have combined with other media outlets to produce their own results. No White House press official can ignore this activity. The Gallup Organization alone conducted 600 presidential approval polls from Eisenhower through Reagan, varying from an annual average of 14 polls for Eisenhower to 23 for Carter.[45]

I will focus on two outcomes in discussing the public standing of Presidents Truman through Bush: elections and the passage of important legislation. For elections, it should be noted that whatever a president's approval rating, the critical factor in the end is what choice the voters have. They may think less of a president than before but be unwilling to choose someone else. They may also decide not to vote at all. For the passage of legislation, one must look beyond the president and his popularity to the legislative product during his term in office. As before, the stimulus for this inquiry is a conception of government that allows the possibility of policymaking regardless of whether presidents have low approval ratings. In many cases, major legislation identified with an administration was, in fact, a result of congressional initiatives or of joint presidential-congressional participation (see chapters 6–7). Any effect of the public standing of the president would be extremely difficult to estimate.

Truman

Truman's presidential approval scores plummeted during his initial months in office as the nation was plagued by strikes and inflation in the immediate postwar period (see figure 4-1). By the third quarter of 1946—

Figure 4-1. *Presidential Approval Ratings, Truman Administration*[a]

Quarterly average (percent)

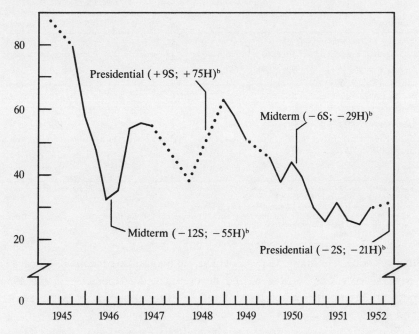

Source: Calculated from Gallup Poll data in the *Gallup Report*, various issues.
a. Dotted lines indicate lack of data.
b. Net electoral gains or losses for the president's party in the Senate (S) and House (H).

just before the midterm elections—his rating had fallen from the initial reading of 87 percent to 32 percent. No other president experienced such a steep drop in so short a time (though Bush came close to matching that record). At this low point, the Republicans captured control of both houses of Congress for the first time since 1928.[46]

There were only two tests of Truman's public standing in 1948 and they were low: 36 percent in April, 39 percent in May–June. His election in November remains one of the greatest upsets ever recorded, primarily because of the widely held perception that the public was dissatisfied with his performance. This perception was bolstered by polls showing Dewey comfortably ahead. Democrats also triumphed in congressional races, recapturing control of Congress. Once Truman had been elected on his own, his approval score climbed to 69 percent, only to suffer substantial decline again

Table 4-2. *Number of Important Laws Enacted,*
by Presidential Administration, 1947–93

Administration	1	2	3	4	5	6	7	8	Total	Annual average
	Year in office									
Truman (1945–53)	n.a.	n.a.	6	4	5	7	3	3	28	4.7
Eisenhower (1953–61)	1	8	2	4	2	9	3	2	31	3.9
Kennedy (1961–63)	9	6	6	. . .	. . .	. . .	. . .	. . .	21	7.0
Johnson (1963–69)	. . .	. . .	. . .	7	15	7	6	10	45	9.0
Nixon (1969–74)	6	16	5	11	11	5	. . .	. . .	54	9.5[a]
Ford (1974–77)	. . .	. . .	. . .	. . .	. . .	6	6	8	20	8.6[a]
Carter (1977–81)	7	5	3	7	. . .	. . .	. . .	. . .	22	5.5
Reagan (1981–89)	2	7	3	4	2	7	5	7	37	4.6
Bush (1989–93)	2	7	n.a.	n.a.	. . .	. . .	. . .	. . .	9	4.5
Total									267	6.1

Source: Calculated from David R. Mayhew, *Divided We Govern: Party Control, Lawmaking, and Investigations,*
1946–1990 (Yale University Press, 1991), pp. 52–73.

a. Nixon's total is divided by 5.67 years; Ford's by 2.33 years.

n.a. Not available. Mayhew does not provide a listing of important laws for the first two years of the Truman administration or the last two years of the Bush administration.

the following January to 45 percent. During his last three years in office, his average score was 33 percent and never reached 50 percent. In the 1950 midterm elections, Democrats suffered substantial net losses in the House and Senate.

Superficially, it would seem that the midterm election results were related to Truman's approval ratings. Congressional Democrats did poorly in 1946 and 1950, when Truman's approval scores were low. The lack of scores in 1948 makes it difficult to draw any firm conclusions about that election. Truman did, however, make the "terrible 80th Congress" an issue in the 1948 campaign, and the Democrats realized very substantial gains in both houses.

A review of major legislation passed during the Truman administration does not lend much credence to presidential approval ratings as a barometer of achievement (see table 4-2).[47] In fact, much of the major legislation identified with Truman was enacted in a period of divided government during that "terrible 80th Congress." The Taft-Hartley Labor-Management Relations Act (over Truman's veto), the Truman Doctrine, unification of the military services in one department, and the Marshall Plan were all passed in 1947–48. Truman's popularity did improve in 1947, possibly in part because of the passage of some of this legislation.

Other major legislation was enacted during the precipitous decline in Truman's popularity following his inauguration. I would include the following from those identified by David R. Mayhew.

—1949: Housing Act of 1949, NATO ratification, Mutual Defense Assistance Act.

—1950: Point Four aid program, social security expansion, creation of the National Science Foundation, McCarran Act (over Truman's veto), Defense Production Act, Excess Profits Tax.

—1951: Mutual Security Act, Reciprocal Trade Act.

—1952: McCarran-Walter Act (over Truman's veto), Japanese peace treaty ratification.

The fact that three of the major enactments listed above (the Taft-Hartley, McCarran, and McCarran-Walters acts) were passed over Truman's veto is a reminder that legislation associated with an administration is often derived from Congress.

Eisenhower

President Eisenhower's public approval ratings are legendary. His quarterly average never fell below 50 percent, and his individual scores fell below that figure just once (March–April 1958), to 48 percent (see figure 4-2). His approval score always exceeded his disapproval score. He experienced one period of sustained erosion in public approval between his reelection in 1956 and the disastrous midterm election for congressional Republicans in 1958. But his personal popularity increased steadily during the next year, then declined somewhat following the U-2 incident and the collapse of the summit talks with the Soviets. It is difficult to determine his effect on the congressional elections, but it seems apparent that his popularity was not transferrable. The Republicans narrowly lost control of Congress in 1954, experienced little change in 1956, but then in 1958 returned to the low numbers experienced during the Roosevelt years. This pattern was to be repeated frequently: a winning Republican president unable to convey his electoral or popular support to his party in Congress to the extent of winning majorities there.

Eisenhower's popularity was also not a good barometer for the passage of major legislation. His administration had the lowest annual production of important enactments of any of the postwar presidents (see table 4-2). During his first year in office, only one major law passed, the Tidelands Oil Act. In the second and sixth years of his presidency, 1954 and 1958, more important legislation was passed than in the other six combined. In 1954 there was a major tax schedule revision, social security expansion, approval of the St. Lawrence Seaway, the Communist Control Act, the Atomic Energy Act,

Figure 4-2. *Presidential Approval Ratings, Eisenhower Administration*

Quarterly average (percent)

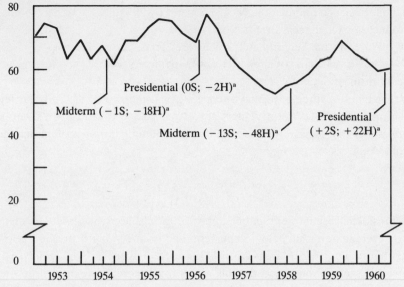

Source: Calculated from Gallup Poll data in the *Gallup Report*, various issues.
a. Net electoral gains or losses for the president's party in the Senate (S) and House (H).

agricultural and housing acts, and the food for peace program. During this time Eisenhower's approval ratings were a bit jagged but remained high.

In 1955 and 1956, Eisenhower realized his highest sustained approval readings, yet very little major legislation was enacted. Of the six pieces identified by Mayhew, only the Federal Aid Highway Act is normally remembered as a great Eisenhower achievement. Substantially more notable legislation was enacted in 1957 and 1958, during Eisenhower's most sustained popularity decrease.

—1957: Civil Rights Act, Price-Anderson Nuclear Industry Indemnity Act.

—1958: Alaska statehood, National Aeronautics and Space Administration established, National Defense Education Act, Department of Defense reorganization.

Eisenhower's solid recovery during his last Congress was not matched by an increase in legislative productivity. Congressional Democrats were actively preparing alternatives that would form an election platform for the 1960 presidential contest.[48] Mayhew lists only five important legislative enactments during the two years, of which four were typically associated with the Eisen-hower presidency.

—1959: Landrum-Griffin Labor Reform Act, Hawaii statehood.

—1960: Civil Rights Act, Kerr-Mills aid for the medically needy aged.

As Richard Neustadt has observed, public prestige is there to be perceived and interpreted by other elected officials, notably the members of Congress.[49] But for high popularity to produce a large volume of legislation there must be presidential interest and intent, as well as a substantial agenda. The president must fit that activist model so admired by many observers of the White House. These years also confirm that limited presidential involvement can, over time, stimulate greater congressional participation in the policy process. James L. Sundquist makes a persuasive case that analysis of the Great Society programs of the Johnson administration should begin with the work of congressional Democrats in the latter years of the Eisenhower admin-istration. And that point elucidates another: most major legislation can be traced to work done over a period of time (see chapters 6–7).

Kennedy-Johnson

I have treated the Kennedy-Johnson administrations together and will do the same with the Nixon-Ford administrations. A good case can be made for policy continuity in each. Further, there were equally dramatic interruptions: an assassination and the first-ever resignation. The patterns of popular ap-proval are fascinating, particularly in juxtaposition to the production of im-portant legislation.

Kennedy had a very good first year at the polls: he was the only elected president whose final reading for the year exceeded that of his first (see figure 4-3). His ratings dropped in the second year but were on the rebound at the point of the midterm elections, when congressional Democrats did excep-tionally well, gaining Senate seats and losing well below the average number of House seats. Kennedy's approval rating fell steadily during his third year.

With Johnson's accession to the White House, presidential approval climbed once again in the mid- to high 70s and remained there through June 1964. No readings were taken before the fall election, but Johnson's over-whelming victory suggests strong public approval as well. As noted earlier, the 1964 election was interpreted as one of the most policy oriented in con-temporary times, as close to the "good election," as defined by the party responsibility advocates, as those in the 1930s. What then followed was a steady decline in public approval (figure 4-3). Increases occurred from time

Figure 4-3. *Presidential Approval Ratings, Kennedy-Johnson Administration*[a]

Quarterly average (percent)

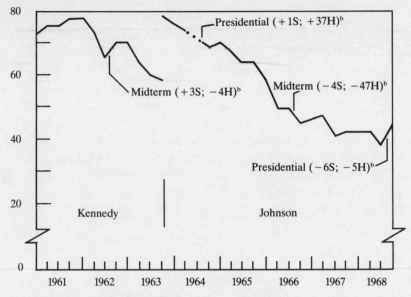

Source: Calculated from Gallup Poll data in the *Gallup Report*, various issues.
a. Dotted lines indicate lack of data.
b. Net electoral gains or losses for the president's party in the Senate (S) and House (H).

to time, but they were followed soon after by decreases, and improvements tended not to recapture the earlier high ground. By the midterm elections in 1966, Johnson had fallen from 80 percent approval in January 1964 to 44 percent. Democrats suffered huge losses in the 1966 elections. However, they had achieved highly inflated margins in the 1964 election. When Nixon was elected to the White House in 1968 (by a very narrow margin), congressional Democrats endured further losses. No one will never know whether Johnson himself could have been reelected.

In terms of legislative productivity, the period from 1961 to 1976 was truly exceptional (see table 4-2). Over half of the total of important laws Mayhew identifies between 1946 and 1990 were passed during these sixteen years. Kennedy's first year was very productive, despite some of the conventional wisdom about his failure to move more legislation early in his administration. In spite of his narrow popular vote margin and questionable mandate, more major bills were passed than in any other first-term president's first year.

Sundquist explains that although the election could not be counted as an endorsement of all of the specific proposals developed by the congressional Democrats in the late 1950s, "it was a clear endorsement of an approach to domestic problems, of a governing temper—and tempo."[50] Thus while Kennedy's popularity remained high, several pieces of legislation that had been in the works were enacted: a housing act; minimum wage and social security increases; the Area Redevelopment Act; and the establishment of the Peace Corps, the Arms Control and Development Agency, and the Alliance for Progress.

During the next two years other important legislation was passed, although so much was in the pipeline that Kennedy was criticized for not producing more. Here is a sample of important measures, some of which were new initiatives:

—1962: Trade Expansion Act, Manpower Development and Training Act, Communications Satellite Act, Revenue Act, public welfare amendments.

—1963: Nuclear Test Ban Treaty ratification, Higher Education Facilities Act, Clean Air Act, Equal Pay Act.

The concept of important enactments takes on an entirely new dimension as one turns to the production of the Johnson years in the White House. The steady slide downward in the president's approval while major legislation flowed from Congress is of particular relevance to this discussion of public standing and legislative products. Johnson's average quarterly approval scores increased in only five of the more than twenty quarters of his presidency. The events in Vietnam and riots in major cities contributed substantially to this decline in popularity, which enhances the view of public approval as subject to forces outside those in Washington itself. Here is a sample of that remarkable record of landmark legislation, much of it representing new initiatives.

—1964: Civil Rights Act, Economic Opportunity Act, tax cut, Urban Mass Transportation Act, Wilderness Act, Food Stamp Act.

—1965: Medical Care for the Aged, Voting Rights Act, Elementary and Secondary Education Act, establishment of the Department of Housing and Urban Development, Appalachian Regional Development Act, immigration reform, Higher Education Act, Housing and Urban Development Act, Water Quality Act.

—1966: Establishment of the Department of Transportation, Clean Waters Restoration Act, Traffic Safety Act, Fair Packaging and Labeling Act, Demonstration Cities Act, social security increase.

—1967: Public Broadcasting Act, Air Quality Act, Age Discrimination Act.

—1968: Open Housing Act, Housing and Urban Development Act, Gun Control Act, Omnibus Crime Control and Safe Streets Act, Truth-in-Lending Act.

The Johnson years produced a domestic policy legacy that continues to dominate the agenda and the budget. Yet the president could not in any significant way reverse the downward spiral of his public approval. The story of this extraordinary legislative production is complicated and can be fully told only by turning back to developments in the 1950s, but it confirms that analysis of public standing is peripheral in the study of national policymaking. High approval does not transform a president's program into law; declining approval does not suspend a policy momentum that has been building for months or years.

Nixon-Ford

During his first three years, Nixon experienced a gradual decline in public approval, starting in the low 60s and bottoming out in 1971 around the 50 percent mark, primarily because of the continued conflict in Vietnam and the poor economy. In the 1970 midterm election, congressional Republicans experienced little change. Going into the 1972 general election, the China and Soviet initiatives tended to balance the continuing bad news from Vietnam, so Nixon had quite positive public approval ratings. However, his recovery in public approval ratings and stupendous victory in 1972 did not transfer to his party in Congress. Thus Nixon's party was in no better position in 1972 with his landslide win than it had been in 1968 with his narrow victory.

Following the inauguration, Nixon's popularity began to plummet—a drop of 40 points in 1973 between the Vietnam peace agreement and the firing of Archibald Cox as special prosecutor (see figure 4-4). It fell even further in 1974 to 24 percent just before his resignation.

Ford entered the White House to a collective sigh of approval. His pardon of Nixon, however, cost him dearly in public support: his rating dropped 21 points in just over a month. Then came the disaster of the 1974 midterm elections. Congressional Republicans were back to the numbers of the Johnson and Roosevelt eras, yet with a Republican president. It seemed that the Republicans in Congress could lose when there were dramatic decreases in presidential approval but could not realize substantial gains when there was high approval. Their position still did not improve in 1976, even though Ford came very close to winning.

Figure 4-4. *Presidential Approval Ratings, Nixon-Ford Administration*[a]

Quarterly average (percent)

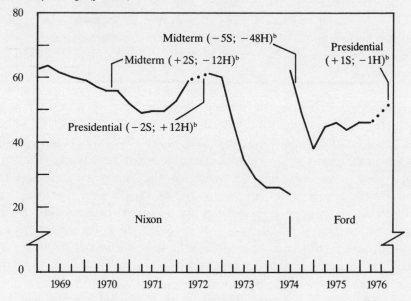

Source: Calculated from Gallup Poll data in the *Gallup Report*, various issues.
a. Broken lines indicate lack of data.
b. Net net electoral gains or losses for the president's party in the Senate (S) and House (H).

Was the production of legislation at all associated with the president's approval ratings? There was an outpouring of major laws, but presidential approval appeared to have little to do with it. These eight years were the most productive of major legislation of the forty-four years included in Mayhew's study, including the single most productive year, 1970 (see table 4-2). Even more remarkable, three productive years—1972, 1973, and 1974—occurred consecutively while the political system was presumably disintegrating. The pipeline was full of legislative proposals, and much of the system operated in spite of a crippled executive. This is convincing evidence indeed that this nation has a government, not just a president.

Paul C. Light points out that Nixon made few legislative requests during his first three months in office and also had the fewest first-year requests of any of the four elected presidents Light studied (Kennedy, Johnson, Nixon, and Carter).[51] Still, the first-year production was impressive: the Coal Mine Safety Act, social security increase, Tax Reform Act, Nuclear Nonproliferation Treaty ratification, and National Environmental Policy Act.

Nixon made even fewer new requests in the second year of his administration but, as noted above, legislative production was outstanding. And none of the pieces was enacted over the president's veto.

—1970: Organized Crime Control Act, postal reorganization, Voting Rights Act extension, Clean Air Act, Water Quality Improvement Act, ban on cigarette advertising, Occupational Safety and Health Act, Rail Passenger Service Act (Amtrak), Narcotics Control Act, Economic Stabilization Act.

In 1971 and 1972 Nixon's new requests were relatively few, but a number of issues carried over from the previous Congress. By Mayhew's count, there were five major laws enacted in 1971, the most notable being a social security increase, the Emergency Employment Act, and a constitutional amendment lowering the voting age to eighteen. The agenda remained full in 1972, and once more the variety of programs enacted by the Democratic Congress with presidential approval was impressive. The pending election was clearly a major factor; for example, social security benefits were increased. Of the eleven major pieces of legislation, only one was passed over the president's veto, although Nixon had begun to use the veto much more frequently in 1972 to check congressional spending.[52]

—1972: Federal Election Campaign Act, Water Pollution Control Act (over Nixon's veto), State and Local Fiscal Assistance Act (revenue sharing), social security increase (COLAs), Equal Rights Amendment, Pesticide Control Act, ABM Treaty ratification, Consumer Product Safety Act, Equal Employment Opportunity Act, Supplementary Security Income, Higher Education Act.

The next two years represent the most serious challenge to the traditional understanding of how the political system works. The White House and many members of Congress became absorbed by the Watergate scandal that was to force many resignations, ultimately that of the president. Yet the 93d Congress matched the 89th Congress as the most productive of major legislation in the postwar period. Clearly both the executive and legislative branches were doing other work. Only two bills were passed over the president's veto, although both Nixon and Ford used that tool frequently as a threat to get amendments adopted or to kill legislation. A sample of legislation again illustrates the manifold issues treated during this tense period in the history of the two institutions.

—1973: War Powers Resolution (over Nixon's veto), Federal Aid Highway Act, Comprehensive Employment and Training Act, social security increase, Trans-Alaska pipeline, Foreign Assistance Act, Regional Rail Reorganization Act (Conrail), Aid for Health Maintenance Organizations, Emergency Petroleum Allocation Act.

—1974: Trade Act, Employment Retirement Income Security, Federal Election Campaign Act, Budget and Impoundment Control Act, Freedom of Information Act (over Ford's veto), creation of Nuclear Regulatory Commission and Energy Research and Development Administration, National Health Planning and Resources Development Act.

The transition to Ford was presumably one of the least favorable arrangements possible for a working government, a takeover by an unelected vice president. His one advantage was dissipated when he pardoned the former president, his public approval declined significantly, and the Democrats gained overwhelming majorities in both houses of Congress in the 1974 elections. Not surprisingly, Ford relied heavily on the threat and practice of the veto (most were sustained). Ford's public approval improved marginally in 1975 and 1976. It was not a factor in the work done by Congress during that time.

—1975: Energy Policy and Conservation Act, Voting Rights Act extension, New York City bailout, Tax Reduction Act, Securities Act Amendments.

—1976: Unemployment compensation overhaul, copyright law revision, Toxic Substances Control Act, Tax Reform Act, Railroad Vitalization and Regulatory Reform Act, National Forest Management Act, Federal Land Policy and Management Act, Resource Conservation and Recovery Act.

What explains the failure of analysts to take note of legislative accomplishments during the Nixon-Ford era? Mayhew argues that what occurred did not fit the "script" and, in addition, there was a great deal of captivating political theater going on in Washington. "Legislation moved along not all that visibly under a canopy of verbal shellfire about Vietnam, Nixon's and Agnew's 'social issues,' the 'imperial presidency,' and Watergate." And so nobody much noticed, nor was anyone much moved to attribute the passage of this legislation to the public prestige of Nixon or Ford.

> Probably most of us, for evidence that vigorous lawmaking is taking place, tend to rely on the familiar narrative in which a presidential candidate presents a program, wins an election, claims a mandate, and then stages a well-publicized "hundred days" of passing laws. . . .
>
> But no such familiar or engaging script fit the Nixon and Ford experience. Nixon entered office without much of a program. . . . There was never a "hundred days." In 1969 and later, statutes tended to pass in a jumble at the close of a Congress rather than according to someone's plan at the start of one.[53]

Figure 4-5. *Presidential Approval Ratings, Carter Administration*

Quarterly average (percent)

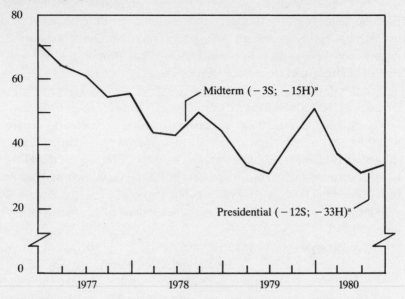

Source: Calculated from Gallup Poll data in the *Gallup Report*, various issues.
a. Net electoral gains or losses for the president's party in the Senate (S) and House (H).

Related to Mayhew's explanation are three facts: the pipeline of issues was full, the Democratic Congress was better prepared to participate actively in the policy process, and the deficit had not yet come to constrain all decisionmaking.

Carter

The 1976 election returned single-party government to Washington. Superficially, the results looked very much like those in 1960: a narrow win for the Democratic president and the return of large Democratic House and Senate majorities elected two years earlier. In terms of public standing, however, the two presidencies look very different. Carter's approval ratings dropped dramatically during the first year. His overall pattern for his four years looks more like that of Truman for his first five years, with almost the same rises and falls. His drop in the first two years is also like that of Reagan (see figure 4-5).

The Democrats' midterm net losses in 1978 were modest, and they retained a 119-seat edge in the House. Carter experienced two peaks after his first year: one associated with the Camp David peace accords and the other with the taking of the hostages in Iran. And in 1980, with his popularity at a low point, Carter lost overwhelmingly to Reagan, the Republicans captured the Senate, and the Democrats' margin in the House was reduced to 51.

Upon entering office, Jimmy Carter essentially acted in accordance with the appropriate script described by Mayhew. Believing he had a mandate to do the right thing, he was extremely determined to enact a lot of legislation, in the tradition of Roosevelt and Johnson. A number of important laws were, in fact, passed in that first year, most of which revised those already on the books: a minimum wage hike, an agriculture program, a social security tax increase, and amendments to the clean air and clean water programs. The principal new initiative was a Surface Mining Control and Reclamation Act. A major energy policy proposal carried over to 1978.

The remaining three years of the Carter administration produced less important legislation than the second year of the Nixon administration (see table 4-2). Much was organizational and regulatory (or deregulatory) in nature. Carter's reduced public standing appeared to be less important in this limited production than the changing nature of the national agenda, including the rise of major fiscal and economic issues associated with government spending and the deficit.

—1978: comprehensive energy package, Panama Canal treaties ratified, Civil Service Reform Act, airline deregulation.

—1979: Chrysler Corporation bailout, Foreign Trade Act extension, creation of Department of Education.

—1980: Depository Institutions and Monetary Control Act, trucking deregulation, Staggers Rail Act (deregulation), windfall profits tax on oil, synthetic fuels program, Alaska Lands Preservation, Toxic Wastes Superfund.

There is very little dramatic to say about single-party government under the Carter administration. Clearly the agenda itself was shifting. Carter's public standing never fully recovered from the decline in the first eighteen months. But other presidents had suffered similar reductions, while many major laws were passed. Quite simply, times had changed and so had the work of the government.

Figure 4-6. *Presidential Approval Ratings, Reagan Administration*

Quarterly average (percent)

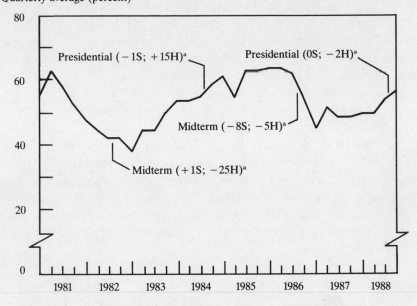

Source: Calculated from Gallup Poll data in the *Gallup Report*, various issues.
a. Net electoral gains or losses for the president's party in the Senate (S) and House (H).

Reagan

There is an extraordinary myth about the public popularity of Ronald Reagan. In fact, his early record is more like that of Truman and Carter than of the other postwar presidents. He had a lower approval rating upon entering office than any of his predecessors (later matched by his successor, George Bush). The reading after the assassination attempt in late March 1981 rose to 68 percent. At the time of the first midterm election in 1982, Reagan's approval rating was 42 percent (see figure 4-6). House Republicans' hopes of finally attaining majority status were dashed; once again the Democrats had a one-hundred-seat majority.

Where Reagan does compare favorably with other presidents is in his recovery following the low point in his popularity in late January 1983. Although his ratings never achieved extremely high levels, they steadily improved until the Iran-contra scandal in 1986. In part, this improvement appeared to be a consequence of his persona. He projected optimism, a mood seemingly in favor with the public. As Ceaser observed:

In the style of monarchies, while one may attack the ministers and the policies of the government, the person of the king remains inviolate. This "rule" was respected even more by Reagan's detractors than his defenders. Detractors discovered that the best way to neutralize Reagan's influence was not to dispute his benevolence. People might love Ronald Reagan, but that implied nothing about his policies.[54]

As it happened, Reagan's approval rating (at 58 percent) was at its highest point in over three years just before the 1984 election. However, his overwhelming victory was accompanied by his party's net loss of one Senate seat and modest gains in the House. Given the lack of issues during the campaign and the coronation-style reelection, it was difficult for Reagan to claim a strong policy mandate akin to that in 1980.

Reagan's approval rating before the 1986 midterm election was higher than it was before his landslide reelection in 1984. That positive standing did not prevent the Senate from returning to Democratic control, however (though Republican losses in the House were the smallest for any Republican president in this century). In the 1988 election Reagan's heir apparent George Bush easily won, but there was virtually no change in party levels in Congress. Reagan's approval rating had recovered modestly from the Iran-contra debacle.

Mayhew would be the first to concede that not all important enactments can be weighed equally. Certainly there is no better illustration of this than the legislative product of Reagan's first year. Only two major pieces of legislation passed in 1981 by Mayhew's measures, thus making it the least productive first year since that of Eisenhower (see table 4-2). But the impact of the Economic Recovery Tax Act and the Omnibus Budget Reconciliation Act was greater than that of a dozen other major pieces of legislation. Just as the Great Society programs reset the agenda for the 1970s and beyond, these two acts shaped policy choices for the 1980s and beyond. Although Reagan's approval ratings had declined after the high mark associated with the assassination attempt, many members of Congress, including many Democrats, believed that Reagan was strong in their states and districts. House Speaker Thomas P. O'Neill recalled it this way:

> I was afraid that the voters would repudiate the Democrats if we didn't give the President a chance to pass his program. After all, the nation was still in an economic crisis and people wanted immediate action. . . .
>
> I was less concerned about losing the legislative battle in the spring and summer of 1981 than I was with losing at the polls in the fall of 1982. I was convinced that if the Democrats were perceived as stalling in the midst of a national economic crisis, there would be hell to pay in the midterm elections.[55]

In regard to the unprecedented tax cut, O'Neill explained that "we will ultimately send a bill to the president that he will be satisfied with."[56] What was going to satisfy the president was a tax cut to trigger the supply-side economic experiment. He got most of what he wanted from Congress, but the supply-side theory did not work as expected and previously unimaginable deficits mounted to produce a very different policy politics.

During Reagan's second year in office—a period in which his approval rating never once exceeded 50 percent—a rather eclectic bundle of laws was enacted. As his public standing improved approaching the 1984 election, the most important piece of legislation to pass was a substantial revision of social security. Here is a sample of the limited production after 1981:

—1982: Transportation Assistance Act, Tax Equity and Fiscal Responsibility Act, voting rights extension, Nuclear Waste Repository Act, Depository Institutions Act, Job Training Partnership Act.

—1983: Martin Luther King holiday, Social Security Act Amendments, antirecession jobs program.

—1984: anticrime package, deficit reduction package, Trade and Tariff Act, Cable Communications Policy Act.

Reagan sustained his longest period of high approval ratings during the first twenty-three months of his second administration. Mayhew records just two pieces of major legislation during the first year: the Food Security Act (agriculture subsidies) and the Gramm-Rudman-Hollings Anti-Deficit Act. The latter was, of course, primarily a congressionally inspired move. The 1986 record was quite different. Two major reform measures passed: the Tax Reform Act and the Immigration Reform and Control Act. Both were enormous undertakings that had been under way for many months. Those measures alone would have marked this session as productive. But also enacted were South African sanctions (over Reagan's veto), an antinarcotics measure, Superfund expansion, the Omnibus Water Projects Act, and another reorganization of the Department of Defense.

The final Congress of the Reagan administration is particularly interesting: it was the most productive of the four, and yet Reagan's approval hovered around the 50 percent mark. Several of the pieces of legislation were attributable to congressional initiative (two, in fact, were passed over the president's veto). But that is precisely the point: the president's public standing is only one factor—and often a marginal one—in the workings of the system. The record of the 100th Congress not only disproved the notion that single-party government is necessary for major legislative production; it also showed that split-party control may actually be favorable for yielding cross-partisan coalitions to deal with controversial reform packages. Here is the record:

—1987: Water Quality Act (over Reagan's veto and a carryover from 1986), Surface Transportation Act (same), deficit reduction package, Housing and Community Development Act, Homeless Assistance Act.

—1988: Catastrophic Health Insurance for the Aged, Family Support Act (welfare reform), Omnibus Foreign Trade Act, Anti-Drug Abuse Act, Grove City civil rights measure, Intermediate Range Nuclear-Force Treaty ratification.

Perhaps part of the explanation for the myth of Reagan as the most popular postwar president is the fact that his exit reading was higher than his entry reading.[57] Unquestionably there was a reservoir of public support for Ronald Reagan. Over the period of his presidency, however, members of Congress apparently came to realize that it did not necessarily extend to his program, nor need it interfere with their taking policy initiatives or going far beyond what the president had proposed. Whatever was proposed, however, had to account for mounting deficits incurred as a consequence of the initial perception by members of Congress (and others, notably the press) that Reagan had won a mandate in 1980 and that he deserved to put his program in place even in the face of steadily declining public support. This experience confirms Neustadt's emphasis on the *perception* of public prestige as the key variable, rather than the approval ratings themselves.

Bush

I began the chapter with the intriguing story of George Bush and public approval and little more needs to be said here. He experienced impressive increases in quarterly averages during his first year in office (figure 4-7). Following a dip to averages that matched Reagan's best showing, Bush's approval rating then broke records at the point of the popular Gulf War. His descent then nearly matched Truman's.

This remarkable record is all the more fascinating because, apart from the Gulf War, the source of Bush's popularity was not exactly clear. He was regularly criticized in the press for lacking a comprehensive program. In my view, although poll respondents had no special, deep-seated reason to think Bush was doing a good job, neither did they have reason to believe he was doing a poor job. Not all that much was going wrong during the first months of the administration. And when one thing went well—the Gulf War—re-

Figure 4-7. *Presidential Approval Ratings, Bush Administration*

Quarterly average (percent)

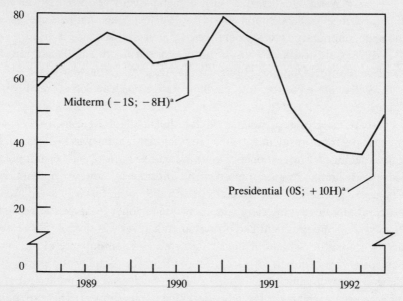

Source: Calculated from Gallup Poll data reported in *American Enterprise*, vol. 4 (March–April 1993), p. 94.
a. Net electoral gains or losses for the president's party in the Senate (S) and House (H).

spondents reacted positively when asked by the pollsters. It is very likely that if an election had been held at that point, instead of a poll, George Bush would have won handily. In this system, however, presidents cannot choose their preferred date for seeking reelection.

During that first year of steadily rising popularity, just two major pieces of legislation were enacted by Mayhew's count—more evidence that approval is not tied to legislative productivity. The two important pieces of legislation were a minimum wage increase for teenagers and an authorization for $50 billion to assist with the savings and loan disaster—notable but hardly earth-moving legislative acts. The second year was much more active and included Bush's breaking of his "no new taxes" pledge. Several of the acts most associated with the Bush presidency were passed in this second year:

—1990: Americans with Disabilities Act; Clean Air Act; deficit reduction package.

Bush's conflicts with Congress were almost certain to intensify following the 1990 election, when the Democrats gained in the House and the Senate. The deadlock that is predicted for divided government was very much in

evidence during the last two years of the Bush presidency. If the president
proposed a program, congressional Democrats typically criticized or ignored
it. If congressional Democrats were successful in passing a program, the
president often vetoed it. Copartisanship gave way to intense partisanship
and stalemate. The president's support score on Capitol Hill dropped from
54 percent in 1991 to 43 percent in 1992, the lowest ever recorded by *Congressional Quarterly*.[58]

Congress's support score with the president, as measured by successful
vetoes, was also low. He vetoed four bills in 1991 and twenty-one in 1992.
Just one of his forty-six vetoes in his four-year presidency was overridden.[59]
The president's strategy of checkmating with the veto was no doubt successful
in part because of problems Congress experienced in 1992. Several scandals
and a vigorous movement to limit terms contributed to low approval ratings
for Congress (down to 18 percent in March 1992).[60]

Mayhew has not yet rated legislation from the 102d Congress. My own
estimate is, however, that the following will be included in a future review of
the Bush years:

—1991: Persian Gulf War authorization; surface transportation reauthorization; banking overhaul; unemployment benefits extension; Civil Rights
Act Amendments (first vetoed by the president in 1990).

—1992: cable television reauthorization (passed over the president's veto);
National Energy Policy; aid authorization for former Soviet republics; Job
Training Partnership Act Amendments.

Most Americans apparently found it easy to approve of George Bush as
a president for good times. They even viewed him more favorably than not
when he left office. But it is hard to know what to make of public approval
as a resource for presidents when a passive president is both rewarded and
punished for inaction.

Public Approval and the Work of Government

The greater attention to public approval of the president can be explained
in part by the desire to have interim readings for presidents whose party is
not in the majority in Congress. The diffusion of responsibility that is characteristic of split-party government is unsatisfying to those who are eager to
assign liability. The reasoning appears to be that a president with a high
approval rating should employ it to get legislation enacted. There is a pre-
sumption that members of Congress will fall into line and support him on

the basis of his public standing. This same reasoning would indicate that presidents with low ratings should not actively press for their policy preferences, but rather allow the majority party in Congress to shape the agenda.

In fact, presidential approval rating has come to be a process with a life of its own. Presidents are tested more often, the media treat the results as relevant to policy and politics, and the White House in turn worries about the ratings and seeks to manage them. Presidents are said to "go public" more often but, of course, presidents *are* public. They cannot fail to be the major political figure, given their treatment by modern-day media.

Reading the public's reaction to presidential job performance for policy consequences is even more difficult than interpreting elections for the same purposes. Therefore, going public as a strategy for a president who is weak on Capitol Hill is unlikely to be very productive or coercive. Still, a president may not have a choice, either because of media demands or because he has so few other advantages. Thus it may come to be a factor in bargaining, although the Bush experience suggests that it does not carry much weight.

How important are the ratings for electoral and legislative outcomes? Congressional candidates from the president's party surely prefer to have the approval scores be positive, but Gary C. Jacobson and others have shown a "declining influence of presidential politics on aggregate House election results."[61] This decrease has hurt Republican congressional candidates. Republican presidents have done well in the postwar period but have not greatly improved the status of their party in Congress. More important, the lawmaking process is clearly not held hostage to the president's popular appeal. Legislative production simply does not turn on the popularity of the president. The Eisenhower years produced the fewest major laws on an annual basis and the Nixon-Ford years, the most (table 4-2). Some presidents want little, others want a lot; and some who want little find they have to react to congressional initiatives. Meager production in one era may spawn significant output later. The work of government hinges more on the nature of the agenda than on the periodic tests of presidential job performance.

Although the public standing of the president is a part of how the system works, it is not a very important part. It provides a spot reading from a sample of respondents as to how things are going. But Harry Truman had it right. A president who seeks to govern by maintaining high approval ratings has been distracted from his main duties. Presidencies are neither destroyed nor saved by these concocted ratings.

CHAPTER FIVE

Presidents, Mandates, and Agendas

PRESIDENTS are expected to govern: to know about, perhaps to manage, the workload of government. Personal and political advantages, organization and appointments, and public backing are resources directed to this governing purpose. Analysts devoted to the perspective of a responsible party and an activist chief executive expect presidents to enter office with policy proposals, perhaps even with a vision. By this perspective, good elections grant mandates, and mandates imply agendas. The good and effective president, then, is one who brings work to the government and aggressively manages the work that is already there. He is a firm and productive leader of the national policy process and therefore can justifiably be held accountable by the voters at election time.

However appealing this formulation might be, there are numerous barriers to its realization. Some are constitutional in nature; others are political or related to an annual budget approaching $2 trillion. I begin with the constitutional impediments that are a part of the fundamental characteristics and workings of a separated system. The Founders were not ignorant of the potential advantages of accountability or responsible government, but they found greater advantages in another system.

Elections and Agendas in the Constitution

The Constitution clearly specifies the terms of office for the president and members of Congress, thereby providing for elections by the calendar, not by the emergence of issues. The president "shall hold his office during the term of four years; The House of Representatives shall be composed of members chosen every second year; The Senate of the United States shall be composed of two senators from each state . . . for six years." For much of the nineteenth century, presidential and congressional elections occurred at different times, further confounding any direct policy message. It was not until the latter years of the nineteenth century that the elections for the three institutions occurred on the same day every four years.

Although longer terms for the president were discussed at the Constitutional Convention, a four-year term was approved, with no limit on the number of terms. A one-term president serves the equivalent of two House terms or two-thirds of a Senate term. Presidents were limited to two terms by precedent until Franklin D. Roosevelt broke with tradition. Following Roosevelt's pathbreaking record, the Twenty-second Amendment was ratified, limiting a president to two terms.

Before the ratification of the Twentieth Amendment, any issue or policy ardor realized from the campaign and election was cooled by the period of time between the election and the taking of office. By precedent, the terms of the president and members of Congress ended on March 4. At that time the new president was inaugurated, but Congress typically did not meet until December (as provided in article I, section 2 of the Constitution). For most members of Congress this first meeting was more than a year after their election.[1]

Nowhere in the Constitution does it even hint at a practice of holding elections as a result of a crisis or some issue configuration. Constitutional provisions for removing a president from office could conceivably have led to issue-based elections. That is, if an early president had resigned for failure to have his program enacted, or had the "inability to discharge the powers and duties of the . . . office" been interpreted as failing to command majorities in Congress, then a precedent for issue-based elections would have been established. This did not happen. And, in any event, the provision for succession was that the vice president would assume the duties of the president. Should both be removed, Congress would then provide for succession. There could be no realization of the potential for an issue-based election arising from a resignation or declaration of incapacity to govern because of policy failure.

These basic characteristics for legitimating the government through elections are highly relevant to agenda setting. The contests are set by the calendar, not by issue emergence or policy failure. Therefore an election should not ordinarily be treated as a national policy test. Yet most elections are interpreted as such: the presidential election for whether and how it endorses proposals made by the winning candidate, and the midterm elections for what they reveal about how the president is doing. Despite constitutional intent, election results are typically read for their effects on the agenda of government. In fact, when the issue content is obscure, as in 1984 or 1988, most analysts are critical of the candidates, the political parties, and even the system and often call for reform. Yet interpreting American elections as issue events that invest presidents and members of Congress with a mandate distorts constitutional intent and practice.

The concept of the "mandate" is vital to the party responsibility perspective because of its agenda-laden implications. Therefore I will discuss it first. Next is consideration of what the agenda is at any one time and how presidential preferences about issues can be and are folded into agenda politics. As commonly used, the term *agenda* refers to several different policy-related matters: a set of continuing problems more or less unaffected by elections; an orientation or a dominant policy preference—sometimes liberal, sometimes conservative; a crisis that overrides or displaces current policy problems; and presidential initiatives, variably interpreted as emanating from a mandate. I attempt to distinguish among these uses of the term, seeking to incorporate the perspective of scholars who view the agenda in dynamic terms.

Finally, I will treat the differences observed among the presidents since World War II and attempt to place each president's policy or programmatic efforts into the ongoing agenda. This latter exercise will identify the opportunities presidents have for influencing and altering the agenda as well as the limitations that may force them to work "at the margins," as George C. Edwards III puts it.

The Mandate

Given the separation of elections and variable term lengths for elected officials, why are mandates discussed at all? Why should one expect that an election would convey a mandate for policy action? What is it that leads people to expect, want, and demand that issue definition be the central purpose of elections? A number of distinguished scholars have thought about these questions, arguing persuasively that the concept is not useful in the American political setting. Of these, Raymond E. Wolfinger is most blunt: "Mandates are inherently implausible. . . . As Chairman Mao might have said, 'Many issues, one vote.'"[2] Henry Jones Ford would have added "several elections" to Wolfinger's paraphrasing of Chairman Mao. He stated this principle: "The greater the number of elections the less is their effect on public policy!"[3] Robert A. Dahl severely challenges the idea of a policy mandate. Here is a sample of relevant propositions:

> On matters of specific policy the majority rarely rules. . . .
>
> Strictly speaking, all an election reveals is the first preferences of some citizens among the candidates standing for office. . . .
>
> We can rarely interpret a majority of first choices among candidates in a national election as being equivalent to a majority of first choices for a specific policy. . . .
>
> Most interelection policy seems to be determined by the efforts of relatively small but relatively active minorities. . . . If you examine carefully any policy decision . . . you will always discover, I believe, that only a quite tiny proportion of the electorate is actively bringing its influence to bear upon politicians.[4]

In a more recent review of the mandate concept, Dahl concluded that the Framers had no such notion in mind in designing an elected executive. "The theory of the presidential mandate not only cannot be found in the Framers' conception of the Constitution; almost certainly it violates that conception." He then concludes that the mandate was not accepted as practice during the nineteenth century by the presidents themselves, most having accepted the Whig perspective that Congress was the representative institution. The president's power was that of an executive. "Even Abraham Lincoln, in justifying the unprecedented scope of presidential power he believed he needed in order to meet secession and civil war, rested his case on constitutional grounds, and not as a mandate from the people."[5]

Yet one renowned political scientist, Woodrow Wilson, articulated a theory of presidential mandate, motivated no doubt by his concern that congressional government was not working well. "By 1908, when *Constitutional Government in the United States* was published, Wilson had arrived at strong presidential leadership as a feasible solution" to the problem of congressional government.[6]

It is worth quoting at length from Wilson's *Constitutional Government* so as to convey both the logic of his argument in favor of the contemporary presidency and the verve with which he formulated it. Clearly the prospect of the mandated president, as leader of his party and the nation, excited him. In the passage quoted below he establishes the public legitimacy of a president's leadership as a basis for his obligation to take charge. If he fails, the responsibility is his: "His capacity will set the limit."

He cannot escape being the leader of his party except by incapacity and lack of personal force, because he is at once the choice of the party and of the nation. . . . Members of the House and Senate are representatives of localities, are voted for only by sections of voters, or by local bodies of electors like the members of the state legislatures. There is no national party choice except that of President. No one else represents the people as a whole, exercising a national choice; and inasmuch as his strictly executive duties are in fact subordinated . . . the President represents not so much the party's governing efficiency as its controlling ideals and principles. He is not so much part of its organization as its vital link of connection with the thinking nation. He can dominate his party by being spokesman for the real sentiment and purpose of the country, by giving direction to opinion, by giving the country at once the information and the statements of policy which will enable it to form its judgments alike of parties and of men.[7]

Having established the president's legitimacy as a representative and policy spokesman, Wilson turned directly to the matter of the president's obligation to exercise leadership and the obligation of others to follow. "The President is at liberty, both in law and conscience, to be as big a man as he can." And how might that be?

Let him once win the admiration and confidence of the country, and no other single force can withstand him, no combination of forces will easily overpower him. . . . He is the representative of no constituency, but of the whole people. When he speaks in his true character, he speaks for no special interest. If he rightly interpret the national thought and boldly insist upon it, he is irresistible; and the country never feels the zest of action so much as when its President is of such insight and calibre. Its instinct is for unified action, and it craves a single leader. It is for this reason that it will often prefer to choose a man rather than a party. A President whom it trusts can not only lead it, but form it to his own views.[8]

Wilson's argument is close to that of a recent president sometimes likened to him. Jimmy Carter described the president's role before winning in 1976: "Congress is inherently incapable of unified leadership. That leadership has got to come from the White House. . . . There's no one in any congressional district in the nation that won't be my constituent if I become President."[9] Later, upon completing his service in the White House, Carter explained in Wilsonian style: "Members of Congress, buffeted from all sides, are much more vulnerable to these groups [powerful lobbies] than is the President. One branch of government must stand fast on a particular issue to prevent the triumph of self-interest at the expense of the public."[10] Wilson and Carter outline a trusteeship of the public interest by which the president is invested with the responsibility of overcoming the natural tendency of members of Congress to accede to the pressures of special interests. Their view is, however, very much in the tradition of strong presidential leadership of party government (with Wilson more than Carter willing to lead through his party, though insistent on defining what his party will support).

How can presidents know that they have been invested with custody of a national purpose? Voter intentions at election time are often not clear, whatever is said on the day after. And as Dahl notes: "The systematic analysis of survey evidence that is necessary (though perhaps not sufficient) to interpret what a presidential election means always comes well after presidents and commentators have already told the world, on wholly inadequate evidence, what the election means."[11]

The 1980 election is illustrative. Analysis of survey data following that election cast serious doubt on whether voters were consciously awarding Ronald Reagan a mandate for his conservative, antigovernment proposals. Many voters were rejecting Carter, not necessarily approving Reagan. And yet under the circumstances of a postelection rush to judgment, it was unlikely that the new president would urge caution. In fact, had he stated that he did not plan to press for his program until he heard from the professional voting behavior analysts, he would have been criticized for betraying the trust conveyed by postelection commentators.

Dahl is surely correct in his judgment that the myth of the mandate is "now too deeply rooted in American political life and too useful a part of the political arsenal of presidents to be abandoned."[12] It is just plain handy during those frantic hours following an election when commentators need a simple explanation of what happened. Here is how one prominent journalist put it: "Elections should be a mandate for something. If elections aren't a mandate for something, then what do they mean?"[13]

Dahl has the answer: An election "confers the legitimate authority, right, and opportunity on a president to try to gain the adoption by constitutional means of the policies the president supports."[14] This formulation is consistent with the constitutional separation of powers as perpetuated by the separation of elections, precisely the alternative perspective I espouse in this book. In fact, it sounds very much like the analysis offered by Richard E. Neustadt in his definition of presidential power as "persuasion," varying among presidents because of differences in personal, public, and political sources of power.[15] I suggest an addendum, however. The "policies the president supports" may not always require expansion of government. Thus analysts need to take account of alternative strategies to those associated with an activist president or one promoting large-scale social programs. Voters sometimes elect—even resoundingly—presidents who have made few policy promises.

Whatever the policy preferences of the president, consideration also must be given to the independent nature of the agenda. As Frank R. Baumgartner and Bryan D. Jones describe it, "Any study of the dynamics of American political institutions must be able to account for both long periods of stability and short, violent periods of change—again, with respect to the processing of issues, not in the basic constitutional framework."[16] These periods do not necessarily coincide with presidential administrations. There is a whole world of policy outside the White House, a world in which presidents seek their place.

Neither the implausibility of the mandate nor the plausibility of power as persuasion is likely to overcome the next-day convenience of the mandate in explaining election outcomes. Accordingly, the mandate can become a kind of reality through its use in interpreting an election by media analysts, members of Congress, and presidents themselves. The mandate is a classic example of an illusion becoming reality in the context of power as persuasion. If others declare that the voters have invested a president with the right to pursue particular policy goals, then he may be expected to rely on that interpretation as a source of power. Indeed, he may well be judged by whether he uses this strength to whatever advantage it has been defined to convey. Further, even if survey data later show that many voters were saying "no" to the loser rather than "yes" to the winner and his program, members of Congress and others in Washington may acknowledge a mandate as a hedge in case the president develops a strongly positive policy standing within their constituencies or among their clienteles. Thus the preposterous can become genuine and may contribute to expectations that cannot, perhaps should not, be met. Accordingly, presidents are well advised to be cautious in accepting the award of a mandate or in declaring one on their own.

Judgments about Mandates

A review of postelection analyses in the postwar era suggests several uses of the mandate concept: the perceived mandate for change, the status quo mandate, the mixed or nonmandate, and the unmandate. The following categories direct attention to how analysts read elections for issue messages.

The Mandate for Change

The preferred outcome for party government advocates is a mandate for change. This is how an election meets the ideal conditions discussed in chapter 1: publicly visible issues, clear differences between the candidates, a substantial victory for the winner and his party in Congress, and a postelection declaration of party unity. Whatever the survey results show later, an election meeting these conditions will be perceived to have conveyed a mandate to the winning president as leader of his party.[17]

The postwar elections that come closest to meeting these conditions are those in 1964 and 1980. A third possibility is the 1952 election, though it did not match the others in regard to candidate differences on issues or substantial gains for the president's party in Congress (despite Republican majorities in each house). If all elections are placed on a continuum, there is little doubt that these three elections fit nearer to the "mandate for change" point. In all three cases, there were those who raised questions about whether the vote was for the new president or against his opponent (particularly in 1980). No analyst doubted, however, that the elections served as a major source of power for the new presidents, with variations as to the legitimacy, clarity, and strength of the mandate.

The 1964 election presented postelection analysts with the most unambiguous case of a mandate for change. Some analysts acknowledged that many voters were rejecting Goldwater, however, and that fact had an effect on reading the returns for purposes of declaring a mandate.

A *Washington Post* columnist wrote, "It is evident that the President's victory could best be interpreted as one either for him personally or against Sen. Goldwater personally, rather than a massive victory for the Democratic Party." *Time* magazine agreed: "As far as figures are concerned, the mandate could hardly have been written more clearly. But since the figures meant anti-Goldwater as much as pro-Johnson, carrying out the mandate will not follow automatically."[18]

But the main emphasis was on the strong policy message of the election, and, following Woodrow Wilson, the attendant responsibility for the president in translating this message into government action. A column by Arthur Krock exemplified this point of view: "President Johnson has four years in which to supply the answer to the great question created by the most emphatic vote of preference ever given to a national candidate: How will he use the mandate to lead and govern that has been so overwhelmingly tendered by the American people?" A *New York Times* editorial proclaimed that the "overwhelming vote for the Johnson-Humphrey ticket reflects popular attachment to the policies of moderate liberalism." And a *Washington Post* editorial described the mandate as "clear and unmistakable" and "essentially, a mandate to pursue a national consensus at home and abroad with restraint and common sense."[19]

The 1980 election required even more attention to whether people had voted "no" or "yes." After all, Jimmy Carter was the first Democratic incumbent to be defeated since Grover Cleveland in 1888. Questions were therefore raised as to exactly what message was being sent by the voters. *Time*'s commentary is typical:

> Though the conservative trend of the country was obvious from the results, Reagan's mandate was a good deal less than indicated by his 489 electoral votes. . . . His victory was surely not so much an endorsement of his philosophy as an overwhelming rejection of Jimmy Carter, a President who could not convince the nation that he had mastered his job.[20]

For James Reston, the election did not convey a policy mandate for Reagan. "Obviously there has been a conservative sweep of opinion in the nation. . . . But it does not follow that a Reagan administration can impose a dramatic, conservative set of policies on a Congress still dominated by Democrats."[21]

Much of the commentary was muted, given that a party declared virtually dead after Watergate had just ousted an incumbent president and won a majority in the Senate for the first time in twenty-eight years. The results both stunned and perplexed the analysts. Could it be that a new era was dawning? Or did the results merely represent voter dissatisfaction with President Carter? Analysts were cautious. According to David Broder, "Victorious Republicans and decimated Democrats looked back yesterday at an election that gave the national government its sharpest turn to the right in a generation and wondered if 1980 would go into the history books as the start of a new era of conservative and Republican dominance." And a *Washington Post* editorial agreed that "Governor Reagan surely has both a strong public mandate and strong personal inclination to do something. . . . But we have no doubt that some large part of Tuesday's Democratic liberal defeat must have been owing to dissatisfaction with [Carter] and his economic and foreign policy handiwork."[22]

It is interesting that even the purest cases of the mandate, by the criteria of party government advocates, do not satisfy their demands. Commentators express caution because of the weakness of the opponent, the lack of clarity of policy positions, the precise intentions of the voters, or the failure to win full control of Congress. Yet they acknowledge that something unusual happened and are willing to use the term *mandate* freely, sometimes with the implication that a president will be tested subsequently by whether he satisfies it, and them.

In the third election in this group, in 1952, a military hero viewed as a political outsider won a substantial victory and his party won majorities in both houses of Congress for the first time since 1928. But reading the returns for policy messages was not simple. General Eisenhower had defeated the true conservative, Senator Robert A. Taft (Ohio), for the Republican nomination. Thus there was no nice, clean choice between conservatism and liberalism. A common interpretation was that the victory was "personal" for Eisenhower, not a real win for the Republican party. The mandate was for a "fresh start" or for "leadership," typically failing to specify toward what goal (which presumably would have been apparent had it been a party, not a personal win). These characteristics naturally cast doubt on the victory as a party government mandate and presumably encouraged analysts to predict problems for the outsider president as he worked with his own party in Congress.

The following selections reflect the analytical themes in the immediate postelection period. Arthur Krock spoke for the view that it was a personal, not party, victory: "That General Eisenhower, and not the Republican Party, was the principal reason for the termination of the Democratic tenure in the White House . . . was made evident by the result of the contests for Congress." *Time* agreed: "Ike generally ran well ahead of G.O.P. Congressmen. . . . Hence his victory was clearly more of a personal victory than a party victory."[23] Yet *Time* used the term "mandate for leadership," and *Newsweek* also supported the notion of a generalized mandate: "The voters chose the future. And they chose Eisenhower and the Republican Party as its custodians. . . . Congress . . . will honor Eisenhower's fresh mandate from the people by giving him almost anything he requests." And pundit Walter Lippmann carried the theme to new heights:

> The mighty majority which the people have given him is conclusive. He is the captive of no man and no faction. He is free, as few men in so high an office have ever been, to be the servant of his own conscience. For his mandate from the people is one of the greatest given in modern times and it is beyond dispute.[24]

The mandate for change carries with it expectations for policy action by the White House. Paul C. Light's recommendation to "move it or lose it" is clearly most appropriate for presidents under these circumstances, assuming, of course, that they have a program to move.[25] However, the act of perceiving a mandate does not annul the continuing set of issues on the national agenda.

Rather, the widespread perception of a license to make change becomes a potential resource that strengthens the president's hand in setting priorities and identifying alternatives. And it is transitory for all of the reasons identified by Dahl and Wolfinger: it was never that presumptive in the first place.

The Mandate for the Status Quo

The persistence of the mandate concept in the lexicon of political analysis is amply illustrated by elections in which the president is reelected by a landslide but his political party fails to garner majorities in Congress. The postwar cases are 1956, 1972, and 1984. (In 1984 the Republicans did have a majority in one house of Congress—the Senate, though with a net loss of one seat.) Working from the expectations of the party government model, analysts insist on employing the term *mandate* when they observe a president being overwhelmingly reelected. In these three elections, that was definitely the case: the combined electoral vote split was Republican candidates, 1,502 (winning 139 states); Democratic candidates, 103 (winning 9 states).

A standard conclusion for the status quo mandate is that the president has won, not his party. Typically the analysis is cast in disapproving terms. In spite of an electoral system and campaigning practices that permit, even facilitate, split-ticket voting, the president is expected to deliver Congress and the state offices for his party. The failure to do so is judged a weakness for him and for the system. In 1956 a typical judgment was that "the Eisenhower victory was a personal endorsement and not a victory for the Republican Party." In 1972 Republican National Party Chairman Bob Dole explained that "this is a personal triumph for Mr. Nixon, and not a party triumph." And in 1984 Haynes Johnson attributed "the great landslide" to "personal affection for Reagan and better feelings about the country" rather than "a strong national tide leading to some great ideological realignment of the two political parties."[26]

There were, however, differences in how postelection analysts viewed the results and their effects. Although there was general agreement that voters supported continuance, whatever was to be continued varied among the three presidents. For Eisenhower, the landslide was said to represent "an opportunity to consolidate his domestic program of moderate social advance in a stable economy, while living up to his pledges to do everything possible to preserve peace in the world."[27] Also reiterated was the voters' "confidence" in his leadership. There was no effort to suggest that Eisenhower voters were really voting against Adlai Stevenson.

For Nixon, however, questions were raised as to whether the size of his victory was attributable to the weakness of his opponent. Arthur Krock concluded that "the huge popular majority was merely registering its judgment that his opponent was not of Presidential caliber." Thus doubts were raised about the extent to which the sweeping victory conveyed much added authority. One editorial put it this way: "There is no evidence from the election at the Congressional level that the country is either seething with discontent or carried away by the glories of the Nixon Administration."[28]

In 1984 there was little suggestion that voting for Reagan was a way of voting against Walter Mondale; in fact, one comment was that "for the first time in at least a dozen years, Americans were voting *for* rather than *against*."[29] Thus his support was considered pure. But there was more of an ideological cast to the interpretations of this election. For some, to continue or to maintain the status quo meant accepting a more conservative approach to public policy, and there was even talk of a "mandate for continuation of [Reagan's] conservative policies." Others questioned the extent to which the results endorsed Reagan's ideology: "Tuesday's mandate, as in most Presidential elections when times are good, is a broad instruction to keep them good."[30]

A fourth postwar election also fits into this category of the "status quo mandate": the interesting and unusual election of 1988. It has many of the characteristics of an approval election. For the first time since 1836, a vice president directly succeeded the president he served, and for the first time since 1928 a party succeeded itself in the White House (not including reelections or a vice president who served as president and won election, such as Truman).

George Bush did not win by the same overwhelming margins as did Eisenhower, Nixon, and Reagan in their reelections. Still he won handily, exceeding Nixon's first-term margin and coming close to Eisenhower's. But House and Senate Republicans both had a small net loss, thus encouraging analysts to downplay any talk of a Bush mandate. According to Broder, "If the voters meant that either as a personal accolade or a policy mandate, they muffled the signal by giving Democrats a renewed vote of confidence in congressional and state elections." The election was described as one "that affirmed the status quo and the reluctance of the American electorate to give either party a real vote of confidence." Thus Bush was said to have won "a decisive victory and a personal vindication, but no clear mandate." And in a frank expression of the perceived importance of political analysts, the *New York Times* editorialized: "Thus it remains for partisans, pundits and, above all, for Mr. Bush to sculpt the mandate. The President-elect can do so only by fashioning ends and means and costs into policies that make sense."[31]

It is fascinating that election outcomes returning the incumbent government are interpreted within the context of a mandate. The search for issue instructions from an election continues in spite of limited evidence that these instructions can often be clearly identified.

The Mixed or Nonmandate

The 1988 election provides a perfect introduction to the third category of interpretations of mandates. It is truly on the borderline between a status quo mandate and no discernable mandate. What encourages one to include it above is simply the size of the victory for Bush. The other four in this category—1948, 1960, 1968, and 1976—feature extremely close presidential elections, among the closest in history. I also include the 1992 election in this group, although, as discussed below, it has a number of special characteristics.

The 1948 election is the most perplexing for analysts because of Truman's surprise victory. Dewey was supposed to win, as most pollsters had predicted. Yet Truman pulled it off in a three-way race, garnering less than 50 percent of the popular vote. At the same time, the triumph for congressional Democrats was impressive. They recaptured control of both houses with a net gain of nine Senate seats and seventy-five House seats. What did it all mean? Interpretations varied.

On the one hand, there was Krock's classical party responsibility interpretation:

> Once more in our history, and at an essential time, a party is in power at both the White House and Congress with definite responsibility for the conduct of the government.
>   The voters of the nation have told the Democratic party to discharge this responsibility. The President's task as the party leader and the party's popular mandate are to compose Democratic differences to the degree required to govern.[32]

On the other hand, Raymond Moley warned that "President Truman should not consider this result a real popular endorsement of his own policies and methods of administration. . . . This election can hardly be taken as a mandate for the repeal of the Taft-Hartley Act or for a continuous increase in the rate of Federal expenditures."[33]

Commentators paid little attention to the discontinuity between the president's narrow win and the huge net gains for House and Senate Democrats.

It was not easy for Truman to claim coattails. Further, J. Strom Thurmond, the Dixiecrat Democrat from South Carolina, won thirty-nine electoral votes, capturing four southern states. All these factors contributed to making the 1948 election one of the most difficult to interpret for those devoted to the mandate concept of American government.

Analyses of the 1960, 1968, and 1976 election outcomes featured interchangeable sentences. Fill in the blanks with John F. Kennedy, Richard M. Nixon, or Jimmy Carter.

In the end, _____ won the election but not the mandate. . . . But an electorate that proved to be more cautious than apathetic, more unimpressed than dispirited, turned out in substantial numbers to produce a collectively narrow judgment.

It is a good thing that the election was so close. It should serve as a restraining force and as a reminder to the _____ Administration that it should proceed with caution and that it has no mandate to embark on drastic changes of policy, either foreign or domestic.

There is not much of a mandate here for anything, except a new face in the White House and that "New Leadership" in the Executive Branch which _____ was promising all along the campaign trail.

The correct match is Jimmy Carter for the first statement, John Kennedy for the second, and Richard Nixon for the third.[34] The Carter and Kennedy elections are remarkably alike. They won with a similar combination of electoral votes from the South and Northeast and pivotal wins in enough midwestern industrial states to ensure victory. A comparison of the popular and electoral votes also shows the similarity of the two elections.

	Popular vote (percent)	*Electoral vote (percent)*
Kennedy	49.7	56.3
Carter	50.1	55.2

In addition, both ran behind most Democratic House and Senate winners. House Democrats won 54.4 percent of the popular vote in 1960—almost 5 points ahead of Kennedy—and they ran 6 points ahead of Carter in 1976. These statistics are not encouraging for presidents seeking automatic support for their programs from members of Congress. Congressional Democrats would not ignore the White House, but their support had to be won on a basis other than the popularity of the president in their districts.

Kennedy and Carter at least had Democratic majorities in Congress and were therefore charged with the responsibility of governing. In fact, Walter Lippmann even found a mandate for Kennedy: "Although the popular vote was very close . . . there is nothing ambiguous about Kennedy's majority. . . . He has a clear mandate to undertake what he promised to do."[35] In the case of Nixon, however, there was no Republican majority in either house of Congress. The judgment was uniform: no mandate "for any particular policy direction," and therefore the president was advised to proceed with caution.[36]

Nixon's win in 1968 was special. No president since the founding of the modern two-party system had entered office with his party in the minority in both houses of Congress. (Bush was to suffer the same condition twenty years later.)[37] There is ample reason to expect different behavior from presidents under these conditions. The election results violate several of the basic requirements of party government, yet are wholly constitutional. Thus it seems only reasonable to search for another model to describe and evaluate presidential-congressional interaction in this type of split-party government. The party government model is of no more value to the analyst in this case than it is to a president who must meet the challenges of governing.

The 1992 election had several characteristics of the other mixed or non-mandate elections and yet was special in many ways. Clinton won comfortably in the electoral college (69 percent of the vote, compared with 57 percent for Truman in 1948, and 56 percent each for Kennedy and Nixon in 1960 and 1968). Because Ross Perot's candidacy split the vote three ways, Clinton garnered a lower proportion of the popular vote than Michael Dukakis had in 1988, but his margin over Bush was substantially greater than that of the other winners in this category over their opponents. Although the House Democrats had a net loss of seats, the Democrats controlled both branches of government for the first time in twelve years and just the second time in twenty-four years. Thus there was the strong temptation to declare an end to "gridlock," with the attendant expectations of a strong policy record for the new administration.

For the most part, analysts doubted that the results constituted a mandate. They did marvel at Clinton's accomplishment, however, since many of them had declared his candidacy to be in deep difficulty along the way.

The truth is that Bill Clinton deserves congratulation not just for prevailing in the contest but for having waged a strong, smart and civil campaign. It is certainly the case that neither the size of his victory nor the nature of his campaign rhetoric provides a clear and specific mandate or 1-2-3 agenda for action that all can agree on.[38]

Elaine Kamarck, a Clinton adviser from the Progressive Policy Institute, emphasized the need for the new president to define a mandate "early and often," in part to override media interpretations. Michael Kramer agreed that it was up to the president to define a mandate because "a majority of Americans voted for someone else" and "there is a vast difference between being an instrument *of* change and being a catalyst *for* change."[39] Meanwhile, journalists covering Capitol Hill advised the new administration that ending political gridlock did not mean that there was "a compliant legislature ready to respond to [Clinton's] every command. Instead, Clinton is likely to be confronted by . . . a largely Democratic but freewheeling group of legislators who hunger for results but chafe at discipline, unaccustomed to dealing with a president of their own party and used to calling the shots for the party themselves."[40] This analysis by a veteran congressional reporter comes as bad news for those expecting smooth sailing under conditions of unified party government. It is not in the least unexpected by those attuned to the nature and workings of a separated system.

The Unmandate

So far I have stressed how the mandate concept—a staple of the responsible party model of governing—is used by analysts for understanding the policy effects of an election. Two points are evident from this review: Despite its popularity for analysis, the concept has limited value for contributing to an understanding of the conditions under which the government works, and most elections turn out not to suit the demanding tests for declaring a mandate. In other words, devotion to the mandate in explaining elections often results in exactly the kind of contorted analysis I have cited above. My journalist friend puts the question: "If elections aren't a mandate for something, then what do they mean?" That is precisely the problem for party government advocates in postelection analysis.

Further evidence for this explanatory conundrum shows up in what typically happens two years into an administration. Again, the Constitution is perfectly clear: "The House of Representatives shall be composed of members chosen every second year," and the Senate "shall be divided as equally as may be into three classes . . . so that one third may be chosen every second year." There is no language accompanying these words to suggest that these elections "every second year" will be tests of either the president's personal popularity or of the mandate he did not receive in the first place. The president, in fact, is not even mentioned in these clauses. Yet the mandate-based analysis persists.

"The nation has, in effect, flashed a 'Caution—Go Slow' signal to the Johnson Administration."[41] This reaction was not uncommon following large Republican gains in the 1966 midterm elections. The voters giveth and they taketh away, according to the theory of the mandate. Seldom are midterm elections interpreted for what they are: state and local contests rather than tests of a presidential administration. The shifts in House seats can usually be explained by the extent to which the president's party, in the presidential election, won seats normally held by the other party. If many such seats were won, then the president's party enters the midterm election in a vulnerable position and losses may be heavy. Bruce I. Oppenheimer, James A. Stimson, and Richard W. Waterman refer to "exposure" of the president's party in congressional elections: "the degree to which a party has more or fewer than its normal complement of seats going into the election." They conclude that "the proportions of strong or vulnerable candidates . . . [are] likely to be very much a function of party exposure levels."[42]

Still it is common to read the midterm results for the political and policy messages they may hold for the president. A sample from analyses of various postwar midterm elections shows this popular interpretation has persisted throughout the period. After the 1950 midterm elections, the *New York Times* proclaimed, "No good reason remains . . . for the President to insist upon his oft-repeated claim that he has a 'mandate from the people'. . . . There is no evidence in Tuesday's elections of such a 'mandate.'" Four years later, William S. White wrote: "The people of the country clearly have registered some anxiety at the course of a Republican Congress that never has exactly typified the president himself. They have not given the Democrats any clear mandate in the Legislative Branch. . . . They have only set the Democrats to watch . . . certain tendencies of the Republicans in Congress." And by 1974 the *Washington Post* was still trying to find a mandate in the midterm results:

> When it comes to extracting "mandates" from elections results we can be as arbitrary as the next person. . . . The voters seem to be saying that they want the President to be more like a President. Their message does not include, of course, an explanation of how he is now supposed to deal, presidentially, with an overwhelmingly Democratic Congress; that's how it often is with "mandates."[43]

This last commentary is one of the most candid in acknowledging the role played by the mandate in election commentary. It goes on to say: "A certain subjective arbitrariness is inherent in the traditional post-election game of figuring out who has been 'mandated' to do what." In other words, an election is often the occasion for analysts to comment on the president's performance. And since the midterm results normally show a net loss for the president's party in Congress, the mandate concept works well as a device for instructing a president what to do next. That the exercise itself is both arbitrary and illogical seldom prevents it from occurring.

The Persistent Concept

Nothing said here will prevent analysts from using the mandate concept for interpreting election results. The preceding review illustrates how entrenched it is as a crutch for postelection commentary. I have shown how it varies and thus comes to be useful for present purposes by illustrating yet again how presidencies differ, even when analyzed by inappropriate concepts. There is no escaping the complexity caused by frequently installing opposite party forces in positions of power. So even if analysts try to stuff an election into a standard mandate container, it pops out again. It seems too much to hope that the concept will be abandoned. As Dahl notes, it is "too deeply rooted in American political life and too useful a part of the political arsenal of presidents." But there are good and bad uses of this inapt concept, depending on whether the analyst acknowledges the parts that spill out of the container and modifies the analysis accordingly.

The Continuing Agenda

So the mandate lives. But is it really necessary to rely on it so heavily in judging how an election affects a president's capacity to govern? Is there a better way to comprehend the set of policy and political constraints within which a president tries to do his job? I believe there is; that better way begins with an understanding of the policy agenda that serves as the context for campaigning, voting, and making choices once the winner takes office.

The national government has an agenda that is continuous because much of it is generated from existing programs. In his masterful review of policy development during the 1950s and 1960s, James L. Sundquist identified the following six issues as "those that appeared to reflect the most pressing concerns of the people": jobs for the unemployed, opportunity for the poor, schools for the young, civil rights for minorities, health care for the aged, and protection and enhancement of the outdoor environment.[44] It is striking that as these words are written all six issues continue to find an important place on the agenda, though not in the same form. Many of the issues of the 1990s are related either to the cost of programs enacted during this earlier period or to the persistence of problems in spite of the expenditure of large sums of money.

Although the government cannot do without a president, most of what government does requires little or no involvement by the White House. There is a momentum to a working government that cannot be stopped or easily redirected. It is useful to remind oneself of this fact as a corrective to the tendency to overstate the role of the president as an agenda setter. Richard E. Neustadt, who has stressed the important agenda-setting function of the White House, acknowledges that the president's choices occur within the limits of ongoing policies. Commenting on the decade before the publication of the first edition of his book, *Presidential Power*, Neustadt observed:

> To sense the continuity from Truman's time through Eisenhower's one need only place the newspapers of 1959 alongside those of 1949. Save for the issue of domestic communists, the subject matter of our policy and politics remains almost unchanged. We deal as we have done in terms of cold war, of an arms race, of a competition overseas, of danger from inflation, and of damage from recession. We skirmish on the frontiers of the welfare state and in the borderlands of race relations. Aspects change, but labels stay the same. So do dilemmas. Everything remains unfinished business.[45]

The notion of cycles places the president in a larger social, political, and policy context, since the cycles are not typically coterminous with presidential administrations. Bert A. Rockman explains:

> The president usually is assumed to be the chief director of goals. As time wears on, however, presidential agendas become susceptible to alteration. The unforeseen consequences of past policies—those of previous occupants of the White House and those of the incumbents—conspire along with unprogrammed events and with changes in the composition of political majorities to provide new problems requiring reaction. Some of these will not be consistent with earlier elements of the presidential agenda.[46]

One obvious conclusion is that the president's agenda—his list of priorities— is influenced by, and has to be fitted into, a larger set of ongoing issues.

Erwin C. Hargrove and Michael Nelson categorize individual presidents as presidents of preparation, achievement, and consolidation. They acknowledge that each type is subject to the policy or political conditions of the time. Presidents of preparation "generate, distill, and present new ideas. The political situation calls on [them] to attempt to build a rising tide of support for such ideas." Presidents of achievement "get an ambitious legislative program passed. [Their] political situation is one of strong but temporary empowerment, and the president must seize the day by mobilizing the public in favor of action." Presidents of consolidation "have the task of rationalizing *existing* programs."[47] Again, the president's role in the agenda is not at all of his own making. In fact, one measure of leadership is the capacity of a president to comprehend the policy environment accurately. Baumgartner and Jones explain it this way:

> Sometimes skillful leaders can foresee an onrushing tide and use their energies to channel it in a particular direction. Others fail to see the tide or attempt to oppose it, virtually always unsuccessfully. Successful political leaders, then, are often those who recognize the power of political ideas sweeping through the system and who take advantage of them to favor particular policy proposals. Leaders can influence the ways in which the broad tides of politics are channeled, but they cannot reverse the tides themselves.[48]

Light offers the most extensive analysis of the president's role in regard to the agenda. He finds that the president is "constrained by the level of both internal and external resources." Presidents naturally vary in their capacity to set and control the agenda.

> It is important to recognize that the agenda changes substantively from administration to administration. However, the President's domestic agenda does have several stable characteristics. . . . The President's domestic agenda is set very early in the term; . . . the timing of agenda requests affects ultimate legislative success; and . . . the size of the domestic agenda varies directly with what I will call presidential "capital."[49]

However much one speaks of "context," it is seemingly tempting to overstate the president's role in agenda setting. In the first place, it suits the common preference for an activist president playing out his role in party government. There is also the related view that a system of separated institutions sharing powers can work only if the president sets the agenda. "Congressmen need an agenda from outside, something with high status to respond to or react against. What provides it better than the program of the President?"[50] This observation by Neustadt also implies a convenience of having an agenda set by the most prominent player in a system of distributed power. John W. Kingdon found confirmation in his interviews with national officials "that the president can single-handedly set the agendas, not only of people in the executive branch, but also of people in Congress and outside of government."[51]

The White House surely does serve to orient others to policy priorities. The president's involvement can be absolutely crucial, given media and public attention to the White House. As Baumgartner and Jones see it:

> The personal involvement of the president can play a key role in further strengthening the positive feedback processes. No other single actor can focus attention as clearly, or change the motivations of such a great number of other actors, as the president. . . . We conclude that the president is not a necessary actor in all cases, but when he decides to become involved, his influence can be decisive indeed.[52]

However reasonable these views may be, one should not lose sight of the context within which the president makes choices. Normally he chooses from among a set of issues that are familiar because they are continuous. Many of these issues are directly traceable to programs already on the books. His alternatives are also increasingly structured by the deficit, which has in recent years come to be recognized as an overarching issue itself. It is also useful to remember that a conscious decision *not* to act represents a policy preference in regard to an issue on the agenda every bit as much as a decision to act, even though by not acting a president may be criticized for failing to meet his obligations as an agenda setter.

Agenda-Related Concepts

Various scholars have sought to clarify the agenda-setting process by distinguishing between types of agendas.[53] I borrow heavily from these scholars in formulating the following concepts.

Agenda Orientation or Context

The concept of agenda orientation simply refers to the policy setting within which a president must try to govern. Some people use the labels "conservative" and "liberal" to denote different eras. What they typically mean in the American setting is support for more or less national government involvement in solving social and economic problems. I do not particularly like those labels for present purposes, however, since other forces are at work that they do not capture. Further, because most Americans resist such labels, conclusions about public support for conservatism or liberalism are based on weak evidence. Finally, conservatism or liberalism as policy preferences may have different meanings in different periods.

Any effort at labeling is subject to exceptions, but I do think it is possible to identify agenda orientations in relation to issue priorities. For example, in social welfare there are periods when conditions support expansion of the role of the national government; these are often followed by periods of consolidation. Baumgartner and Jones speak of "lurches and lulls" in policymaking.[54] Expansion is characterized by new programs, consolidation by reorganization and occasional retrenchment. The two notable periods of expansion were during the Roosevelt and Johnson administrations: the New Deal and the Great Society. These were followed by consolidative efforts during the Truman and Eisenhower administrations and the Nixon, Ford, and Carter administrations.

Until 1980 there had not been a contractive orientation. The cutbacks during consolidative periods are normally to make government programs more effective, not to eliminate them altogether. In 1980, however, a president was elected who not only doubted government's capacity to solve social welfare problems but believed that government contributed to these problems. In 1981 President Reagan was successful in enacting policies that definitely established the contractive agenda orientation. Tax cuts, increases in defense spending, and limited cuts in domestic programs created huge deficits. Even liberals had to consider how to cut back in order to go forward.

Once it was no longer politically feasible to cut back further, and as deficits mounted, attention turned to taxes—a fiscal orientation. George Bush campaigned on the slogan "read my lips, no new taxes," but he was forced to renege on that promise because of the continued failure to control the growth of government spending. In 1992 Congress seriously considered a constitutional amendment to balance the budget, a measure acknowledged by many to be an admission of incapacity to deal with increasing deficits. The amendment failed by just nine votes in the House to get the required two-thirds majority.

In summary, I have identified four agenda orientations within which presidents prepare programs: expansion, consolidation, contraction, and fiscal. None of these categories is pure. Consolidative and contractive efforts, for example, can expand government through regulation. The point here is simply to characterize policy and political conditions associated with a presidency that serve to constrain or define the president's program.

Proposals and Programs

John Kingdon finds it useful to distinguish between an agenda and alternatives. The first is "the list of subjects or problems to which governmental officials, and people outside of government closely associated with those officials, are paying some serious attention at any given time." He identifies a governmental agenda ("the list of subjects that are getting attention") and a decision agenda ("the list of subjects within the governmental agenda that are up for an active decision").[55]

Alternatives, for Kingdon, are the various proposals being considered for acting on a problem on the agenda. Proposals may be generated in many places in and out of government: within agencies with responsibility for the issue, within the Office of Management and Budget, among White House aides, within think tanks, within congressional committees, or among clienteles for existing programs. Kingdon's point is that presidents do not control the production of alternatives. In fact, for most major issues there are many alternatives available, readily offered by support groups or bureaucratic agencies. The election of a new president is an occasion for policy advocates to reach down into that bottom desk drawer and pull out the great idea whose time has finally come.

The president may select among proposals; he may also ignore them. He may select one from many or create a blend. At the beginning of each year he is expected to offer policy choices, preferably as part of a larger program that lends itself to labeling (the New Deal, Fair Deal, New Frontier, Great Society, Reaganomics). It is usually easier to name a program that expands government than one that is more consolidative or contractive in nature. And a president who prefers limited government is often said not to have a program. Put otherwise, choosing not to act, encouraging others to act, or thwarting an action judged inadequate or even harmful is typically not considered to be a presidential program, however internally consistent these choices may be.

As used here, *proposals* refer to the various alternatives that are available for acting on a problem; *program* refers to the set of presidential choices among proposals, including not to act or to defer government action. Note that *program* is used to refer to the president's choices. Because Congress is a two-house legislature with no single leader, it is not normally thought of as having a program, though certain leaders, such as Democratic House Speaker James Wright of Texas, have sought to offer one in competition with that of the White House.

Consensus

The concept of consensus directs attention to the level of agreement between members of Congress and the president in regard to the agenda ori-

Table 5-1. *Characteristics of Presidents and the Agenda, Truman–Bush*

President	Agenda orientation	President's program	Agenda consensus	Major events	Impact on subsequent agenda
Truman	Consolidation	Active	Low	Korean War	Significant
Eisenhower	Consolidation	Permissive	Moderate to low	Little Rock, U-2, recession	Limited
Kennedy	Expansion	Active	Low	Civil rights, missile crisis	Significant
Johnson	Expansion	Active	High	Vietnam War, urban riots	Massive
Nixon	Consolidation	Active	Moderate to low	Vietnam War, China initiative, Arab oil embargo, Watergate	Significant
Ford	Maintenance	Permissive/reactive	Low	Nixon pardon	Limited
Carter	Consolidation	Active	Moderate to low	Camp David, Iran hostages, recession	Limited
Reagan	Contraction to fiscal	Active to permissive	High to low	Tax and budget cuts, assassination attempt, Iran-contra	Massive
Bush	Fiscal	Permissive/reactive	Low	Persian Gulf War, recession	Limited

entation and a program for acting on problems on the agenda. Elections naturally can have a major influence on the level of agreement. For example, as previously discussed, the 1964 and 1980 elections resulted in a high level of agreement on the agenda and substantial concurrence that the president had the approval of the public to proceed with his program. There was no such agreement following the 1960, 1968, or 1988 elections. Thus consensus is characteristic of elections that are perceived as conveying a mandate for change. It is built on superficial evidence of congruity between the policy messages of presidential and congressional elections. That is, it is assumed that the public was sending strong policy signals, whether or not that conclusion can be sustained by a survey of true voter intentions.

Modern Presidents and the Agenda

In his final State of the Union message, President Eisenhower observed that "progress implies both new and continuing problems and, unlike Presidential administrations, problems rarely have terminal dates."[56] Thus, as he exited the White House in 1961, Eisenhower left to Kennedy the existing set of new and continuing problems as the context within which the new president would set his priorities. How much any one president shapes the agenda is not easy to determine. In his review of the Eisenhower-Kennedy-Johnson period, Sundquist concluded:

The ultimate results were, in a sense, compelled by the circumstances of the problems themselves. Though the imagination and skill and doggedness of the political actors were indeed remarkable, these men nevertheless seem as actors, following a script that was written by events.[57]

As in other discussions of the individual presidents, the distinction between the takeover and elected presidents is relevant here. The latter have an issue-orienting experience during the campaign. They have an opportunity to test ideas and probe for openings in a crowded calendar of issues. Takeover presidents do not have the same kind of experience since loyalty to their leader precludes an effort to fit their policy preferences into the ongoing agenda. And in two cases—Truman and Ford—they had little time even to acquaint themselves fully with their predecessor's orientation and style.

An overview of each postwar administration is shown in table 5-1, which characterizes the agenda orientation, the ambitiousness of the president's program, the degree of consensus, major events that influenced the agenda, and the president's impact on later agendas.

Truman

The agenda at the time of Roosevelt's death was clear enough. First it was necessary to bring the war to a close; then a substantial set of foreign and domestic issues required attention. The list of issues was not difficult to compile. Whole nations required assistance in rebuilding, and a great many domestic problems had been put aside during the war. The orientation, therefore, was consolidative, one of postwar reassembly. The emphasis was not on creating new programs but on making up for lost time in regard to programs enacted during the New Deal. Truman himself was active in proposing legislation to deal with the postwar issues of housing, employment, farm support, and public works. His surprise win in 1948 was partially based on portraying himself as facing a "do-nothing" Republican Congress.[58] New proposals were introduced as a part of Truman's Fair Deal, and some were enacted. However, the boldest of these—a national health care program—did not pass.

The Truman administration was characterized by significant policy conflict. His own unexpected election in 1948 did not carry with it a consensus on policy direction, and in 1950 Republicans once again increased their numbers in Congress. The principal events affecting Truman's management of the agenda were the labor disputes immediately following the end of World War II and the Korean conflict in the last years of the administration. Throughout his term in office Truman struggled to maintain control of the policy agenda, to preclude events from overtaking him. The mark of his leadership is that despite limited resources, or "political capital" in Light's terms, he remained a major actor throughout, if not always in charge.

Eisenhower

Truman's agenda legacy for Eisenhower was the Korean conflict. In one of his few campaign promises, the new president said that, if elected, he would "go to Korea." This was an engrossing issue for the new president and one that he was, by training, well prepared to deal with. An armistice was signed July 27, 1953, just six months after Eisenhower's inauguration. As for the domestic agenda, most of the issues were consolidative in nature: extensions and refinements of existing programs, along with a number of reorganizations. New problems began to emerge toward the end of the administration in the domestic economy, civil rights, and medical care. And, as well documented by Sundquist, congressional Democrats actively worked to prepare proposals responsive to the emerging agenda.

Eisenhower himself was more permissive than active in proposing alternatives to deal with the consolidative issues of the time. He was more a manager or commander than an initiator or promoter. Although there appeared to be a moderate degree of consensus in 1952 with the election of Republican House and Senate majorities, the president's own limited program was unlikely to result in major change in the consolidative agenda inherited from Truman. For example, there would probably not be significant cutbacks in the New Deal programs that continued to define the work of the national government.

Several major events during the period had a definite effect on the agenda. Senator Joseph R. McCarthy, Republican of Wisconsin, began an anticommunist crusade that charged many prominent public officials with conspiracy. His campaign had a chilling effect throughout the government.[59] The confrontation in Little Rock, Arkansas, between state and federal officials reflected growing discontent over civil rights and presaged passage of legislation in 1957 and 1960 during the Eisenhower years and in 1964 and 1965 during the Johnson years. The economic recession brought huge majorities of Democrats to Congress in 1958 and encouraged them to prepare for recapturing the White House in 1960. The U-2 incident created a rift with the Soviet Union that would be exacerbated in the early months of the Kennedy administration.

President Eisenhower was seemingly content to conform to the agenda as it moved through his years in the White House. Events made a difference, but the president settled for guidance more than innovation, with the ultimate effect of permitting, perhaps encouraging, congressional Democrats—particularly the liberals—to participate actively in policy development. Legislative production was limited, but the congressional Democrats identified an agenda to take to the voters in 1960.

Kennedy

The agenda was full following the rather tranquil 1950s. As a candidate, Kennedy was anxious to convey a sense of command and therefore created a group of advisory committees following his nomination. Task forces worked on proposals during the campaign and immediately following the election.[60] The expansionist agenda orientation encouraged an activist program by the president. Kennedy's desire for control was fortified substantively by the work of the Democrats (mostly liberal senators) in the 86th Congress.

However impressive this early effort was, agenda consensus, as defined here, was relatively low. It was not easy for Kennedy to sell the idea that the presidential and congressional election results represented a congruous policy message. He won narrowly, and the Democrats' margins in both houses suffered a net loss. Theodore Sorenson believed that the 87th Congress was the most conservative since the Republican-controlled 83d. "The balance of power appeared to have swung decisively in the direction of the conservative coalition of Republicans and Southern Democrats who had since 1937 effectively blocked much of the progressive legislation of four Presidents."[61]

Events also had a negative effect for a president eager to clear the agenda. In particular, the Bay of Pigs disaster was inimical to an image of bold and effective leadership. Other preoccupying events included civil rights demonstrations, the erection of the Berlin wall, a confrontation with the steel industry, and, above all, the Cuban missile crisis. In the meantime, however, a substantial foundation was being laid for the enactment of new programs in many policy areas. Therefore there was a significant effect on subsequent agenda management. The difficulty in making a firm judgment is that no one can know what might have happened had Kennedy lived.

Johnson

Seldom have personal, political, and policy forces converged so positively as in 1964–66. Important factors—the agenda preparation by Kennedy, national contrition for the shooting of the president, the legislative mastery of the new president—were bolstered by an overwhelming Democratic victory at the polls in 1964. The result was the Great Society. The expansionist agenda orientation was fulfilled as Johnson added to the already activist Kennedy program and benefited from perhaps the greatest agenda consensus since the 1932 election.

Johnson's triumph in enacting the Great Society led to a shift in agenda orientation. After the expansionist calendar was cleared a more consolidative set of issues naturally arose. It was now time to make these many new programs work. Then events like the escalation of the Vietnam War and inner-city riots diverted attention from the previous agenda and Johnson's remarkable success on Capitol Hill. What began as the ideal activist party government disintegrated in the face of foreign and domestic policy challenges.

The Kennedy-Johnson years had a massive impact on the national policy agenda. The next administration did not have to search for issues. A quantum increase in domestic programs had generated a full calendar of work at the White House. Civil unrest among minority groups and antiwar activists would have to be dealt with. And like Eisenhower, the next president would be left to close down a war—one even more unpopular, yet more of a political labyrinth, than that in Korea.

Nixon

The former vice president, long identified as a strong partisan, was commissioned to cope with this new and challenging agenda. So as not to make it that easy for him, voters also returned a Democratic Congress. At this critical juncture, then, the public appeared to go in two directions at once, thus defying any interpretation of an agenda consensus. The circumstances and results of the 1968 election are ample grounds for questioning the usefulness of the mandate concept.

The national government had become a much larger enterprise as a result of the enactment of the Great Society. Administering, reorganizing, extending, and refining these programs required substantial work by the Nixon administration. The Nixon administration faced the enormously complex task of consolidating the Great Society. In addition, however, were the fresh issues generated by these many programs and defined by the clienteles that had been created. In particular, there were new emphases on the environment, energy, and safety. It was not a set of issues that instinctively attracted Nixon, but as president he could not ignore their politics: they were a major part of the agenda during his administration.

The Vietnam War was nearly as difficult for Nixon to resolve as it had been for Johnson, but there was a promise of settlement by the time of the 1972 election. Nixon's initiatives with China and the Soviet Union were to have a significant effect on the foreign policy agenda for subsequent presidents. Another major event of agenda-setting importance was the Arab oil embargo imposed October 18, 1973. The price of imported oil quadrupled, sending reverberations through most of the domestic economy for several years. Finally, the Watergate scandal that marks the Nixon years in history diverted executive and congressional attention from the more substantive agenda.

Clashes between the president and Congress were frequent throughout the period but did not forestall legislative productivity.[62] In many cases members of Congress were not content to await presidential initiative. They participated more actively in all phases of the policy process and enacted congressional reforms to increase their ability to analyze policy and perform oversight. One major consequence was a Congress prepared psychologically and materially to play the role of an alternative government, adapting itself to split-party control and to the incapacitation of the president because of Watergate.

There is ample evidence that this period was one of the most important in the postwar era for understanding the dynamics of the agenda. Even a relatively superficial review suggests that a complex, independent, consolidative agenda had been created as a result of the Great Society programs. This agenda dominated domestic policy politics in the White House and on Capitol Hill and had the force to carry beyond Nixon's service. Much of the puzzle of high legislative productivity during the Nixon-Ford administrations (see chapter 4) may well be solved by inquiry into the extent to which the agenda guided policy action. In both foreign and domestic policy, a focus on the effects of agenda continuity and change on institutional response would contribute materially to understanding the context within which the president and Congress do their work. Such analysis would also clarify institutional adaptation to the variable political conditions encouraged by the separation of elections.

Ford

Of the three modern takeover presidents, Ford clearly had the least opportunity to escape the legacy of his predecessor. Most of what he had to cope with was set in motion by the Nixon administration or by Congress before he entered the White House. The agenda orientation was maintenance of the consolidative efforts already under way. It was extremely difficult for Ford to fashion a program of his own.[63] He had little choice but to be permissive or reactive, allowing a Democratic Congress to work its will and vetoing measures that went too far. "During his brief tenure Ford undoubtedly vetoed more bills raising important substantive issues than any previous president."[64] Unlike the other takeover presidents, Truman and Johnson, he did not have an opportunity to establish or to reset an agenda consensus. The momentum already in place continued to carry through the final years of the truncated Nixon administration. The environmental and energy agendas remained active throughout the Ford presidency, accounting for six major pieces of legislation.

The event with the greatest impact on Ford's capacity to influence the agenda was, of course, his pardon of Nixon. Whatever political or policy advantage he may have had from taking over was lost almost immediately. "In the wake of the Nixon pardon, Congress showed little inclination to respond to Ford's promises of 'communication, conciliation, compromise, and cooperation.'"[65] Already sizable Democratic majorities in the House and Senate grew substantially in 1974, further isolating the president politically. Ford's presidency will be correctly analyzed as that of filling out the Nixon term, essentially as Nixon's "lame duck." In a continuum of presidential influence and management of the agenda, Ford will forever be placed at the low end. That is not to say that his presidency was a failure, but it acknowledges the context for judging his options as a leader.

Carter

Had Nixon not been compelled to resign, it is conceivable that his completed term in office would not have looked very different from that of Carter. The consolidative agenda orientation of the post–Great Society era and the aftereffects of events like the Arab oil embargo continued to influence policy choices beyond the Nixon and Ford administrations. The major legislation enacted during the Carter administration dealt predominantly with environmental, energy, reorganizational, and deregulatory issues (totaling fourteen of Mayhew's count of twenty-two important laws passed).

In this context, Carter himself was an activist, proposing a large number of consolidative proposals. Members of Congress were also actively engaged in dealing with these same issues, and not always to the president's liking. They were unwilling to shut down the policy apparatus on Capitol Hill that had been created during the Nixon-Ford years. Thus not only did the agenda look very much like it had in those years, but frequently so did the politics. Democratic control of both branches made less of a difference than many people had expected. "Congress never did hit it off with Carter . . . who as president remained a stranger to much of official Washington."[66] The Carter years demonstrated that there is nothing automatic about party government when one party manages to win control of Congress and the White House.

None of the three elections in which Carter was involved conveyed a high degree of agenda consensus. Carter himself won narrowly against a weak Republican opponent in 1976, by choice he was not heavily involved in the 1978 congressional elections, and he suffered a substantial loss in the 1980 presidential race. Again, as had happened in previous Republican administrations, there was no obvious evidence that Congress conceded agenda-setting authority to the president, however much the president may have believed that he had such a prerogative.

The Camp David accords and the taking of hostages in Iran were events receiving the most press coverage during the Carter administration. Neither had the effect of, say, the Arab oil embargo for restructuring the agenda, however. It was the recession in 1980 that dominated the presidential election and provided a favorable agenda orientation for the contractive policy message of Ronald Reagan.

Reagan

Never before 1980 had there been conditions so favorable to a contractive agenda orientation. In this century, expansion has typically been followed by consolidation or maintenance. In 1980, however, Reagan reiterated his view that government was not the solution; it was, in fact, the problem. Therefore he believed it was essential that programs be cut back, regulation and bureaucracy be reduced substantially, and federal taxes be cut sharply. The 1980 election results were interpreted as affirming this policy approach and representing a consensus for the Reagan program. Support for the new president was enhanced by the assassination attempt, which occurred at the critical point when Reagan had introduced his budget and tax-cutting proposals.

Comparison with the Johnson presidency is informative. As described, conditions in 1964–66 allowed Johnson to have a massive impact on the subsequent agenda. But the repercussions would come later as succeeding presidents sought to administer the new programs put in place. Reagan also enjoyed high agenda consensus at the beginning of his first term. However, the reordering of priorities in 1981 had significant effects on the agenda during his terms in office. The combination of reduced taxes, significant increases in defense expenditures, and a failure to achieve compensatory decreases in domestic expenditures produced deficits that then constrained the choices available to policymakers for the remainder of the Reagan presidency and for many years that followed.

The Iran-contra scheme, which came to light toward the end of Reagan's second term, had the potential, not unlike that of Watergate, for paralyzing the White House. The president acted quickly to defuse this plausible result by appointing a commission and by having his administration cooperate with congressional investigations. Even so, the event had important policy effects. Congressional Democrats, led by Speaker Jim Wright, became more active than they had been in Reagan's first term, taking initiatives in defining and acting on the agenda. In order to preserve an active policy role for himself in this atmosphere, the president had to take these initiatives seriously. The effect was to produce more than the expected amount of important legislation on major issues. As was the case in the last Congress in the Eisenhower era, a capacity for initiative and productivity was displayed under circumstances of divided government and during the lame-duck months of a two-term administration.

Once it was no longer possible to significantly reduce major social welfare or entitlement programs, attention naturally turned to fiscal issues. The agenda orientation shifted to how to improve the economy and increase revenues. That orientation persisted into the Bush and Clinton administrations. New programs are severely constrained by the reality of the deficit. If cuts cannot be made, or if additional spending is agreed upon, then taxes have to be raised (as they have been several times) or more jobs must be created, or both. These options have defined the choices for Reagan's successors.

Bush

It was difficult for many analysts to judge what the 1988 election was about. Bush was said not to have a mandate in spite of his impressive personal victory. Expectations were low, and George Bush did what was expected. Given his limited political capital and the limited agenda identified during the 1988 campaign, it would have been surprising had he sought to rival predecessors who had won by large margins.

The limited agenda during the first year of the Bush administration is amply demonstrated by the fact that only two major pieces of legislation were enacted (see chapter 4). In Bush's second and subsequent years, the domestic agenda was dominated by a growing realization that the deficit was substantially greater than had been anticipated. Thus, although Bush worked with the Democratic Congress to enact a number of important laws—rights for the disabled, clean air, child care support, immigration, affordable housing— his second year will be most remembered for the passage of a bipartisan deficit reduction package. A major part of the package sought to respond to the fiscal agenda that was carried over from the last years of the Reagan administration. An unfortunate political by-product of the agreement was that Bush had to renege on his famous "no new taxes" pledge. However much he was praised at the time for this action, it symbolized his loss of even the limited control he had of the domestic agenda. He did not regain even a small edge during his last two years in office.

Initiative was clearly centered on Capitol Hill during the last two years of the Bush administration. At first the president was triumphant in gaining support for his actions in the Persian Gulf. But congressional Democrats then established a pattern of sending to the president legislation that they believed either was in the best interests of the country or would give them a political edge if the president exercised his veto power. Bush did not disappoint them in regard to the latter strategy. In 1992 alone he vetoed twenty-one bills, including several that fit the "political issue" category: conditional most favored nation status for China (twice), a tax-the-rich bill, campaign finance reform, fetal tissue research, motor voter registration, family leave, family planning, and funding for abortions. All these vetoes were sustained in at least one house.[67]

An end-of-term review of Congress had this to say about the last two years of Bush's presidency:

> Scandal, special interests, sagging poll ratings, divided government, presidential election politics. They all share the blame for the 102nd Congress' meager record of legislative accomplishment. But the real culprit may be more fiscal than political, and that problem will remain even if voters change the players Nov. 3.[68]

Much of Bush's agenda was fiscal in nature. He was constrained in dealing with it by limited political resources and by having bound himself by a pledge to forgo one potential solution: higher taxes. Therefore he found it difficult throughout his term to take charge of the crucial certification process in agenda setting and could only act defensively with the veto to thwart Democratic initiatives. The agenda for a complex government remained in place, awaiting those with sufficient political support to certify particular items for attention.

Summary

I have not argued that the president plays an unimportant role in agenda setting, nor does the evidence support this conclusion. Rather, I have sought to identify how presidents fit into the government's work when they take office. I have raised doubts about their capacity to set the agenda at that point. Most of the policy issues a president faces upon entering the White House preceded him, and, indeed, these issues typically were central to the

up in 2000

rhetoric and debate of the campaign. Seldom can the president interpret the election results as providing a mandate. However, because others make this interpretation, the mandate comes to have political and policy consequences for how his record will be evaluated and for the resources he may have available in dealing with Congress.

The president becomes part of a continuous though changing government. He has significant influence in setting priorities, certifying certain issues, proposing policy solutions, and reacting to policy initiatives of others (such as those increasingly offered by more policy-active members of Congress). These are vital functions for a busy government. Under most circumstances, the agenda is full to overflowing. Since it is not possible to treat all issues at once, members of Congress and others anxiously await the designation of priorities. These presidential choices are typically from a list that is familiar to other policy actors. Nonetheless, a designator is important, even if he is a Republican having to work with a Democratic Congress. As in any organization with too much to do, there is a need for someone in authority to say: "Let's start here." Without that initiative by the president, a two-chamber Congress finds it very difficult to act. But a president who says "Let's start here and here and here and here" also fails as a designator. Carter committed this second designation error, as did Clinton, at least in the early months of his administration.

I have also stressed here that presidents vary markedly in their capacity to alter the agenda during their term in office. Occasionally a president has sufficient political resources to reset the agenda: examples are Johnson's quantum expansion in social programs in 1964–65 and Reagan's major contraction in revenues in 1981. But most presidents are substantially more constrained in the policy choices available to them. Analysis of their role suitably begins with the continuing agenda and the way each incumbent employs his limited resources for influencing outcomes.

CHAPTER SIX

Presidents and Lawmaking in a Separated System

AGENDAS identify the substantive work of government. I turn next to a major and uniquely complex task in a separated system: creating the laws that tax, benefit, and regulate the public. Mark A. Peterson and George C. Edwards III strike the proper note for this chapter:

> The settings in which the Congress assesses and responds to presidential initiatives vary enormously. . . .
> There is no question that the successes and failures of each [presidency are] tied to forces beyond the manipulation of the individual incumbents.[1]

> Clearly, the conditions for successful presidential leadership of Congress are contingent, and the president's strategic position uncertain. If circumstances are not serendipitous, the potential for leadership is diminished. In such a context it becomes all the more necessary for the president to take advantage of whatever opportunities do appear.[2]

There is no one formula for presidential participation in lawmaking; presidents vary in the advantages they possess for working with Congress; and forces outside the president's influence may be the deciding factor in what gets done. Presidents do have programs that often become the focal point of congressional action. But members of Congress can, and do, prepare proposals on their own initiative or in response to those offered by the president. Few, if any, major policy proposals are likely to pass both houses unchanged. Presidents rarely expect that to happen, and if they do, they are inevitably disappointed.

The very first words of the text of the Constitution itself are among the more clear and straightforward in the document: "All legislative Powers herein granted shall be vested in a Congress of the United States, which shall consist of a Senate and House of Representatives" (article I, section 1).

Knowing no more than these words, and understanding that they were written with a serious purpose, one might expect that those who want laws passed must seek to influence Congress. The words bestow upon that institution a legitimacy regarding a fundamental power of government: lawmaking.

To acknowledge that Congress has the ultimate authority to make law is not to dismiss the president's influence in that process. After all, he has both constitutional and political standing to participate. Rather, the purpose is to offer a way to assess this influence. This exercise is meant to correct a tendency by many analysts to overstate the president's strategic position. Many view the president as agenda setter and program initiator and director, rather than as designator or certifier of priorities. A president's record of achievement is typically scored by how much of his program is enacted into law and sometimes simply by the number of laws passed, whether or not he initiated the proposals that became law. Should he fail to propose a large and innovative program, or should circumstances not demand such action, the president will score low on what John B. Bader refers to as the "FDR scale"—essentially the first-one-hundred-days test.[3] This test may even be applied at regular intervals throughout a president's term. There is, therefore, a real need to identify the characteristics of lawmaking as a first step in calculating what presidents do in the lawmaking process and how they do it.

Misinterpreting or oversimplifying the president's role in lawmaking may be a consequence of a failure to account fully for the complex features of the lawmaking process and the legislature. Lawmaking in a democratic system of separated institutions will be substantially more intricate and variable than in a unified, parliamentary structure. The many arenas of decisionmaking provide multiple points of access and foster a permeability that makes it difficult to predict either participation or outcomes.

The Nature of Lawmaking

Lawmaking represents an effort toward public resolution of societal issues. Typically, democratic lawmaking is speculative: no one is absolutely certain of the outcome or the effect of implementation. By identifying the varying political and structural conditions for participation, a review of the characteristics of lawmaking in a separated system aids in defining the challenge facing presidents.

Lawmaking is *continuous*. Most laws create tangible programs, benefits, regulations, organizations, or processes. They authorize the spending of money, then appropriate the funds. They instruct agents how to collect taxes. There are behavioral, organizational, and structural residues once laws are passed. As a political system matures, much of the agenda will be generated from within the laws already on the books. Most of what a president proposes builds on what is already there, for example, in education, agriculture, health, or housing. There are very few new initiatives, and virtually no new programs originate, live, and die within one presidential administration. Presidents do have options, to be sure, but they are typically exercised within the constraints of ongoing commitments.

Lawmaking is *iterative* and *alterative*. Iteration is commonly defined as repetition. One dictionary, however, defines it as "a computational procedure in which replication of a cycle of operations produces results which approximate the desired result more and more closely." Alteration is therefore implied in the repeated exercises of exploring problems, developing solutions, and testing options. A substantive element is introduced, making iteration a purposeful rather than a mindless activity. A proposal is worked and reworked to approximate the interests of those participating. This use of the term is familiar to bureaucrats engaged in planning and policymaking.

Iteration is not simply the passage of time. Thus, for example, computation or approximation does not necessarily occur just because a problem has been on the agenda over a period of time. And efforts to block lawmaking, as occurred for decades in civil rights and federal aid to education, do not constitute iteration. However, faithful representation of the complex dimensions of an issue can result in significant delay as efforts are made to compute and recompute formulas that "approximate the desired result more and more closely."

Iteration is not limited to partisan interactions, that is, one party repeating a policy exercise engaged in by its opposite. It can and does occur within one party, one institution, or one committee. It may be politically motivated or inspired solely by substantive policy concerns. Lawmaking is not a one-stage or one-shot process, and iteration may occur over a period of months or years. Therefore, if the president is interested in a piece of legislation, he will have to be involved at many intervals over time in order to exert influence. He cannot simply announce his position when a bill is introduced or when roll call voting begins and expect to have influence.

Lawmaking is *representative*, and differentially so. The variation in representation for Congress and the president—in the length of terms, the constituencies represented, and the means for election—is a familiar feature of the U.S. system. This variation produces elected officials whose representational perspectives will differ significantly. In a system of separated institutions competing for shared powers, lawmaking as an iterative process cannot be restricted to one branch, one party, or a few participants. Because of representation and the legitimacy it confers, this competition and iteration take place even when one party controls both branches of government.[4] It would be extremely odd to have established a two-house legislature and legitimized each house by anchoring it in a representational form, only to ignore that arrangement for purposes of lawmaking. So the several forms of representation guarantee that lawmaking will be iterative, within and between legislative bodies. For presidents to misunderstand that fundamental characteristic of the system is to invite disappointment. Examples abound of presidents who failed to account for the different representational bases in the House and Senate.[5]

Lawmaking is *informational*. More than forty years ago, J. Willard Hurst identified three related advantages of the legislature in a democratic political system: "its legitimacy in public opinion"; "its broad authority under the Constitution"; and "its power . . . to inquire into matters of public concern." Regarding the third advantage, Hurst explains:

> Law represents an effort—however short of the ideal—to order men's affairs according to rational weighing of values and the means of achieving them; how the lawmaker learns the facts of the living society in which he intervenes, is therefore, a point of fundamental importance regarding the manner of lawmaking. No agency in our government inherited a fact-gathering authority in any degree comparable to that of the legislature.[6]

Making law implies "the power to look for facts" so a reasonable choice can be made and so that judgments can be rendered as to how current laws are working.

A contemporary explication of the informational function of lawmaking is offered by Keith Krehbiel. He identifies a "legislative signaling game" that is both sequential and informational. "The committee proposes a bill. The legislature updates its beliefs. The legislature chooses a policy." Krehbiel conceives of congressional committees as having power primarily because of their informational advantages: they signal facts needed by lawmakers. "In instances of informational committee power, a committee credibly transmits private information to get a majority to do what is in the majority's interest."[7] This purpose of defining society's needs through representational lawmaking is rarely appreciated for its contribution. In fact, presidents often decry the inevitable fact gathering by lawmakers.

Lawmaking is *sequential*: laws are made in a series of stages, and because several institutions are legitimately involved, there are sequences within and between the institutions. The budget process is a notable example of an elaborate sequence. The executive produces a budget document that is then introduced in each house of Congress. The House and Senate each have a sequence of action leading to a budget resolution, which eventually must be approved by the other chamber. The sequence by which the two houses act can make a difference and therefore is a factor in developing lawmaking strategies.

There are several types of sequences. Those that are required by the Constitution include origination of revenue measures in the House and the requirement of action by both houses to enact a law. Some sequences are institutionally created to allow the House, Senate, and White House to do their work, such as legislative clearance in the White House or the movement of bills from subcommittee to committee to scheduling for floor consideration in each house of Congress. And some sequences are cross-institutional between the House and Senate or between the White House and the two houses of Congress, such as the budget process.

Decisions about sequence are typically strategic in nature. Who acts first may make an important difference. Yet before the split-party Congresses of the Reagan presidency, when an effort was made to build momentum by having the Republican Senate act first, little attention had been paid to this matter.

Lawmaking is *orderly* in the sense of setting priorities. When decisions are made regarding the order in which legislation will be taken up, preferences are established among the bills themselves. Major battles may be fought over which legislation will be considered first. Even where there is little or no conflict over status, decisions have to be made simply to facilitate the flow of work in a legislative body, to suit timing demands (for example, for reauthorizations or other legislation subject to deadlines), or to accommodate various interests.

An important function of leadership is to set priorities in scheduling in consultation with the committee chairmen. Presidents may participate in these decisions but are by no means in command. Crises typically have the effect of displacing the expected order, often to the advantage of the president.

Lawmaking is *declarative*. An iterative, informational, and sequential process within a two-house, representative legislature requires displays of agreements reached along the way. Thus declaration, even publication to display the most recent iteration, is crucial to lawmaking in a representative system. Publication can stimulate a response from other interests not represented in earlier stages. If these interests have a legitimate claim, they may contribute to reaching the desired goal of building majority support for a proposal. Here is a familiar pattern: an agreement is reached in a subcommittee; the results are displayed for participants in subsequent stages in the sequence; further changes are made as new interests are represented; an agreement is reached and the results are published; previously nonparticipating interests may try for an advantage in the rules for floor debate; an agreement is reached on how the proposal will be debated and that is published; and still further interests may require representation in the settlement on the floor. The media play an important role for important legislation in advertising the agreements reached along the way, and this in turn contributes to the number of interests participating at each stage.

The president's strategy must account for the probability of greater participation with the publication of agreements. Estimates must be made regarding who is likely to respond and how. He cannot wait to see what happens, nor can he ever trust that agreements will remain confidential. The budget agreement of 1990 is a particularly dramatic example of a failure to estimate the effects of publishing the understandings reached; President Carter's energy package in 1977 is an example of poor judgment in excluding interests before the introduction of the program.

In summary, representation justifies iteration, iteration produces information and occurs in sequence, an iterative-informational-sequential process requires publication of prior results, and legislative agreements will be taken up in an order that is itself subject to influence. Viewing the lawmaking process in this way has the distinct advantage of directing attention to the role of the many participants who are legitimately involved. The president is often one of the most important participants. But no one who has read the Constitution or watched this government work expects him to be the sole actor. The process just described is often one of "legislating together," as Peterson has it, and the role of the president frequently is "at the margins," as Edwards puts it. But Congress also has the power to act alone, even when the president decides to exercise a veto.

This chapter will examine a number of topics so as to show how presidents work on Capitol Hill. The first is presidential "success." Part of the governing problem for presidents is that of calculating how to manage their participation in an ongoing legislative body with multiple dependencies. Success for presidents, as Steven A. Shull points out, may require an understanding of what happens at several stages of the policy process.[8] To assess the role of the president requires study of more than roll call voting; study of compromise and change along the way is also needed.

Table 6-1. *Major Legislation, by Institutional Influence, 1873–1940*

Institutional influence	1873–1990		1901–10		1911–20		1921–30		1931–40		Total	
	Number	Percent	Number	Percent	Number	Percent	Number	Percent	Number	Percent	Number	Percent
Presidential preponderant	1	6	4	29	4	20	0	0	10	36	19	21
Congressional preponderant	12	75	4	29	10	50	6	50	3	11	35	39
Joint presidential-congressional preponderant	1	6	5	36	6	30	3	25	14	50	29	32
Pressure group preponderant[a]	2	13	1	7	0	0	3	25	1	4	7	8
Total	16	100	14	101[b]	20	100	12	100	28	101[b]	90	100

Source: Developed from the summary of legislation in Lawrence H. Chamberlain, *The President, Congress and Legislation* (Columbia University Press, 1946), pp. 450–52.
a. If the "pressure group preponderant" category is dropped, the percentages for the other three categories ($N = 83$) are: presidential preponderant, 35 percent; congressional preponderant, 42 percent; joint president-congressional preponderant, 23 percent.
b. Numbers have been rounded.

Easton — can see his influence on Jones.

Next is the production of laws in a separated system. Replacing the presidency-centered, party responsibility mode of analysis with a more system-oriented perspective prepares one to receive evidence that production does not cease under split-party control. If a president does not act, perhaps Congress will.

The evidence of legislative productivity also encourages one to consider the continuity of issues. Perhaps the system produces in ways not predicted by party responsibility advocates because legislative work occurs over time, coming to fruition at a particular moment rather than in four- or eight-year segments coincident with a president's term or terms.[9]

Presidential Success with Congress

There is an understandable interest in judging how well the president is doing on Capitol Hill, for all of the reasons that analysts focus on the president in the first place. If the president is supposed to lead the political system, then people naturally want to know how he is doing. As stressed throughout this book, this concentration both emerges from and encourages a presidency-centered framework of analysis, leaving scholars unprepared to see the president as a lesser player because of political circumstances, personal policy preferences, or both. Jon R. Bond and Richard Fleisher acknowledge: "The present arrangement between the branches makes it extremely difficult for the president to fulfill promises made during the election period. Yet the public tends to hold the president accountable if he fails to deliver."[10] When this happens, harsh judgments about presidential performance are typically the result, and reform proposals designed to get the president to lead often follow.

Comparing Two Eras

In the most extensive study of presidential-congressional interaction on legislation before World War II, Lawrence H. Chamberlain examined ninety pieces of legislation. Having familiarized himself with what happened in Congress with each of these acts, he then categorized them as shown in table 6-1. There are relatively few instances where presidential influence was preponderant, but the number of such cases increased greatly during the New Deal decade of the 1930s, with a concomitant drop in the cases where congressional influence was preponderant. Pressure group influence was preponderant mostly on tariff acts. Twelve of the 90 acts (13 percent) were passed under divided government. By contrast, 152 of 267 acts (57 percent) chosen by David R. Mayhew (see below) were passed under divided government. This reflects the difference in the frequency of split-party results in the two eras.

Chamberlain's findings have received little notice in contemporary empirical studies of presidential-congressional interaction on legislation. Yet his conclusions deserve attention for at least two reasons. First, they represent painstaking analysis of an earlier era and therefore provide a most interesting basis for comparison. Second, many of his findings about the system are relevant today.

Chamberlain concluded that his results "indicate not that the President is less important than generally supposed but that Congress is more important."[11] This important role for Congress is attributable in large part to the fact that most issues are treated over a period of time. So his findings demonstrate not only "the joint character of the American legislative process," but also that Congress nurtures proposals.

> One of the points brought out most clearly by the case studies . . . was the depth of the legislative roots of most important statutes. For instance, a law is hailed as something new at the time of passage but further examination reveals that the proposal had been discussed more or less continuously in Congress for several years.

The president's role often is one of designating or certifying an issue or proposal as worthy of further attention, according to Chamberlain.

> Presidential attention had led to [a bill's] elevation from the obscurity of just another bill to the prominence of an administration measure. Administrative experts had participated by drafting a new bill but there was not very much in the new bill that had not been present in one or more earlier drafts. At all events, driven by the power now behind it, the bill becomes law without great difficulty or delay, while in the absence of presidential action years might have gone by without its adoption.[12]

Chamberlain estimated that seventy-seven of the ninety acts were traceable to bills previously introduced in Congress by members themselves. He judged this "long germinative period" as "one of the most valuable contributions that a legislative body can make."[13] I will have reason to return to these important observations later in this chapter and in the chapters that follow.

In the postwar period, many analysts have concluded that Congress is no longer able to perform the type of active role that it played during the period of Chamberlain's study. Power shifted to the White House: some even spoke of the "imperial presidency" and of "presidential government."[14] In a particularly critical analysis of Congress, Samuel P. Huntington argued that "momentous social changes have confronted Congress with an institutional 'adaptation crisis.'" Huntington observed that Congress was in a fight with itself in trying to preserve its autonomy relative to the executive.

> Apparently Congress can defend its autonomy only by refusing to legislate, and it can legislate only by surrendering its autonomy. [When] Congress balks, criticism rises, [and] the clamoring voices of reformers fill the air with demands for the "modernization" of the "antiquated procedures" of an "eighteenth century" Congress so it can deal with "twentieth century realities." The demands for reform serve as counters in the legislative game to get the President's measures through Congress. Independence thus provokes criticism; acquiescence brings approbation. If Congress legislates, it subordinates itself to the President; if it refuses to legislate, it alienates itself from public opinion. Congress can assert its power or it can pass laws; but it cannot do both.[15]

Ronald C. Moe and Steven C. Teel sought to test Huntington's assertions by reviewing legislation passed during 1940–67 (after Chamberlain's study). Relying primarily on case histories in twelve categories of legislation, Moe and Teel conclude that their review does not support Huntington's observations.

> Our conclusion challenges the conventional wisdom that the president has come to enjoy an increasingly preponderant role in national policymaking. The evidence does not lend support to Huntington and his thesis that Congress ought to recognize its declining state and forego what remains of its legislative function. Quite the contrary, the evidence suggests that Congress continues to be an active innovator and very much in the legislative business.[16]

In seeking to explain the continued importance of Congress in lawmaking, Moe and Teel identify the "decentralized structure of both chambers." They believe that "Congress provides innovation in policy through 'successive limited comparisons.'" Congress, it seems, is a lawmaking institution organized to do its job. In the process, and not surprisingly, the members and their staffs come to know a lot about what public policy is and who it affects.

During the 1970s, after both the above studies were published, Congress engaged in substantial reform. One main purpose was to enable Congress to be even more heavily involved in contemporary policymaking. Increased personal and committee staff, new and enhanced policy analytical units, new budget procedures, and committee and party reorganizations all contributed to creating an enormous policy factory on Capitol Hill. Coincident with this development was the start of an era of presidents, who, for several reasons, were less likely to propose extensive new programs or were forced by the sheer magnitude of administering the Great Society to offer proposals that were more consolidative than innovative.

These developments—a more policy-active Congress, a less policy-active president—would seem to invite even more contextual analysis of lawmaking to account for the characteristics identified above. Yet many contemporary studies rely on roll call votes as a basis for gauging presidential-congressional interaction.[17] Roll call results surely afford a tempting test of presidential success in legislating. And, indeed, they would be a most convenient and meaningful measure if presidents submitted proposals to be voted up or down in a one-house legislature. Such conditions would satisfy the avid sports fans among political analysts who like to have winners and losers in the game of politics. Alas, the Founders were not engaged in preparing an eighteenth century version of contemporary sports contests.

Presidential Support Scores

Congressional Quarterly publishes a presidential support score that is supposed to make it easy to keep track of how well presidents have worked with Congress. When the score is announced each year, it typically gets considerable press attention, including comparisons with other presidents. The fact is, however, that the scores must be used cautiously in research. They are based on roll call votes on matters on which the president has taken a position. *Congressional Quarterly* itself issues caveats advising that the scores "must be interpreted with care." It notes, for example, that the scores do not account for "matters approved by voice vote or that are killed or bottled up in committee"; the administration sometimes does not take a position on an important issue; equal weight is given to all issues and to all votes (that is, whether narrow or by a wide margin); and a proliferation of votes on a single issue can skew the composite score for a president.[18]

Many scholars perceive other dangers in relying too heavily on these scores.[19] The judgment about the president's position may not always square with how those in the White House see a particular vote. The president's position may shift along the way (*Congressional Quarterly* uses the position at the time of the vote). The number of noncontroversial votes that are included in calculating the scores varies across presidents (between 12 and 51 percent, according to Bond and Fleisher).[20]

Additional concerns about using these scores arise when one reviews the votes that are included in any one year. The votes included for the House and Senate are not the same, thus reducing the potential for comparison between the two houses. The amendments being voted on are seldom the same in each chamber, and the bills subject to conference are, perforce, different. Sometimes the actual votes that are the basis for the scores are heavily skewed to a few issues. For example, in 1989 eleven of fourteen of President Bush's victories and eight of his eleven defeats on domestic policy came on two bills. Also in 1989, twenty-one of Bush's total of seventy-four victories on Senate roll call votes were on nominations, which typically come in a large group in the first year of an administration. Had nominations not been included (he suffered one defeat), his Senate support score would have dropped by 6 percent.

Examination of specific pieces of legislation and how the votes were scored also raises questions about the utility of the scores for interpreting a president's success in getting what he wants from Congress. Consider the Civil Rights Act of 1957. Six Senate and four House votes were selected for purposes of determining presidential support. Four of the Senate votes were counted as victories for the president: rejection of two amendments and adoption of two motions (one was to adopt the House version of the bill). Two of the Senate votes, both on amendments, were counted as defeats for the president. The four House votes were counted as presidential victories: the rejection of a motion to recommit and the rule, initial passage, and subsequent approval of a modified bill. So this was a case of eight victories for the president out of the ten roll call votes, a highly respectable batting percentage. Yet Eisenhower signed the bill without comment, and the *New York Times* reported that his silence "reflected in part his dissatisfaction with the drastic revision of the Administration measure as it passed through the Senate."[21] There was, in fact, substantial question as to the strength of the president's commitment in this area.[22]

President Carter's experience with his proposed Department of Education offers another interesting example of the potential distortion in analysis based on presidential support scores. Carter was credited by *Congressional Quarterly* with seventeen victories and two defeats on this measure for purposes of calculating his 1979 score. The wins were the most for a president on any of the twenty-eight bills included here, and they constituted 7 percent of Carter's total roll call victories in 1979. Yet the legislative history of this proposal suggests anything but sure-handed presidential control. In fact, the debate was almost comical at times, especially in the House, where twelve of the seventeen victories were registered (see chapter 7 for details).

Study of the substance of decisions and the process of lawmaking raises questions about these scores as indicators of presidential preference and achievement even in the final stages of action on legislation. Their creation is driven by a faulty premise regarding the operation of the political system—

that it should be tested by the extent to which Congress approves of an identifiable White House program. Even if this premise were correct, the support scores fail for the reasons listed above. But the premise itself is wrong, and therefore so is the test. As discussed, U.S. lawmaking is, by design and practice, iterative and sequential. The president plays a role in this process, but so, equally, does each house of the Congress. How all of that works at any one time depends heavily on political and policy factors.

Other Indicators

Scholars have sought to overcome the problems inherent in the presidential support scores and other indexes. Edwards offers four indexes of presidential support for the House and Senate for 1953–86, from "the comprehensive to the very selective."[23] He provides scores for both the House and Senate in each case. Overall support includes all the votes on which the president has taken a stand (as determined by *Congressional Quarterly*). Nonunanimous support includes the votes on which the president has taken a stand and the winning side numbers less than 80 percent of those who voted. Single-vote support includes only the most important nonunanimous vote on each bill, thus avoiding the problem of distortion caused by many votes on amendments to a bill. And key votes include those on which the president has taken a stand among those selected by *Congressional Quarterly* as being of particular importance. This produces a small number of votes for each Congress.

Each of the four measures permits the calculation of a score for the members of Congress as well as for the House and Senate. There are differences among the indexes, to be sure, but overall one is struck more by the similarities than the differences, most notably the similarities between the indexes of nonunanimous and single-vote support. Edwards concludes that "including more than one vote per issue in an index of presidential support has little impact on the index."[24]

However one develops and uses indexes of support, it is vitally important to recall precisely what the data represent: aggregated individual decisions on an unsystematic sample of the questions dealt with in the lawmaking process. To avoid the problems with scores, Bond and Fleisher simply rely on the roll call votes that are the bases for the presidential support scores. They then make distinctions between conflictual and nonconflictual votes and between important and less important issues.[25] These refinements enable them to offer a more reliable test of presidential "success." Peterson draws a sample from *Congressional Quarterly*'s list of important issues (updating their list to include the Carter and Reagan administrations) and specifies a wide range of explanatory variables for how Congress responded to presidential initiatives. His approach, the least presidency-centered of the empirical studies of Congress, eschews a search for "success" in favor of several potential outcomes: inaction, opposition dominance, compromise, presidential dominance, and consensus. As I do here, Peterson accepts that "the president's role in legislative policy making, and the response to the executive's initiatives, depend on the type of policy under consideration, because the structural implications of the tandem-institutions setting differs across policy domains."[26]

It is interesting and relevant that those who rely on floor voting in the House and Senate typically conclude their analysis by challenging the conventional wisdom about presidential command of Congress. For example, Edwards concludes that even those presidents who appeared to dominate "were actually facilitators rather than directors of change." And Bond and Fleisher attribute doing well on Capitol Hill more to "Congress-centered" than to "presidency-centered" variables. The implications are clear. As Edwards explains: "By examining the parameters of presidential leadership and not assuming that presidents will succeed in influencing Congress if they are just skillful enough in employing their resources, one is better positioned to understand the consequences of leadership efforts."[27]

However they are interpreted, roll call votes cannot be more than they are: one form of floor action on legislation. If analysts insist on scoring the president, concentrating on this stage of lawmaking can provide no more than a partial tally. But I want to raise questions about focusing on "presidential success" to the exclusion of other important topics associated with how the government makes law. An emphasis on scoring in this way contributes to a presidency-centered appraisal that prevents analysts from accounting for how the system works under the variable conditions permitted by the Constitution.

Legislative Production: What Gets Done and When

A concept of presidential success that is questionable and limited under unified party conditions is bound to be even more so when the two parties settle in at each end of Pennsylvania Avenue. If one believes that the system can only work well when one party is in control of the White House and Congress, then divided control is a serious problem. Woodrow Wilson be-

lieved that "You cannot compound a successful government out of antago-
nisms."[28] James L. Sundquist agrees, concluding that presidents and Congresses of opposite parties will produce stalemate.[29] James MacGregor Burns
has long believed that "the majority party should be the perfect instrument
for carrying out a popular mandate." In 1990, when various Eastern European regimes were collapsing, he updated his distress that the American
political system was not working correctly. Burns advised these regimes to
pay little heed to the American political system: "Our system of checks and
balances, with the resulting fragmentation of power, frustrates leadership,
saps efficiency, and erodes responsibility. . . . The governing party is failing
to govern and the opposition party is failing to oppose. . . . We can, para-
doxically, learn from [Eastern Europe]."[30]

In reading such analyses one would think that the system had ground to
a halt: the "deadlock of democracy," as Burns once described it, the end of
politics by other accounts.[31] Yet presidents continue to make proposals and
Congress still legislates, even when voters return divided government to
Washington. In fact, studies of the volume of lawmaking show very little
difference between the two arrangements.

The Mayhew Study

It is precisely this matter of whether the system passes important laws that
is of interest to David R. Mayhew. He looked at the period from 1946 to 1990
to find out how many and when such laws were passed. Mayhew acknowledges the importance of ideological differences that may be associated with
the parties and their control of one or both branches. "But the basic concern
in this work, as regards lawmaking, is not with direction but with motion—
whether much gets done at all."[32]

In addition to the usual concerns about relying on presidential support
scores, Mayhew asks, "Why should we care whether presidents got what they
wanted?" He doubts that is "the appropriate question." He understands that
not all laws are a part of a president's program, and, indeed, some are exactly
contrary to what the White House wants to have done. "But laws are laws.
System production should be the final test, not whether presidents happened
to get what they wanted."[33] That is exactly the perspective I am promoting
here. Presidents are a part of a government, and so is Congress. Both have
the right to participate in lawmaking, and both do. As stressed earlier, concentration on *presidential* success treats only one participant in the system.
The ultimate test is the success of that system in treating public problems. A

president whose proposals score well in roll call voting may find that the programs do little to solve problems. Conversely, presidential proposals substantially changed by Congress may do the job. In this case the president's lack of success in the short run may result later in a respectable record for his administration, if presidents are to be scored by what happens during their terms in office, not merely by whether they win roll call votes.

Mayhew understands that he cannot begin to answer his central question without establishing criteria for important legislation. In a meticulous accounting, he "sweeps" twice through the period. First he relied on contemporary judgments, mostly those by journalists doing an end-of-the-year wrap-up story on Congress. Next he relied on retrospective judgments of policy specialists in forty-three policy areas. He used the second sweep to validate choices from the first sweep and also to identify further important acts. In the end, he identified 267 important enactments.[34]

There are two problems with Mayhew's technique for my purposes. First, it cannot easily account for preventing the passage of a law as a form of system production. Some presidents do not want a law enacted and will count it among their achievements if they stop it. They may even hope that failure to act at the national level will result in private action or legislation at the state or local level. Second, there is a natural tendency to treat all important legislation as equal when in fact there are tremendous differences in impact among the 267 enactments included in Mayhew's list. He would be the first to acknowledge this point, yet he does not weight the laws in drawing conclusions about the differences between single- and split-party government, and I will not do so in reviewing specific pieces of legislation in chapter 7. However, aggregating these enactments as though they were all equal is misleading in calculating legislative production

Laws and Mandates

Having issued these caveats, and confessing an inability to correct for them apart from the narrative discussion to follow, I turn now to a highly aggregative exercise. First I categorize Mayhew's list of important enactments, as he does, by president and by whether the government or Congress was single- or split-party (table 6-2). The years and circumstances of greatest production are clear. Under unified control the range of enactments is from six during the last two years of the Truman administration to twenty-two during the first two years of Johnson's full term. For divided control, the range is from five during the last two years of the Eisenhower administration

Table 6-2. *Major Legislation Passed, by Type of Presidential Mandate and Party Control, 1946–91*

Type of mandate and president[a]	Number of enactments	Party control
Change		
Eisenhower (1953–55)	9	Single
Johnson (1965–67)	22	Single
Reagan (1981–83)	9	Split/Democratic House
Total	40	
Annual mean	6.7	
Status quo		
Eisenhower (1957–59)	11	Split/Democratic Congress
Nixon-Ford (1973–75)	22	Split/Democratic Congress
Reagan (1985–87)	9	Split/Democratic House
Total	42	
Annual mean	7.0	
Mixed (presidential year)		
Truman (1949–51)	12	Single
Kennedy (1961–63)	15	Single
Nixon (1969–71)	22	Split/Democratic Congress
Carter (1977–79)	12	Single
Bush (1989–91)	9	Split/Democratic Congress
Total	71	
Annual mean	7.1	
Mixed (midterm)		
Truman (1951–53)	6	Single
Eisenhower (1955–57)	6	Split/Democratic Congress
Kennedy-Johnson (1963–65)	13	Single
Johnson (1967–69)	16	Single
Nixon (1971–73)	15	Split/Democratic Congress
Carter (1979–81)	10	Single
Reagan (1983–85)	7	Split/Democratic House
Total	73	
Annual mean	5.2	
Unmandate		
Truman (1947–48)	10	Split/Republican Congress
Eisenhower (1959–61)	5	Split/Democratic Congress
Ford (1975–77)	14	Split/Democratic Congress
Reagan (1987–89)	12	Split/Democratic Congress
Total	41	
Annual mean	5.1	

Source: Developed from list in David R. Mayhew, *Divided We Govern: Party Control, Lawmaking, and Investigations, 1946–1990* (Yale University Press, 1991), pp. 52–73.

a. See chapter 4 for explanation of mandate types.

to twenty-two during two Congresses under Nixon (91st and 93d). As Mayhew emphasizes, by this gross measure there is very little difference in production of important legislation between single- and split-party control. If split-party control is divided into two groups—that in which both houses of Congress have opposition party majorities and that in which just the House is controlled by the opposition party—the Reagan years show a substantially lower annual production when only one house was under Democratic control (1981–87) and an increase when both houses were won by the Democrats.

Mayhew draws attention to the "bulges in the middle" of the forty-four-year period.[35] The sixteen years from the beginning of the Kennedy administration to the end of the Nixon-Ford administrations (36 percent of the period) produced 52 percent of the important enactments. A review of the laws themselves suggests an agenda explanation like that presented in chapter 5: significant expansion during the 1960s, followed by various consolidative and regulatory actions during the 1970s.

I now add to Mayhew's findings a categorization of presidents by the interpretation of their mandates (see table 6-2). The first category—that of the perceived mandate for change—illustrates the problems of ideological direction that are raised but not managed as such by Mayhew. Over half the important enactments were a product of the first two years of Johnson's full term. This was the core of the Great Society. By comparison, Eisenhower hardly had a program. As for Reagan, to count either the Economic Recovery Tax Act or the Omnibus Budget Reconciliation Act (both passed in 1981) as one enactment clearly shows the need for a weighting system.[36] These two enactments had virtually as much effect on the subsequent agenda as did the twenty-two enactments of the 89th Congress. In Mayhew's defense, however, such weighting would only lend further support to his overall conclusion regarding the lack of independent effect of unified or divided party control.

The perceived mandate for the status quo is restricted to the reelected presidents: Eisenhower, Nixon, and Reagan. In each case the voters returned the whole government, which meant a party split (except in 1984, when the Republicans retained their Senate majority). Again the range within this group is considerable, from nine for Reagan to twenty-two for Nixon-Ford. The Nixon-Ford period is particularly fascinating to ponder since it surely violates every conceivable condition for responsible party government. A Republican president won reelection by one of the widest margins in history, but voters returned a Democratic Congress. The president was then severely handicapped by the resignation of his vice president, by the Watergate scandal that led to resignations and indictments of many in his government, and finally by his own resignation. And yet through it all a sizable number of important laws were enacted. Major legislative initiatives that were under way during this period were successful in spite of the media and public preoccupation with what was interpreted as a constitutional crisis. How could that be? Possibly because the president is not the whole government, nor was he ever intended to be so. The political system was intentionally designed to weather such predicaments.

The third category, a mixed mandate, is the largest. It includes the cases following a presidential election that produced incongruous results—for Congress in one direction and the president in another, or less in the same direction—thus causing problems for the mandate readers. Also included are cases following midterm elections in which a declared mandate is more muted (1954, 1966, 1982) or a previously mixed result is confirmed (1950, 1962, 1970, 1978). Together, the annual mean production does not vary greatly from the other categories.

Differences do emerge when the two types are separated. The first-term mixed-mandate presidents—Truman, Kennedy, Nixon, Carter, and Bush—have the highest annual average production of any group. Two of them, Nixon and Bush, faced split-party government. Perhaps lack of clarity in the policy messages of an election is a good thing for the passage of major legislation. If so, there is not much solace in that finding for party government advocates. The second group, those following midterm elections, has a significantly lower annual mean production, perhaps because in some cases the first two years were quite productive.

The "unmandate" refers to those conditions when analysts declared governing capabilities to be seriously jeopardized. Three of the four cases come at the second midterm election of an eight-year administration when Republicans suffered major losses: 1958 for Eisenhower; 1974 for Ford, who was completing the second Nixon administration; and 1986 for Reagan, whose party lost its majority in the Senate. The only other case included is that of Truman after the 1946 election, when Republicans won control of both branches for the first time since 1930. These were not highly productive Congresses, and yet not even under these dire political circumstances did the system cease operating. In fact, contrary to what most analysts would predict, major legislation was enacted during such periods: the Taft-Hartley Act and Marshall Plan during the 80th Congress (1947–48); the Landrum-Griffin Labor Reform Act and a civil rights act during the 86th Congress (1959–60); energy and environmental laws and a tax reform act during the 94th Congress (1975–76); and welfare, medicare, and trade reform in the 100th Congress (1987–88).

Mayhew also asked this relevant question: Do important laws enacted during unified control pass by large margins while those enacted during divided control pass by small margins? The answer is that most laws drew either bipartisan or cross-partisan support; more were passed with majorities of two-thirds or more during split-party control than during single-party control. This outcome is actually what Mayhew expected, because under divided government "wider assent is needed to permit action."[37] But, of course, his thinking runs counter to that of the party government advocates who predict stalemate. Mayhew also found cross-partisan politics in two directions: southern Democrats joined Republicans (the conservative coalition) and moderate Republicans joined northern Democrats (most often on civil rights legislation).

Two points need reiterating. First, neither Mayhew in his work, nor I in my use of it, is suggesting that it makes no difference who is in control of which parts of the national government. The product of Lyndon Johnson's Great Society is very different from that of the great consolidation of the Nixon period and the great deficit of the Reagan period. To show that there are no substantial differences between single- and split-party governments in the quantity of important enactments is not to say that the laws themselves do not differ in substance, kind, and direction. But the system does move under both types of governments, and it appears to move rationally toward an expanded role under some circumstances and toward consolidation, even contraction, under other circumstances. Critics may not like the policy decisions that are made at any one time or under a particular set of circumstances (such as a Republican president and a Democratic Congress), but such concerns differ from conclusions that the system is deadlocked and cannot act.

Second, nothing in this discussion is meant to suggest that the president is an unimportant player in national policymaking and politics. My search is for the variable role that a president plays in a system of separated institutions competing for shared powers. The presumed goal of that competition is the resolution of problems on the government agenda, which has a dynamic all its own.

Legislative Timelines

Chamberlain stresses that study of legislation reveals that "new" proposals typically have been "discussed more or less continuously in Congress for several years." John W. Kingdon describes a continuous process of policy initiation, testing, and change, often involving a "recombination of already-

familiar elements." Richard E. Neustadt acknowledges that "everything remains unfinished business." Former senator (and White House chief of staff)
Howard Baker, Republican of Tennessee, observed that "issues are like
snakes—they just refuse to die! They keep coming back, time after time."
Richard Rose refers to the president as a "policy taster." "When a President
goes [to] Washington, he does not have to bring a new set of policy proposals
with him. There are lots of ideas circulating in executive agencies and Congress. . . . From the viewpoint of a President who is a professional cam-
paigner and an amateur in government, it is just as well that a pile of ideas
awaits him."[38] Serious students of national policymaking concede that what
has gone on before helps immeasurably in explaining what will happen next.

A related notion is that of the "idea whose time has come."[39] It was the
explanation given by Republican Senator Everett M. Dirksen of Illinois for
the passage of the Civil Rights Act of 1964. When told that Republican
Senator Barry M. Goldwater of Arizona, the odds-on favorite in 1964 to run
against President Johnson, refused to support the bill, Dirksen reportedly
told Goldwater: "You just can't do it [vote against the bill], not only for
yourself, but you can't do it for the party. The idea has come!"[40]

One former House member identified a policy cycle for major issues that
is independent of the electoral cycle.

> The issue governs. . . . Some things have a shelf-life in Congress and they
> don't have to fit the quadrennial patterns of elections. Clean air was one
> of those. After we'd screwed around with it long enough, it was going to
> come due. Trade Act of 1988. [After] four years [it] eventually came to a
> point where it suddenly came to life and it was an important policy piece.[41]

Yet there are calendar markings derived from the Constitution that encourage categorizing policy by presidential administration, legislative session, or Congress. Those are, indeed, useful dividing points. But they should
not deter scholars from inquiring into policy lineages, particularly for the
purpose of better understanding how institutions cope with public issues. In
other words, the convenience of, say, a presidential term should not mislead
anyone about how a particular legislative initiative fits into its policy context
or when an issue may suddenly come to life.

Most of the current studies of presidential-congressional interaction raise
serious questions about the extent to which the president controls the agenda
and manages Congress. The White House is not a bad place to start in
identifying the agenda, to be sure, but one must move on. Nor, as Mayhew
has shown, can one rely solely on single-party government to produce policy
results.

All of this is by way of justifying the next exercise, which is itself a prelude to more detailed treatment of selected laws in the post–World War II period. In understanding how a president does his job, how he tries to find his place in government, it is useful to consider the policy setting within which his actions and preferences have force and meaning. He must judge how to fit himself and his policy preferences into ongoing institutional, political, and policy processes. I will concentrate here on the latter, drawing specific attention to timelines for the enactment of legislation.

I selected twenty-eight laws from Mayhew's list to illustrate variation in issues and represent the nine presidencies of the period. Like Richard F. Fenno, Jr., in choosing his cases for *Home Style*, I did not know which laws would best serve my goals since I was not fully certain what I was looking for. Like Fenno, I did not know the answers in advance, nor was I very clear about the questions.[42] But I knew why I wanted to study laws. I was dissatisfied with my own understanding of the variable role of the president in lawmaking under different types of party control and under varying partisan conditions as discussed in chapter 1. The number of laws I selected for each administration is not in proportion to the years involved. I was more intent on choosing cases that reflected those judged to be the achievements of the time and those normally associated with a particular president. Many policy issues are included: labor, foreign policy and trade, health and welfare, education, taxation and budgeting, transportation and energy, environment, civil rights, regulation, and crime. Defense and agriculture are, perhaps, the principal omissions (although the War Powers Resolution was as much about defense as foreign policy and the Food Stamp Act, when passed, was as much a farm surplus as welfare program).

The first exercise in regard to these bills was to establish a timeline for each (see figure 6-1). Was it a new idea? Was it an extension of a basic law passed earlier? Was there an immediate precursor? Did the legislative history carry over from one administration to the next? The overwhelming conclusion is that most of these enactments were part of a continuing legislative story within an issue area. There are two clear cases of legislation without obvious precursors in either a previously enacted basic law or efforts that trace to previous administrations. The Marshall Plan and the War Powers Resolution of 1973 were developed within the Truman and Nixon administrations, respectively. The first was a proposal of the administration, originating within the Department of State with the approval of the president. The second was a proposal originating in Congress and vehemently opposed by the president, who vetoed the resolution when it reached his desk.

Figure 6-1. *Legislative Timelines, Twenty-eight Selected Enactments, 1947–90*

Truman (1945–53)
Taft-Hartley (T-H)
Marshall Plan (MP)
National Housing Act (NHA)
Excess Profits Tax (EPT)

Tenure

Labor Act → Bill → T-H (1947)
Truman Doctrine → MP (1948)
Housing Act → Bills → Act → NHA (1949)
Revenue Act → Act → EPT (1950)

Eisenhower (1953–61)
Atomic Energy Act (AEA)
Highway Act (HA)
Civil Rights Act (CRA)
Landrum-Griffin Act (LGA)

Tenure

Atomic Energy Act → Hngs → AEA (1954)
Highway Act → Amdts → Proposal → HA (1956)
Proposal → Proposal → CRA (1957)
Labor Act → T-H → Bill → LGA (1959)

Kennedy (1961–63)
Manpower Dev. & Tng. Act (MDTA)
Revenue Act (RA)
Clean Air Act (CAA)

Tenure

Voc. Ed. Act → Amdts → NDEA → Amdts → MDTA (1962)
Revenue Acts → Int. Rev. Code → RA (1962)
Air Pollution Act → Amdt → Amdt → CAA (1963)

Johnson (1963–69)
Food Stamps (FS)
ESEA
Medicare (MD)

Tenure

AAA → Amdts → Food Stamps → Bills → Pilot → FS (1964)
Lanham Act → NDEA → Bills → ESEA (1965)
SSA → Proposals → Bills → Kerr-Mills → Bills → MD (1965)

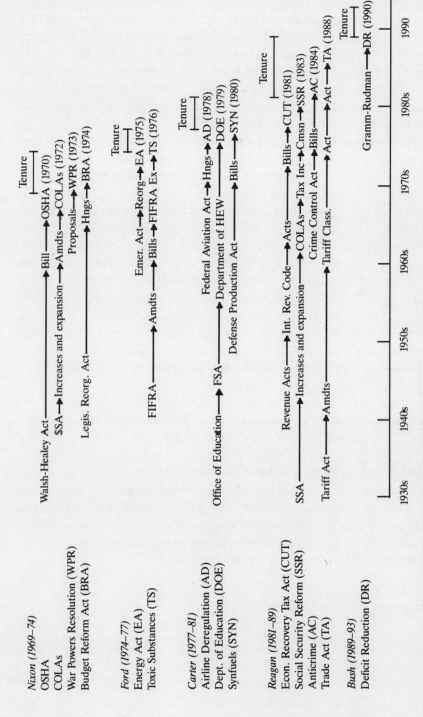

Source: Developed from information on legislation in *Congressional Quarterly Almanac*, various vols.; and Congressional Quarterly, *Congress and the Nation*, various vols.

The Budget and Impoundment Control Act of 1974 is somewhat of a special case inasmuch as it proposed substantially new reforms. The Legislative Reorganization Act of 1946 provided for a legislative budget, but the experiment did not work. It could hardly be considered a precursor to the 1974 act. This was a reorganizational effort conceived on Capitol Hill as a response to congressional inadequacies and fear of presidential usurpation of a fundamental legislative power.

There are five other cases of a relatively short-term legislative heritage, even though they carry through from one administration to the next. The Energy Policy and Conservation Act of 1975 and the Toxic Substances Control Act of 1976 had relatively short histories (although in the latter case the legislative history bears some relation to the Federal Insecticide, Fungicide, and Rodenticide Act of 1947). Had it not been for Watergate, action on both bills presumably would have been completed in the Nixon administration. That both were passed following Watergate is itself evidence of the continuity of the legislative process in the face of an institutional crisis. Airline deregulation in 1978 and the synthetic fuels program of 1980 also had relatively short legislative histories, carrying over as proposals from the Ford administration to Carter—from a split- to a single-party government. The one Bush administration case also had a relatively short lineage, directly traceable to the congressionally initiated Gramm-Rudman-Hollings deficit control efforts during the second Reagan administration.

As for the rest, each had a substantial legislative heritage, traceable to a basic law and typically exhibiting a short-term history of the immediate bill. Battle lines are already drawn on most important pieces of legislation: committee and subcommittee members and staff are familiar with the issue, other members have participated in previous debates, agency personnel know the administrative and legislative history, and interest group representatives are knowledgeable about who did what and who voted how. The problem then for the president and his advisers is to find a place in this network in order to obtain favorable action: enacting their proposals, modifying the proposals of others, or killing a bill they oppose.

Summary

This chapter has moved from the organizational, public, and agenda contexts discussed in earlier chapters into the direct workings with Congress. A review of the basic characteristics of lawmaking showed the complexity of decision points beyond roll call voting. Scholars need to look beyond roll call votes and simple measures of success to other points in the legislative process where presidents interact with members of Congress.

Some scholars judge that split-party government produces stalemate or, worse, bad decisions. Mayhew has shown that "it does not seem to make all that much difference whether party control of the American government happens to be unified or divided."[43] Mayhew's study takes one a step further from presidency-centered analysis than do those of roll call voting. The message is: understanding the production of laws requires analysis of lawmaking. The system is now, and always has been, one of "separated institutions sharing powers" as Neustadt puts it.[44] In a lengthy period of split-party government, Neustadt's formulation might better be cast as "separated institutions competing for shares of power."[45] Either way, efforts to comprehend presidential power in public policy require study of congressional power (and vice versa).

I identify the legislative lineage of selected enactments in the postwar period to confirm the continuous nature of lawmaking. This exercise moves the analysis from abstract formulations of presidential-congressional interaction to the concrete setting that awaits a president or member of Congress who wants to make change, and it introduces a set of important enactments that will serve as the basis for an in-depth examination of the iterative, sequential, and partisan differences in the lawmaking process of a representative legislature.

CHAPTER SEVEN

Making Laws

CLEARLY ONE can only go so far in equating one piece of legislation with the next. It is important to look at the actual variations in legislative action on specific laws. I have developed legislative histories for each of the twenty-eight laws chosen from Mayhew's longer list of important enactments in the postwar era. I gathered information on each stage of the lawmaking process and, where available, reactions by the press, elected officials, and other relevant actors to each stage. This legislative history allowed me to identify the lawmaking sequence, extent of iteration, and nature of partisan interaction for each of the principal steps in the process. I then sorted the twenty-eight laws into four categories, very close to those relied on by Lawrence H. Chamberlain: preponderant presidential influence in enacting a bill into law, preponderant congressional influence, or joint presidential-congressional influence.[1] I use these categories with one alteration: in joint influence, I distinguish between cases in which the president is particularly active and those that represent more of a true balance between the branches.

I do not have a direct measure of influence as such. Rather, I rely on the apparent involvement and activity of each branch on the specific pieces of legislation. I am less interested in influence than in identifying presidential and congressional participation at different action points in the lawmaking process. One major purpose is to direct attention to the developmental nature of lawmaking so as to better place the president in his relationship to Congress.

In some cases it was difficult to estimate which institution was preponderant, even after several reviews of the legislative history. That is not unexpected in a system of separated institutions competing for shared power. Both Congress and the president have a legitimate right to participate actively at any number of decision points. It is unreasonable to expect that such a system will be tightly managed and controlled at either end of Pennsylvania Avenue, especially under conditions of split-party government. The purpose in making the choices is not to offer a definitive decision but rather to provide a convenient means for identifying patterns and discussing the legislation. I want to clarify the challenge facing the president in leading Congress and adjusting to a moving process of legislative decisionmaking.

In my sample, the number of cases of presidential preponderance is less than the number of congressional preponderance, and those two combined are less than the cases of institutional balance (see table 7-1).[2] Here is confirmation that presidency-centered analysis of lawmaking is misleading if it conveys the impression of presidential dominance, either as an empirical fact or as a normative conclusion growing out of the principles upon which the system is built.

As noted in chapter 6, 152 of Mayhew's 267 bills became law when the two parties each controlled one branch. As expected, my sample reflects Mayhew's findings: 16 of the 28 laws were enacted during periods of split control. I also show in table 7-1 the sequence of decisionmaking for each enactment. As expected, most of the proposals emanated from the president. But a surprising number came from other sources: the House or Senate, a congressional directive, a joint committee, or a commission. Further, in several cases when the president initiated a proposal, members of Congress may have been preparing an alternative at the same time (for example, the Taft-Hartley labor-management relations legislation) or the president may have borrowed substantially from a proposal emanating from the Hill (such as the Reagan tax package in 1981 and the Kemp-Roth tax proposals offered earlier). The lawmaking sequences vary substantially: measures moved from the Senate to the House to conference in ten instances; from the House to the Senate to conference in six instances; and other sequences in twelve instances. Most, but not all, important bills go to a conference between the two houses. Three did not in this sample, and one (the anticrime package of 1984) went to an appropriations conference rather than a conference between the two Judiciary committees.

For each piece of legislation I made a number of judgments about the degree of iteration, partisan interaction, sequence of lawmaking, closeness of the final enactment to earlier versions, and number of presidential victories and losses as measured by *Congressional Quarterly*. The details are shown in the appendix to this chapter. The exercise of rating bills by degree of iteration and nature of partisanship was repeated several times to increase the likelihood that the same criteria were used throughout. The process is

Table 7-1. *Institutional Interactions, Party Control, and Sequence for Twenty-eight Selected Enactments, 1947–90*

Legislation and institutional interaction	Congress	President	Party control	Lawmaking sequence[a]
President preponderant				
European Recovery Act (1948)	80th	Truman	Split	Pres.→Sen.→House→Conf.
Federal Aid Highway Act (1956)	84th	Eisenhower	Split	Pres.→House→Sen.→Conf.
Airline Deregulation (1978)	95th	Carter	Single	Pres.→Sen.→House→Conf.
Food Stamp Act (1964)	88th	Johnson	Single	Pres.→House→Sen.→House
Elementary and Secondary Education Act (1965)	89th	Johnson	Single	Pres.→House→Sen.
Economic Recovery Tax Act (1981)	97th	Reagan	Split	Pres.→Sen.→House→Conf.
Congress preponderant				
Labor-Management Relations Act (1947)	80th	Truman	Split	Pres.→House→Sen.→Conf.→Veto→Override
Labor Reform Act (1959)	86th	Eisenhower	Split	Pres.→Sen.→House→Conf.
Social Security Benefit Increases (1972)	92d	Nixon	Split	Pres.→Sen.→Conf.→House
Toxic Substances Control Act (1976)	94th	Ford	Split	Sen.→House→Conf.
Omnibus Trade Act (1988)	100th	Reagan	Split	Congress→House→Sen.→Conf.→Veto→House→Sen.

War Powers Resolution (1973)	93d	Nixon	Split	Sen.→House→Sen.→Conf.→Veto→Override
Budget and Impoundment Control Act (1974)	93d	Nixon	Split	Joint comm.→House→Sen.→Conf.
Balance with president active				
Medicare (1965)	89th	Johnson	Single	Pres.→House→Sen.→Conf.
Department of Education (1979)	96th	Carter	Single	Pres.→Sen.→House→Conf.
Synthetic Fuels (1980)	96th	Carter	Single	House→Pres.→Sen.→Conf.
Energy Act (1975)	94th	Ford	Split	Pres.→Sen.→House→Conf.→House→Sen.
Anticrime Package (1984)	98th	Reagan	Split	Pres.→Sen.→House→Conf.
True balance				
National Housing Act (1949)	81st	Truman	Single	Pres.→Sen.→House→Conf.
Excess Profits Tax (1950)	81st	Truman	Single	Congress→House→Sen.→Conf.
Civil Rights Act (1957)	85th	Eisenhower	Split	Pres.→House→Sen.→Neg.→House→Sen.
Revenue Act (1962)	88th	Kennedy	Single	Pres.→House→Sen.→Conf.
Atomic Energy Act (1954)	83d	Eisenhower	Single	Pres.→Joint comm.→House→Sen.→Conf.→Conf.
Manpower Development (1962)	88th	Kennedy	Single	Pres.→Sen.→House→Conf.
Clean Air Act (1963)	89th	Kennedy	Single	Pres.→House→Sen.→Conf.
Occupational Safety and Health Act (1970)	91st	Nixon	Split	Pres.→Sen.→House→Conf.
Social Security Reform (1983)	98th	Reagan	Split	Cmsn.→Pres.→House→Sen.→Conf.
Deficit Reduction (1990)	101st	Bush	Split	Pres.→House→Sen.→Conf.→Neg.→House→Neg.→House→Sen.

a. Pres. = president; Sen. = Senate; Conf. = conference; Joint comm. = Joint committee; Cmsn. = commission; Neg. = negotiation outside conference.

qualitative and judgmental, to be sure. Given the nature of the search, however, it proved difficult to devise shortcuts. No doubt someone else engaging in the same exercise would produce somewhat different results, and thus the advantages of replication are surely reduced. On the other hand, anyone making these judgments would also find variations in iteration and partisanship, even if not exactly those I offer. And it is these differences in sequence, iteration, and partisan interaction that encourage one to search for an alterative perspective for understanding and explaining national policy politics.

Presidential Preponderance

The six cases discussed here reveal several conditions for presidential preponderance in lawmaking. The first set exemplifies those occasions when an issue is accepted as sufficiently vital to require bipartisan support for an administration plan. The European Recovery Act of 1948 and the Federal Aid Highway Act of 1956 are striking examples. When that occurs, congressional support follows. Neither Congress nor the opposition party forgoes its prerogatives, but all sides have reasons to work with the administration. Under these conditions, split-party government does not appear to be a major roadblock. Airline deregulation in 1978 was less momentous, perhaps, but it also attracted substantial support from both parties.

In my second set are examples of the fascinating cases when presidents are said to be entrusted with a mandate and therefore normal presidential-congressional politics is suspended. These circumstances presumably lead to the kinds of policy breakthroughs so prized by those devoted to the party responsibility perspective.

Bipartisan Support

The first two entries in the first set show similar characteristics occurring for very different issues. In both cases, presidential or executive influence was significant despite split-party government, and a consensus developed in favor of the proposal. Congress made moderate changes in both cases. There was bipartisan support at crucial times for both proposals. Airline deregulation had broad support but did not have the smooth sailing experienced by the other bills even though it was enacted under single-party government.

EUROPEAN RECOVERY. The Marshall Plan is a prime example of the benefits of bipartisanship in foreign policy, stimulated by a White House initiative. Secretary of State George Marshall visited Moscow in April 1947 and returned to Washington "gravely worried and upset" that the leaders of the Soviet Union "were quite content to see uncertainty and chaos prevail in Europe." Marshall instructed George Kennan to prepare a report that could serve as a basis for establishing policy. Meanwhile, President Truman asked Under Secretary of State Dean Acheson to fill in for him in giving a speech at a small college in Mississippi. Acheson used the occasion to stress the importance of rebuilding Europe. "The speech ⸙ . . . was the alarm bell that Truman wanted sounded."[3]

Kennan's report, issued in late May 1947, provided the basis for developing a recovery plan. When Marshall received an honorary degree at Harvard University in early June, he used the occasion, with Truman's approval, to announce the plan. Marshall emphasized that the Europeans themselves had to agree on a plan for recovery that would then receive support from the United States.

> It would be neither fitting nor efficacious for this government to undertake to draw up unilaterally a program designed to place Europe on its feet economically. . . . The initiative, I think, must come from Europe. The role of this country should consist of friendly aid in the drafting of a European program and of later support of such a program so far as it may be practical for us to do so. The program should be a joint one, agreed to by a number, if not all European nations.[4]

A positive response from Europe was immediate and a meeting took place in July 1947. The Soviet Union sent a delegation, then withdrew and refused to allow its satellite nations to participate (Czechoslovakia and Poland were particularly eager to be included). "By refusing to take part in the Marshall Plan, Stalin had virtually guaranteed its success. Sooner or later congressional support was bound to follow now, whatever the volume of grumbling on the Hill."[5]

A report to Marshall on September 22 triggered action by the White House and Congress. The situation in Europe was critical, particularly in France and Italy. The president called a special session of Congress on November 17, 1947, to provide for stop-gap aid until a long-range program could be put in place. On December 19, 1947, he then outlined a comprehensive plan and called on Congress to act quickly.

The president managed the politics carefully since the Republicans had majorities in both houses of Congress and hoped to recapture the White

House in 1948. Truman's strategy in the face of a split-party government was to make the plan Marshall's plan. "Although Truman's firm backing of the plan was never in doubt, . . . he subordinated his own role and emphasized that of the general. Because his domestic programs were unpopular and Marshall's prestige was high, this stance helped gain supporters for the plan."[6] Truman also relied on outside support from citizen committees, including business leaders, bankers, and foreign affairs specialists like Dean Acheson (now in private life). This was an early example of building outside support for an important foreign policy move, not unlike that by President Carter in his effort to get the Panama Canal treaties ratified in 1977 and 1978.[7]

Leading the bipartisan effort on the Republican side was Senator Arthur Vandenberg (Michigan). The president, in his memoirs, credited Vandenberg and his counterpart chairman in the House, Charles A. Eaton: "In a Congress dedicated to tax reduction and the pruning of governmental expenditures, they championed this program in a truly bi-partisan manner."[8] The issue for most members of Congress was not whether to support the proposal, but whether such a large aid program might harm the U.S. economy.

Committee and floor action was moderately iterative, with floor amendments adopted in each house. Members of Congress were interested in who would be aided, how much aid would be authorized, where the money would be spent, the duration of the program, the program as a potential curb against communism, and the loyalty of those administering the program. Bipartisanship characterized committee and floor action, thanks to the leadership of the committee chairmen. But there were holdouts on the floor and the final vote was cross-partisan in nature. Senate and House Republicans voted in favor of the plan by over 70 percent; Senate and House Democrats, by over 90 percent. Given the partisan balance in each house, neither party's support was sufficient itself to ensure victory; thus the vote in both houses met the conditions of classic cross partisanship. Passage of the Marshall Plan was a remarkable achievement under the circumstances: a Republican Congress anxious to win the White House working with a Democratic president eager to win a full term on his own, all occurring during an election year.

INTERSTATE HIGHWAYS. In 1956 an aid program of a very different nature was enacted into law. The Federal Aid Highway Act was correctly described by President Eisenhower as "the biggest peacetime construction project of any description ever undertaken by the United States or any other country."[9] A marvelously distributive program, it would bring money, roads, and jobs to every state in the nation. Following a report by a presidential advisory commission headed by General Lucius Clay, Eisenhower recommended enactment of the program in his 1956 State of the Union message. Like Truman, he faced a Congress controlled by the other party and it was, once again, a presidential election year. But here was a program bound to warm the political hearts of members of both parties in Congress.

The only important dispute between the White House and Congress was over the financing of the project. General Clay's group had recommended issuance of $20 billion in government bonds. Eisenhower preferred self-financing toll highways. Many members of Congress preferred paying for the system out of appropriations. In the end, the financing was through increased taxes on gasoline, diesel oil, tires, trucks, buses, and trailers.

The bill was considered by two committees in each chamber: the public works and taxing committees. Committee action was moderately iterative, mostly regarding the financing provisions and, as expected, the apportionment of funds among the states. Further changes were made on the Senate floor and only minor changes were made on the House floor. The bill had bipartisan support throughout the process. It passed by 388-19 in the House and by a voice vote in the Senate. *Congressional Quarterly* credited the president with two wins for this measure in his support score for 1956.

AIRLINE DEREGULATION. Airline deregulation was seemingly an idea whose time had come. President Ford was the "original champion of deregulation," but he was defeated in 1976. "Even members of the Civil Aeronautics Board, individuals who had authority over airline regulation, lobbied to decrease their board's power."[10] Given the widespread support for this step, the new Carter administration meant to score a "quick hit" by deregulating the airlines.[11]

Deregulating an entire industry was no small step: this was a reform with major economic implications, not to mention significant opportunities within the highly competitive airline industry. According to Martha Derthick and Paul J. Quirk, "reform advocacy" of this type has "to neutralize or overcome [the] potential sources of resistance inherent in a congressional perspective." They conclude that a combination of forces had exactly this effect. For example, one normally does not expect to get agreement, let alone unanimity, among economists on any major issue, and yet "deregulation was, in effect, a recommendation of the economics profession as such." Endorsements also came from government agencies, congressional support units (the General Accounting Office and Congressional Budget Office), and a coalition of interest groups. The result was that "widely shared interests and values converged in support of reform."[12] Other developments contributed to the momentum for change. President Carter appointed as chairman of the Civil Aeronautics Board Alfred Kahn, a Cornell University economist who favored deregulation. United Airlines broke with its competitors and supported deregulation. And the predictions of dire economic consequences were belied when CAB policies that encouraged competition before the passage of deregulation appeared to increase business.[13]

This momentum was naturally reflected in Congress. Early conflicts that delayed approval of Carter's proposals were resolved. The president did not get the "quick hit" he wanted, but he did get a bill that was close to what had been proposed. Much of the delay occurred in the House, where a member of the Aviation Subcommittee of the Committee on Public Works, Elliott Levitas from Carter's home state of Georgia, was successful in substituting a watered-down bill for Carter's plan. This action led to a lengthy and complex markup of the legislation. Meanwhile, the Senate passed a bill more to the president's liking, and the conference agreement favored the Senate version.

Iteration in Congress on this legislation was in the moderate range (perhaps higher in the House), with very few changes on the House and Senate floor. The fact that a piece of legislation develops the kind of momentum described above certainly does not preclude congressional involvement, particularly for a regulatory measure with widespread constituency effects. The final votes in favor of airline deregulation were overwhelming in both houses, suggesting bipartisanship. However, the pattern was more cross-partisan than bipartisan in the earlier crucial stages of preparing the legislation. *Congressional Quarterly* awarded Carter six victories and no defeats for this legislation.

Presidential Mandates

The other three pieces of legislation in this first group are the most representative products of mandated, classic responsible party government in the sample of twenty-eight. That is, they were passed relatively quickly during periods when it was widely perceived that the president had a mandate to act. In two cases there was not even a need for a conference. In the cases of food stamps and the Elementary and Secondary Education Act, Lyndon Johnson had first the self-designated responsibility of enacting Kennedy's uncompleted program and then the advantage of his own landslide victory, which was seemingly an endorsement of an activist domestic agenda. In the case of the Economic Recovery Tax Act of 1981, Ronald Reagan capitalized on what was widely interpreted as a mandate for altering the government's role in the economy.

FOOD STAMPS. The food stamp idea was not new in 1964. It was tried in 1939 for the same dual purposes identified later: distributing surplus food and improving the diets of the poor. Several problems with the program ended the experiment in 1943. Still, the idea was attractive to many in Congress, and bills were introduced in every session until one passed in 1964.[14] In 1956, Secretary of Agriculture Ezra Taft Benson was directed to study the idea. He recommended against it. Democratic Representative Leonor Sullivan of Missouri, a particularly strong advocate of the plan during the 1950s, finally won congressional approval in 1959 to authorize the secretary of agriculture to conduct a two-year program. Since he was not *directed* to implement the plan, Secretary Benson, a strong opponent, simply did not act.

Thus when John Kennedy became president "the program's political history before 1961 made it ideally suited for adoption by an administration that deplored its predecessor's resistance to innovation and preoccupation with economy."[15] Kennedy had been a supporter of food stamps while in the Senate. Once inaugurated, he initiated a pilot program under existing executive authority. Republicans strongly criticized the program because it was tested only in Democratic congressional districts.[16] Kennedy requested a permanent program in 1963. After Johnson assumed office, he endorsed Kennedy's plan and meant to see it enacted in 1964 once the civil rights bill passed.

Getting the bill passed proved to be no simple matter, however. Republicans were strongly opposed and had not yet suffered the devastating losses of the 1964 election. Thus cross-partisan voting, with southern Democrats joining Republicans, could potentially defeat the bill. Republicans questioned why a welfare bill should be assigned to the Committee on Agriculture. Further, they sought to define the food stamp program as a wedge for forcing desegregation in the South by denying food stamps to areas that did not meet federal standards.[17] "It took overt, almost crude logrolling . . . to get the 1964 food stamp legislation out of the Agriculture Committee and then passed on the floor of the House."[18] The program was coupled with a cotton and wheat bill to get it passed in committee (by a narrow vote of 18–16). The logrolling to hold southern Democratic support also worked on the floor, where 89 percent of Democrats voted for the bill against 92 percent of Republicans opposing it. The president actively lobbied for the bill.

Senate action was much less contentious. The bill was reported out of committee with some changes, passed by voice vote, and returned to the House. The Senate version was then accepted by the House, thus avoiding a conference. Passage of the program was hailed as a victory for President Johnson's antipoverty program, a conclusion Johnson himself confirmed in signing the bill.[19]

The lawmaking process in Congress was moderately iterative within and between the House and Senate committees, with no important changes made subsequently. However, one cannot ignore what had gone on before: the program had been tested in the past and most of the arguments on both sides were fully developed. Likewise, the partisan nature of this issue was not invented in 1964. Republicans and northern Democrats had established their positions, making the southern Democrats the critical bloc. Johnson's old-fashioned horse trading ultimately secured the support of 75 percent of the southern Democrats. Since most of the debate and all of the roll call votes occurred in the House, the president's three victories for his support score came there.

ELEMENTARY AND SECONDARY EDUCATION ACT. Few pieces of legislation in modern times have a lineage to match that of the Elementary and Secondary Education Act of 1965. How, to what extent, and, indeed, whether, to provide federal aid to education were unresolved issues dating back at least to the 1930s, when President Roosevelt asked his Advisory Committee on Education to report on educational needs. The committee documented significant inequalities among the states in 1938, stimulating introduction of a Senate bill to provide federal aid to the states in proportion to needs. Hearings were held, but the bill went no further. General school aid bills were introduced in every subsequent session of Congress. Sometimes the bills reached the floor; seldom did they pass even one house. In 1960 bills passed both houses, but the House Committee on Rules prevented a conference.

After more than two decades of effort to pass a bill, the full dimensions of the issue were apparent to all policymakers by 1961, and no one was certain how they were to be overcome. In their review of the history of federal aid to education before 1965, two scholars concluded that "the struggle over federal aid has not been a single conflict, but rather a multiplicity of controversies only loosely related to one another. The situation might be compared to a better-than-three-ring circus, although, in view of the tactics at times employed, a multiple barroom brawl might make a more apt analogy."[20]

An accounting of the efforts to pass legislation during this period was entitled "Race, Religion, and the Rules Committee."[21] The racial issues were paramount, involving the question of whether federal aid would be provided to segregated schools in the South. The Powell amendment, named for Democrat Adam Clayton Powell of New York, who chaired the House Committee on Education and Labor, specifically prohibited any such allocation. Passage of a House bill with the Powell amendment meant that it faced a potential filibuster by southern Democrats in the Senate. Southern Democrats also had a lock on the House Committee on Rules.

The religious dimensions were equally troublesome. Catholics were well represented on the House Committee on Education and Labor and in the Democratic leadership, and in 1961 they held the balance of power in a House Committee on Rules that had been expanded to give President Kennedy a majority. Catholics were bound to ensure that parochial schools were included in the first, precedent-setting federal aid bill.

The political landscape for this issue changed dramatically in 1964. The Civil Rights Act of that year prohibited the use of federal funds for segregated public facilities, thus eliminating the racial hurdle to federal aid. The Economic Opportunity Act of 1964 provided a method for avoiding the constitutional problem of church-state relations by linking aid to education with poverty. School districts would receive aid based on the number of low-income families, for both parochial and public school children. And the Republicans were in no position to block much of anything, having suffered losses that left them with less than a third of the seats in each chamber.

Thus passage of the Elementary and Secondary Education Act in 1965 was almost an anticlimax. It passed virtually as introduced. Amendments by Republicans and southern Democrats were turned back in the House Committee on Education and Labor, and several Republican amendments were defeated in the Senate. A conference was avoided by resisting all amendments in the Senate, much to the chagrin of Republicans. In the House committee changes favorable to northern Democrats were made in the formula for allocating aid, but overall the process was less iterative than for any bill of the twenty-eight included in the sample. That fact should not mask the efforts over the years to fashion a bill that would win a majority of votes, however. Nor should it convey the impression that the process had produced the perfect formula for federal aid. One member of Congress described what happened: "The question Congress had to settle in 1965 was whether there was ever to be federal aid to the elementary and secondary schools of this nation. The 1965 bill, in all candor, does not make much sense educationally; but it makes a hell of a lot of sense legally, politically, and constitutionally."[22]

A number of House and Senate Republicans voted in favor of the bill, and a number of southern Democrats in each chamber voted against it.

Ordinarily one might label this a case of classic cross partisanship. However, the Republican votes were not needed in either chamber because a sufficient number of southern Democrats voted with their party. House Republican leaders decided to let their members vote their districts, and 27 percent of them voted in favor of the bill.[23] It was because of this type of case that I distinguish between classic, or primary, cross partisanship and free, or secondary, cross partisanship (see appendix for an explanation of this distinction).

The president scored well with this legislation. His fourteen victories came mostly from the defeat of eleven amendments in the Senate (all but one from Republicans). In this case the support score is influenced by procedural differences between the two chambers. The president's House wins came mostly in committee and were then ratified by two roll call votes on the floor. His Senate wins came on the floor, with many recorded votes on amendments. The results in each chamber were similar, but this support score measure cannot reflect similar outcomes differentially processed.

Not unexpectedly, the passage of the bill was marked as a triumph of Johnson's Great Society. After so many years of struggle, the bill had become law in just four months. Whether this is the recommended process for passing legislation is surely a legitimate question, but it is extraordinary and not in the least characteristic of most lawmaking, whether by a single- or split-party government.

ECONOMIC RECOVERY. One does not normally expect large policy change as a product of the American political system. The constitutional structure itself encourages incremental moves. This is particularly true for economic issues, where the high probability of unanticipated ripple effects induces caution among those likely to be held responsible for adverse consequences of bold decisions. Thus the passage of a multiyear tax cut in 1981 seemed a remarkable exception. The bold "supply-side" plan had its antecedents in proposals by Senator William Roth, Republican of Delaware, and Representative Jack Kemp, Republican of New York. Reagan endorsed this approach, in conjunction with severe budget cuts, during the campaign. Reagan's overwhelming defeat of an incumbent president, combined with sizable gains for House and Senate Republicans, led to expectations that the Reagan program would be put into effect.

Of course, no matter how successful the Republicans had been in the election, the house of origin for tax bills—the House of Representatives—still had a majority of Democrats. Thus serious negotiations could be expected among the new chairman of the Committee on Ways and Means,

Democrat Daniel Rostenkowski of Illinois, the new Senate Republican leaders, and the White House. At the urging of Speaker Thomas P. O'Neill, Rostenkowski made a serious attempt at copartisan politics by fashioning an alternative to the Reagan tax cut proposal, but he was forced to rely on partisan support at the committee stage. All Republicans signed the minority report and were prepared to support a Reagan substitute plan on the floor. In order to hold southern Democrats, a tax break for oil-producing states was included in Rostenkowski's plan. Republicans countered with other sweeteners. "The Republican cosponsor of the administration bill, Barber Conable, publicly expressed dismay over the bidding contest that had developed, but stated that it had become unavoidable under the circumstances in order to ensure adoption of the president's basic economic program."[24]

The Republican-controlled Senate Committee on Finance acted first, attaching the Reagan program to a House-passed debt limit measure so as not to violate the constitutional provision requiring that revenue measures originate in the House. The strategy was clearly to put pressure on the House by building momentum for the Reagan proposal. A vigorous lobbying effort by the White House supplemented the sequential strategy of having the Senate act first.

Meanwhile, in the House, the president gained the support of a group of southern Democrats, the "boll weevils," and thus had a working majority to reject the Rostenkowski plan and substitute his own proposal (a modified version of the Kemp-Roth plan). Although each point in the sequence of legislative action in the House was highly iterative, the changes made in the committee were actually negated on the floor and much of the president's original plan was restored. A cross-partisan coalition thwarted the copartisan strategy by House Democratic leaders, who no longer had a working majority. Near-perfect Republican unity in the House capitalized on Democratic defections to produce a cross-partisan win. Similar levels of Republican unity in the Senate made Democratic support superfluous, but huge numbers of Democrats crossed over anyway.

Press reaction to the passage of the Economic Recovery Tax Act emphasized Reagan's mastery over Congress, the disarray among the Democrats, and the uncertainty of its economic effects.[25] On the one hand, columnists, editorial writers, and others in Washington were impressed with the exercise of power as an expression of the perceived mandate for change; on the other hand, the boldness of proposals designed to produce a real difference worried them.

The Economic Recovery Tax Act resulted in thirteen victories for President Reagan in calculating his support score. Most of these victories came in the Senate, where the highly cohesive Republicans rejected amendments from Democrats. House Republicans were also unified.

Congressional Preponderance

A comparison of the legislative characteristics of the acts I categorize as "Congress preponderant" with those just discussed is striking (table 7-1). For example, all the Congress-preponderant legislation was enacted in a split-party government, including one with a split between a Democratic president and a Republican Congress (Taft-Hartley in 1947). In four instances, the initiative for the legislation came primarily from Capitol Hill, not the White House. It is clear that Congress is fully capable of producing legislation on significant and complex issues. The president was essentially an observer for much of this legislation—an active observer and monitor, to be sure, but hardly serving as leader or manager of the lawmaking process. And the sequences for the president-preponderant bills were more or less standard (varying only in which house acted first and whether a conference was required), but the Congress-preponderant acts show considerable sequential variation. Only one (Landrum-Griffin in 1959) followed what is thought of as a standard pattern.

This group also contains the only cases of presidential veto in the sample of twenty-eight: three, of which two were overridden. The veto, and most certainly its threat, is a strategic weapon in the overall lawmaking process, not merely a method of rejecting proposals offered by congressional majorities. Finally, with the single exception of the Budget and Impoundment Control Act of 1974, the lawmaking process was highly iterative and typically cross-partisan (sometimes copartisan at the committee level). Again, I have divided the cases into two sets. The first five cases all demonstrate variable conditions under which Congress is the preponderant actor. The two cases in the second set involve congressional reforms aimed at an assertive president, Richard Nixon.

Variable Cases

In the first set, the Taft-Hartley Act of 1947 and the Landrum-Griffin Act of 1959 illustrate the making of labor law under obverse conditions of split-party government: a Democratic president and a Republican Congress with the first, a Republican president and a Democratic Congress with the second. Social security benefit increases (1972), Toxic Substances Control (1976), and Omnibus Trade (1988) provide interesting examples of presidential-congressional interaction when the president has an interest but is more reactive than active. These latter cases all occurred in a presidential election year: the first two when the incumbent was seeking reelection (Nixon) or election (Ford), the third when an incumbent vice president was seeking election (Bush). The passage of each of these five pieces of legislation defies the standard assumption about lawmaking derived from a presidency-centered, party responsibility model.

LABOR-MANAGEMENT RELATIONS ACT. Labor-management relations following World War II were bound to be contentious. Labor unions were anxious to improve the status of workers, strikes were frequent, and industry was concerned that unions were already too strong as a result of the protections provided by the National Labor Relations Act of 1935 (the Wagner Act). "Anti-labor sentiment, inflamed by John L. Lewis's defiance of the government in the fall of 1946, was gaining new strength, and labor legislation became a prime issue in 1947."[26] Legislation to curb strikes and provide for bargaining was introduced and passed in the 79th Congress, but President Truman vetoed what he called "that repressive measure." Congress was not able to override the veto.

In the 1946 midterm elections, the Republicans won majorities in both the House and the Senate for the first time since 1930. They looked forward to recapturing the White House in 1948. Therefore, when Truman requested a revision of the Wagner act, one could expect a highly iterative lawmaking process, featuring co- and cross-partisan politics. Certainly the congressional Republicans, who supported the bill Truman had vetoed, were unlikely simply to endorse the president's moderate proposals. And some southern Democrats were as eager as Republicans to go beyond the president's recommendations. On opening day of the 80th Congress, seventeen labor bills were "dropped into the hopper" of the House; more than a hundred eventually were introduced into the House and Senate.[27]

Led by Chairman Fred Hartley of New Jersey and Charles A. Halleck of Indiana, Republicans on the House Committee on Education and Labor prepared a bill that Democrats claimed was "aimed at the heart of industrial democracy."[28] They won the support of southern Democrats on the committee, presaging what was to follow on the House floor. Confirmation of the strength of cross-partisan support came on the rule, which passed 319-47.

Northern Democrats tried unsuccessfully to soften the bill; southern Democrats succeeded in making it tougher. The bill passed by a cross-partisan margin greater than that needed to override a presidential veto, 308-107. Support by southern Democrats was not needed for passage, but it would be required for a veto override.

Senate action on this issue was led by Republican Robert A. Taft of Ohio, chairman of the Committee on Labor and Public Welfare. As a prospective presidential candidate himself in 1948, he found the issue sensitive. Taft crafted a bill that was less objectionable to the president than the House bill but designed more to win support within the committee than to win Truman's signature. Although the Republicans had an 8-5 edge, Taft had to work between the far right on this issue, represented by Joseph Ball, Republican of Minnesota, and the more moderate position, represented by Irving Ives, Republican of New York. Ives reflected the views of Governor Thomas E. Dewey, Taft's likely opponent for the 1948 presidential nomination. In a demonstration of legislative mastery, Taft succeeded in building a winning coalition. The committee supported the bill 11-2, and after three weeks of intense debate, Taft's omnibus bill passed by a veto-proof margin of 68-24, again with substantial support from southern Democrats.

The final product as it emerged from the conference could hardly be satisfactory to Truman, in either policy or political terms. After all, the compromises being made were between two Republican versions, one only slightly less objectionable to labor than the other. The more moderate, but still tough, Taft version dominated the conference deliberations. "Taft's stubbornness irritated the House conferees, but Hartley knew that he had to give in—or risk a presidential veto that the Senate would fail to override."[29]

The rhetoric in the aftermath of final passage was predictable on both sides. Labor leaders denounced the bill and, along with several congressional Democrats, called for a veto. The volume of mail, overwhelmingly supporting a veto, "was the greatest ever received in the White House on any issue," exceeding 750,000.[30] A labor rally was held in Madison Square Garden with 35,000 in attendance. Few were neutral about the legislation. The scope and shrillness of the public debate were extraordinary.

The editorial reaction to the campaign for a veto was critical of labor. Both the *New York Times* and the *Washington Post* expressed the view that labor was misrepresenting the bill.[31] History tends to confirm these judgments. As James T. Patterson concluded: "In retrospect, it is clear that the unions grossly exaggerated the adverse effects of the law."[32]

Still, the pressure was on for Truman to say "no." And, in the end, politics dictated his decision.

> If he approved the bill one year after his proposal for drafting rail strikers and seventeen months before the 1948 election, his standing with labor would have been destroyed. . . . If he vetoed the bill, his previous sins in the eyes of labor would be absolved. At the same time he might counteract certain liberal support still building for a possible third party under Wallace. Moreover it was evident from the voting on the bill in both houses that Congress probably would override a veto. What did Truman have to lose, therefore, by vetoing it and winning labor's acclaim, if the bill was going to become law anyhow?[33]

The House overrode his veto the same day it was received. A majority of Democrats (60 percent) voted with 95 percent of the Republicans. The Senate override came three days later, following a filibuster. The Senate Republicans were as unified as their House colleagues. They were joined by just less than half of the Senate Democrats.

LABOR-MANAGEMENT REPORTING AND DISCLOSURE ACT. Enacting labor-management relations legislation in 1959 was not as contentious as in 1947, but neither was it a simple matter. As before, there was a stimulus for action. The Senate Select Committee on Improper Activities in the Labor or Management Fields (the McClellan committee, named for its chairman, Democrat John McClellan of Arkansas) was established in 1957 to investigate corruption in labor unions, "focusing its attention primarily on unsavory activities of leaders in the Teamsters' union." Hearings were televised, producing considerable public support for cleaning up the unions. "Many liberal and pro-labor spokesmen were dismayed and astonished at the impressive bill of particulars accumulated by the committee."[34] Yet the political situation was not apparently conducive to getting a bill passed. The Democrats won huge majorities in both the House and Senate in 1958, and President Eisenhower was about to retire. Further, as was true in 1947, it was not an issue that Democrats wanted to manage since it inevitably led to conflict with their labor constituency.

Conditions favored a highly iterative and copartisan process between the president and Congress as well as within Congress. Early in 1958, President Eisenhower called for anticorruption legislation and for amendments to the Taft-Hartley act. Meanwhile, the McClellan committee offered an interim report that proposed controls over union management that were not in the least popular with organized labor. Democratic Senator John F. Kennedy of Massachusetts chaired the Subcommittee on Labor of the Committee on Labor and Public Welfare and therefore could be expected to propose his own bill. Kennedy sponsored a wages and pension disclosure act in 1958, successfully shepherding it through both houses. Working with Republican Senator Irving Ives, he also succeeded in getting Senate approval of an anticorruption act, but it failed in the House amidst recriminations all around.[35]

All of this hostility and anxiety, along with a Democratic triumph at the polls in the midterm elections, constituted the setting for high politics in 1959. The president repeated his requests (including changes in the Taft-Hartley act), Kennedy reintroduced a modified version of his bill (excluding Taft-Hartley amendments), and McClellan was prepared to strengthen whatever bill reached the floor. Kennedy's bill passed in committee, with compromises on Taft-Hartley changes to pick up Republican votes. On the Senate floor, McClellan introduced his "bill of rights" amendment to protect union members. According to Samuel C. Patterson, "McClellan now clearly had charge of the debate," taking over from Kennedy.[36] The McClellan amendment split the Democrats and passed by the narrowest of margins, 47-46, supported by 94 percent of the Republicans and 25 percent of the Democrats. After acrimonious debate and the approval of a substitute bill of rights, the bill had been sufficiently modified to gain cross-partisan support and passed by a wide margin, 90-1. Only Republican Senator Barry Goldwater of Arizona, who had introduced the administration's bill, voted "no." He revealed, however, that Eisenhower told him: "Had I been in the Senate, I would have voted with you."[37]

The same contending forces were at work in the House, but conservative southern Democrats were in key positions on the critical committees. Further, "there was a good deal of personal jealousy and ill-feeling among some committee members, especially on the Democratic side." Yet, as Patterson notes, by the time of House action the Democrats were under substantial pressure to overcome these divisions and produce legislation.[38] The Kennedy bill, with many amendments, passed the House committee by a narrow, cross-partisan majority of 16-14. But that result alone hardly revealed the complex and varied views on this issue. The committee report, which included separate statements and "supplementary views" from at least seven subsets of members, was "among the strangest that has ever come from the Congress."[39]

What happened next confirmed the signals being sent by the report. The modified Kennedy bill was managed on the floor by Democrat Carl Elliott of Kentucky rather than Committee Chairman Graham Barden, Democrat of South Carolina, who favored a much tougher bill. It was debated under an open rule. Before the debate, both AFL-CIO President Meany and President Eisenhower addressed the nation.[40]

Two members of the House Education and Labor Committee, Democrat Phil Landrum of Georgia and Republican Robert Griffin of Michigan, introduced a substitute to the Elliott bill on the floor. The Landrum-Griffin substitute included the Taft-Hartley changes that Eisenhower favored. After two further amendments were rejected, the Landrum-Griffin substitute passed with cross-partisan support, 229-201; 89 percent of the House Republicans and 34 percent of the Democrats voted in favor. The conference modified the House bill somewhat; it then passed both houses and was signed by the president on September 14, 1959. George Meany claimed that it was "the most damaging anti-labor bill since the Taft-Hartley Act," but President Eisenhower was reportedly "very pleased" with the bill, as was Secretary of Labor James Mitchell.[41]

The president's pleasure with the result does not qualify for placing this act in the category of "president preponderant." Although Eisenhower was more active on this than on most legislation, still the action was primarily in Congress, with the president as one of the important players. That he got much of what he wanted in the end was a consequence of the political dynamics within Congress, where this legislative drama took place beginning with the McClellan hearings. What this story illustrates so well is that major legislation can be enacted under highly variable political conditions and against all odds.

The president's support scores for this piece of legislation show its importance for his record in 1959. He had four wins and no losses in the House, two wins and four losses in the Senate. The Senate losses include several amendments for changes that eventually made their way into the legislation in the House but did not include the crucial vote on the McClellan bill of rights. Given the political dynamics of this legislation, so much of it occurring within Congress, it is misleading for political analysts to characterize this battle in terms of presidential wins and losses.

SOCIAL SECURITY BENEFIT INCREASES. The social security benefit increases in 1972 illustrate the crucial importance of context in lawmaking. Martha Derthick describes the policy context for this legislation:

> The interest in antipoverty legislation during the Johnson years, which carried over during the Nixon administration into the campaign for the family assistance plan (FAP), encouraged the expansion of the social se-

a policy train, no one at the controls

curity program in two ways. It lent momentum to welfare legislation generally, and because social security was the most popular and feasible form
of such legislation, it won support when more controversial forms were
stymied. . . . Incremental changes in well-established programs do not
attract attention.[42]

The political context was easy to spot: the 1972 election was approaching,
and it is now clear how badly Richard Nixon wanted to win, and win big.
And Congress was populated with prospective Democratic opponents.

What took place in 1972 was a lawmaking process seemingly out of control, a policy escalation unchecked by the normal controls that contribute to
incrementalism. This race to satisfy the social security clienteles occurred
not in a single-party government, free to work its will or to fulfill its mandate.
It occurred in a split-party government with a strongly partisan president and
ambitious congressional Democratic leaders. Derthick refers to what happened as "the disintegration of policymaking."[43] It is an amazing story.

In his budget message to Congress in 1972, President Nixon proposed
increased spending for the aged. He initially proposed a 5 percent increase,
on top of a 10 percent increase that had been approved by Congress in 1971.
The response on Capitol Hill favored an increase, but Nixon's proposal was
criticized as inadequate. Several Democrats proposed increases ranging from
12 to 25 percent.

The principal legislative action occurred within the Senate in spite of the
constitutional provision that revenue measures must originate in the House.
A debt limit increase passed by the House was to act as a vehicle for the
social security benefit increases (as it had in 1971). The Senate Committee
on Finance approved a 10 percent increase, moderately larger than that
preferred by the president. Everyone expected that a larger increase would
be proposed on the Senate floor, and it was. Democratic Senator Frank
Church of Idaho introduced an amendment that increased benefits by 20
percent, raised social security taxes, and set in place automatic cost-of-living
adjustments (COLAs), a mechanism favored by the Nixon administration.
The Church amendment passed overwhelmingly. And so it was that COLAs
came into being.[44]

The increases in benefits and taxes, and the new indexation procedure,
were attached to the debt limit increase passed earlier by the House. Thus
the conference agreement now included the Church proposals as nongermane
amendments, which had to be approved in the House. They were, by a large,
cross-partisan margin. No one could stop this bandwagon as it rolled toward
the 1972 elections. John Byrnes, ranking Republican on the Committee on

Ways and Means, was aghast at the acquiescence of his long-time friend and chairman, Wilbur Mills. He expressed his disappointment on the House floor and warned of the future consequences: "We are contemplating taking steps that can lead us into very serious problems as far as this system and the many people involved in it are concerned."[45]

This is a good example of the point that an unrestrained lawmaking process does not necessarily produce the best legislation. COLAs were one more contribution to what R. Kent Weaver calls "automatic government." President Nixon reportedly considered a veto, "but he was in a politically impossible situation."[46] The bill had passed both houses by more than the two-thirds majorities required to override, the national conventions were about to take place, the election was just four months away, and the popular increases were attached to a debt ceiling bill that had to be approved to keep the government running. And so Nixon satisfied himself by warning of the effects of inflation and of attaching "seemingly attractive, politically popular but fiscally irresponsible riders" to future debt ceiling increases.[47] These warnings proved prescient (see the subsequent discussion of the Social Security Amendments of 1983).

Congressional Quarterly did not include any roll call votes from this legislation in calculating President Nixon's support score for 1972. An absolutely crucial piece of social welfare legislation, with major budget implications, is not accounted for in evaluating Nixon. The case illustrates yet again the perils of relying on roll call votes for this purpose. But the political dynamics also show the fallacy of testing the system from a presidency-centered perspective. Nixon was a major player in this legislative contest, but he did not manage it—nor, it seems, did anyone else.

TOXIC SUBSTANCES CONTROL. Many have labeled the 1970s as the environmental decade, a deserved title given the number of major enactments during the period. The Council on Environmental Quality (CEQ) issued a report in 1971 drawing attention to the many new untested chemicals that go on the market each year. The Nixon administration submitted a proposal to Congress in 1971 that was changed substantially as it worked its way through Congress. A bill passed both houses, but because the House failed to agree to the revised Senate version, the bill died in 1972. Another effort was made in 1973. Again both houses passed a bill, but conferees could not reach an agreement.

By 1975, this issue was being primarily treated within Congress. The original initiative may have come from the CEQ and Nixon's early proposals, but subsequent action was on Capitol Hill, with the Ford White House primarily playing the role of monitor. The issue had strong potential for attracting public attention. The term *toxic* has an arresting quality to it. And though not all effects are known of emitting chemicals into the air and spilling them into the water, such uncertainty causes concern. As one specialist observes: "Latency and uncertainty make chronic toxic substances difficult to recognize and control."[48] These characteristics, like those of AIDS, encourage policymaking.

A new effort to pass a bill began in 1975, with the Senate acting first. Democratic Senators Vance Hartke of Indiana, John Tunney of California, and Philip Hart of Michigan sponsored a bill in the Senate Committee on Commerce. The principal conflict concerned premarket testing of chemicals, with the administration apprehensive about having the Environmental Protection Agency (EPA) regulate the chemical industry. By now the committee had ample practice in building floor support for the bill; it was approved 60-13, gaining majority support among Republicans and nearly unanimous support among Democrats. The question was: What would happen in the House?

The administration's reaction to the Senate-passed bill was not altogether clear. A letter from the White House stated opposition to the bill because it "unnecessarily overburdens both the regulatory agency and the regulated industry." On the other hand, it was reported that EPA Administrator Russell Train thought that "this legislation requires the industry to test chemicals in the lab rather than in the marketplace. They should test mice rather than people."[49]

A less stringent bill more clearly acceptable to the White House was reported out by the House Committee on Interstate and Foreign Commerce. An effort was made to win Republican support, perhaps to avoid a veto. The bill then passed the House with moderate but important changes (one of which banned PCBs). There was uncertainty regarding both the possibility of a Ford veto and whether the House and Senate could reach an agreement.

The conference was highly iterative as House and Senate conferees worked out an agreement on the EPA's role as to the marketing of tested chemicals. The agreement was approved by large majorities in both houses and signed by President Ford, who identified it as "one of the most important pieces of environmental legislation that has been enacted by Congress."[50] In the House, 84 percent of Republicans voted for the conference report; in the Senate 80 percent of Republicans voted for the report.

Only one roll call vote was included in President Ford's support score for 1976: the early Senate passage of the Hartke-Tunney-Hart bill, which was counted as a defeat for the president. The subsequent modification of the bill to suit the president's concerns was therefore not reflected in the support score, in spite of the overwhelming support given to the final bill by House and Senate Republicans and the president's own endorsement of the legislation as an important achievement.

OMNIBUS TRADE. Few policy issues have a longer history than that of trade. Developing a strategy that will maintain America's competitive position without downgrading the domestic economy has never been a simple matter. A dramatically worsening trade and investment deficit in the 1980s encouraged many in Congress to fashion a comprehensive policy to stabilize and improve the American position. Many Democrats identified this issue as potentially having major political appeal, perhaps enough to recapture the White House in 1988. This was an issue requiring analysis of enormous scope since trading problems involve the nation's economic, political, and social structure. No one would recommend that such sensitive and comprehensive policy be developed in Congress. And yet that is what happened during the second Reagan administration.

As with so many of the bills examined here, the Omnibus Trade Bill was several years in the making. A congressional Democratic task force began work in 1985. In 1986 a bill "was stitched together from individual bills drafted by six committees."[51] The bill invited a veto because of its heavily punitive nature. It never reached the president's desk, however, because it passed the Democratic House but did not reach the floor in the Republican Senate.[52]

In the 1986 midterm elections, Senate Democrats increased their numbers by ten seats, giving them a 55-45 majority. Party leaders announced that Democrats would make trade a priority issue in the 100th Congress. The continuing trade deficit and concern about unfair trade practices ensured that there would be Republican support for a bill unless the Reagan administration strongly objected. The White House sent clear signals in 1986 that a strongly punitive, highly protectionist bill would be vetoed. Thus party leaders on both sides could hardly fail to understand the terms for reaching an agreement.

Action within the House Committee on Ways and Means was directed by Chairman Daniel Rostenkowski and Trade Subcommittee Chairman Sam Gibbons, Democrat of Florida. Together they revised the 1986 trade bill by removing many of the features the White House objected to. As a result, the bill attracted cross-partisan support from committee Republicans.

A Democratic member of the Committee on Ways and Means, Richard Gephardt of Missouri, was planning to run for president in 1988, primarily on the basis of a tough trade policy. He proposed severe penalties for countries that failed to eliminate unfair trade practices. Gephardt decided not to press for his amendment at the committee stage primarily because of opposition by Rostenkowski and Gibbons. When offered on the floor, the Gephardt amendment passed by a narrow margin, 218-214. The winning margin was supplied by seventeen Republicans; fifty-five Democrats voted against the amendment. Thus the bill on final passage included the Gephardt amendment. The Democrats were nearly unanimous in supporting the bill, as amended, providing enough votes for passage even without Republican support (a secondary cross-partisan vote, as defined in the appendix). However, enough Republicans voted in favor to override a potential veto.

Senate action closely paralleled that in the House. The bill was reported out of the Senate Committee on Finance by a wide margin. The debate on the Senate floor, which took four weeks, included the adoption of 120 amendments (most noncontroversial). The president warned that the bill contained too many objectionable features, but it passed with cross-partisan support, 71-27. As in the House vote, the Senate Democrats supplied sufficient votes for passage, but Republican support meant that a veto override in the Senate was also a possibility.

The sheer size of the bill, its legislative origins in several committees, the significant differences between the two versions, and the pressure from the White House to make modifications all led to one of the largest and most complex conferences in history. In effect, the two houses created a new legislative body with 199 members and 17 committees (or subconferences). The conference worked intermittently over a period of months, finally producing a bill that removed the Gephardt amendment and modified other provisions so as to avoid a veto. It was the most highly and continuously iterative process of any bill of the twenty-eight in this sample and surely one of the most iterative in history.

President Reagan still opposed provisions in the bill, however, and vetoed it. He particularly objected to a provision requiring notice of plant closings. At the same time, he indicated that he would sign a "responsible" bill, virtually inviting Congress to try him again. "By this time, the Administration's negotiators, especially [the Trade Representative], had a vested interest in the compromise, and quietly worked to make it more acceptable to the White House." The House voted to override, with even more Republicans joining Democrats than on the earlier vote. The Senate, however, sustained the veto. Further changes were made, including removal of the plant-closing provision, and the bill was signed into law "in the pre-election atmosphere . . . that makes prompt action possible."[53] The Democrats passed a separate plant-closing bill immediately and held up action on the trade bill until Reagan agreed to allow the plant-closing bill to become law without his signature. Forcing the president's hand in this way substantially compromised the president's earlier rationale for vetoing the original trade bill.

It was an extraordinary achievement for a bicameral Congress: a 1,128-page law that "changed the face of U. S. relations with its trading partners for the rest of this century."[54] Once again a split-party government acted on a major issue as a presidential election neared. In fact, the Senate cleared the bill for the president's signature just before the Republican convention, and Reagan signed the measure the week after the convention.

Even this brief description raises doubts about the reliability of selected roll call votes to characterize the complex politics of the issue. A total of twelve votes were included in the president's support score for the two years. In 1987 Reagan was credited with two wins and three defeats in the Senate and two defeats in the House. The Senate wins and losses were on various amendments favored by the president. The House losses were first on the Gephardt amendment, then on passage of the bill with that amendment. Even though the Gephardt amendment was later removed in conference, there was no way to record that action as a win for the president without a roll call vote on that specific conference decision.

In 1988 Reagan was credited with one win and four losses on this legislation. The scoring for that year is even more distorted. Two of the losses were the result of House and Senate approval of the conference report that had excluded the Gephardt amendment but included the plant-closing notification. A third loss was the result of the House overriding the president's veto. But sustaining a veto requires only a one-third plus one vote in one house, which the president got in the Senate (recorded as his only win). Logic would suggest that what was recorded as a loss in the House was not, in fact, a loss if the other chamber sustained the veto.

Finally, the president's fourth loss in 1988 came on a cross-partisan Senate vote favoring the plant-closing notification bill. The House roll call vote on the same legislation was not included among those used to calculate the president's 1988 support score. Just as puzzling is the fact that the vote on final passage of the trade bill, which the president announced in advance that he would sign, was not included as a victory for the president. The legislative tangle that characterized the enactment of the Omnibus Trade Act of 1988 cannot be unsnarled simply by creating scores. To say that Reagan won 25 percent of the votes selected for inclusion on this issue reveals nothing of importance about the lawmaking that occurred.

Institutional Reform

The second set in this group of "congress-preponderant" laws includes two instances of reform: one primarily directed at the executive (the War Powers Resolution of 1973) and one directed at both the executive and Congress (the Budget and Impoundment Control Act of 1974). Both occurred during the Nixon administration for the very good reason that many members of Congress viewed this presidency as a threat to Congress because of Nixon's personal interest and expertise in foreign policy and a style of decisionmaking that was more exclusive than inclusive. In both of these cases, therefore, the initiative naturally came from members of Congress and not the executive. However, the executive had a strong interest in what was being proposed.

Though both laws were passed during a period of presidential weakness caused by scandal, each had a much longer lineage. Indeed, both issues touch at the very core of executive-legislative interaction on national policy. Had the Vietnam War continued under a Democratic president, it is just as likely that there would have been a War Powers Resolution. The case for budget reform was equally strong no matter who served in the White House, because of the sheer magnitude and complexity of government spending and the chaotic congressional methods for dealing with it. Impoundment control, however, represented a more strictly partisan response to a Republican president by congressional Democrats.

WAR POWERS. According to Robert A. Katzmann, "few issues so graphically illustrate the problems of allocating responsibility between Congress and the executive as the power to make war." The War Powers Resolution of 1973 represents an effort to define and refine that allocation and illustrates "the difficulties of defining the balance of authority."[55] No one could expect a president to favor efforts to expand the congressional role in foreign and defense policymaking. President Nixon wrote later that any such action was clearly at odds with the intentions of the Founders.

> The President's power was wisely limited by the Founders in the Constitution. . . . The President's power has been further limited by Congress in ways the Founders would not have approved. . . . Along with most Presidents who have succeeded me, I believe [the War Powers Act] is clearly unconstitutional and contrary to the intent of the Founders.[56]

This issue, like so many, was not created *de novo*. The resolution passed in 1973 reflected a legacy of congressional concern about the erosion of authority during the post–World War II period. A major difficulty was that the constitutional authority of Congress to declare war had become passé in a world of alliances, United Nations resolutions, and fast-strike military capability. Congress found itself having to support military commitments in Korea and Vietnam without ever having had an opportunity to declare war. In 1969 a "sense of the Senate" resolution was passed that a national military commitment should not be made by the president alone. The resolution was a second effort by Democratic Senator J. William Fulbright of Arkansas, chairman of the Committee on Foreign Relations, to define presidential-congressional responsibilities and was "only an admonition to the President to consult with Congress; he still was not bound to do so." It had the support of many Republicans despite the characterization of the resolution by Senate Minority Leader Everett Dirksen of Illinois as "a bundle of mischief."[57]

The incursion of American forces into Cambodia in 1970 again raised the issue of the extent of the president's independent authority to commit military forces. The House passed joint resolutions in 1970 and 1971 defining Congress's role, but the Senate did not act beyond holding hearings in 1971. In 1972, the Senate took the initiative on this issue and passed the precursor to the 1973 resolution. The House passed its less restrictive 1970 and 1971 versions in 1972. Nixon endorsed the House action as the lesser evil. The differences between the two chambers were not resolved in conference, so no resolution was enacted.

The House Committee on Foreign Affairs made significant changes in the resolution in 1973. This high degree of iteration was the result of an effort to toughen the measure as earlier passed by the House. The Senate more or less endorsed its work of 1972. The Senate Committee on Foreign Relations unanimously approved and reported a resolution jointly sponsored by Republican Jacob Javits of New York and Democrat John Stennis of Mississippi. This bipartisan action in the committee virtually ensured floor approval.

Minor changes were made on the House floor, but no changes were made on the Senate floor, as opponents counted on a presidential veto. Passage in both chambers was with cross-partisan support (40 percent of House Republicans joining 74 percent of House Democrats; 61 percent of Senate Republicans joining 93 percent of Senate Democrats). The Senate margin was more than needed to override a veto, but the House margin fell substantially short of the two-thirds required to override. The conference was active in reaching a compromise between the two versions of the resolution, and the conference report was agreed to by margins in each house similar to those for the original bill.

Editorial reaction urged the president to sign the resolution.[58] Nixon ignored this advice and vetoed the resolution as posing a serious threat to presidential prerogatives in foreign policy. The great concern, of course, was what would happen in the House of Representatives, given the previous votes in that chamber. Certainly it was within the power of the House Republicans to sustain the veto because they held 44 percent of the seats. In the final tally, however, nearly half the Republicans (46 percent) voted to override—more than had voted for the resolution in either of the previous votes. And so the veto was overridden by a slim four-vote margin in the House. The question naturally arose as to why Republicans would switch their votes. *Congressional Quarterly* found that most switchers changed their vote "to assert more independence."[59] Another reason was that Nixon's veto raised the prospect of having no clarification of institutional responsibilities in this important area.

Other events occurring during this same time were highly damaging to the Nixon administration. During the month in which both houses voted on the conference report and on the override of the veto, Vice President Spiro Agnew resigned, Gerald R. Ford was nominated by Nixon to be vice president, Nixon ordered the dismissal of the special Watergate prosecutor, House Democratic leaders tentatively agreed to begin an inquiry into impeachment proceedings, and Leon Jaworski was appointed as the new special Watergate prosecutor. It was, to say the very least, a time of confrontation between the two branches. The *Congressional Quarterly* survey of House members failed to establish that Watergate was the principal reason for overriding the president's veto, but there is no ignoring the context in which the vote took place.

The president suffered seven defeats for his presidential support score: one in 1972, the other six in 1973. The three votes in the Senate in 1973 hardly varied in the vote split, raising a question of why three votes were included in the score.

BUDGET REFORM. By the 1970s, members of Congress had become just as frustrated with their budgetmaking role as with their foreign policymaking role. The Nixon administration sought to streamline the budgeting process by reorganizing the administrative apparatus and introducing new budgeting procedures. In 1973 Nixon proposed serious reductions in domestic programs, most of which were to be achieved administratively for programs that had strong congressional support. The president also criticized congressional budgetmaking procedures for contributing to spending that was out of control. He wanted a cap on expenditures and the authority to make cuts if Congress exceeded the statutory limit. Finally, he threatened to impound funds if Congress failed to set a limit and appropriated funds for programs the administration did not want.

Congressional leaders essentially agreed with the president that their procedures needed overhauling, in part for the reasons Nixon outlined and in part for fear that failure to act would result in a significant loss of institutional power. A Joint Study Committee on Budget Control, made up mostly of members from the two appropriations and two tax-writing committees, was created in 1972 to propose changes in congressional organization and procedures. Al Ullman, chairman of the House Committee on Ways and Means, chaired the Joint Committee. He observed that "timing in the political arena is of utmost importance. This is the time for Congress to accomplish a purpose which it has not been willing to face up to for 100 years."[60]

A major overhaul of the budget process was proposed, including the creation of budget committees, a congressional budget office, budget resolutions, a change in the fiscal year, and limits on impoundments by the president. The action in both houses was most iterative at the committee stage. Substantial bipartisanship characterized the legislation throughout (less so at early stages in the House). Liberal House Democrats, concerned that the new Committee on the Budget might lock in a conservative majority, insisted on changes in the makeup of the committee. Once an agreement was worked out by which all legislative committees would be represented on the new panel, the bill, as reported by the Committee on Rules, passed handily.

In the Senate there was a jurisdictional tug-of-war between two committees: Government Operations and Rules and Administration. Following an agreement, the Rules and Administration Committee "conducted unprecedented negotiations among staff representatives from 10 Senate committees, four joint committees and the House Appropriations Committee."[61] Both committees then managed the bill to an 80-0 approval on the Senate floor. The conference negotiations also included input from staff representatives. The final product was agreed to overwhelmingly in both houses.

The reaction to passage of the Budget and Impoundment Control Act of 1974 contained warnings about the workability of the timetable and the possibility of escape hatches, but most reaction was positive.[62] Nixon signed the bill in "an air of joviality," in spite of the new controls on his power to impound funds. At the signing ceremony he observed: "This bill is the most significant reform of budget procedures since Congress began."[63] This was less than a month before his resignation, and Watergate now dominated his administration. In all probability, a Nixon veto would have been quickly overridden.

Several years later, Nixon expressed views quite different from those at the signing ceremony: "I used impoundment to restrain some of the willy-nilly spending of the massive, and now largely discredited, Great Society programs I inherited. . . . In 1974 Congress took the impoundment power away, thus reserving to itself the right to spend irresponsibly without con-straint."[64] *Congressional Quarterly*'s calculation of Nixon's 1974 presidential support score did not reflect these thoughts: the only vote included was on an amendment in the House to delete the impoundment control sections of the bill, which was registered as a defeat for the president. None of the final votes on the budget reform act was included in Nixon's support score.

Joint Participation

I now review fifteen important enactments that reflect more balanced participation in lawmaking by the White House and Congress. As indicated in chapter 6, I introduce a distinction here between the issues in which the president was particularly active in designating the proposal as a high priority, although members of Congress were actively involved in the legislation at all critical stages, and the cases that demonstrate genuine balance, arguably even greater congressional involvement. The total number of cases of joint participation is itself noteworthy, more than any other category. Try as I might, I found it difficult to assign clear preponderance of involvement by one branch over the other in over one-third of the laws, an unlikely conclusion about any other national political system.

Substantial Presidential Activity in Single-Party Government

Three of the laws in this first category of balanced participation were passed under single-party government: medicare in 1965 (Johnson), creation of the Department of Education in 1979 (Carter), and the synthetic fuels program in 1980 (Carter).

MEDICARE. As shown in figure 6-1, medical care for the aged was a familiar issue for public policymakers. It was also extremely contentious because it pitted a powerful professional group, the American Medical As-sociation, against what was then a sleeping giant of political pressure, senior citizens. "Socialized medicine" was a frequent slogan whenever proposals were made. President Truman proposed a comprehensive national health care program in 1949, but no action was taken in Congress. In 1957 Democratic Representative Aime Forand of Rhode Island introduced a health care program for those eligible for old age and survivors insurance, to be paid for by an increase in social security taxes. The Forand bill had its roots in a plan devised by the AFL-CIO. Forand introduced it "with some reluctance . . . and a legislative star was born."[65]

President Eisenhower had earlier proposed reinsuring private insurance companies against heavy losses for health claims. Because of growing interest in the Forand bill, the Eisenhower administration first studied the problem; then Secretary of Health, Education, and Welfare Arthur Flemming proposed a state-administered, voluntary, means-tested program for those over sixty-five. He called it "medicare." It was not even introduced in the House. "Although scarcely anyone but its authors liked" the Flemming plan, there had been movement in both parties toward accepting the importance of the issue and devising a solution.[66] Under the pressure of election-year politics, a mild version of the Flemming plan was enacted, limiting coverage to the medically indigent. It was called the Kerr-Mills act after its authors, Senator Robert Kerr, Democrat of Oklahoma, and Representative Wilbur D. Mills, Democrat of Arkansas.

A highly iterative, developmental phase then ensued with the election of a new president in 1960. President Kennedy favored a plan financed through social security, and there was some cross-partisan support led by Republican Senator Jacob Javits of New York. But Wilbur Mills, chairman of the House Committee on Ways and Means, remained opposed and thus this proposal (named for its sponsors, Representative Cecil King, Democrat of California, and Senator Clinton Anderson, Democrat of New Mexico) did not pass.

The 1964 election was, in part, about medicare. Johnson was for it and Goldwater was against it. Johnson's overwhelming victory, combined with a significant increase in House Democrats, "practically" all of whom were "committed to medicare," virtually ensured passage of the King-Anderson bill.[67]

Still, it was essential that Wilbur Mills be persuaded to support the social security approach. A key player within the administration was Wilbur Cohen, then assistant secretary of health, education, and welfare for legislation. Cohen believed that winning over Mills required "the adaptation of the legislative proposal to satisfy Mills' prestige and his own personal creativity."[68] Others in the administration believed that pressure on other members would eventually force Mills to support King-Anderson, but Cohen did not support humiliating him with a defeat or making him into a messenger for the administration. Mills was as capable as others in Washington of reading the 1964 election returns. If there was a mood to act on this issue, then Mills was eager to "put his own stamp upon the program, rather than merely accepting the Administration's proposal as it was submitted to Congress."[69] A portrayal of Mills during this period points out: "The decisions of the Committee are shaped and articulated by Mills, but his word comes close to being law in the Committee because he has listened to others, particularly to the ranking Republican, John Byrnes."[70]

Meanwhile, Republicans countered with a proposal of their own, sponsored by Representative Byrnes of Wisconsin that provided for a voluntary health insurance program financed by premiums, state contributions, and federal appropriations. A third plan was offered by the American Medical Association. Called "eldercare," it was an extension of the existing Kerr-Mills program. Representatives of the Department of Health, Education, and Welfare (HEW) viewed these programs "as mutually exclusive alternatives," but instead Mills "suggested that the committee consider a 'medi-elder-Byrnes bill' . . . [to] combine the three programs." The HEW representatives "were stunned by Mills' combination of the several programs."[71]

Mills now wanted Johnson's support for his copartisan strategy, which was designed to provide maximum cross-partisan support on the House floor. The key vote came on the recommittal motion by Byrnes, which would have sent the compromise package back to the committee with instructions to report the Republican plan back to the floor. Byrnes's motion was defeated by a vote of 191-236. The closeness of the vote confirmed the need for Mills's copartisan strategy. The Democrats had a huge, two-thirds majority in the House, but sixty-three Democrats sided with Byrnes on the recommittal vote. The House Republican Policy Committee endorsed Byrnes's recommittal motion but took no position on the final passage of Mills's bill. Nearly half of the Republicans voted in favor of the bill, and forty-two Democrats voted against it.

Although an advance count in the Senate showed a ten-vote margin for the bill, including three Republicans, the immediate problem was getting the bill reported out of the Committee on Finance, chaired by Democrat Harry F. Byrd of Virginia, an announced opponent of medicare. In a celebrated televised meeting, the president got a public commitment from Byrd to hold hearings on the bill.[72] The committee voted it out by a 12-5 count. The bill passed the Senate by a substantial, cross-partisan margin, 68-21 (48 percent of the Senate Republicans joined 89 percent of the Senate Democrats in favor). A number of liberalizing amendments were passed on the Senate floor. The conference agreement greatly favored the House version of the bill. President Johnson went to Independence, Missouri, to sign the bill in the presence of former president Harry S. Truman, whose early efforts at promoting a national health plan had failed.

The legislation contributed fourteen victories and no defeats to Johnson's 1965 presidential support score. Eleven of the fourteen wins were in the Senate; nine of these were on amendments offered by Republicans or procedural motions. The one successful amendment that was opposed by the floor managers of the bill was not counted among those on which the president took a stand. All of the liberalizing amendments passed by voice vote, and many of these changes were then removed in the conference.

Support scores are not calculated for chairmen of the Committee on Ways and Means, but no one doubted that Wilbur Mills had performed well in what began as a difficult political situation for him. It is relevant that Mills joined the effort in his own way, substantially altering the administration's proposal and essentially taking charge of the policy process for this issue. Accepting the bold changes fashioned by Mills made it possible for the president to claim victory in the House roll call votes.

Medicare was judged to be an outstanding achievement of the Johnson administration. It is no diminution of that accolade to point to the major contribution made by members of Congress or to the progression of this issue over time.

DEPARTMENT OF EDUCATION. One test of responsible party government is whether the president fulfills his promises. In the 1976 presidential campaign, Jimmy Carter "endorsed the idea of creating a cabinet-level department [of education]" because "for those educators who came to Washington to seek help or resolve a question or dispute, it was almost impossible to locate the federal official who was supposed to be responsible."[73] Yet after Carter became president, his proposal for creating the new department was subjected to considerable criticism, even among Democrats, some in his own cabinet. Being responsible in the classic mode does not always pay off for presidents.

The Republican opponents of a new department hardly had to act, given the nature and source of the conflicts over Carter's proposal. The two principal education lobbies were on opposite sides of this issue. The National Education Association (NEA) favored the proposal and had worked for Carter's nomination in 1976 because of his support for the idea.[74] The American Federation of Teachers (AFT) opposed the proposal. President Carter's principal cabinet representative on education issues, Secretary of Health, Education, and Welfare Joseph A. Califano, strongly opposed rending his department in this way.[75]

A serious effort was made in 1978 to get the plan approved. Both House and Senate committees reported bills, but only the Senate acted, approving the plan, 72-11. Opponents in the House prevented action as the 1978 midterm elections were approaching.[76] The most serious issue was the scope of the new department's jurisdiction. Carter and Democratic Senator Abraham Ribicoff of Connecticut, chairman of the Committee on Government Operations and a former secretary of HEW, favored a broad department. But each program had its advocates for special status.[77] Califano's account illustrates how iteration proceeds. "As the Education Department proposal worked its way through the Congress, each special interest moved to carve out its own independent fiefdom, with legislative power and protection. This had the effect of making it virtually impossible for the Education Secretary to run the new department efficiently."[78]

The White House renewed and redoubled its efforts in 1979, with the president actively and personally involved in lobbying. "The president . . . badly needed a major legislative victory to offset several losses he had encountered on Capitol Hill."[79] The bill again passed by a wide margin in the Senate (72-21), with significant support from both parties. Clearly the House once again "provided a sterner test."[80] The proposal barely got out of the committee (by 20-19 with two Republicans providing the winning margin).

The AFT became active in a loose coalition of groups opposing the new department. The coalition sought to delay floor action in order to build opposition to the bill.[81] Floor consideration took on the characteristics of an auction as opposition forces tried to split liberal and black support. A highly iterative amending process resulted in the approval of amendments against quotas, forced busing, and abortion, along with those favoring voluntary school prayer and limits on departmental growth. Even with all of these changes or perhaps because of them, the bill passed with cross-partisan support by just four votes, 210-206. Republicans supplied a crucial thirty-five votes; eighty-nine Democrats, most of them from the North, voted against the president.

The conference dropped all of the controversial amendments; thus more liberal votes were gained than conservative votes were lost. The House agreed to the conference report by the cross-partisan vote of 215-201, Republicans again supplying a crucial thirty votes and northerners casting the largest share of the seventy-seven Democratic votes against the report. The nature of the cross-partisan voting between conservatives and liberals remained curious throughout the long consideration of the legislation.

President Carter signed the bill on October 17, 1979. Joseph Califano was not present since he had been fired as secretary of HEW some months earlier. The NEA expressed satisfaction with the passage of the bill and confirmed its support for Carter in 1980.[82] As discussed in chapter 6, the support scores on this proposal—seventeen wins and two losses—would mislead one into believing that Carter was in full command of this legislative battle.

SYNTHETIC FUELS PROGRAM. No issues frustrated President Carter more than those associated with energy supply and demand. Carter recorded in his diary that he found "the Congress . . . disgusting on this particular subject."[83] It was, in large part, his bafflement about how to solve energy issues that led to the Camp David retreat in the summer of 1979. Once the retreat was under way, more systemic issues were raised about Carter's leadership and the state of the nation more generally. A debate ensued among Carter's staff as to what should be said once the president returned to Washington. Carter's chief domestic policy adviser, Stuart Eizenstat, was adamant that the president's speech should contain a specific energy proposal since gas lines had made that issue a top priority among the American people. Eizenstat got his way. The transitional sentence in Carter's famous "crisis of confidence" speech reads: "Energy will be the immediate test of our ability to unite this Nation and it can also be the standard around which we rally."[84]

One of Carter's energy proposals was a long-term program to produce synthetic fuels. This was a new proposal but not a new idea. "During World War II, the federal government had begun a program to develop synthetic fuels, and the Truman administration considered them to be nearly commercially feasible."[85] More recently, President Ford had supported synthetic fuels proposals in 1975 and 1976, but Congress did not follow through. In 1979, spurred by a continuing energy crisis, the House had already passed a bill supporting the synthetic fuels industry when Carter made his proposals.

Thus this was a case of the president enthusiastically endorsing a congressional initiative. The president expanded the House proposal and provided a means for funding and managing government support. A windfall profits tax was to pay for the plan, and an energy security corporation (later changed to the Synthetic Fuels Corporation) was to administer the funds. Carter asked for an $88 billion program over a period of twelve years. "This would have been the most expensive technological gamble in U.S. history."[86] The strategy appeared to work. Initial reaction by members of Congress was favorable. Speaker Thomas P. O'Neill predicted that "Congress will pull together in this time of crisis"; House Majority Leader Jim Wright of Texas said that the president's goals were high "but we can keep them"; and Senate Minority Leader Howard W. Baker of Tennessee pledged that "I am willing to work with the president if he would let me."[87]

The lawmaking sequence was somewhat unusual, given that the House had already passed a synthetic fuels bill when the president's program was introduced. The Senate had both the House-passed bill and the president's proposal. The House bill was sponsored by Democrat William Moorhead of Pennsylvania, a member of the Committee on Banking, Finance and Urban Affairs, which sponsored the bill on the floor. Therefore the Moorhead bill went to the Senate Committee on Banking, Housing and Urban Affairs. Because the president's program had been introduced in the meantime, the House bill also went to the Senate Committee on Energy and Natural Resources along with the president's bill. A jurisdictional dispute caused delay in the consideration of both bills.[88]

Decisionmaking in the Senate and the conference was highly iterative and featured cross-partisan support. Two very different bills were reported out of the Senate committees. Carter's program, as revised, emanated from the Energy Committee and was passed by the Senate. Funding was not tied to the windfall profits tax, as Carter requested, and the program was cut back from $88 billion to a start-up authorization of $20 billion. Following agreements reached in conference, the House was forced to adopt legislation that it had not really fully considered under its regular procedures, although Majority Leader Wright played an important role in framing a compromise.[89] The conference report was agreed to by substantial cross-partisan majorities in both houses.

The president scored six victories and one defeat on this bill. The votes used by *Congressional Quarterly* for calculating the 1979 support score were taken primarily in the Senate because of the peculiar sequence of the legislation (five of the six votes). That is, a House bill had already passed when the president made his proposal, and he had not taken a position on a synthetic fuels program at the point of House passage.

Although President Carter identified the program as "the keystone of our national energy policy," President Reagan did not consider the synthetic fuels program a priority. In 1985 the Synthetic Fuels Corporation was dismantled, significantly affecting the longer-range "success" for Carter on this issue.[90]

Substantial Presidential Activity in Split-Party Government

The Energy Policy and Conservation Act of 1975 and the anticrime legislative package of 1984 were close to being free-for-alls in the lawmaking process. Unquestionably the president in each case was active in proposing legislation, but his offerings were viewed as starting points on Capitol Hill. The difference between these two cases and the three above lies in the nature of party control.

ENERGY ACT. It is hard to conceive of political circumstances less hospitable to classic responsible government than those in 1975. Gerald Ford was nominated by Nixon in October 1973 to be vice president when Spiro T. Agnew resigned. When Nixon himself was threatened by a possible impeachment, "a handful of Democrats wanted to stall the [Ford] confirmation procedure" since Speaker Carl Albert would become the president if Nixon resigned or was impeached.[91] Thus Gerald Ford became the first unelected vice president under highly partisan circumstances. Then he took over for a president forced to resign in disgrace and pardoned him. House and Senate Democrats realized substantial net increases in the 1974 elections, further separating the two branches.

This context of partisanship and institutional instability was the political setting for an effort to create a national energy policy. The nation faced serious energy problems in the aftermath of the 1973 Arab oil embargo.[92] This least responsible government, by standard criteria, had to manage one of the most complex policy issues of the postwar period. In January 1975 President Ford sent the Congress "a comprehensive 167-page proposal to deal with the nation's energy crisis."[93] Ford also announced that he would remove all controls on domestic oil prices on April 1, a highly controversial action. The partisan nature of these issues was signaled immediately when the Democrats sought to upstage the president by presenting their program two days before the annual State of the Union message. Ford quickly responded by addressing the nation on the same day the Democrats presented their program.

These political shenanigans were a prelude to a year-long battle between the White House and Congress. The oil price decontrol issue, in particular, came to be a running story through 1975. It included postponement of the president's decision to decontrol, an extension of controls by Congress, a presidential veto of the congressional extension, a House veto of a subsequent presidential thirty-month decontrol plan, congressional passage of another price control extension, a second presidential veto, and finally two temporary extensions of controls agreed to by the president.[94]

No one doubted that some action was required. "The country was in the throes of a veritable economic crisis; unemployment was at its highest level since the Great Depression, and inflation was raging at an annualized rate of 12.2 percent." Rising energy prices contributed substantially to inflation. "To much of Congress the energy problem seemed to be essentially one of exorbitant price. This was not the view of the Ford administration, which regarded high prices as a bitter but necessary antidote for wasteful consumption and sluggish domestic production of energy."[95] The president had to be active on this issue, but whatever he proposed would have to compete with solutions proffered by others. This was not stalemate; it was intense competition by separated institutions for shares of power regarding a critical policy matter.

The Senate acted first. Four bills were produced by two committees: Interior and Insular Affairs and Commerce. The House produced just one comprehensive bill. Iteration and partisanship in the Senate varied substantially among the bills, both within the committees and on the floor. Two of the bills passed on the floor with no opposing votes. The other two were more controversial and yet received substantial majorities.

On the House side, the legislation was considered by just one committee: Interstate and Foreign Commerce. Oil price controls were the most controversial issues, resulting in a partisan division (with three Democrats joining all Republicans in opposition to the committee report). Floor debate and amendment occurred intermittently over a period of more than two months. One Republican expressed his view of the bill: "bad," "controversial," "inadequate," and "unattractive."[96] Democrats were also not altogether satisfied, and therefore the bill was subjected to many changes on the House floor, but it finally passed and was then substituted for one of the four Senate bills.

A conference ensued after each house refused to accept the amendments of the other. After a month of deliberations, an agreement was reached without the support of any Republican (or of three Senate Democrats). The House rejected the report on a cross-partisan vote of 300-103 (96 percent of the Republicans joining 63 percent of the Democrats. The House then made further changes and sent a clean bill to the Senate for approval. Perhaps as much out of exhaustion as genuine approval, the Senate approved the House changes following a debate that ridiculed the bill. Republican Senator Lowell Weicker of Connecticut called it "a political energy cop-out," Republican

Senator Henry Bellmon of Oklahoma referred to it as the "Energy Hash Act," and Republican Senator John Tower of Texas called it the "Cold Homes and Dark Factories Act."[97]

The Energy Policy and Conservation Act is an example of a copartisan effort in the early stages, with separate proposals and independent sources of authority on each side, that did not produce cross-partisan support. Although the roll calls show Republicans voting for the final bills, they faced the same dilemma as the president in his decision to sign or veto the bill (see below). Overall, however, this was a partisan battle in which the large Democratic congressional majorities produced a piece of legislation very different from that which the president requested.

The president faced substantial cross-pressures in judging whether to sign the bill. Ford described himself as caught between his economic advisers, urging him to veto the bill, and his political advisers, urging him to sign it.[98] Senate Republicans reportedly reminded the president that with the election year ahead, western conservatives would leave him for Ronald Reagan if he signed the bill. "Enactment of the Energy Policy and Conservation Act might give Ford New Hampshire, but it would lose him Texas, they prophesied."[99] Secretary of the Treasury William Simon urged him at the last minute to veto the measure. Ford thanked him for his late-night call and signed the bill the next day. Simon later wrote that the Energy Policy and Conservation Act was "the worst error of the Ford administration."[100]

Constructing a support score for this legislation is, as expected, no simple task. President Ford was credited with three wins and four losses, perhaps an accurate reflection of the politics of the issue. Yet the final, critical votes on the conference report in the House, the changes made before rejecting the conference report, and the final acceptance of the House changes in the Senate are not included in calculating the support score. It would not be easy to determine the president's position at this stage of action, but that merely makes the larger point that analyzing and interpreting how laws are made cannot rely solely on presidential position taking or judgments about his success.

ANTICRIME PACKAGE. Like many presidents, Ronald Reagan called for national action to curb crime. In recent years, bills had been introduced in 1973, 1977, 1980, 1981, and 1982, but they either died in Congress or were vetoed. In his 1983 State of the Union message, Reagan called for "an all-out war on big-time organized crime and the drug racketeers who are poisoning our young people."[101]

Since crime occurs in every state and congressional district, legislation relating to it is highly constituency oriented. No president can expect that members of Congress will simply ratify his proposals. And, after all, a presidential election was approaching. Therefore several bills were introduced in both houses as counterproposals to those offered by the Reagan administration. What happened then is what discourages those wishing to understand American politics.

The Republican Senate acted first, as was common during the years when Republicans were in the majority. Action within the Committee on the Judiciary was highly iterative and copartisan. Senate Democrats introduced their own proposals. A cross-partisan majority emerged that gained widespread support for several bills on the Senate floor. Taken as a package, the bills met with the approval of the president, who then complained about the failure to act in the House. Others were not so persuaded of the correctness of Senate action. A *New York Times* editorial declared that the Senate bill "rode pell-mell over the Constitution."[102]

The House Committee on the Judiciary reported fourteen separate anticrime bills, an action interpreted by the Reagan administration as parliamentary maneuvering to prevent a vote on the whole package. The last of the Judiciary Committee measures was reported in September.

In late September, House Republicans moved to attach a bill identical to the Senate anticrime package to a fiscal year 1985 continuing resolution (an appropriations measure to keep the government running). Their maneuver succeeded with the support of over a third of the House Democrats. The Democratic leadership then offered an omnibus bill containing most of the Judiciary Committee proposals, which passed by a wide margin. However, the legislative vehicle for the anticrime program was still the continuing resolution. Therefore the conference was not between the two Judiciary committees but rather between the two Appropriations committees, with House Judiciary Committee members playing only a consultative role.

Reaction to passage acknowledged the far-reaching nature of the anticrime package and credited both parties.[103] Yet *Congressional Quarterly* gave the president eight victories and one defeat, a ratio that would surely surprise those on Capitol Hill who worked hard on this legislation.

Institutional Balance on Familiar Issues

The final group of ten bills represents genuine balance between president and Congress. I have divided my discussion of them into three sets. First is a group of old-line issues that were well understood in the White House and Congress, if not easily resolvable in either place. The National Housing Act of 1949; two tax measures, the Excess Profits Tax in 1950 and the Revenue Act of 1962; and the Civil Rights Act of 1957 each displayed the expected joint participation by those in each institution. Of the four, the Civil Rights Act represented something new—the first such act to be passed in many decades—but the issue itself was certainly not novel.

NATIONAL HOUSING ACT. President Truman wrote in his memoirs that "housing was one of the acute postwar problems with which I had to deal. . . . The immediate demand for new housing was far in excess of the industry's capacity to produce."[104] Work on housing proposals had been proceeding since the end of the war in both the White House and Congress. The effort in the Senate had bipartisan leadership: Democrats Robert Wagner of New York and Allen Ellender of Louisiana and Republican Robert Taft of Ohio. Yet in Congress as a whole, the politics of the issue was more cross-partisan than bipartisan, that is, it was more a matter of building a majority from both parties than being able to rely on one from the start. The alliances cut across the parties: "Northern Democratic senators and congressmen and some nationally known Southern Democrats have usually combined with the Northeast urban Republican senators and congressmen from urban areas to support housing legislation. Opponents . . . are drawn from Southern Democrats and Midwest and rural Republicans."[105]

A number of bills had been enacted to give temporary housing relief to homecoming veterans. A long-range housing policy, however, was more difficult to enact because of intense opposition by the real estate and home-building interests. The principal stumbling block was public housing.

Everyone had ample opportunity between 1945 and 1949 to observe and absorb the politics of this issue. In 1946 the Senate passed a bill by a voice vote, but the House Committee on Banking and Currency did not report a bill. In 1947, when the Republicans were in the majority, a joint committee studied the problem but produced no legislation. In 1948 the Senate passed a bill with a public housing provision, but the House Committee on Rules refused to grant a rule to debate the bill in the House. A limited bill was passed and signed by Truman even though he judged it inadequate. In 1948 Truman was elected, to everyone's surprise, and congressional Democrats regained their majorities in both houses.

In 1949 the cross-partisan characteristic of earlier action in the Senate was replaced by copartisanship: both parties offered serious proposals. The administration's bill was introduced by Wagner, Ellender, and five other

Democrats. "Democrats, cavalierly assuming they could enact a public housing bill by themselves, drew up a draft at the start of the session, then gave Taft but one hour to study it before they introduced it. Taken aback, he refused to lend his name to it, and joined [Senators Irving] Ives and [Ralph] Flanders in submitting a plan of his own."[106]

Senator Ives doubted that the two versions could be reconciled because the Democrats had "slammed the door by not giving Senator Taft a proper chance to join them."[107] However, Wagner, Ellender, and Taft had worked on this issue too long not to reach an agreement. Cross partisanship was reestablished. The two proposals were melded and sent to the floor and passed.

The true test was to come in the House. As in the Senate, the Republicans offered their own bill (essentially the Taft alternative). But there was less compromising, and the bill as reported by the committee was closer to the president's original requests. The Committee on Rules first voted to deny a rule. Speaker Rayburn then threatened to invoke the newly adopted twenty-one-day rule by which the Committee on Rules could be circumvented.[108] The committee then reversed itself and voted a rule.

Floor debate on the rule began with the eighty-three-year old Rules Committee chairman, Adolph Sabath, Democrat of Illinois, denouncing the "unholy alliance and coalition" of Republicans and southern Democrats for blocking public housing legislation in the past. "Representative Eugene Cox, Democrat, of Georgia, sixty-nine years old, called Sabath a liar and punched him in the mouth. Sabath's glasses flew off, and he swung blindly at Cox until the two men were pulled apart."[109] Amid cries of "socialism" by opponents, the bill did pass with cross-partisan support. The key vote came on a motion to eliminate the public housing section of the bill. The Democrats could not win this vote on their own, but twenty-four Republicans voted against the motion and it failed, 209-204. On final passage, Republicans supplied a crucial thirty-four votes, without which the bill would have met defeat.[110] The conference report, slightly favoring the Senate bill, was approved by voice vote in both houses. The new housing act was hailed "as one of the most important achievements of the present Congress and one of the most gratifying."[111] Upon signing, Truman marked the legislation as opening up "the prospect of decent homes in wholesome surroundings for low-income families." There were, however, doubts as to how committed Truman was to liberal housing policy.[112] He made no mention of the act in his memoirs.

EXCESS PROFITS TAX. On June 25, 1950, North Korea launched a full-scale invasion of South Korea. Two days later, President Truman committed

U.S. forces to aid South Korea. These events had a significant impact on tax policy in a year that John F. Witte refers to as "one of the most active and confusing . . . in the history of American taxation."[113] One of the issues in the enactment of the Revenue Act of 1950 was an excess profits tax, a popular levy during war but politically questionable during a midterm election year. The president favored such a tax but wanted it enacted after the election, preferably in 1951. After much maneuvering, a provision was included in the Revenue Act to direct the two taxing committees to prepare an excess profits tax either in a special postelection session or in the next Congress, with the tax to be retroactive to 1950.

Congress did reconvene following the 1950 midterm elections and quickly began to work on the legislation. Truman wrote to the chairman of the House Committee on Ways and Means: "To preserve the integrity of the government's finances, our revenue system must keep pace with our defense expenditures." Senate Majority Leader Scott Lucas of Illinois explained: "We're going to see that no one gets rich just because he happened to get a defense contract, or because he cornered a market on something which is in short supply."[114] Predictably, labor groups supported the tax and business groups opposed it. Action in the House was strongly partisan. The opposition was not even allowed to testify before the Committee on Ways and Means, though a Republican plan was introduced that "allowed corporations a choice between increased regular corporate rates of 45 to 55 percent or the excess profits tax."[115] The plan was defeated. After modest changes were made in the administration's proposal, it was reported out by a party-line vote. The Rules Committee granted a closed rule for debate on the floor. The Republicans sought support for their plan in the motion of recommittal. It was defeated, again on a strongly partisan vote. The bill then passed by a wide margin.

As the bill moved to the Senate, Secretary of the Treasury John Snyder warned that defense costs were escalating and more money would be needed. The Senate Committee on Finance accordingly made a number of changes in the House bill to raise more revenue. Republicans did not seriously object, since President Truman had declared a national emergency on December 16 in response to China's involvement in the war. The bill passed the Senate on a voice vote. Conferees quickly reached an agreement, followed by voice vote support in both houses. In a statement released at the signing, Truman praised Congress and its committees for acting with "commendable speed," but others sharply criticized the legislation for containing too many loopholes and not providing sufficient additional revenue.[116]

The Excess Profits Tax of 1950 is an example of emergency legislation responding to events as they occurred. The procedure of having Congress direct itself to act later was unusual. Normal partisan or copartisan behavior over tax policy was suspended in the face of the threat of war with China. The president expressed the need for the legislation and the secretary of the treasury identified the revenue requirements, but the formula itself was written on Capitol Hill.

CIVIL RIGHTS ACT. Lawmaking in a democracy often can be reduced to numbers: the number of voters who support one candidate over another, the number of legislators who align with one party over another, the number of amendments, the number of votes a bill receives. In the case of civil rights lawmaking, an important number for decades was sixty-four—two-thirds of the Senate (which had ninety-six members from 1912 to 1959). It required a two-thirds vote to break a filibuster, and southern and border states nearly had the one-third needed to prevent cloture. A strong cross-partisan alliance was needed to overcome the filibuster, and it was not forthcoming. Therefore attempts by Roosevelt and Truman to pass various civil rights measures were rebuffed by Congress.

The new Eisenhower administration had narrow Republican majorities in Congress and thus "had little interest in spending their energy blowing on the embers of their predecessors' disasters" in civil rights since southern Democratic support might well be required to enact the president's program.[117] Eisenhower had committed himself in his 1953 State of the Union message "to use whatever authority exists in the office of the President to end segregation in the District of Columbia, including the federal government, and any segregation in the armed forces." He believed that "much could be done by Executive power alone," thus avoiding the bruising, and losing, battles on Capitol Hill.[118]

Pressured by congressional northern Democrats and events (such as the Montgomery bus boycott), Attorney General Herbert Brownell, with cabinet approval, began formulating a civil rights proposal in 1955. Cabinet reaction was mixed, as was that of the president, who remained skeptical about taking a legislative initiative in this area. Brownell was forced to moderate his proposal in sending it to Congress in 1956, but he nonetheless worked for support of the whole package, virtually against Eisenhower's wishes.[119] It seems apparent in retrospect that Eisenhower's cautious approach reflected a sensitivity to the politics of the issue, combined with a hope that equality would happen without a fight. The solution appeared to be a kind of hesitant support by the president combined with toleration of more active involvement by Attorney General Brownell. An encouraging increase in his share of the black vote in 1956 contributed to Eisenhower's endorsement of the full Brownell proposal in his 1957 State of the Union message.

Congressional reactions to Eisenhower's more active support of the Brownell proposal were as expected. The powerful leader of the southern Democratic bloc, Senator Richard B. Russell of Georgia, vowed uncompromising opposition, and the leader of the liberal northern Democrats on this issue, Senator Hubert H. Humphrey of Minnesota, welcomed "the President's support of our civil rights program." Senate Majority Leader Lyndon B. Johnson of Texas announced his opposition to the bill, but explained that he would not block efforts to have it debated on the floor.[120]

The House acted first and passed the Eisenhower program after approving a few amendments that weakened the bill. The bill passed by a greater than two-to-one margin, with 90 percent of the Republicans joining 52 percent of the Democrats in favor.

As predicted, the Senate was the stumbling block once again. Efforts were made, as they had been in 1953, to have new rules adopted, based on the view that the Senate was not a continuous body (thus providing an opening for changing the cloture rule). Johnson pleaded with the Senate not to take this action so as to preserve the two-thirds vote on cloture as an important protection for minorities. At the same time he indicated that a civil rights bill could pass the Senate if a majority supported it. In essence he was guaranteeing a vote on the bill, but was also promising there would be no filibuster. With the support of Minority Leader William Knowland of California, Johnson carried the day. Sundquist explains: "The interest of the South in 1957 was therefore *not* to filibuster but to accept as weak a civil rights bill as they could get away with."[121]

The first hurdle in the Senate was the Committee on the Judiciary, chaired by James Eastland of Mississippi. The plan was to avoid the committee altogether. Minority Leader Knowland objected on the floor to sending the House bill to the Judiciary Committee, Senator Russell raised a point of order against the objection, and the Senate, by a vote of 39-45, rejected Russell's point of order. The result was to place the House bill on the Senate calendar, thus allowing it to be taken up by majority vote. Knowland's motion to take up the bill was the subject of eight days of debate, after which the bill itself was debated for twenty-four days.

Two important changes were made on the Senate floor, both weakening the bill by reducing the attorney general's authority and providing for jury trials in criminal contempt cases. Senator Russell led the efforts to cripple the enforcement provisions of the bill. After an impassioned speech foresee-ing the forced "commingling of white and Negro children in the state-sup-ported public schools of the South," "Russell had the civil rights forces in full retreat."[122]

Eisenhower was of little help during this period. Asked in a news confer-ence about Senator Russell's charges, he responded that he found such a reaction "rather incomprehensible, but I am always ready to listen to anyone's presentation to me of his views." Asked if the bill should be changed, the president responded that he had been reading the bill and "there were certain phrases I didn't completely understand."[123] Biographer Stephen E. Ambrose concluded:

> It was a stunning confession of ignorance. Eisenhower had been pushing the bill for two years, had managed to get it through the House and considered by the Senate, and yet now said he did not know what was in it. Eisenhower's admission was an open invitation to the southern senators to modify, amend, emasculate his bill, and they proceeded to do just that.[124]

Following the passage of the crippling amendments, the Senate passed the bill on August 7 by a substantial cross-partisan margin, 72-18. The House then refused to meet in conference or to accept the Senate amendments. On August 22, Speaker Rayburn agreed to negotiations. A bipartisan group from both houses met to work out the differences, and on August 23 Lyndon Johnson called the president to announce an agreement. Both houses then adopted the compromise, delayed in the Senate by the longest filibuster in history, by Strom Thurmond, Democrat of South Carolina.

Reactions to passage were uniformly unenthusiastic. Those supporting a stronger bill were disappointed, and editorial comment was flat.[125] Eisen-hower signed the bill without comment. However, the president was credited with 80 percent support on votes for this bill he did not much like, suffering only two defeats.

Ambrose believes that "the whole experience was one of the most ago-nizing of [Eisenhower's] life. . . . He had waged two successful campaigns to become the nation's leader, but he did not want to lead on the issue of civil rights."[126] On September 21, twelve days after signing the Civil Rights Act of 1957, Eisenhower sent federal troops into Little Rock, Arkansas, to enforce court-ordered integration of the schools.

Not all presidents like the expectations that they will lead in regard to all issues on the agenda. The civil rights policy process in 1956–57 is a good example of presidential reluctance in the face of an issue that was being carried along and framed by others. Eisenhower's certification of the issue was very important, but his passivity otherwise had an effect on the debate and final result. There are few better illustrations of the human factor in presidential participation in governing.

REVENUE ACT. Presidents who win during periods of recession naturally want to get credit for subsequently improving the economy. The state of the economy had been a major issue during the 1960 campaign, so President Kennedy proposed a tax reform program in 1961 to provide greater investment incentives. He planned a two-phased effort: quick action on his 1961 proposals, followed by greater deliberation on a more comprehensive tax reform proposal that would be offered in 1962. The first set of proposals included an investment tax credit, restrictions on deductions for business expenses, and tightening of several loopholes, the most controversial of which was a withholding plan for dividends. Reaction to the president's initial proposal ranged from strong opposition to mild approval. Business, labor, and the financial industry all had criticisms, as did Republicans.[127]

The Committee on Ways and Means held hearings in 1961, but the lesson from this early action was that the president's proposals were sufficiently controversial that legislation would have to be held over until 1962. Witte described a process by which the Committee on Ways and Means assumed leadership of the legislation: "Ways and Means, under the leadership of Wilbur Mills, broadened the investment credit, dropped repeal of the dividend deduction and credit and then adjourned in August 1961, sending a clear message to the administration that depreciation revision was necessary before passage would be possible."[128] The president's role along the way became that of an accommodator or facilitator. Throughout the next several months, Kennedy accepted whatever was being agreed to on Capitol Hill. This acquiescence may have been due in part to the fact that he "had no taste for economic theory."[129]

Action in the House in 1962 was swift. The bill was reported out of committee on March 16, an action praised by President Kennedy. The Committee on Rules granted a closed rule on March 22. The bill passed the House a week later by a relatively narrow vote of 219-196. Only one Republican voted for the bill.

The Senate Committee on Finance held twenty-nine days of hearings on the bill, then made substantial changes "on votes reflecting an unusual coalition of liberals and conservatives."[130] These changes "further sweetened the pot," according to Witte, and thus guaranteed passage. Only one minor amendment was accepted on the floor. As in the House, the bargains were made and the bargains held. In contrast to action in the House, however, the bargains were cross-partisan rather than partisan, with substantial support among Republicans.

Secretary of the Treasury Douglas Dillon called the Senate bill (now quite far from Kennedy's original proposal) "a significant first step toward the reform of our outmoded tax laws," but Senator Albert Gore of Tennessee, criticized the administration, saying that it "had lifted not a finger" to fight the changes made in the Senate.[131] The conference largely accepted the Senate version, and Kennedy signed the bill on October 16. There were many "it's a good start" statements, including one by the president himself. But the nature of the process in 1961 and 1962 led analysts to be pessimistic about future comprehensive reform in the Kennedy administration. Once again, when it comes to tax policy, it is well to be reminded that decisions are made by two institutions, each with a great deal of interest, experience, and political sensitivity.

Institutional Balance on New Issues

The second set of cases dealt with issues that were relatively new and emerging, yet ones in which members of Congress could be expected to be very active because of constituency pressures or other interests. This set includes the Atomic Energy Act of 1954, the Manpower Development and Training Act of 1962, the Clean Air Act of 1963, and the Occupational Safety and Health Act of 1970. The manpower training and worker safety proposals related to familiar issues associated with the labor force, but there had been limited experience with these problems at the federal level.

ATOMIC ENERGY ACT. Atomic energy policy following World War II was fraught with a number of serious and difficult issues. To what extent should the United States cooperate with other nations, notably its former ally, the Soviet Union? How much nuclear military power was sufficient? How might peaceful uses of atomic energy be developed? Would civilians or the military manage development of atomic energy? What role would be played by the private sphere, and what were the implications for the spread of nuclear weapons?

Nelson W. Polsby observes that "the principle of civilian control [of atomic energy] emerged very late in a complicated process of deliberation."[132] Civilian control inevitably introduced the whole set of policy issues to the world of politics. Sensitive to this fact, the designers established an independent regulatory commission, the Atomic Energy Commission (AEC), and a joint congressional committee, the Joint Committee on Atomic Energy (JCAE).

The JCAE was "the only body in Congress that could draft and submit its own legislation and then act as a joint House and Senate 'conference committee' to prepare the legislation for final vote. [It] thus was able to practice a take-it-or-leave-it attitude towards the Congress as a whole regarding nuclear legislation."[133] The AEC, charged with a highly defense-related function of developing nuclear weapons, was hardly the typical regulatory commission, either. Therefore atomic energy politics would be played out in a special organizational setting, but politics there would be.

Because the Republicans won majorities in both the House and the Senate in the 1952 elections, it was reasonable to expect greater involvement by private industry in atomic energy. Two Republican conservatives, Representative W. Sterling Cole of New York and Senator Bourke Hickenlooper of Iowa, took over as chairman and ranking senator, respectively, of the JCAE. President Eisenhower nominated Lewis Strauss, "a die-hard conservative with an ideological devotion to pure private enterprise," to be AEC chairman in 1953.[134] All three—Cole, Hickenlooper, and Strauss—were anxious to revise the Atomic Energy Act of 1946 so as to permit greater private-sector involvement in the development and application of atomic power.

The president set the context for the privatization of atomic power and endorsed "the peaceful uses of atomic energy" in his "Atoms for Peace" speech to the United Nations on December 8, 1953.[135] However, the executive branch became caught up by delays in the controversial Strauss nomination. The JCAE was unwilling to wait. It held hearings during 1953 to lay the foundation for important changes in atomic energy policy. This anxiety to act on Capitol Hill spurred the AEC to prepare legislative proposals sooner than they might have otherwise. The AEC proposal was sent to Congress in February 1954, but was not actually introduced. Instead in April Cole and Hickenlooper introduced their own bill, which incorporated much of what the administration asked for.[136] Closed, then open, hearings were held in May.

The issue of public versus private power came to be contentious and highly partisan. Democratic Representative Chet Holifield of California, a member and later chairman of the JCAE, was a strong and active supporter of public power and a vigorous opponent of the Cole-Hickenlooper bill.[137] The partisan nature of the debate within the JCAE carried over to both the House and Senate floor, in part, perhaps, because of members' lack of knowledge of the subject. According to Harold P. Green and Alan Rosenthal, floor debate in the House was "generally superficial." The Senate debate was no more edifying and did not really address the complex issues involved in establishing a national policy for peaceful uses of atomic energy. "In the Senate, too, debate on particular provisions was overshadowed by polemic and partisan maneuvering. . . . Thus, Congressional debate, especially in the Senate, was more a study in political strategy and parliamentary tactics than a close scrutiny of atomic-energy legislation."[138]

The Senate debate, which lasted 181 hours, featured a filibuster by the public power advocates, led by Democrat Warren Magnuson of Washington.[139] The debate was fueled in part by criticism of the Dixon-Yates power contract, an AEC-supported agreement with private contractors to supply power to the Tennessee Valley Authority. When the debate ended, Republicans in both chambers voted overwhelmingly in favor of the bill (97 percent in both chambers). The Republican vote alone was sufficient in each chamber to pass the legislation. However, amendments were passed in each chamber, so different versions of the bill were returned to the JCAE, now acting as a conference. Partisanship continued to dominate, and three Democrats refused to sign the conference report (once again because of disagreement on public versus private power). The House accepted the conference report, but the Senate rejected it on a partisan vote (although five Republicans actually provided the necessary margin). After a second conference removed the most objectionable provisions, the report was approved in both chambers. President Eisenhower signed the bill on August 30.

Peaceful use of atomic energy was a relatively new policy issue. The federal government had supported the development of this new energy source for military purposes. The crucial decision regarding domestic development of atomic energy was one in which Congress would naturally be heavily involved, given the constituency-related effects and the ideological division between advocates of public and private power. The president's role was relatively small once he delivered his "Atoms for Peace" speech and appointed an AEC chairman to his liking. In fact, the 1954 act barely received mention in his memoirs.[140] However disengaged he may have been, he did receive credit from *Congressional Quarterly* for seven victories and just two defeats in his presidential support score for 1954.

MANPOWER DEVELOPMENT. During the 1960 presidential campaign, Kennedy had been "shaken by the misery he witnessed first hand in West Virginia."[141] Upon winning the White House, he was determined to effect change. In 1961 an Area Redevelopment Act to assist depressed regions was passed, including authorization for job training programs. On May 25, 1961, the president announced to Congress that he was sending a Manpower Development and Training Program to train "workers whose skills became obsolete as a result of industrial change."[142] Here was a new type of program, "the first major effort to train and retrain unemployed workers."[143] Such a program was likely to find favor on Capitol Hill with Republicans as well as Democrats. As historian James T. Patterson observed, "Sold as a way of helping people help themselves and thereby get off welfare, the program was popular with Congress."[144]

The Senate acted first on Kennedy's request. The principal issue came to be whether "retraining of adults should be organized and administered as a new category within the existing federal-state vocational education program . . . or embody some major new departures."[145] The American Vocational Association (AVA) was represented by a particularly vigorous lobbyist, who was successful in getting changes made. The bill enjoyed significant cross-partisan support and passed 60-31 (Republicans providing a crucial sixteen votes).

Developments in the House were somewhat more complicated. The House Committee on Education and Labor had studied the general problem of unemployment, as had a House Republican Policy Committee Task Force. The bill that resulted was a compromise between Elmer Holland of Pennsylvania, the Democratic chairman of the subcommittee with responsibility for the measure, and the principal Republican activist on this issue, Charles E. Goodell of New York. The Education and Labor Committee failed to consider the changes desired by the AVA, however, and the bill was stalled in the Committee on Rules at adjournment (with the AVA lobbyist taking credit for the delay). At this point, Goodell essentially took over, using the Senate-passed bill as a model and eventually forcing Holland to accept the changes. Released by the Rules Committee, the Goodell bill passed the House by a wide bipartisan margin, 354-62 (well over 80 percent of each party voting in favor). Here was an unusual case of partisanship at the committee stage, copartisanship leading to cross-partisan support in floor maneuvering, and eventual bipartisan voting.

Though it was later to be the subject of criticism, the new act was hailed at the time as a major accomplishment for the Kennedy administration.[146] Members of Congress were equally active in the development of the program, however. There were relatively few votes to be counted in the presidential support score, primarily because the important changes were made within the committees or between the key actors in floor maneuvering, not in amendments subject to roll call voting.

CLEAN AIR. A federal role in pollution control was also a relatively new issue. Therefore policymakers in both institutions had to familiarize themselves with the nature of the problem, the feasibility of solutions, and the advantages or disadvantages of locating a program in various agencies. A small program enacted in 1955 provided limited federal support for state and local governments to control air pollution. In 1960 the few members of Congress interested in air pollution were successful in authorizing the surgeon general to conduct a study of automobile exhaust. But basically this issue remained one for the states and localities, not the federal government.

President Kennedy was interested in expanding the federal role. In February 1961 he asked for "an effective Federal air pollution control program now."[147] His ally in the Senate on this issue was Republican Thomas Kuchel of California, who was successful in getting a modest bill passed. However, Democrat Kenneth Roberts of Alabama, chairman of the Subcommittee of Health and Safety of the House Committee on Interstate and Foreign Commerce, was opposed to federal enforcement and thwarted action on Kuchel's bill in the House.

Within the administration, conflict existed between those supporting an enforcement role for the federal government and those in the Public Health Service (with allies in the Bureau of the Budget) who were reluctant to serve as the enforcers. Partly because of these internal battles, those favoring an enforcement role decided to have the president recommend legislation but rely on Congress to prepare the bill. Randall B. Ripley describes what happened:

> Virtually all the supporters of the legislation favored not introducing an administration bill. [They] did not want to become involved in the formal legislative clearance process with the Public Health Service and the Bureau of the Budget. . . .
>
> What legislation would emerge, if any, was now up to the Congress. The executive at this point was speaking timidly and with reservations.[148]

Meanwhile, the situation had changed in the Senate. Kuchel's Democratic colleague from California, Clair Engle, introduced legislation in the fall of 1962. In November, Abraham Ribicoff, Kennedy's former secretary of HEW, was elected to the Senate from Connecticut. Ribicoff sponsored a clean air bill in 1963 (with nineteen cosponsors), but he was not appointed to the Committee on Public Works, which had jurisdiction for the bill. Still his bill became "a major focus of debate throughout the year."[149] In the House, Roberts changed his mind and introduced a bill, as did Democrat Peter Rodino of New Jersey and Republican James Fulton of Pennsylvania, whose joint proposal was the same as the Ribicoff bill. Dean Coston, a special assistant from HEW, worked with all interested members in promoting the legislation and working out compromises. Roberts was successful, following modifications, in getting unanimous committee endorsement of his bill providing grants to the states and enforcement measures. The bill then passed the House without change by a cross-partisan vote of 273-102 (42 percent of Republicans joining 95 percent of Democrats in support). Republican votes were not crucial to the passage of the bill, given the unity of House Democrats.

Senate approval seemed a foregone conclusion, given bipartisan support for the legislation. The issue was the extent to which the bill would be strengthened. A new figure came to champion the legislation: Democratic Senator Edmund S. Muskie of Maine had become the chairman of a Special Subcommittee on Air and Water Pollution of the Committee on Public Works. Six bills were available: those by Ribicoff and Engle, the House bill, and three others. Following hearings, the Muskie subcommittee strengthened the House bill and reported it to the Senate, which passed it with only minor changes by a voice vote on November 19, three days before Kennedy was assassinated.

Muskie and Roberts communicated frequently in working out the differences between the two versions. The conference agreed on the changes, most of which favored the Senate version, on December 4. The conference report was agreed to in the House by very much the same vote as the Roberts bill had received and by a voice vote in the Senate. It was one of the first bills signed by Lyndon Johnson on December 17.

This bill is a fascinating instance of a conscious strategy by the administration, with presidential acquiescence, to work through Congress, fully aware of the support available there, rather than to prepare a bill. Clearly the principal work on this legislation occurred in the congressional setting, and Ripley concludes that "without Congress, the executive would have produced legislation less far-reaching in its provisions than what was produced with the help of Congress."[150] Little attention was paid to the bill in the press, preoccupied with the death of the president and the succession of Lyndon Johnson. In calculating presidential support for 1963, *Congressional Quarterly* counted only two votes, both as wins for the president and both in the House since Senate action was by voice vote.

OCCUPATIONAL SAFETY AND HEALTH. In 1968 President Johnson offered an occupational safety and health proposal that would authorize the secretary of labor to set mandatory standards and to close down plants that did not meet these standards. Business and industry lobbied intensely and successfully to kill the proposal. A bill was reported from the House

Committee on Education and Labor but was bottled up in the Committee on Rules. The Senate Committee on Labor and Public Welfare held hearings but took no further action. The problem to which this legislation was directed was generally acknowledged to be severe, but little had been done at the federal level to establish regulations. A mine disaster in Farmington, West Virginia, in November 1968 drew more attention to worker safety, but Congress had already gone home without having enacted President Johnson's proposal.

By 1970 President Nixon and the Republicans were receptive to proposals that might attract blue-collar support, and an occupational safety and health program seemed a good prospect.[151] Graham K. Wilson counts the 1970 legislation as an example of congressional influence: "The notion that all important bills are drafted in the Executive Branch dies hard. The OSH Act was indeed sired by President Johnson. . . . The form that his brain-child took was determined much more by its gestation in Congress, however, than by the Executive Branch under Nixon."[152] Nixon proposed that a national occupational safety and health board be established to set standards. Congressional Democrats essentially reintroduced the Johnson proposal. They preferred to have the secretary of labor in charge of regulation since a regulatory board might well come under the influence of industry. Initial reactions to the Nixon proposal reflected exactly those concerns.

The House acted first. The Committee on Education and Labor reported a bill that adopted the Johnson approach. However, on the floor a cross-partisan coalition supported a substitute amendment introduced by Republican William Steiger of Wisconsin and Democrat Robert Sikes of Florida that was very close to the original Nixon proposal. The amendment passed with the support of 90 percent of the Republicans, who were joined by sixty southern Democrats to form a majority.

The Senate Committee on Labor and Public Welfare also reported out a bill favoring the Johnson approach of giving the secretary of labor the authority to create and enforce standards. On the Senate floor, Republican Jacob Javits of New York proposed an amendment that split the difference. The secretary of labor would set standards and a presidentially appointed board would enforce them. As in the House, the amendment passed with cross-partisan support, eleven southern Democrats joining all Republicans in favor. Once President Nixon accepted the compromise, the bill passed by a wide margin. The conference agreement favored the Senate approach, to the chagrin of certain House members.[153]

Both business and labor praised the passage of the bill, surely an unusual response regarding labor legislation. It is a classic case of copartisanship leading to a cross-partisan compromise. Only two votes were counted in the presidential support sweepstakes, both in the House, which then did not succeed in having its way in conference. The vote on the Javits substitute was not counted, presumably because the president publicly favored the House bill at that point.

Institutional Balance under Unusual Procedures

The third set of cases in this group of balanced participation between the branches offers two of the most interesting enactments in the whole set of twenty-eight. The Social Security Amendments of 1983 and the Deficit Reduction Package of 1990 represent the use of extraordinary policymaking procedures in response to the political, partisan, and institutional conflicts associated with these issues. It was necessary to go outside the normal lawmaking procedures in order to build cross-partisan majorities.

SOCIAL SECURITY AMENDMENTS. As noted earlier (see discussion of COLAs), reforming the social security system is a highly participatory activity. Certainly no member of Congress can opt out. Each is expected to have an opinion and to be engaged when any change in benefits is proposed. And yet Congress is not well designed as a planning body. It is a political body, designed to represent interests in making decisions about plans offered by others. Thus rational reform of large-scale programs is not easily managed in Congress. In addition, as Martha Derthick concludes, congressional "action is *never* complete. Constantly changing in composition, torn always between its roles as policymaker for the nation and representative of particular constituencies and constituents, . . . Congress engages endlessly in lawmaking."[154]

Unfortunately, a problem of grand scale had been developing in social security financing for some time.[155] It was unlikely to be dealt with solely by Congress, yet any administration proposal that recommended cuts would probably be defeated, if considered at all. It was not even clear that members of Congress could publicly acknowledge a problem, for to do so would invite politically unacceptable solutions.

The triumph of the Republicans in the 1980 elections seemingly provided a stimulus for change. President Reagan campaigned on cutting the budget and reducing taxes. Since the burden for program cuts had to be shared, perhaps a bipartisan agreement could be reached to include social security beneficiaries in an overall package of programmatic cutbacks. The problem itself had been studied to death. According to Paul C. Light, "there was no shortage of potential solutions, but no place to hide. In the two short years before Reagan's inauguration, there had already been three major study reports on the social security crisis."[156] The issue was developing policy momentum. Democrat J. J. Pickle of Texas, chairman of the Subcommittee on Social Security of the House Committee on Ways and Means, had prepared a bill. Republican Senator Pete Domenici of New Mexico was gathering support in the Senate Committee on the Budget for a cross-partisan plan. And the administration was prepared to move in order to take advantage of its perceived mandate for change. Conditions seemed right for copartisan politics leading to a cross-partisan compromise solution.

However, for this result to be achieved on such a politically sensitive issue, everyone involved had to be protected. Both parties had to share in taking credit and avoiding blame. That goal proved impossible to achieve. Reagan's budget director, David Stockman, was eager to show immediate savings, principally through severe reductions for early retirees, while the Pickle plan projected reductions in the future. Neither Stockman nor Chief of Staff James Baker liked the Domenici initiative, and they worked actively to have the president express his opposition at a meeting on Capitol Hill.[157] Confident that speed was of the essence, Stockman controlled the input and "tightened secrecy around his decisions. . . . The [White House] legislative staff did not see the final proposal until just three days before the formal announcement. . . . Pickle . . . was not informed about the Stockman proposal, nor were key Republicans on the Ways and Means Committee. There was no warning of what was to come."[158] Stockman did get signals of difficulties from within the White House itself, and House Republicans complained of being blindsided. The president had little interest in the whole subject.

Partisan or copartisan politics begins with support from within one's own party. Stockman did not have that support, and his style antagonized many congressional Republicans. The Democrats, reeling from defeats on other budget-related issues, pulled back from proposing their solution so as to attack the president's plan. Speaker O'Neill "urged Pickle to hold back from any favorable response."[159] And then they hit the president with both barrels. The plan was called a "breach of contract," "insidious" and "cruel," "despicable."[160] Democratic Senator Patrick Moynihan of New York introduced a "sense of the Senate" resolution condemning the administration proposal as "a breach of faith." It was defeated by just one vote. Republican Senator

Robert Dole of Kansas then introduced a resolution, without the partisan rhetoric, that simply opposed an unfair cut in benefits for early retirees. It passed 96-0.[161] "The next day's *Washington Post* front-page headline was "Senate Unanimously Rebuffs President on Social Security." This created a permanent axiom in the Reagan White House: "Never go it alone on social security."[162]

After suffering this self-inflicted political defeat, the Reagan White House had to back up and try again. The president accepted the proposal by Republican Senator William Armstrong of Colorado to create a bipartisan National Commission on Social Security Reform, with the members appointed by the president, the Speaker of the House, and the Senate majority leader. Meanwhile the Democrats continued to pound on the president, carrying their social security message into the 1982 elections, where they increased their House seats by almost the number lost in 1980.

Thus the national commission became the institutional base for policy development.[163] The commission eventually produced a package that was accepted by President Reagan and Speaker O'Neill, each of whom promised to deliver the necessary votes so that the credit and blame would be shared. Once an agreement was reached in mid-January 1983, the emphasis was on speedy action in Congress lest the cross-partisan support collapse. The House Committee on Ways and Means immediately scheduled hearings and then approved the plan with amendments. The floor debate centered on whether to manage the fiscal future of the program by adding taxes or by raising the retirement age and reducing benefits for early retirees. In a bitter debate, the latter won. Democrat Claude Pepper of Florida, champion of the aged, proposed the former and was defeated, 132-296. J. J. Pickle proposed the latter and won on a cross-partisan vote, 228-202. The Pickle amendment garnered 92 percent of the Republican vote, 60 percent of the southern Democratic vote, and 13 percent of the northern Democratic vote.

The Senate Committee on Finance modified the House bill but basically accepted the Pickle approach. One further change was made on the Senate floor, but the bill itself passed by a cross-partisan vote of 88-9. The results of the conference favored the House bill. The resulting report was agreed to by the House (243-102) and Senate (58-14). In both the House and Senate, a higher proportion of Democrats than Republicans supported the final version. President Reagan and Speaker O'Neill stressed the importance of conciliation and compromise at the signing ceremony.

The president was credited by *Congressional Quarterly* with six victories and one defeat. Although Reagan favored certain amendments and opposed others, one can question how accurate it is to conclude that he won 86 percent of the time on this issue, or, for that matter, what exactly victory meant in the case of a hard-fought compromise agreement. It also stands as an extraordinary case of breaking a political stalemate between the president and Congress. As Light concluded, "Congress and the President had created a new form of government."[164]

DEFICIT REDUCTION. Officially titled the Omnibus Budget Reconciliation Act of 1990, the deficit reduction package passed at the end of the 101st Congress will surely go down in history as one of the most fascinating lawmaking stories ever. What happened in 1990 cannot be understood without some attention to what had gone on before. Among the more important defining factors were these:

—Passage in 1974 of the Budget and Impoundment Control Act, which provided for a congressional budget process (see earlier discussion). The act directed Congress to enact budget resolutions, thereby providing a tracking device for congressional action.

—Passage in 1981 of the Economic Recovery Tax Act, which contributed to sizable deficits that kept the pressure on Congress to make cuts in expenditures.

—Passage in 1985 of the Gramm-Rudman-Hollings (GRH) deficit reduction process by which targets were set and failure to meet them resulted in sequestration.

—A pledge in 1988 by presidential candidate George Bush not to raise taxes: "Read my lips, no new taxes."

These four realities predictably led to high politics. As with the social security issue in 1981, it was not clear how an agreement could be reached within the normal workings of presidential-congressional interaction. Conditions were excellent for producing a political stalemate. And yet that was not an acceptable outcome since the GRH mechanism would then be triggered, requiring severe cuts in domestic and defense programs. Thus there were copartisan incentives to fashion a cross-partisan majority. Doing so proved to be arduous, conflictual, and tense.

As required by the GRH provisions, the president presented a budget in late January 1990 that met the deficit target for fiscal year 1991. As dictated by the political realities, the Democrats heaped scorn on the president's plan (a reaction that had come to be routine in the Reagan years). "Democrats had derided President Bush's budget, but they found it next to impossible to come up with one of their own."[165] The House acted first, producing a budget resolution that, in spite of the criticism, incorporated much of the president's plan. It even adopted the administration's economic assumptions. Still, the changes that were made, primarily cuts in defense, found disfavor among congressional Republicans, who voted to a person against it in the Budget Committee and on the House floor. And by the time the resolution passed the House, both sides were backing away from whatever was on paper because it appeared that the July budget review from the Office of Management and Budget would show a sizable increase in the projected deficit for the year. Eventually the president's plan was withdrawn from the floor, "much to the glee of the Democrats."[166] Earlier the president had ruled out a summit; now one seemed the only way out.

Given what had already happened, it was going to be even more difficult for the Senate to produce a budget resolution. The Republicans signaled their opposition to any Democratic proposal. All participants appeared to be waiting for the right time to meet at a summit. Defense, in particular, divided the Democrats, whose majority was rather slim to start with. A document was produced that met the deficit targets, but no one knew for certain just how that would happen. Meanwhile, the president and congressional leaders agreed to meet. Therefore the Senate, by a voice vote, passed a skeletal, policy-neutral resolution.

Charade now seemed the appropriate word to describe events. The House refused to meet the Senate in conference on their resolution. The prospect of a summit agreement obviated passage of any budget resolution. Yet the Appropriations committees required such a triggering mechanism to enact appropriations bills. The solution was to produce a "deeming resolution" in each house by which the appropriations process would be authorized to proceed on the basis of the resolution that each house had passed but not agreed to in conference.

"Democrats were wary about another summit, but . . . their leadership could not refuse the president's request to talk."[167] In particular, the Democrats wanted Bush to go first, to rescind his pledge of no new taxes. The president agreed that the talks would proceed with no preconditions, thereby upsetting many Republicans who had already fixed their antitax position for the upcoming 1990 congressional elections. In the initial presummit sparring, Democrats pressed for an even stronger statement by the president on increasing taxes. As Barbara Sinclair observed, "Democrats had been tarred as high taxers too often; they were united in their unwillingness to propose increasing taxes."[168] As the jockeying proceeded, both the Office of Management and Budget and the Congressional Budget Office agreed that earlier deficit projections were again too low and that there were troubling signs in the economy.[169] Finally, the president issued a statement backing away from his campaign pledge. He explained that all of the following were required in a budget package: "entitlement and mandatory program reform; tax revenue increases; growth incentives; discretionary spending reductions; orderly reductions in defense expenditures; and budget process reform."[170]

Now meetings began in earnest to prepare a budget package, but were interrupted by the August recess of Congress. Two days before members left town, Iraq invaded Kuwait, producing a serious Mideast crisis that would affect the economic assumptions so vital to producing a workable plan. When Congress reconvened, the summiteers secluded themselves at Andrews Air Force Base outside Washington. Early optimistic reports gave way to pessimism, and the consultations returned to the Capitol with a reduced group of participants.

Representative Bill Frenzel of Minnesota observed: "No one wants to concede anything until the last minute. We have to declare a last minute."[171] The approaching mandatory sequester seemingly was such a last minute, so the president and congressional leaders finally announced an agreement on September 30, and each house passed continuing resolutions to keep the government going. A week later a cross-partisan alliance between liberal Democrats and conservative Republicans rejected the agreement in the House. Both houses then passed a second continuing resolution, which was vetoed by the president, who insisted that a budget resolution be enacted first.

During the next three weeks, Congress passed a skeletal budget resolution, a series of continuing resolutions, and, at long last, a reconciliation package on October 27. The final agreement split both parties. The final House majority was made up of 181 Democrats and 47 Republicans; the Senate majority included 35 Democrats and 19 Republicans. The product itself was unquestionably a compromise, but Democrats were pleased with the tax program in which the rich would bear most of the increases. It included significant new procedures for future budget making and, as a multiyear agreement, promised to avoid a replay of the 1990 exercise for at least two years.

In the end, Sinclair probably is correct in asserting that "because the president needed action, he was eventually forced to capitulate and renege on the major promise of his campaign. The decision was clearly necessary to get an agreement, yet it eventually led to a reframing of the debate so as to disadvantage the president."[172] In this case, the president was credited by *Congressional Quarterly* with three victories and four defeats. But among the defeats was the early House budget resolution that was no more than a negotiating position, as stated by the Speaker himself, and among the victories was the final agreement, which was judged at the time to be a victory more for Democrats than for the president.

Sequence, Iteration, and Partisanship

I began this discussion by stressing that our representative system makes laws through a mostly public process that is variably iterative, sequential, and partisan. I also raised questions, as have others, about the utility of roll call votes as reliable measures of presidential success with Congress, and have even challenged the concept of "success," given the complexity of major issues as they are acted on over time. Presidents have important roles to play in lawmaking, but most of the time they deal with issues that are familiar on Capitol Hill. Legislative proposals are typically designed to alter programs already on the books. There are relatively few new proposals for new problems. In order to make change, presidents must determine how to manage existing forces, most of which have established access on Capitol Hill and within the bureaucracy. It is time to identify some of what has been learned by an examination of lawmaking in twenty-eight instances.

Sequence is clearly part of the strategic environment. Presidents do often initiate the proposals that form the basis of legislative action, though as John Kingdon and others have noted, they may represent ideas that have been around for some time. When presidents are reluctant to act, Congress is a source of legislative initiative, even for highly significant issues like trade and energy. Further, as has been frequently illustrated, presidential initiative by no means guarantees presidential dominance in lawmaking. Members of Congress rightfully believe they are charged to make laws, and they act on this understanding of their authority.

The matter of which house acts first may be a result of other work that is scheduled, strategic considerations, constitutional mandate (as with revenue legislation), or issue preferences of the majority. In the cases studied here, the House acted first fifteen times, the Senate thirteen times. A summary of the various sequences is shown in appendix table A-1. There were sixteen cases of what might be called a "pure sequence," that is, presidential initiative followed by action in the two houses and either a conference or acceptance by one house of the bill passed by the other (one of the sixteen resulted in a veto). The other twelve cases were extraordinary in that no two were alike. It is intriguing that this simple distinction among these major laws displays significant variations in the president's role and a rich assortment of legislative sequences.

That lawmaking is iterative would hardly be a point worth making except that it is so often ignored in analyzing presidential-congressional interaction. A summary of my judgments concerning the amount of iteration at the committee and floor stages for both houses is shown in appendix table A-2. As expected, the cases of high iteration are fewest (just two) in the category of presidential preponderance and greatest (sixteen) among those in the category of congressional preponderance. Iteration in the cases of balanced institutional participation is moderate to high in a large majority of instances.

Normally one expects the committees to function in a manner that would reduce the degree of iteration on the floor. That happened in over half the cases in each house (see appendix table A-3). In one instance in the House (the Elementary and Secondary Education Act) and two in the Senate (again, the Education Act and the Economic Recovery Tax Act), there was limited iteration at either stage. In a surprisingly high number of instances, the iterative process either continued at a moderate or high rate or actually intensified when the bill was treated on the floor. These include the most interesting and important pieces of legislation, such as the Taft-Hartley act, the Omnibus Trade Act, the Energy Policy and Conservation Act, the creation of the Department of Education, COLAs, and the Deficit Reduction Act. And, as discussed, the Civil Rights Act of 1957 was brought directly from the calendar to avoid the committee stage and thus was highly iterative on the Senate floor.

The patterns of partisanship at the committee and floor stages for the twenty-eight bills are shown in appendix table A-4. The rich variety of inter-party relations in the congressional lawmaking process is remarkable. This evidence of the flexibility of the party structure calls into doubt the applicability to American national institutions of the classic party responsibility model. There are also interesting differences among the four categories of branch participation. The cases of presidential and congressional preponderance show the least variety. For the first, presidents either have the party support to get their way, are successful in gaining bipartisan support for an overriding issue, or gain enough support from the other party to win the day. For the congressional cases, the greater openness in participation encourages substantially more cross partisanship in lawmaking. It is not easy for a two-house legislature to form policy solutions through single-party action, particularly given the voters' habitual production of split-party governments. The cases of balanced participation also show substantial cross-partisan activity, either directly or as a result of initial copartisan politics. These cases also display the full range of partisan methods for building majorities and the differences between the two chambers in these patterns.

The voting patterns for final passage or the conference report for the twenty-eight major bills (shown in appendix table A-5) confirm many of the same differences noted in the earlier stages. In only one-fourth of the cases of presidential preponderance did the president require the votes of the other party for passage. In the cases of congressional preponderance or balanced participation the voting often showed mixed patterns of partisanship, again indicating its inconstant nature in lawmaking. And there are only two instances that meet my criterion for partisan voting (80 percent of each party on opposite sides), both in the House: the Food Stamp Act of 1964 and the Revenue Act of 1962.[173]

These patterns indicate a highly dynamic process of partisan interaction that is not well portrayed by studies of party voting. An intensive look at the process by which twenty-eight major laws were passed reveals a set of party-based negotiating activities. The president is often an active participant in this process, but sometimes he is not, even if he was originally responsible for the proposal that is being negotiated. Therefore in some instances there is a progression from a presidential policy initiative to a congressionally developed proposal that is monitored and responded to by the White House. These developments cannot be captured by roll call votes or by scores based on those votes.

A particularly interesting result of this analysis is the identification of copartisan and cross-partisan patterns. Eighteen cases in the House and twenty in the Senate predominantly fit these patterns (that is, I characterized them as such in two or more of the committee, floor, and voting stages). Of those cases, twelve in each house occurred in split-party governments. Given that such governments are common, more attention should be paid to how legislation is formed under these circumstances. Just as absorbing, however, is that six House cases and eight Senate cases of these patterns occurred during single-party governments.

In his study of political parties in the postreform House of Representatives, David W. Rohde points out that "partisanship was not muted by divided government, although compromises were eventually reached in some instances. Nor was stalemate the result, and certainly not inaction. Clearly the president did not set this agenda; he opposed it. Yet not only did every one of the ten items on [Speaker] Wright's list of priorities pass the House; every one of them eventually became law in one form or another."[174] Rohde's description of relations between President Reagan and a Democratic Congress in the late 1980s could easily be a summary of legislative interaction between President Truman and the Republican Congress in 1947–48. A review of twenty-eight laws over several decades shows the full range of partisan variations.

The examination of these twenty-eight laws also produces an important distinction between bipartisanship and cross partisanship. Bipartisanship—where both sides are substantially agreed and involved in policy development—does not occur often (see tables A-4 and A-5). Cross partisanship—where a critical portion of one side joins the other to form a majority—occurs frequently. In some cases the coalition shows up in the early stages of the legislation; in other cases it is the result of initial position taking by each side, followed by compromise and agreement to support a modified version of the proposal.

The analysis in this chapter has also explored the reliability of presidential support scores as indicators of presidential involvement in and success with individual pieces of legislation. Disaggregating these scores for specific pieces of legislation raises serious questions as to what they represent. Often reliance on them for an important bill results in a distorted view of the president's role, as I have explained throughout. The wins and losses for twenty-four major bills are summarized in appendix table A-6 (the four Truman cases are not included since presidential support scores were not calculated then).

There is a stark difference in batting average between the cases of presidential and congressional preponderance. The presidents suffered no losses in the first category and had wins in just two of the cases in the second category. Clearly these scores do provide gross indicators for distinguishing between the primary involvement of the president and Congress in major legislation. The presidents' batting averages were impressive in both types of balanced participation, dropping below 78 percent in only three cases. However, throughout this chapter I have raised questions concerning what this scoring means, given the variability in the data. For example, the range of votes included for calculating the support score is from zero for the social security increases in 1972 to nineteen for the creation of the Department of Education in 1979. The number of votes used for calculating the support score was greater in the Senate than the House, and, of course, these votes frequently were not directly on the issue but rather on procedural matters. The weight of a set of votes on a particular issue in relation to the president's overall score for the year varied substantially, from 1 percent to 28 percent (the latter being the losses for Kennedy in votes for the Revenue Act of 1962). But the relative weight of any one set of votes depended on how active the president was in making proposals and taking positions along the way. For example, Eisenhower's six wins on the Landrum-Griffin Act of 1959 accounted for 7 percent of his wins for that year, but Carter's six wins on airline deregulation in 1978 accounted for just 3 percent of his wins. Support scores should be viewed skeptically as indicators of presidential performance.

This examination of the making of major laws during the postwar era illustrates the true nature of the U.S. national political system. Presidents must fit themselves into an ongoing lawmaking process. They may be key actors in this process, but it can, and often does, operate without or alongside them. Those interested in measuring presidential success in this process are advised to refine their measures to account for the important differences in policy, political, and institutional conditions associated with each administration. Even more useful, perhaps, would be the development of a means for measuring success of the system. For when it comes to making laws in Washington, it is never done solely in the White House, it is sometimes done largely on Capitol Hill, and it is normally done with a substantial amount of cross-institutional and cross-partisan interaction through elaborate sequences featuring varying degrees of iteration. A first step in understanding how that happens is to resist oversimplification.

Appendix

For each of the twenty-eight pieces of legislation I made the following judgments and observations.

1. A composite rating of the degree of iteration in committee and on the floor for each house, based on the number of serious and credible alternatives offered, the number of amendments introduced, and the changes made.

2. A judgment regarding the partisan interaction in committee, on the floor, and in voting, using the four categories of partisanship discussed in chapter 1: partisan, copartisan, bipartisan, and cross-partisan. For the committee and floor stages, I made a composite judgment based on bill sponsorship, alternative proposals, announced support, and the source of amendments. For voting, I used the following criteria to classify the votes (on final passage and on the conference report unless otherwise noted):

Partisan = 80 percent of each party on opposite sides.

Bipartisan = 80 percent of each party on the same side.

Cross-partisan 1 = votes of other party *needed* for a majority (classic or primary cross partisanship).

Cross-partisan 2 = substantial other-party votes (20 percent or more) present but *not needed* for a majority (free or secondary cross partisanship).

3. The sequence of lawmaking between the two houses–which chamber acted first.

4. A judgment about whether the final product was closer to the House version or the Senate version or was balanced between the two.

5. The number of presidential wins and losses from the roll call voting on the bill, as identified by *Congressional Quarterly* for calculating the presidential support score.

Table A-1. *Lawmaking Sequence, Twenty-eight Selected Enactments, 1947–90*

Sequence	Legislation
Presidential initiative (pure sequence)	
Pres.→House→Sen.→Conf.	Highway Act (1956), Medicare (1965), Revenue Act (1962), Clean Air Act (1963)
Pres.→Sen.→House→Conf.	European Recovery (1948), Airline Deregulation (1978), Economic Recovery (1981), Labor Reform Act (1959), Department of Education (1979), Anticrime (1984), National Housing Act (1949), Manpower Development (1962), Occupational Safety and Health Act (1970)
Pres.→House→Sen.	Education Act (1965)
Pres.→House→Sen.→House	Food Stamps (1948)
Pres.→House→Sen.→Conf.→Veto→Override	Labor Management Relations Act (1947)
Presidential initiative (uncommon sequence)	
Pres.→Sen.→Conf.→House	Social Security Benefit Increases (1972)
Pres.→Sen.→House→Conf.→House→Sen.	Energy Act (1975)
Pres.→House→Sen.→Neg.→House→Sen.	Civil Rights Act (1957)
Pres.→Joint comm.→House→Sen.→Conf.→Conf.	Atomic Energy Act (1954)
Pres.→House→Sen.→Conf.→Neg.→House→Neg.→House→Sen.	Deficit Reduction (1990)
Congressional initiative (varying sequence)	
Sen.→House→Conf.	Toxic Substances (1976)
Congress→House→Sen.→Conf.→Veto→House→Sen.	Omnibus Trade Act (1988)
Sen.→House→Sen.→Conf.→Veto→Override	War Powers Resolution (1973)
Joint comm.→House→Sen.→Conf.	Budget Reform (1974)
House→Pres.→Sen.→Conf.	Synthetic Fuels (1980)
Congress→House→Sen.→Conf.	Excess Profits Tax (1950)
Joint initiative	
Cmsn.→Pres.→House→Sen.→Conf.	Social Security Reform (1983)

Table A-2. *Degree of Iteration at the Committee and Floor Stages,*
Twenty-eight Selected Enactments, 1947–90[a]

Institutional interaction and degree of iteration	House		Senate		Total	
	Committee	Floor	Committee	Floor	Number	Percent
President preponderant						
High	1	1	0	0	2	8
Moderate	4	1	4	2	11	46
Limited	1	4	2	4	11	46
Congress preponderant						
High	6	3	4	3	16	62
Moderate	0	2	3	1	6	23
Limited	0	1	0	3	4	15
Balance with president active						
High	4	3	3	1	11	55
Moderate	1	0	2	1	4	20
Limited	0	2	0	2	4	20
Variable	0	0	0	1	1	5
True balance						
High	3	2	5	3	13	33
Moderate	6	2	3	2	13	33
Limited	1	6	0	5	12	31
Variable	0	0	1	0	1	3

a. One case (Social Security Benefit Increases, 1972) was not considered in the normal process in the House, and another (Civil Rights Act, 1957) was acted on directly on the Senate floor.

Table A-3. *Progression of Iteration from Committee to Floor,*
Twenty-eight Selected Enactments, 1947–90[a]

	Number of cases	
Progression	House	Senate
From more to less		
High to moderate	3	3
High to limited	4	3
High to variable	0	1
Variable to limited	0	1
Moderate to limited	8	8
Same degree (limited)	1	2
Same degree (moderate)	1	3
Same degree (high)	7	5
From less to more		
Moderate to high	2	0
Limited to moderate	1	1

a. One case (Social Security Benefit Increases, 1972) was not considered in the normal process in the House and another (Civil Rights Act, 1957) was acted on directly on the Senate floor. Thus the number in each chamber was reduced to twenty-seven.

Table A-4. *Partisan Interaction Patterns at the Committee and Floor Stages, Twenty-eight Selected Enactments, 1947–90*

Institutional interaction and pattern[a]	House		Senate		Total	
	Committee	Floor	Committee	Floor	Number	Percent
President preponderant						
Partisan	3	2	1	1	7	29
Bipartisan	2	2	2	2	8	33
Cross partisan	1	2	3	3	9	38
Congress preponderant						
Bipartisan	0	0	2	1	3	12
Copartisan to cross partisan	2	1	2	1	6	23
Copartisan to partisan	1	0	0	0	1	4
Cross partisan	3	5	3	5	16	62
Balance with president active						
Partisan	1	0	0	0	1	5
Bipartisan	0	0	0	1	1	5
Copartisan	1	1	0	0	2	10
Copartisan to cross partisan	0	0	1	0	1	5
Copartisan to partisan	1	0	0	0	1	5
Cross partisan	2	4	3	3	12	60
Mixed	0	0	1	1	2	10
True balance						
Partisan	5	5	2	1	13	33
Bipartisan	0	0	1	2	3	8
Copartisan	1	0	2	1	4	10
Copartisan to cross partisan	0	2	2	1	5	13
Copartisan to partisan	1	0	0	0	1	3
Cross partisan	3	3	3	5	14	35

a. Partisan = bargaining and coalition building occuring primarily within the president's party; bipartisan = active and cooperative involvement of both parties; cross partisan = an important segment of one party supports the other party on an issue; copartisan = parallel development of proposals by each party; mixed = various combinations of above.

Table A-5. *Partisan Voting Patterns, Twenty-eight Selected Enactments, 1947–90*

Institutional interaction and pattern[a]	House	Senate	Total Number	Percent
President preponderant				
Partisan	1	0	1	8
Bipartisan	2	2	4	33
Cross partisan 1	2	1	3	25
Cross partisan 2	1	3	4	33
Congress preponderant				
Bipartisan	0	2	2	14
Cross partisan 1	1	0	1	7
Cross partisan 2	1	0	1	7
Mixed	5	5	10	71
Balance with president active				
Bipartisan	0	1	1	10
Cross partisan 1	1	0	1	10
Cross partisan 2	1	3	4	40
Mixed	3	1	4	40
True balance				
Partisan	1	0	1	5
Bipartisan	1	2	3	15
Cross partisan 1	3	5	8	40
Cross partisan 2	2	0	2	10
Mixed	3	3	6	30

a. Partisan = more than 80 percent of each party on opposite side; bipartisan = more than 80 percent of each party on same side; cross partisan 1 = votes of other party needed for a majority; cross partisan 2 = 20 percent or more of other party supporting but not needed for a majority; mixed = various combinations of above.

Table A-6. *Presidential Support Scores, Twenty-four Selected Enactments, 1953–90*[a]

| | House | | Senate | | Total | | Batting |
Institutional interaction and legislation	Wins[a]	Losses[b]	Wins[b]	Losses[b]	Wins[b]	Losses[b]	average[c]
President preponderant							
Federal Aid Highway Act (Eisenhower)	1 (4)	0	1 (2)	0	2 (3)	0	100
Food Stamp Act (Johnson)	3 (7)	0	0	0	3 (2)	0	100
Elementary and Secondary Education Act (Johnson)	2 (2)	0	12 (8)	0	14 (6)	0	100
Airline Deregulation (Carter)	2 (3)	0	4 (3)	0	6 (3)	0	100
Economic Recovery Tax Act (Reagan)	4 (7)	0	9 (8)	0	13 (8)	0	100
Total	12	0	26	0	38	0	100
Congress preponderant							
Labor Reform Act (Eisenhower)	4 (13)	0	2 (3)	4 (7)	6 (7)	4 (5)	60
Social Security Benefit Increases (Nixon)	0	0	0	0	0	0	0
Toxic Substances Control Act (Ford)	0	0	0	1 (5)	0	1 (2)	0
Omnibus Trade Act (Reagan)	0	4 (3)	3 (3)	5 (8)	3 (2)	9 (4)[d]	25
War Powers Resolution (Nixon)	0	3 (4)	0	4 (4)	0	7 (4)[e]	0
Budget and Impoundment Control Act (Nixon)	0	1 (2)	0	0	0	1 (1)	0
Total	4	8	5	14	9	22	29

(continued)

Table A-6 (Continued)

Institutional interaction and legislation	House Wins[b]	House Losses[b]	Senate Wins[b]	Senate Losses[b]	Total Wins[b]	Total Losses[b]	Batting average[c]
Balance with president active							
Medicare (Johnson)	3 (3)	0	11 (7)	0	14 (6)	0	100
Energy Act (Ford)	1 (2)	3 (7)	2 (3)	1 (4)	3 (3)	4 (6)	43
Department of Education (Carter)	12 (12)	2 (5)	5 (4)	0	17 (7)	2 (3)	89
Synthetic Fuels (Carter)	1 (1)	0	5 (6)	1 (3)	6 (3)	1 (2)	86
Anticrime Package (Reagan)	3 (5)	1 (2)	5 (8)	0	8 (6)	1 (2)	86
Total	20	6	28	2	48	8	86
True balance							
Atomic Energy Act (Eisenhower)	2 (7)	1 (13)	5 (8)	1 (6)	7 (8)	2 (8)	78
Civil Rights Act (Eisenhower)	4 (11)	0	4 (9)	2 (17)	8 (10)	2 (5)	80
Manpower Development (Kennedy)	1 (1)	0	3 (1)	0	4 (1)	0[f]	100
Revenue Act (Kennedy)	4 (8)	0	5 (4)	5 (28)	9 (6)	5 (19)	64
Clean Air Act (Kennedy)	2 (3)	0	0	0	2 (1)	0	100
Occupational Safety and Health Act (Nixon)	2 (4)	0	0	0	2 (2)	0	100
Social Security Reform (Reagan)	5 (13)	0	1 (1)	1 (8)	6 (5)	1 (2)	86
Deficit Reduction (Bush)	1 (3)	4 (6)	1 (2)	0	2 (2)	4 (4)	33
Total	21	5	19	9	40	14	74

Source: Calculated from data in *Congressional Quarterly Almanac*, various years.

a. The four bills enacted during the Truman administration are not included. *Congressional Quarterly* did not begin to calculate support scores until the Eisenhower administration.

b. Numbers in parentheses are the percentage of the total wins and losses for the year.

c. How well the president did on this piece of legislation: wins divided by total decisions.

d. Calculated for two years since the votes were counted in 1987 and 1988.

e. Calculated for two years since the votes were counted in 1972 and 1973.

f. Calculated for two years since the votes were counted in 1961 and 1962.

CHAPTER EIGHT

Thinking about Change

THE PRESIDENT is authorized to shape the presidency. The presidency is in a continuous search for its role in the government. Ours is a separated system.

The American presidency carries a burden of lofty expectations that are simply not warranted by the political or constitutional basis of the office. Presidents are important actors in national and world politics, but governments here and abroad must adjust to their inevitable comings and goings. Effective presidents are those who know and understand their potential and variable role in the permanent and continuing government. The natural inclination is to make the president responsible for policies and political events that no one can claim a legitimate right to control. Presidents are well advised to resist this invitation to assume a position of power as though it conveyed authority. Rather they need to identify and define their political capital, and must do so repeatedly in a search for the limits of their influence.

Why are the status and power of the president exaggerated? Why are the constraints of the separation ignored or the president commonly expected to overcome them? Why are the abundant variations of separation not acknowledged as the system's strengths rather than presidential weaknesses? I have puzzled about these questions throughout this volume. My experience in trying to understand just the president's relationships to Congress may offer partial answers. The complexity of a separated system at work is truly imposing, if not always inspiring. It is like an Escher drawing: what rises from one perspective sinks from another. Political analysts, particularly those with deadlines, understandably try to simplify what they observe, and then they criticize when the system does not work as simply as has been described.

For scholars, a presidency-centered, party responsibility perspective may be the consequence of the historical trends in the frequency of split-party government. It was a rarity during the first half of the twentieth century after having occurred often in the latter half of the nineteenth century. Perhaps observers believed that a single-party, presidency-centered government was evolving in the new century as the common solution to the problems identified with the separated system. This hypothesis may have been encouraged by the common interpretation that the Franklin D. Roosevelt administration was the beginning of the modern presidency. With Roosevelt as the model for an evolutionary system of strong presidential leadership, one can then imagine the disillusionment of many scholars with presidents in the post–World War II era. Most presidents, and surely those governing with opposite-party majorities in Congress, were bound to fail the FDR test, yet it continued to be applied. Finally, one can imagine the frustration for those who believed that presidentialism had arrived, only to discover that the Roosevelt years were the exception, not the rule.

Sidney M. Milkis offers little comfort for the evolutionary perspective, and, indeed, he identifies in the Roosevelt years an emergent separation between presidential government and party government. "Roosevelt's party leadership and the New Deal mark the culmination of efforts, which begin in the Progressive era, to loosen the grip of partisan politics on the councils of power, with a view to strengthening national administrative capacities and extending the programmatic commitments of the federal government." For Milkis, "this shift from party to administrative politics" did not secure single-party government, nor did it usher in an "imperial" presidency. Presidents of either party found "themselves navigating a treacherous and lonely path, subject to a volatile political process that makes popular and enduring achievement unlikely."[1] Thus the big government of the post-New Deal era continues to pose a challenge for presidents that is not met by reconstituted "responsible" political parties.

Principal Observations

I have provided concluding comments for individual chapters but will now summarize my principal observations.

—There are substantial differences in the personal and political background of presidents and how they come to serve in the White House (for example, as elected, reelected, nonelected, and heir apparent presidents and elected vice presidents). These differences can lead to strategies (assertive, compensatory, custodial, guardian, and restorative) that aid in explaining performance in office.

—Organizing a presidency is an adaptive process associated with the circumstances of how a president enters the White House and the set of problems he then encounters in doing the job. Several observations are relevant:

Many postwar presidencies involve same-party transitions: Roosevelt to Truman, Kennedy to Johnson, Nixon to Ford, and Reagan to Bush. These transitions have important organizational implications: the new president in each of the four cases faced the task of adapting to or replacing an existing structure.

Commonly used models of White House organization (the circle or pyramid) fail to account for the substantial variations experienced by postwar presidencies or the changes that are made through a term in office. The variables that should be accounted for in characterizing the organization of the presidency include the nature of access, the president's organizational concepts (if he has any), the degree of interaction between the president and the staff, the nature of staff relations, and, for takeover presidents, the nature of the transition.

Cabinet secretaries represent a public manifestation of a president's effort to connect his White House to the permanent government. But turnover is high among these secretaries, and measuring a president's effectiveness on the basis of a series of one-on-one interactions with the secretaries is difficult. Most presidents do not meet the challenge of effectively managing the separated system.

—Public standing of presidents, as measured by public approval ratings, is inexactly related to job performance and effectiveness in working with Congress, as would be expected in a separated system of diffused responsibility and a continuing agenda. Still, tests of public approval have increased substantially in recent years, with evaluations typically equating a president's relative standing with his influence in the separated system.

—However inapt the concept of a mandate in American national politics, it will continue to be used in interpreting election results. Three renditions— the mandate for change, the status quo mandate, and the mixed or nonmandate—are commonly employed at election time and then become tests for performance. A fourth concept, that of the "unmandate," may accompany midterm losses by the president's party or other negative events later in a presidency.

—Presidents perform important agenda-setting functions in setting priorities, certifying issues, proposing policy solutions, and reacting to others' policy initiatives. For the most part, the agenda of government itself is continuous from one year to the next. Presidents are judged by their effectiveness as designators within the ongoing policy process.

—Law in the separated system is made by a process, primarily centered in Congress, that is continuous, iterative, representative, informational, sequential, orderly (in setting priorities), and declarative. Most important legislation is worked on over time and is connected with precursory laws that are familiar to those in the permanent government. To be effective, presidents must take these characteristics of the lawmaking process into account so as to judge how, when, and where to participate.

—An analysis of twenty-eight major pieces of legislation in the postwar period reveals the rich variety of presidential-congressional interaction in lawmaking. It demonstrates that presidents are important actors in lawmaking, but there is substantial variation in which branch is preponderant and there are many instances of balanced participation. The engrossing variations in the degree and place of iteration, the sequence of legislative action, and, above all, the mix of partisan strategies at different stages reveal how little is learned from restricting analysis to roll call votes (particularly studies based on presidential support scores).

Taken as a whole, these observations advise presidency watchers against isolating one branch from the other or concentrating on only one president or Congress. Understanding the workings of a separated system of diffused responsibility and mixed representation logically requires attention to the institutional context within which any one part of the system does its work. A presidency-centered perspective is insufficiently attentive to the challenge facing the president in finding his place in the permanent government. Often this perspective invites questioning the legitimacy of other participants, who may be identified as obstructionists. This then leads to the proposal of reforms to orient Congress and the bureaucracy more toward presidential policy preferences, or those preferences it is assumed that presidents should have.

Much of this presidency-centered analysis concludes that the system is not working well, when in fact only a part of the system has been studied—and the most temporary part, at that. One measure of whether the system is working is the production of important legislation. David R. Mayhew challenges those who doubt the capacity of the government to produce important laws under conditions that might be expected to result in stalemate (as in

1973–74).[2] My detailed examination of 28 of Mayhew's list of 267 laws shows an astonishing array of sequences, patterns of iteration, and partisan connections. There is a saying that one does not want to look closely at how either sausage or laws are made. I agree when it comes to sausage. I strongly disagree when it comes to laws. Careful study of how important laws are made impresses one with the creativity and flexibility of the system of separated institutions competing for shared powers. It is an extraordinarily mature process, with a seemingly infinite number of mutations that are bound to challenge the analyst and the reformer.

Reform and Change

Should the separated system be reformed? First, one should understand that it is ever changing. One of the special features of separated institutions is that they are constantly undergoing modification as they compete for shares of power in dealing with policy issues. Further, since there is no one formula by which president and Congress do their work, the object of reform is not easy to stipulate, nor are the effects of reorganization highly predictable. The system changes without reforms, and reforms do not necessarily lead to desired change.

It is reasonable to demand that those advocating change clarify the perspective serving as a basis for their recommendations. Throughout this book, I have stressed an alternative perspective to that of the advocates of responsible party, presidency-centered, unified government: a perspective of a separated system that I judge to be consistent with the constitutional order and historical practice. The original separationist design provided for distinct elections, which in turn allow various forms of split-party control that contribute partisan checks as supplements to the institutional balances already in place. Therefore, if one accepts that split-party government is as legitimate as single-party government (and some do not), then the analyst as reformer should be interested in making each of these authentic forms work well.

Normally the system should provide checks on excesses without substantially interfering with the capacity of the government to act on major public problems. This formulation suggests two outcomes to be avoided: policy escalation (when policy exceeds its real support as a result of an overmandated administration); and policy stalemate (when there is a failure to act on serious policy issues because of an undersupported administration and a weakened Congress).

Policy Escalation

The conditions leading to policy escalation include election results that are typically perceived as providing a mandate for significant change: A presidential landslide, complemented by major gains for the president's party in Congress, and striking issue differences between the presidential candidates. The two principal cases in the postwar period occurred in 1964 and 1980. Each administration—Johnson and Reagan—was associated with major policy breakthroughs, substantial enough to affect the agenda for later decades.

These are the elections that come closest to satisfying the responsible party, presidency-centered perspective, yet they represent a failure of the separated system. Proposals of enormous impact are enacted on a fast track. This sets an example for other presidents and encourages such advice as "hit the ground running," or "move it or lose it." It is not a simple matter to devise means for curbing an overmandated president. Not only is the White House likely to take advantage of the opportunity to act, but failure to do so may well bring criticism from those in the Washington community who defined the mandate in the first place. There is, in brief, a self-fulfilling quality to the mythical mandate.

The greater responsibility in these cases lies where it is constitutionally set: with Congress. As difficult as it may be to accomplish, congressional leaders should devise means for a serious examination of election results for their policy meaning. There is, for example, substantial evidence that in both 1964 and 1980 many voters were casting their ballots against Barry Goldwater and Jimmy Carter, respectively, rather than for the winner's policy program in each case.

Of course, no one is eager to stand in front of a speeding truck. The president in these cases is commonly expected to have a chance to enact his program (a point made even for presidents for whom there is no mandate). Yet why should that be so without careful analysis of whether voters actually intended that the new president's program be enacted? There is no good constitutional, political, or policy reason for members of Congress to abrogate their responsibilities under any circumstances. When those first readers of election results say that the president has a mandate for large change, members of Congress have an even greater responsibility to bring their judgment to bear on the formulation and legitimation of these proposals.

There is now considerable understanding of the effects of the Great Society programs, as well as those of the multiple-year tax cuts of the early Reagan era. Deficits of historical proportions have come to dominate national politics and policymaking. The claims presidents make for such sweeping proposals ought to be subjected to careful scrutiny by members of Congress, with detailed projections of the costs and benefits. A decent case can even be made for the president exercising caution when a mandate for change is declared to exist. By enacting the bulk of their program early in the term, overmandated presidents can overdraw their policy bank accounts, thus leaving little for the remainder of their time in office. Or they may establish expectations that can never again be met. Meanwhile they may find themselves ill suited to manage the inevitable adjustments that occur as a consequence of the policy breakthroughs. This curious policy trap seemingly had a greater effect on Johnson, who marked success by getting programs enacted in Congress, than Reagan, who was satisfied to cede policy enterprise to others.

Policy Stalemate

Just as serious may be the failure to act when there are pressing public issues. As Mayhew has shown, there are fewer such cases than was imagined with split-party government. But they do exist and they, too, represent a failure of the separated system. If the separation is working well, it can serve as a counterbalancing mechanism. That is, when one institution is either not motivated to act or is incapable of acting, the other institution takes the initiative. Legislation can be and is initiated by both the White House and Congress, with reaction from the other.

The extreme case of stalemate is that of the last two years of the Bush administration (the last months of the Ford administration is a second case). President Bush took few initiatives, congressional Democrats passed some legislation that was then vetoed by the president, and the president's vetoes were sustained in all but one case. Seemingly neither the Republican president nor the Democratic Congress was willing to permit the other side to gain a policy advantage, and "gridlock" came to be a common expression during the 1992 presidential and congressional campaigns.

James L. Sundquist argues that stalemate is the expected outcome of split-party government:

If the president sends a proposal to Capitol Hill or takes a foreign policy stand, the opposition-controlled House or houses of Congress—unless they are overwhelmed by the president's popularity and standing in the country—simply *must* reject it. Otherwise they are saying the president is a wise and prudent leader. . . . By the same token, if the opposition party in control of Congress initiates a measure, the president has to veto it.[3]

Mayhew's study of important legislation and my sample from his listing show that the contenders in a split-party government do not typically act as Sundquist predicts. Neither side tends to view lawmaking as a zero-sum game. The president and the opposition party leaders often view the process as one of partial win-partial win or as a guarantee of protection from full accountability should the policy be subject later to severe criticism. Further, Sundquist's analysis assumes a greater perceived association between policy action and election outcomes for president and Congress than is typically possible under the present system.[4]

What, then, are the conditions under which policy stalemate does occur, where each side seeks to block the other? The last two years of the Bush administration provide important clues for answering this question. The president was perceived as having little or no positive program for dealing with an economy that was very slow to recover. Republicans in Congress suffered further losses in the 1990 midterm elections. And the president lost his advantage of expertise in foreign and defense policy issues as a result of the dramatic changes in Eastern Europe and the former Soviet Union. The cold war was at an end. The problems that George Bush might justifiably be returned to office to solve were dissipating, replaced by economic troubles at home.

Meanwhile, on Capitol Hill, congressional Democrats faced a series of scandals, most of which were mismanaged. The most widely publicized one concerned a banking service for members of the House of Representatives that allowed many members to overdraw their accounts. The exposure of these banking privileges encouraged examination of other advantages enjoyed by members in both chambers. And the revelations fueled an already vigorous national movement to limit the terms of legislators. Seldom in recent memory were members of Congress more concerned about their status and that of their institution.[5]

The condition for stalemate was perceived weakness in both the presidency and Congress. Neither institution was well positioned to take up the slack for the other, as, for example, occurred during the last two years of the Reagan administration, when congressional Democrats were aggressive in taking policy initiatives. In the Bush case, each institution lacked confidence in itself at the same time it perceived weakness in its opposite. Bargaining can take place when strength is pitted against strength, but it is unlikely to occur between two weak and irritable contenders.

There is no simple remedy to policy stalemate that is the result of under-supported institutions. Of course, elections are always just around the corner in the American system. As noted, institutional gridlock came to be a major talking point during the 1992 elections. The problem in this case, however, is that the rational remedy is two-directional: voting Democratic to correct for a weak president and Republican to correct for a scandal-ridden Congress.

Can anything be done at the time? Although Congress bears the responsibility for curbing policy escalation, it is not well designed to lead the government out of stalemate. Only the president can try to break the partisan gridlock of an undersupported government. He should take the initiative to overcome partisanship, given the need for policy action on major public issues. It may well be that he cannot succeed or that he simply is not capable of leading in that manner. After all, there is no constitutional requirement that presidents know what do to and when to do it. But when there is a larger national interest at stake, the president should be willing to forgo short-term political considerations in a relentless effort to convince congressional party leaders to participate in copartisan politics. This leadership may have to be highly personal, with the president possibly ignoring the counsel of his political advisers. It may even result in sacrificing his political career if it is required during the first term. (In George Bush's case, his effort in 1990 to get a cross-partisan budget agreement surely was at the cost of political support within his own party.) The risk of such bold actions, however, must be weighed against the effects of not acting or of contributing further to stalemate.

A Plurality of Governments

I turn next to the potential for reform and the reality of change in the presidency and its work with Congress. My purpose is less to propose specific reforms than to promote understanding of the plurality of legitimate forms of governing, and, quite candidly, to discourage illusions that the separated system can easily be transformed into a presidential system through institutional or procedural tinkering.

The first point to make is simply this: universal reforms are discouraged by a Constitution that allows for different types of governments. One of the most important lessons from this study is that presidents enter the White House and participate in the policy process in very different ways, all sanctioned by the Constitution. Therefore any suggested changes must account for these permissible variations in legitimate governments. I acknowledge that some reformers want to change the constitutional structure itself so as to prevent this multiplicity of governments.[6] My personal view is that these efforts will, and probably should, fail. Rather than bemoan the legitimate outcomes provided for in the separated system, it is more constructive to judge how the various forms of single- and split-party government might be made to work more effectively.

The variations in the postwar governments and the strategies that I deduce from the strengths and weaknesses of the presidents upon entering the White House were discussed in chapter 2 (see table 2-5). In a somewhat broader perspective, it is useful to identify various patterns of governments for the postwar presidents (see table 8-1). Note first that balanced participation is the most common type of government, as expected in a separated system. Note further the tendency for split-party government under Republican presidents to move from balanced participation to congressional preponderance. The experiences in single-party government are mixed. Clearly, presidents face very different strategic conditions and there is no standard formula for presidential performance. For purposes of illustration, I will discuss reform under three situations in presidents' working relationships with Congress, essentially drawing from the categories I developed in the discussion of the twenty-eight cases of major legislation.[7]

PRESIDENTIAL PREPONDERANCE. Presidential preponderance is the relatively rare situation when the election appears to have conveyed a congruent policy message for both president and Congress: the perceived mandate for change. Such a presidency, which most closely fits the ideal of the party responsibility advocates, has been discussed above as potentially resulting in policy escalation. The cases that fit into this category are those of the Johnson and Reagan administrations (principally the early years for each).

When presidents have significant political advantages, reforms should strive to preserve the distinctive contributions of the separated institutions and ensure effective communication between the president and his congressional majority. Because of the inexactitude in reading policy messages from diverse and disconnected elections, both institutions must work at deciphering their meaning.

Table 8-1. *Institutional Interaction and Party Control of Modern Governments, 1945–93*

President and Congress	Institutional interaction[a]	Party control
Truman		
79th	Balanced	Single
80th	Congressional	Split
81st	Balanced	Single
82d	Balanced/congressional	Single
Eisenhower		
83d	Balanced	Single
84th	Balanced	Split
85th	Balanced	Split
86th	Congressional	Split
Kennedy-Johnson		
87th	Balanced	Single
88th	Balanced/presidential	Single
89th	Presidential (escalation)	Single
90th	Balanced	Single
Nixon-Ford		
91st	Balanced	Split
92d	Balanced	Split
93d	Balanced/congressional	Split
94th	Congressional (stalemate)	Split
Carter		
95th	Balanced	Single
96th	Balanced/congressional	Single
Reagan		
97th	Presidential (escalation)	Split[b]
98th	Balanced	Split[b]
99th	Balanced	Split[b]
100th	Congressional	Split
Bush		
101st	Congressional	Split
102d	Congressional (stalemate)	Split
Clinton		
103d	Balanced	Single

a. Types drawn from discussion in chap. 7: presidential preponderance, congressional preponderance, and balanced participation.
b. Split-party control between House and Senate.

Since policy escalation can be the result of presidential preponderance, stringent tests of representation and responsiveness should be applied, with the members of the president's party in Congress communicating their perspectives drawn from their own representational expertise. Congress should never vacate its deliberative responsibility. This view undoubtedly will be interpreted as an argument against change. I do not agree. It is, rather, a brief in favor of change realized through the cross-institutional processes that characterize the separated system. Neither is it counsel against presidential leadership. It is rather an acceptance of the special conditions under which leadership works in the separated system.

CONGRESSIONAL PREPONDERANCE. In congressional preponderance, the president is substantially weakened by his party's losses in the midterm elections, emboldening the opposition party in Congress to take policy initiatives. These are most often instances of split-party government when the president's party has done poorly in a second midterm election (such as the 86th Congress, Eisenhower's last, and the 100th Congress, Reagan's last), or when a takeover president has to manage public dissatisfaction and a mood for change (such as the 80th Congress, Truman's second; the 94th, Ford's post-Watergate Congress; and the 101st and 102d Congresses, both during Bush's term).

Under these circumstances members of Congress are tempted to compensate for a weakened president. However instinctive this reaction may be, reform in such cases should be attentive to the maintenance of the separated system. Therefore an enhanced congressional capacity for setting the agenda, taking policy initiatives, and overseeing executive actions should be constructively developed to prevent the tendency toward policy stalemate noted earlier. However, the opposition majority party in Congress should not assume this role at the expense of further erosion of the president's position or status, particularly when midterm results cannot reasonably be interpreted as a referendum on presidential performance. This is not a recommendation to eliminate politics, but rather a further exhortation to preserve the advantages of the separated system.

BALANCED PARTICIPATION. Most often there are balanced advantages between the president and Congress, as befits the separated system. Interestingly, this balance may exist whether there is single- or split-party government. The source of the equilibrium, however, is not always the same. In single-party cases, balance is associated with a relatively weak electoral performance by a Democratic president and substantial Democratic majorities in the House and Senate (such as Truman in 1948, Kennedy in 1960, Carter in 1976, and Clinton in 1992). In each case the president had advantages associated with a surprise win or the freshness of his message. But at the same time most congressional Democrats had ample reason to conclude that they won independently of the president and thus the policy connection between the presidential and congressional elections was weak at best. In split-party cases, balance is associated with congressional Democrats successfully maintaining their majorities in the face of Republican presidential victories (such as Eisenhower in 1956, Nixon in 1968 and 1972, and Reagan in 1984). In three of these cases Democratic House and Senate majorities were returned despite landslide reelection victories by Republican presidents.

It is vital for comprehending the workings of the separated system in the postwar period to acknowledge that balanced participation is the most frequent of the three situations and that it characterizes both single- and split-party governments. Reforms in these situations should be aimed at strengthening the capacity of both the president and Congress to participate effectively. At times, realizing that goal has meant having to undertake major reforms, such as in the 1970s, when both Congress and the executive made significant changes designed to manage a number of large issues like budget making, civil rights, the environment, energy, the economy, trade, and taxes. It is remarkable how much adjustment does take place when institutions are stimulated to compete for shared powers. In some cases this arises out of a concern for loss of status, as was the case for Congress in 1946 and in the 1970s. Balanced, competitive participation in the separated system does not produce gridlock. Instead, it facilitates the identification and treatment of major public issues, often working through intricate processes of co- or cross partisanship (as illustrated in chapter 7).

PERMUTATIONS. For six consecutive years during the Reagan administration Congress itself experienced split-party control: a Republican Senate and a Democratic House of Representatives. Although this form of split control occurred many times in the past, never in the history of the modern two-party system had it been repeated for three successive Congresses. This is another variation in governing, and it has a decent prospect of being repeated, given the competitiveness of Senate elections in recent times.[8] To my knowledge, there has been little or no systematic study of what is yet another form of government allowable under the Constitution, as amended by the Seventeenth Amendment.

Lessons for Presidents

Virtually everything I have said here counsels that generic advice to presidents is to be viewed with the utmost suspicion. Presidents differ, and each is free to judge how best to make his personal, political, and policy traits work for him. Still, there are lessons related to the workings of the separated system that may be usefully reiterated. I turn initially to the cases of elected presidents.

The first lesson is the most obvious, yet possibly the one most difficult to absorb in the election aftermath. Newly elected presidents are fresh from an experience that is all-consuming and extraordinarily self-centered. A presidential campaign of perpetual motion focuses exclusively on the candidate. Every activity is directed toward decisions that occur by the calendar: primary dates, a convention vote, election day. The time arrives when the candidate-centered organization can congratulate itself and hand over its victor to the permanent government. It is at that precise point of triumph that a new leader must be the most disciplined in acknowledging the requirements of a transition from candidate to president. After heading a temporary, highly convergent, and concentrated organization, he will now participate as a central figure in a permanent, divergent, and dispersed structure. The first lesson, then, for a president in a separated system is to learn what is required to do the new job, understanding that campaign experiences and campaign workers have little to offer toward that end.

A second, related lesson is that presidents should not be misled by the importunings of many in the Washington community about how they want politics to work. For various reasons, these permanent residents may wish the president to exceed his capacity and resources. Presidents must be stubbornly realistic in understanding who they are, how they came to be in the Oval Office, their strengths and weaknesses, and the strengths and weaknesses of others authorized to participate in decisionmaking. This reflective assessment will help guide prospective achievements.

A third advisory is that estimating status and resources is not a one-time activity. Little remains in place in the separated system. The pace of change may have quickened through the postwar era, but there has always been change. That feature should surprise no one since a major purpose of representative democracy is to bring the outside in on a continuing basis. Even so, the sources and types of change during a presidential administration are astonishing, in people, issues, organization, processes, and public support.

Presidents typically have more than one presidency; in some cases the change is significant enough to require new leadership. And even with high incumbent return, one Congress is seldom exactly like the one before.

Fourth, a frequently cited source of power, that of public support as measured by approval ratings, should be viewed skeptically by presidents, for all of the reasons cited in chapter 4. Richard E. Neustadt's concept of public prestige is perhaps more useful, because it rests on more substantial grounds and is tested qualitatively by other actors in the separated system.[9] A high approval rating does not create an advantage in presidential persuasion if it is not translatable into clear effects for, say, members of Congress. President Bush can be authoritatively consulted on that point. Likewise, a low approval rating need not result in gridlock or even the judgment that the president has lost prestige as an actor in policymaking. President Clinton, for example, maintained prestige as a knowledgeable policy analyst throughout a year in which his approval rating seldom rose above 50 percent. Prestige cannot be invented by polls, nor is it likely to be demolished by them.

Fifth, all things considered, presidents are well advised to beware of mandates. They come with high expectations of performance that seldom can be met in the separated system. Further, mandates typically last only until those declaring them to exist rediscover how separationist politics works, a process that may take only a few short months. In some cases, notably in 1965 and 1981, those declaring a mandate have included members of Congress, who then find it difficult to undo what they agreed to during the short life of the sanction. Meanwhile, the decisions themselves have lasting effects, even resulting in significant agenda shifts that the mandated presidents may be ill suited to manage (for example, the fiscal politics of huge deficits).

Sixth, an analysis of how laws are made confirms ordinary expectations that the president and members of Congress are legitimate participants in the full range of policy activities. The lesson for presidents is apparent. Whenever powers are shared, attention must be devoted to the other decisionmakers. How do they view the problem? What are their present commitments? On what basis will they compromise? The test in a separated system is not simply one of presidential success. It is rather one of achievement by the system, with presidents and members of Congress inextricably bonded and similarly judged. Solo triumphs for presidents in the separated system are, and should be, rare.

Many of these lessons are also applicable to presidents not elected for the first time. But there are additional observations to make about these others.

Reelected presidents have presumably found their place in the permanent government and therefore campaign both as candidates and incumbent leaders. As it has happened, only Republicans have been reelected in the postwar period, all serving in split-party governments. Approval for them occurs within the context of continued public tolerance for split-party government. The president's term limit upon reelection alters the policy dynamics, inviting him to indulge and adapt to the policy initiatives of a congressional majority party looking forward to an open presidential election.

Takeover presidents face enormous challenges in managing an organization created to fit their predecessor into the separated system. As vice presidents, they were associated with and often held responsible for an administration to which they made marginal contributions. Lacking a concentrated and self-centered campaign experience, they are unlikely to overestimate their status. After all, their campaign activity was also oriented toward the presidential candidate. The principal lesson appears to be that such presidents must carefully weigh the complex strategic situation, assessing the expectations of their guardianship and moving cautiously from the designs of their predecessor to making their own connections with the government. Experience suggests that how and when these things happen will vary, depending heavily on the circumstances of the takeover. For Truman, the sheer magnitude and pace of major events necessitated decisiveness, virtually to the exclusion of deliberation at times. For Johnson, a substantial agenda awaited his legislative mastery. For Ford, restoration of the president's trusted role in the separated system was required and demanded.

Elected vice presidents (including the one heir apparent) appear to include those persons who could not have been elected on their own before serving as vice president. Harry Truman did not try. There is no evidence to my knowledge that Truman harbored presidential ambitions before he was selected as Roosevelt's running mate in 1944. Lyndon Johnson tried in 1960 and lost badly to his younger Senate colleague. George Bush tried in 1980 and won just four primaries in competition with Reagan. They were then elected president as a consequence of already being in the White House: Truman and Johnson as president, Bush as vice president and the heir apparent. The six lessons noted above are all applicable to these presidents, but there is one more that is especially apt. The rationale for having the vice president serve as president may be more transitory than for having an elected president serve in the first place. Little in the job description or in historical experience suggests that vice presidents are prepared to serve well as presidents. They have their place in the separated system, and that place is as a temporary replacement for elected or reelected presidents. I am not intimating that vice presidents who take over as presidents should stand down at the completion of their predecessor's term. I am, rather, challenging the assumption that they should then be elected to the presidency by reason of their unanticipated incumbency or of being a patient understudy.

The Presidency in a Separated System

I come away from this study quite in awe of the American national government. That is not to say I believe it is faultless; angels are not available to govern, as James Madison explained long ago. It does mean that I am impressed with the capacity of a complex set of political institutions to adjust to a remarkable variation in political and policy circumstances. E. E. Schattschneider explained that "democracy is a political system for people who are not too sure that they are right."[10] His formulation draws attention to decisionmaking rather than to the decisions themselves. It is no simple matter to create, maintain, or reform a government forged to represent uncertainty and to approximate, but not necessarily achieve, policy solutions.

The capacity of the separated system to adjust is reflected in the classifications developed throughout this book. Regardless of the topic—how presidents came to be there, how they organized their presidency, their public standing and role in agenda setting, and the patterns of partisan and institutional interactions—I found the differences among and within presidencies to be striking. It simply was not possible to generalize across all postwar presidencies. The manifold determinants of the president's strategic position assist in specifying his advantages for certifying and managing items on a continuous agenda, which may be oriented in strikingly different ways, and for participating in a lawmaking process that mostly takes place in another, independent branch of government.

I conclude that it is more important to make the separated system work well than to change systems. The preferred institutional interaction is that of balanced participation, with both branches actively involved in the policy process. The United States has the most intricate lawmaking system in the world. It will not be made better through simplification. Preponderance of one branch over the other should be a cause for concern, not celebration. Presidents are well advised to appreciate the advantages of the separated system and to define their role in it. Most do not have to be counseled on the legitimacy of Congress, but some do. Most know instinctively that their advantages are in certifying the agenda and persuading others to accept their proposals as a basis for compromise, but some have grander conceptions of presidential power. Most understand that they are temporary leaders of a convention of policy choice already in session, but some lack the skills to define the limits or realize the advantages of that status. Most realize that patience, persistence, and sharing are required for effective work in the separated system, but some are overly anxious to take immediate credit for change. And most grasp the purposes of a diffused-responsibility system of mixed representation and shared powers, but some believe that the president is the presidency, the presidency is the government, and ours is a presidential system. Those who believe these things may even have convinced themselves that they are right. They will be proven to be wrong.

Notes

Chapter One

1. Lyndon Baines Johnson, *The Vantage Point: Perspectives of the Presidency, 1963–1969* (Holt, Rinehart and Winston, 1971), p. 18.

2. Quoted in Ruth Marcus, "In Transition Twilight Zone, Clinton's Every Word Scrutinized," *Washington Post*, November 22, 1992, p. A1.

3. I should note, however, that comparative scholars typically classify the United States as a presidential system. Often, in fact, it is designated as the "model and prototype of presidential government." Classifications of democratic systems are typically limited to parliamentary or presidential government. See, for example, the introduction and essays by Douglas V. Verney, Juan J. Linz, and G. Bingham Powell, Jr., in Arend Lijphart, ed., *Parliamentary versus Presidential Government* (Oxford University Press, 1992); and by Scott Mainwaring in Gyorgy Szoboszlai, ed., *Flying Blind: Emerging Democracies in East-Central Europe* (Budapest: Hungarian Political Science Association, 1992). See also Matthew S. Shugart and John M. Carey, *Presidents and Assemblies: Constitutional Design and Electoral Awareness* (Cambridge University Press, 1992). Many comparative scholars argue that the parliamentary system is superior to the presidential system (which is the label typically given to a separated system), as do many reformers in the United States. For a counterargument, see Thomas O. Sargentich, "The Limits of the Parliamentary Critique of the Separation of Powers," *William and Mary Law Review*, vol. 34 (Spring 1993), pp. 679–739.

4. Just as several scholars have said to expect, notably Richard E. Neustadt, *Presidential Power: The Politics of Leadership* (Wiley, 1960); George C. Edwards, III, *At the Margins: Presidential Leadership of Congress* (Yale University Press, 1989), chaps. 1, 11; Paul Charles Light, *The President's Agenda: Domestic Policy Choices from Kennedy to Carter (with Notes on Ronald Reagan)* (Johns Hopkins University Press, 1982), chap. 1; Erwin C. Hargrove and Michael Nelson, *Presidents, Politics, and Policy* (Johns Hopkins University Press, 1984), chap. 4; Mark A. Peterson, *Legislating Together: The White House and Capitol Hill from Eisenhower to Reagan* (Harvard University Press, 1990), chap. 3; and Bert A. Rock-

man, *The Leadership Question: The Presidency and the American System* (Praeger, 1984), esp. chap. 4.

5. Imagine the nerve required to create a government that would foster criticism by preventing full satisfaction for any one group. It was truly an imaginative and bold experiment, this American system of government.

6. "The Johnson Landslide," *New York Times*, November 4, 1964, p. 38.

7. Richard E. Neustadt has pointed out to me that President Johnson was "conscious at the time that he only had two years." In notes by Neustadt summarizing a meeting at the White House in December 1964, the president "made clear his own awareness of the character of his election victory: a sharp defeat for screw-ballism and an endorsement of sanity, but by no means an overwhelming mandate for a Hundred Days a la 1933. . . . Yet, the Liberals and interested groups of every sort would now be calling for another Hundred Days. And the columnists would be watching, counting days, and keeping score."

8. "Republican Renascence," *New York Times*, November 13, 1966, p. E10.

9. David S. Broder, "Somber '68 Message Is a Contrast to Optimism of '64," *Washington Post*, January 18, 1968, p. A13.

10. Johnson, *Vantage Point*, pp. 532–33.

11. ". . . and Empty Landslide," *New York Times*, November 9, 1972, p. 46.

12. Arthur Krock, "The Unmandate," *New York Times*, November 10, 1972, p. 39.

13. "Mr. Nixon's Victory," *New York Times*, November 8, 1972, p. 46.

14. "The Nixon Resignation," *New York Times*, August 9, 1974, p. 32.

15. Richard Nixon, *In the Arena: A Memoir of Victory, Defeat and Renewal* (Simon and Schuster, 1990), p. 25.

16. Arthur M. Schlesinger, Jr., *The Age of Roosevelt*, vol. 3: *The Politics of Upheaval* (Houghton Mifflin, 1960), p. 242.

17. Landon told a story of the Kansas farmer reacting to his farm having been swept away by a tornado. He was found laughing at "the completeness of it." Ibid., p. 643.

18. "The President's Message," *New York Times*, January 5, 1939, p. 22; and "The President's Budget," *New York Times*, January 6, 1939, p. 20.

19. Johnson, *Vantage Point*, p. 443.

20. Richard Rose, *The Postmodern President: The White House Meets the World* (Chatham, N. J.: Chatham House, 1988), p. 46.

21. Walter Lippmann, *Public Opinion* (Macmillan, 1950), p. 25.

22. Mark J. Rozell, *The Press and the Carter Presidency* (Boulder: Westview Press, 1989), p. 4.

23. "Congress and President," *New York Times*, January 3, 1947, p. 26.

24. "President and Congress," *New York Times*, November 6, 1948, p. 12.

25. "Tuesday's 'Mandate': For the President . . ." *Washington Post*, November 7, 1974, p. A30.

26. James L. Sundquist, *Constitutional Reform and Effective Government*, rev. ed. (Brookings, 1992), p. 1.

27. Ibid., p. 10.

28. Ibid., p. 11.

29. Ibid., p. 16.

30. Robert A. Dahl and Charles E. Lindblom, *Politics, Economics, and Welfare* (Harper and Brothers, 1953), pp. 335–36 (emphasis in original).

31. American Political Science Association, *Toward a More Responsible Two-Party System: A Report of the Committee on Political Parties* (New York: Rinehart, 1950), pp. 1–2.

32. James L. Sundquist is one of the few. In an influential article, he explained his own devotion to party government, identified it to be the dominant perspective among American political scientists, and challenged political scientists to "provide a new body of theory" if it is to be abandoned. "Needed: A Political Theory for the New Era of Coalition Government in the United States," *Political Science Quarterly*, vol. 103 (Winter 1988–89), pp. 613–35.

33. Neustadt, *Presidential Power*, p. 33 (emphasis in original).

34. Peterson, *Legislating Together*, pp. 8, 9.

35. Since the 1970s, congressional Democrats have increased staff, added analytical units (like the Office of Technology Assessment and the Congressional Budget Office), and changed scheduling and floor procedures so as to participate more actively in all phases of policymaking.

36. Thus, for example, the 100th Congress, the last for the Reagan administration, was highly productive of reform legislation in the areas of trade, welfare, and health care. Few predicted that there could be such an outpouring of legislation since the president was in the last two years of his term.

Chapter Two

1. Edward S. Corwin, *The President, Office and Powers, 1787–1948: History and Analysis of Practice and Opinion* (New York University Press, 1957), p. 30.

2. *Time*, April 7, 1986, p. 27.

3. A recent example is Fred I. Greenstein, ed., *Leadership in the Modern Presidency* (Harvard University Press, 1988). Nine very different presidents are analyzed. The concluding essay by Greenstein is a "search" for the "modern presidency," emphasizing the contributions of presidents to the institution.

4. Thomas A. Bailey, *Presidential Greatness: The Image and the Man from George Washington to the Present* (New York: Appleton-Century, 1966), p. 36.

5. Quoted in Michael Nelson, ed., *Guide to the Presidency* (Washington: Congressional Quarterly, 1989), p. 148. For example, how is one to rate Gerald Ford—an unelected vice president, having to take over for Richard Nixon in the wake of the Watergate scandal? One ranking among historians placed him the "average" category along with McKinley, Taft, Hoover, and Carter in this century (ibid., p. 146). What can that possibly mean?

6. See Charles O. Jones, "Nominating 'Carter's Favorite Opponent': The Republicans in 1980," in Austin Ranney, ed., *The American Elections of 1980* (Washington: American Enterprise Institute, 1981), chap. 3, esp. p. 63.

7. For details, see Charles O. Jones, *The Trusteeship Presidency: Jimmy Carter and the United States Congress* (Louisiana State University Press, 1988), chap. 2.

8. *New York Times*, April 15, 1945, p. E3.

9. "President Truman," *New York Times*, April 14, 1945, p. 14.

10. Quoted in David McCullough, *Truman* (Simon and Schuster, 1992), p. 353.

11. "President Johnson," *New York Times*, November 23, 1963, p. 28.

12. "The Next President and Inflation," *Washington Post*, August 9, 1974, p. A30.

13. "The Presidential Pardon," *Washington Post*, September 10, 1974, p. A20.

14. A shift of 6,000 votes in Ohio and 4,000 votes in Hawaii would have elected Ford. But the new Senate had 61 Democrats and the new House, 292 Democrats (67 percent).

15. Harry S. Truman, *Memoirs: Years of Trial and Hope* (New York: Doubleday, 1956), p. 222.

16. A third case is slightly different. Walter Mondale ran as the heir apparent within the Democratic party in 1984 following the defeat of the president with whom he served until 1980. He was overwhelmingly defeated.

17. Humphrey, however, would have faced greater problems simply because of the nature of the agenda in 1968 and the dominance of President Johnson over that agenda. Eisenhower's greater distance—real or perceived—from the agenda would have permitted greater freedom for Nixon.

18. James David Barber, *The Presidential Character: Predicting Performance in the White House*, 4th ed. (Prentice-Hall, 1992).

19. Actually Clinton first ran for public office in 1974, seeking (unsuccessfully) the Democratic nomination for a seat in the House of Representatives.

20. See Joseph A. Schlesinger, *Ambition and Politics: Political Careers in the United States* (Chicago: Rand McNally, 1966), chap. 1; and David T. Canon, *Actors, Athletes, and Astronauts: Political Amateurs in the United States Congress* (University of Chicago Press, 1990), chap. 3.

21. One might reasonably identify Bush with a custodial strategy, much like that of Truman following Roosevelt. I decided on the guardian strategy primarily because Bush won on his own in an election that had many features of a reelection (and, of course, Bush was associated with the Reagan administration for eight years as vice president, to a much greater extent than was Truman with Roosevelt).

Chapter Three

1. President's Committee on Administrative Management, *Administrative Management in the Government of the United States* (Government Printing Office, 1937), p. 5.

2. Bradley H. Patterson, Jr., *Ring of Power: The White House Staff and its Expanding Role in Government* (Basic Books, 1988), p. 11.

3. Peri E. Arnold, *Making the Managerial Presidency: Comprehensive Reorganization Planning, 1905–1980* (Princeton University Press, 1986), pp. 361–63.

4. Many with White House staff experience agree with this formulation. See, for example, Clark Clifford, *Counsel to the President: A Memoir* (Random House, 1991), pp. 76–77; and Jack Watson, chief of staff in the last months of the Carter presidency, in Samuel Kernell and Samuel L. Popkin, eds., *Chief of Staff: Twenty-Five Years of Managing the Presidency* (Berkeley: University of California Press, 1986), p. 70.

5. Richard E. Neustadt, personal correspondence, July 13, 1993.

6. Neustadt points out that both Roosevelt and Truman left to the departments much of what is now managed by the presidential branch "with no obvious loss, in relative terms, of personal influence on outcomes." Ibid.

7. It should be noted that compiling precise figures for the White House staff is a daunting task. Figures from the budget do not include so-called detailees from the departments and agencies. Further, there are a number of special funds available to the president that do not get reported as White House appropriations. See John Hart, *The Presidential Branch* (New York: Pergamon, 1987), pp. 97–109.

8. For a listing of the various functions now performed by the White House staff, see Patterson, *Ring of Power*, pt. 2; Hart, *Presidential Branch*, chap. 4; and George C. Edwards III and Stephen J. Wayne, *Presidential Leadership*, 2d ed. (St. Martin's Press, 1990), p. 179.

9. Nelson W. Polsby, "Some Landmarks in Modern Presidential-Congressional Relations," in Anthony King, ed., *Both Ends of the Avenue: The Presidency, the Executive Branch, and Congress in the 1980s* (Washington: American Enterprise Institute, 1983), p. 20.

10. Edwards and Wayne, *Presidential Leadership*, p. 175.

11. Hart, *Presidential Branch*, pp. 96–97.

12. Hedrick Smith, *The Power Game: How Washington Works* (Random House, 1988), p. 301.

13. See Robert H. Salisbury and Kenneth A. Shepsle, "Congressional Staff Turnover and the Ties-That-Bind," *American Political Science Review*, vol. 75 (June 1981), pp. 381–96.

14. Interview with Eisenhower and Nixon staff person, conducted by Stephen Hess. I have transcribed a selection of Hess's interviews with his permission.

15. George E. Reedy, *The Twilight of the Presidency* (New York: World Publishing, 1970), pp. xiv–xv.

16. Stephen Hess, *Organizing the Presidency*, 2d ed. (Brookings, 1988), p. xi.

17. These and the subsequent model are presented in ibid., p. 254.

18. Quoted in Kernell and Popkin, *Chief of Staff*, p. 62.

19. Hess, *Organizing the Presidency*, p. 254.

20. These forms, primarily those of Richard Tanner Johnson and Roger Porter, are reviewed in John P. Burke, *The Institutional Presidency* (Johns Hopkins University Press, 1992), pp. 54–58. See also Michael Nelson, ed., *Guide to the Presidency* (Washington: Congressional Quarterly, 1989), pp. 934–39.

21. I will limit my discussion to the secretaries of the established cabinet departments in this analysis. Every president appoints other officials to the cab-

inet, typically as a reflection of his interest in a particular issue or sometimes as a signal that the agency in question will later be proposed for departmental status. My interest is in those high-level appointments that represent the president's effort to gain control of the permanent government. These appointments can be compared across presidencies.

22. However, this feature should not be oversold. Governments in many parliamentary systems are formed by coalitions among political parties, thus obscuring accountability.

23. See Hugh Heclo, "The In-and-Outer System: A Critical Assessment," in G. Calvin Mackenzie, ed., *The In-and-Outers: Presidential Appointees and Transition Government in Washington* (Johns Hopkins University Press, 1987), p. 195.

24. Dean Rusk, Oral History Interview, Lyndon Baines Johnson Library, July 28, 1969, p. 7.

25. Nelson W. Polsby, "Presidential Cabinet Making: Lessons for the Political System," *Political Science Quarterly*, vol. 93 (Spring 1978), p. 15.

26. See Jeffrey E. Cohen, *The Politics of the U. S. Cabinet: Representation in the Executive Branch, 1789–1984* (University of Pittsburgh Press, 1988), p. 169.

27. Data collected by the National Academy of Public Administration show a decline in the average tenure of cabinet secretaries from 3.3 years in 1933–65 to 1.9 years in 1964–84. In the latter period, the average tenure for cabinet secretaries was slightly below the average for all top-level appointees (cabinet and subcabinet positions). Linda L. Fisher, "Fifty Years of Presidential Appointments," in Mackenzie, ed., *In-and-Outers*, pp. 22–23.

28. Hugh Heclo, *A Government of Strangers: Executive Politics in Washington* (Brookings, 1977), p. 104.

29. Richard E. Neustadt, *Presidential Power and the Modern Presidents: The Politics of Leadership from Roosevelt to Reagan* (Free Press, 1990), pp. 222–23.

30. Robert J. Donovan, *Conflict and Crisis: The Presidency of Harry S Truman, 1945–1948* (Norton, 1977), pp. 22–23.

31. Clifford, *Counsel to the President*, p. 77.

32. Patrick Anderson contrasted the Roosevelt and Truman White House staffs in this way: "Roosevelt often seemed to be plotting against his aides, playing them off against one another; in Truman's White House most of the plotting was done by the aides, as opposing factions fought an underground battle to shape the President's decisions." *The Presidents' Men: White House Assistants of Franklin D. Roosevelt, Harry S. Truman, Dwight D. Eisenhower, and Lyndon B. Johnson* (Doubleday, 1968), p. 87.

33. Clifford, *Counsel to the President*, pp. 79, 260.

34. Stephen J. Wayne, *The Legislative Presidency* (Harper and Row, 1978), pp. 35–36.

35. G. Calvin Mackenzie, *The Politics of Presidential Appointments* (Free Press, 1981), p. 11.

36. Harold Ickes resigned with Truman's blessing. "He got too big for his breeches," is how the president put it. Cabell Phillips, *The Truman Presidency: The History of a Triumphant Succession* (Macmillan, 1966), p. 157. Henry A.

Wallace was fired. Truman wrote that "Henry is the most peculiar fellow I ever came in contact with." Harry S. Truman, *Memoirs: Year of Decisions* (Doubleday, 1955), p. 560.

37. Mackenzie, *Politics of Presidential Appointments*, p. 11.

38. Hess, *Organizing the Presidency*, p. 41.

39. Anderson, *The Presidents' Men*, p. 133. This is not to say that the Eisenhower White House staff was operating from the first day. It, too, evolved, though with much greater direction.

40. Quoted in Kernell and Popkin, *Chief of Staff*, p. 67.

41. Dwight D. Eisenhower, *Mandate for Change: The White House Years, 1953–1956* (Doubleday, 1963), p. 87.

42. Fred I. Greenstein, *The Hidden-Hand Presidency: Eisenhower as Leader* (Basic Books, 1982), pp. 140, 141.

43. Louis W. Koenig, *The Chief Executive* (Harcourt, Brace and World, 1964), p. 403.

44. Having Adams in charge did not mean that no other staff had access, only that it was controlled and coordinated. One staff aide noted: "President Eisenhower was highly approachable. And there was no clearance necessary. I just went in and out of the president's office." (Interview with former Eisenhower White House staff aide, conducted by Stephen Hess.)

45. Koenig, *The Chief Executive*, p. 400.

46. Eisenhower, *Mandate for Change*, p. 134.

47. Patterson, *Ring of Power*, p. 29.

48. Eisenhower, *Mandate for Change*, p. 99 (emphasis added).

49. Wayne, *The Legislative Presidency*, p. 39. One important modification, as cited in an interview with a Kennedy aide conducted by Stephen Hess, was that Kennedy "did not put people in competition with each other. He was not manipulative in a personal, psychological sense."

50. Cited in Hess, *Organizing the Presidency*, p. 75 (emphasis in original); and Clifford, *Counsel to the President*, p. 329.

51. Quoted in Kernell and Popkin, *Chief of Staff*, p. 76.

52. Arthur Schlesinger, Jr., *A Thousand Days: John F. Kennedy in the White House* (Houghton Mifflin, 1965), p. 687. See also Douglass Cater, *Power in Washington: A Critical Look at Today's Struggle to Govern in the Nation's Capital* (Random House, 1964), p. 98; and Theodore Sorenson, *Kennedy* (Harper and Row, 1965), pp. 259, 262.

53. Sorenson, *Kennedy*, p. 258 (emphasis in original).

54. Ibid., p. 262.

55. Lyndon B. Johnson, *The Vantage Point: Perspectives of the Presidency, 1963–1969* (Holt, Rinehart, and Winston, 1971), p. 19.

56. Wayne, *The Legislative Presidency*, p. 42.

57. Harry McPherson, Oral History Interview, Lyndon B. Johnson Library, December 19, 1968, p. 17.

58. Doris Kearns, *Lyndon Johnson and the American Dream* (Harper and Row, 1976), pp. 174–75.

59. Ibid., p. 173.

60. Hess, *Organizing the Presidency*, p. 103.

61. Quoted in Schlesinger, *A Thousand Days*, p. 127.

62. For details of cabinet selection, see ibid., pp. 127–45; and Sorenson, *Kennedy*, pp. 265–79.

63. Eric F. Goldman, *The Tragedy of Lyndon Johnson* (Alfred A. Knopf, 1969), p. 264.

64. Kearns, *Lyndon Johnson and the American Dream*, p. 253.

65. Hess, *Organizing the Presidency*, pp. 104–05.

66. Kernell and Popkin, *Chief of Staff*, p. 46.

67. Hess, *Organizing the Presidency*, pp. 106, 113. The conflict between Arthur Burns, counselor to the president, and Daniel Patrick Moynihan, assistant to the president for urban affairs, is typically pointed to as an example of multiple advocacy. Yet neither aide stayed very long in his original staff position.

68. H. R. Haldeman (with Joseph DiMona), *The Ends of Power* (Times Books, 1978), p. 58.

69. Interview with former Nixon White House staff aide, conducted by Stephen Hess.

70. Haldeman, *Ends of Power*, p. 52.

71. Alexander P. Butterfield in testimony before the House Committee on the Judiciary, as noted in Wayne, *The Legislative Presidency*, p. 47; and John Ehrlichman, *Witness to Power: The Nixon Years* (Simon and Schuster, 1982), p. 78.

72. Ehrlichman, *Witness to Power*, p. 80.

73. Author's notes from a session with Ehrlichman held at the White Burkett Miller Center, University of Virginia, November 20, 1984.

74. Hess, *Organizing the Presidency*, pp. 116–17.

75. Haldeman, *Ends of Power*, pp. 59, 61.

76. Gerald R. Ford, *A Time to Heal: The Autobiography of Gerald R. Ford* (Harper and Row, 1979), p. 148.

77. Mark J. Rozell, *The Press and the Ford Presidency* (University of Michigan Press, 1992), p. 12.

78. Ford, *A Time to Heal*, p. 24. This group continued to meet, with the president present.

79. Quoted in Kernell and Popkin, *Chief of Staff*, p. 74.

80. Henry Kissinger, *Years of Upheaval* (Little, Brown, 1982), p. 435. In the fall of 1975 Ford appointed General Brent Scowcroft as national security adviser, a decision Kissinger resented bitterly.

81. Ehrlichman, *Witness to Power*, p. 110.

82. Richard M. Nixon, *RN: The Memoirs of Richard Nixon*, vol. 1 (Warner Books, 1978), p. 418.

83. Ibid.

84. Ehrlichman, *Witness to Power*, p. 88 (emphasis in original).

85. See, in particular, Ehrlichman's account of the firing of Walter Hickel as secretary of the interior and the effort to remove George Romney as secretary of housing and urban development. Ibid., pp. 97–101, 104–10.

86. Ibid., p. 111.

87. Stephen E. Ambrose, *Nixon: Ruin and Recovery, 1973–1990* (Simon and Schuster, 1991), p. 14.

88. Henry Kissinger, *White House Years* (Little, Brown, 1979), pp. 1406–07.

89. Ford, *A Time to Heal*, p. 126.

90. Philip W. Buchen, "Reflections on a Politician's President," in Kenneth W. Thompson, ed., *Portraits of American Presidents*, vol. 7: *The Ford Presidency* (New York: University Press of America, 1988), p. 29. Many of those who had given Ford advice on White House organization, including cabinet relationships, discussed their experiences in a day-long conference at the University of Virginia. White Burkett Miller Center at the University of Virginia, *The Ford White House* (Lanham, Md.: University Press of America, 1986).

91. Buchen, in Thompson, ed., *The Ford Presidency*, p. 32.

92. Richard B. Cheney, "Forming and Managing an Administration," in ibid., p. 68.

93. See David R. Mayhew, *Divided We Govern: Party Control, Lawmaking, and Investigations, 1946–1990* (Yale University Press, 1991), chap. 4, esp. pp. 61–67. He shows the Nixon-Ford years to be among the most productive of major legislation of any in the postwar period.

94. James P. Pfiffner, *The Strategic Presidency: Hitting the Ground Running* (Chicago: Dorsey Press, 1988), p. 29.

95. Kernell and Popkin, *Chief of Staff*, pp. 70, 71.

96. Hess, *Organizing the Presidency*, p. 254.

97. Jimmy Carter, *Keeping Faith: Memoirs of a President* (Bantam Books, 1982), pp. 40, 41, 42.

98. Finlay Lewis, *Mondale: Portrait of an American Politician* (Harper and Row, 1980), p. 239.

99. Erwin C. Hargrove, *Jimmy Carter as President: Leadership and the Politics of the Public Good* (Louisiana State University Press, 1988), pp. 23–24.

100. Ibid., p. 26.

101. Haynes Johnson, *In the Absence of Power: Governing America* (Viking Press, 1980), pp. 154–55.

102. John H. Kessel, "The Structures of the Carter White House," *American Journal of Political Science*, vol. 27 (August 1983), p. 460.

103. Charles O. Jones, *The Trusteeship Presidency: Jimmy Carter and the United States Congress* (Louisiana State University Press, 1988), pp. 7–8 (emphasis in original).

104. Hargrove, *Jimmy Carter as President*, p. 31.

105. Carter, *Keeping Faith*, p. 115.

106. Ibid., p. 117.

107. Joseph A. Califano, Jr., *Governing America: An Insider's Report from the White House and the Cabinet* (Simon and Schuster, 1981), pp. 430–31.

108. Hamilton Jordan, *Crisis: The Last Year of the Carter Presidency* (Putnam, 1982), pp. 300–01.

109. Kessel, "Structures of the Carter White House," p. 461.

110. Hargrove, *Jimmy Carter as President*, p. 32.

111. Ibid., p. 30.

112. Carter, *Keeping Faith*, p. 58.

113. Hess, *Organizing the Presidency*, p. 156.

114. One difference was that Carter sought to provide more diversity. He appointed the fourth, fifth, and sixth women, and the first African-American woman. Kennedy appointed no women.

115. Califano, *Governing America*, pp. 429–30.

116. Neustadt, *Presidential Power*, p. 287.

117. Ronald Reagan, *An American Life* (Simon and Schuster, 1990), pp. 222, 225.

118. Lou Cannon, *President Reagan: The Role of a Lifetime* (Simon and Schuster, 1991), p. 70.

119. Ibid., pp. 70, 71.

120. Colin Campbell, *Managing the Presidency: Carter, Reagan, and the Search for Executive Harmony* (University of Pittsburgh Press, 1986), pp. 94, 101–03. Campbell notes that the "triumvirate . . . became a quadrumvirate when William Clark joined the White House in 1982."

121. Donald T. Regan, *For the Record: From Wall Street to Washington* (Harcourt Brace Jovanovich, 1988), pp. 223–29 (quote on p. 227); also see Cannon, *President Reagan*, pp. 558–59.

122. Cannon, *President Reagan*, p. 564.

123. *Report of the President's Special Review Board*, February 27, 1987, p. IV-11. This paragraph is quoted in Regan, *For the Record*, p. 364.

124. Reagan, *An American Life*, pp. 536–37 (emphasis in original).

125. See Cannon, *President Reagan*, pp. 567–69. Cannon also points out that Regan was insufficiently protective of Reagan, not understanding how vulnerable the president was if left on his own (p. 565).

126. Hess, *Organizing the Presidency*, p. 151.

127. Cannon, *President Reagan*, p. 733.

128. Walter Dean Burnham, "The Legacy of George Bush: Travails of an Understudy," in Gerald M. Pomper, ed., *The Election of 1992: Reports and Interpretations* (Chatham, N. J.: Chatham House, 1993), p. 2.

129. Michael Duffy and Dan Goodgame, *Marching in Place: The Status Quo Presidency of George Bush* (Simon and Schuster, 1992), pp. 112, 116–17.

130. For details on staff relationships under Sununu, see Colin Campbell, "The White House and Cabinet under the 'Let's Deal' Presidency," in Colin Campbell and Bert A. Rockman, eds., *The Bush Presidency: First Appraisals* (Chatham, N. J.: Chatham House, 1991), pp. 197–216.

131. Cannon, *President Reagan*, p. 183.

132. William Earl Walker and Michael R. Reopel, "Strategies for Governance: Transition and Domestic Policymaking in the Reagan Administration," *Presidential Studies Quarterly*, vol. 16 (Fall 1986), p. 734.

133. Martin Anderson, *Revolution* (Harcourt Brace Jovanovich, 1988), pp. 197–99.

134. See Peter M. Benda and Charles H. Levine, "Reagan and the Bureaucracy: The Bequest, the Promise, and the Legacy," in Charles O. Jones, ed., *The Reagan Legacy: Promise and Performance* (Chatham, N. J.: Chatham House, 1988), p. 108.

135. Pfiffner, *The Strategic Presidency*, p. 75.

136. Benda and Levine, "Reagan and the Bureaucracy," p. 108 (emphasis in original). See also Campbell, *Managing the Presidency*, pp. 96–101.

137. John H. Kessel, "The Structures of the Reagan White House," *American Journal of Political Science*, vol. 28 (May 1984), p. 246.

138. Anderson, *Revolution*, p. 226.

139. James P. Pfiffner, "Establishing the Bush Presidency," *Public Administration Review*, vol. 50 (January–February 1990), p. 68.

Chapter Four

1. Unless otherwise noted, the approval ratings relied on in this chapter are those of the Gallup Organization, as reported in *The Gallup Opinion Index*, *Public Opinion*, or *American Enterprise*.

2. Jeffrey H. Birnbaum, "Politics and Policy: Bush's Surging Across-the-Board Popularity May Translate into Greater 'Clout' in Congress," *Wall Street Journal*, March 4, 1991, p. A10.

3. "That Was the Easy Part," *Economist*, November 12, 1988, p. 9. The next sentence was more prophetic: "This new president . . . will find that ruling is often a mocking word whose substance will elude him for much of the next four years." Note, however, that the predicted failure to rule is associated with low popularity.

4. As reported in "Rating George Bush," *American Enterprise*, vol. 2 (January–February 1991), p. 96.

5. It should be noted, however, that he had experienced impressive ratings earlier in his administration. From June 1989 to October 1990, his approval score ranged from 60 to 80 percent.

6. Haynes Johnson, "A Nation's Sense of Failure Swept Away by Victory," *Washington Post*, March 1, 1991, p. A2.

7. Birnbaum, "Bush's Surging Across-the-Board Popularity."

8. Mark J. Rozell, *The Press and the Ford Presidency* (University of Michigan Press, 1992), p. 209.

9. Quoted in Birnbaum, "Bush's Surging Across-the-Board Popularity."

10. Quoted in Richard L. Berke, "Democrats to President: Focus on Issues at Home," *New York Times*, March 5, 1991, p. A18.

11. Janet Hook, "Bush Inspired Frail Support for First-Year President," *Congressional Quarterly Weekly Report*, December 30, 1989, p. 3543.

12. Text in "Bush Calls on Postwar Congress for Reform and Renewal," *Congressional Quarterly Weekly Report*, March 9, 1991, p. 624.

13. See Janet Hook, "Hill's Acclaim for Bush in War Won't Bring Peace at Home," *Congressional Quarterly Weekly Report*, March 9, 1991, p. 581.

14. Quoted in ibid.

15. Quoted in Chuck Alston, "Bush's High Public Standing Held Little Sway on Hill," *Congressional Quarterly Weekly Report*, December 28, 1991, p. 3751.

16. Gary C. Jacobson, *The Electoral Origins of Divided Government: Competition in U.S. House Elections, 1946–1988* (Westview Press, 1990), p. 134.

17. Charles O. Jones, "The New, New Senate," in Ellis Sandoz and Cecil V. Crabb, Jr., eds., *A Tide of Discontent: The 1980 Elections and Their Meaning* (Washington: Congressional Quarterly Press, 1981), p. 97.

18. Raymond E. Wolfinger, "Dealignment, Realignment, and Mandates in the 1984 Election," in Austin Ranney, ed., *The American Elections of 1984* (Duke University Press, 1985), p. 295.

19. James W. Ceaser, "The Reagan Presidency and American Public Opinion," in Charles O. Jones, ed., *The Reagan Legacy: Promise and Performance* (Chatham, N. J.: Chatham House, 1988), p. 207.

20. Richard A. Brody, *Assessing the President: The Media, Elite Opinion, and Public Support* (Stanford University Press, 1991), p. 19.

21. Quoted in Rozell, *Press and the Ford Presidency*, p. 220.

22. Richard A. Brody and Benjamin I. Page, "The Impact of Events on Presidential Popularity: The Johnson and Nixon Administrations," in Aaron Wildavsky, ed., *Perspectives on the Presidency* (Little, Brown, 1975), p. 146.

23. John E. Mueller, "Presidential Popularity from Truman to Johnson," *American Political Science Review*, vol. 64 (March 1970), p. 21. For the specific changes in approval coincident with rally events, see Brody, *Assessing the President*, pp. 57–58. Not all events that one might predict to rally the public result in an increase. Summits in particular can result in a loss. See also George C. Edwards III (with Alec M. Gallup), *Presidential Approval: A Sourcebook* (Johns Hopkins University Press, 1990), tables 2.1 and 2.2, pp. 147–49.

24. Rozell, *Press and the Ford Presidency*, pp. 219–20.

25. Charles W. Ostrom, Jr., and Dennis M. Simon, "Promise and Performance: A Dynamic Model of Presidential Popularity," *American Political Science Review*, vol. 79 (June 1985), p. 356.

26. Douglas Rivers and Nancy L. Rose, "Passing the President's Program: Public Opinion and Presidential Influence in Congress," *American Journal of Political Science*, vol. 29 (May 1985), p. 187.

27. George C. Edwards III, *At The Margins: Presidential Leadership of Congress* (Yale University Press, 1989), p. 125.

28. Rivers and Rose, "Passing the President's Program," p. 187.

29. Personal interview, March 27, 1991.

30. Harvey G. Zeidenstein, "Varying Relationships between Presidents' Popularity and Their Legislative Success: A Futile Search for Patterns," *Presidential Studies Quarterly*, vol. 13 (Fall 1983), p. 547.

31. Harvey G. Zeidenstein, "Presidents' Popularity and Their Wins and Losses on Major Issues in Congress: Does One Have Greater Influence over the Other?" *Presidential Studies Quarterly*, vol. 15 (Spring 1985), p. 287.

32. Edwards, *At the Margins*, p. 114.

33. Jon R. Bond and Richard Fleisher, *The President in the Legislative Arena* (University of Chicago Press, 1990), p. 194 (emphasis added).

34. Samuel Kernell, *Going Public: New Strategies of Presidential Leadership* (Washington: Congressional Quarterly Press, 1986), pp. 1, 98.

35. See, for example, Edwards, *At the Margins*, chap. 7; Doris A. Graber, ed., *The President and the American Public* (Philadelphia: Institute for the Study of Human Issues, 1982); and Gary King and Lyn Ragsdale, *The Elusive Executive: Discovering Statistical Patterns in the Presidency* (Washington: Congressional Quarterly Press, 1988), chap. 5.

36. Kernell, *Going Public*, pp. 3–4, 37.

37. Lyndon B. Johnson, *The Vantage Point: Perspectives of the Presidency, 1963–1969* (Holt, Rinehart and Winston, 1971), p. 450.

38. Mueller, "Presidential Popularity," pp. 18–34. Eisenhower's ratings declined less than the others, possibly because of his lesser identity with policies during his years in office.

39. Samuel Kernell, "Explaining Presidential Popularity," *American Political Science Review*, vol. 72 (June 1978), pp. 520, 521. See also Henry C. Kenski, "The Impact of Economic Conditions on Presidential Popularity," *Journal of Politics*, vol. 39 (August 1977), pp. 764–73; and Kristen R. Munroe, *Presidential Popularity and the Economy* (Praeger, 1984).

40. Barbara Hinckley, *The Symbolic Presidency: How Presidents Portray Themselves* (New York: Routledge, 1990), chap. 1; and Lyn Ragsdale, "The Politics of Presidential Speechmaking, 1949–1980," *American Political Science Review*, vol. 78 (December 1984), pp. 971–84.

41. See Edwards, *Presidential Approval*, table 1.2, p. 119.

42. Dean Keith Simonton, *Why Presidents Succeed: A Political Psychology of Leadership* (Yale University Press, 1987), pp. 91–92.

43. Harry S. Truman, *Memoirs: Years of Trial and Hope* (Doubleday, 1956), p. 196.

44. Brody, *Assessing the President*, p. 44.

45. See Edwards, *Presidential Approval*, p. 1.

46. Actually, the Republicans won majorities in both the House and Senate in the 1930 elections by narrow margins, but deaths of Republican House members enabled the Democrats to organize that chamber.

47. For each of the presidents, I rely on Mayhew's list of important enactments, selecting from those programs most often identified with the administration in question. See David R. Mayhew, *Divided We Govern: Party Control, Lawmaking, and Investigations, 1946–1990* (Yale University Press, 1991), pp. 52–73.

48. See James L. Sundquist, *Politics and Policy: The Eisenhower, Kennedy, and Johnson Years* (Brookings, 1968), especially chap. 9.

49. Richard E. Neustadt, *Presidential Power: The Politics of Leadership* (Wiley, 1960), chap. 5.

50. Sundquist, *Politics and Policy*, p. 470.

51. Paul Charles Light, *The President's Agenda: Domestic Policy Choice from Kennedy to Carter* (Johns Hopkins University Press, 1982), pp. 42, 45.

52. Ibid., pp. 112–13. Nixon's overall average number of vetoes was, however, the lowest among postwar Republican presidents. Robert J. Spitzer, *The Presidential Veto: Touchstone of the American Presidency* (State University of New York Press, 1988), p. 75.

53. Mayhew, *Divided We Govern*, pp. 89–90.

54. Ceaser, "The Reagan Presidency," p. 198.

55. Thomas P. O'Neill, Jr. (with William Novak), *Man of the House: The Life and Political Memoirs of Speaker Tip O'Neill* (Random House, 1987), p. 344.

56. Quoted in Gail Gregg, "Reagan Proposes Dramatic Role in Federal Role," *Congressional Quarterly Weekly Report*, March 14, 1981, p. 445.

57. George Bush, too, had a higher exit than entry reading, yet he is unlikely to be remembered as the popular president that his scores would suggest.

58. Bush's average of 52 percent for four years was also the lowest recorded by *Congressional Quarterly*.

59. The vetoes are listed in *Congressional Quarterly Weekly Report*, December 19, 1992, pp. 3925–26.

60. Ratings reported in "Congress's Ratings at an All-Time Low," *American Enterprise*, vol. 3 (November–December 1992), pp. 86–87.

61. Jacobson, *The Electoral Origins of Divided Government*, p. 82. For a review of the literature on the effect of presidential approval, see ibid., pp. 79–82; and Barbara Hinckley, *Congressional Elections* (Washington: Congressional Quarterly, 1981), pp. 116–23.

Chapter Five

1. Since Congress did not meet until late in the odd-numbered years, a number of states held elections in those years. Occasionally these elections occurred *after* a special session of Congress (that is, after March 4), therefore denying the state representation. In 1867 Congress had two special sessions before California's election and therefore the state was not represented in either. See Congressional Quarterly, *Guide to U. S. Elections* (Washington: Congressional Quarterly, 1975), p. 520.

2. Raymond E. Wolfinger, "Dealignment, Realignment, and Mandates in the 1984 Election," in Austin Ranney, ed., *The American Elections of 1984* (Washington: American Enterprise Institute, 1985), p. 293.

3. Henry J. Ford, *Representative Government* (Henry Holt and Company, 1924), p. 271 (emphasis deleted).

4. Robert A. Dahl, *A Preface to Democratic Theory* (University of Chicago Press, 1956), pp. 124, 125, 127, 130.

5. Robert A. Dahl, "Myth of the Presidential Mandate," *Political Science Quarterly*, vol. 105 (Fall 1990), pp. 358–59.

6. Ibid., p. 360.

7. Woodrow Wilson, *Constitutional Government in the United States* (Columbia University Press, 1908), pp. 70, 67–68.

8. Ibid., pp. 70, 68.

9. Quoted in Donald Smith, "Transcript of Carter Interview," *Congressional Quarterly Weekly Report*, September 4, 1976, pp. 2380–83.

10. Jimmy Carter, *Keeping Faith: Memoirs of a President* (Bantam Books, 1982), p. 88.

11. Dahl, "Myth of the Presidential Mandate," p. 363.

12. Ibid., p. 365.

13. Personal interview, July 17, 1989.

14. Dahl, "Myth of the Presidential Mandate," pp. 365–66.

15. Richard E. Neustadt, *Presidential Power and the Modern Presidents: The Politics of Leadership from Roosevelt to Reagan* (Free Press, 1990), chap. 3.

16. Frank R. Baumgartner and Bryan D. Jones, *Agendas and Instability in American Politics* (University of Chicago Press, 1993), p. 4.

17. In a most inventive and interesting study of several countries, John T. S. Keeler examines the opportunities of an election interpreted as providing a strong mandate for change. He shows that "mandate size alone . . . is a very useful predictor of [opportunity] and hence scope of legislative achievement." "Opening the Window for Reform: Mandates, Crises, and Extraordinary Policy-Making," *Comparative Political Studies*, vol. 25 (January 1993), p. 478.

18. Chalmers M. Roberts, "Goldwater Takes Five of Southern States, Withholds Concession," *Washington Post*, November 4, 1964, pp. A1, A12; and "The Vote: Mandate, Hard and Clear," *Time*, November 4, 1964, p. 3.

19. Arthur Krock, "In the Nation: Two Questions in the Wake of the Landslide," *New York Times*, November 5, 1964, p. 44; "The Johnson Landslide," *New York Times*, November 4, 1964, p. 38; and "The Voters Answer," *Washington Post*, November 4, 1964, p. A20.

20. "Reagan Coast-to-Coast," *Time*, November 17, 1980, p. 24.

21. James Reston, "Reagan's Startling Victory," *New York Times*, November 5, 1980, p. 31.

22. David Broder, "A Sharp Right Turn," *Washington Post*, November 6, 1980, p. A1; and "Tidal Wave," *Washington Post*, November 6, 1980, p. A18.

23. Arthur Krock, "Personal Victory," *New York Times*, November 6, 1952, p. 1; and *Time*, November 10, 1952, p. 11.

24. "The Will of the People," *Time*, November 17, 1952, p. 25; "Landslide Sweeps Eisenhower into White House," and "Significance: It Was Time for a Change," *Newsweek*, November 10, 1952, pp. 3, 7; and Walter Lippmann, "A Mighty Majority," *Washington Post*, November 6, 1952, p. 11.

25. Paul Charles Light, *The President's Agenda: Domestic Policy Choice from Kennedy to Carter* (Johns Hopkins University Press, 1982), p. 218.

26. "The Landslide," *Newsweek*, November 12, 1956, p. 62; Dole quoted in Haynes Johnson, "Democrats Battered But Strong," *Washington Post*, November 9, 1972, p. A1; and Haynes Johnson, "Voters Send Up Caution Flags," *Washington Post*, November 8, 1984, p. A48.

27. "The Winner's Burden," *Washington Post*, November 7, 1956, p. A22.

28. Arthur Krock, "The Unmandate," *New York Times*, November 10, 1972, p. 39; and ". . . and Empty Landslide," *New York Times*, November 9, 1972, p. 46.

29. *Time*, November 19, 1984, p. 39.

30. David Broder, "Victory Shows Broad Appeal of President," *Washington Post*, November 7, 1984, p. A1; and "The Mandate, the Mandate," *New York Times*, November 8, 1984, p. A30.

31. David Broder "Voters Again Opt for a Divided Government," *Washington Post*, November 9, 1988, p. 1; David Broder and Paul Taylor, "Once Again, Democrats Debate about Why They Lost," *Washington Post*, November 10, 1988, p. 1; Larry Martz, "The Tough Tasks Ahead," *Newsweek*, November 21, 1988, p. 9; and "A Mandate to Make Sense," *New York Times*, November 11, 1988, p. A30.

32. Arthur Krock, "President Can Claim Big National Triumph," *New York Times*, November 7, 1948, p. E3.

33. Raymond Moley, "The Road Ahead," *Newsweek*, November 8, 1948, p. 8.

34. The sources are, respectively, James M. Naughton, "A Victory, but Not a Mandate," *New York Times*, November 4, 1976, p. 21; "The Presidential Election," *New York Times*, November 10, 1960, p. 46; and "President-elect Richard M. Nixon," *Washington Post*, November 7, 1968, p. A20.

35. Walter Lippmann, "On the Day After," *Washington Post*, November 10, 1960, p. A25.

36. David Broder, "Democratic Edge in House, Senate Trimmed Slightly," *Washington Post*, November 7, 1968, pp. A1, A6.

37. There have been several cases in which the president's party failed to capture a majority in one house in his first term. And both Eisenhower in 1956 and Nixon in 1972 entered their second terms with their party failing to capture a majority in either house. There are also many instances of a president's party losing its majority in one house or both in a midterm election. Finally, there are a few cases when the minority party stayed so after the midterm elections.

38. "The Presidency . . .," *Washington Post*, November 5, 1992, p. A22.

39. Michael Kramer, "What He Will Do," *Time*, November 16, 1992, p. 32 (emphasis in original).

40. Helen Dewar, "On Hill, Clinton Will Find Neither Gridlock Nor Compliance," *Washington Post*, November 5, 1992, p. A25.

41. "The Republican Tide," *New York Times*, November 9, 1966, p. 38.

42. Bruce I. Oppenheimer, James A. Stimson, and Richard W. Waterman, "Interpreting U.S. Congressional Elections: The Exposure Thesis," *Legislative Studies Quarterly*, vol. 11 (May 1986), pp. 227, 243.

43. *New York Times*, November 9, 1950, p. E32; William S. White, "Rayburn to Be Speaker; No Clear Mandate Seen in Results," *New York Times*, November 4, 1954, p. A1; and "Tuesday's 'Mandates': For the President . . .," *Washington Post*, November 7, 1974, p. A30.

44. James L. Sundquist, *Politics and Policy: The Eisenhower, Kennedy, and Johnson Years* (Brookings, 1968), p. 6.

45. Neustadt, *Presidential Power*, p. 5.

46. Bert A. Rockman, *The Leadership Question: The Presidency and the American System* (Praeger, 1984), p. 185.

47. Erwin C. Hargrove and Michael Nelson, *Presidents, Politics, and Policy* (Johns Hopkins University Press, 1984), pp. 196, 197, 198 (emphasis added).

48. Baumgartner and Jones, *Agendas and Instability*, p. 237.

49. Light, *The President's Agenda*, p. 10.

50. Neustadt, *Presidential Power*, p. 8.

51. John W. Kingdon, *Agendas, Alternatives, and Public Policies* (Little, Brown, 1984), p. 25.

52. Baumgartner and Jones, *Agendas and Instability*, p. 241.

53. In particular, see Baumgartner and Jones, *Agendas and Instability*; Kingdon, *Agendas, Alternatives, and Public Policies*; Light, *The President's Agenda*; Roger W. Cobb and Charles D. Elder, *Participation in American Politics: The Dynamics of Agenda-Building* (Boston: Allyn and Bacon, 1972); and Roger Cobb, Jennie-Keith Ross, and Marc Howard Ross, "Agenda Building as a Comparative Political Process," *American Political Science Review*, vol. 70 (March 1976), pp. 126–38. These concepts are presented in slightly different form in Charles O. Jones, "Presidents and Agendas: Who Defines What for Whom?" in James P. Pfiffner, ed., *The Managerial Presidency* (Pacific Grove, Calif.: Brooks/ Cole, 1991), pp. 197–213.

54. Baumgartner and Jones, *Agendas and Instability*, p. 250.

55. Kingdon, *Agendas, Alternatives, and Public Policies*, pp. 3–4.

56. Dwight D. Eisenhower, "State of the Union Message," *Public Papers of the Presidents of the United States: Dwight D. Eisenhower, 1960–61* (Government Printing Office, 1961), p. 930.

57. Sundquist, *Politics and Policy*, p. 507.

58. In fact, the 80th Congress "produced a great deal of legislation." *Congressional Quarterly* lists sixteen items, including the Truman Doctrine, the Marshall Plan, the Taft-Hartley Act, a farm price-support program, and reorganization of the Department of Defense. Congressional Quarterly, *Congress and the Nation, 1945–1964*, vol. 1 (Washington: Congressional Quarterly, 1965), p. 9.

59. Fred I. Greenstein reviews Eisenhower's role in countering McCarthy, arguing it is an example of his "hidden-hand" style of leadership. *The Hidden-Hand Presidency: Eisenhower as Leader* (Basic Books, 1982), chap. 5.

60. For details see Theodore Sorenson, *Kennedy* (Harper and Row, 1965), pp. 236–37.

61. Ibid., p. 340.

62. For a summary, see Congressional Quarterly, *Congress and the Nation, 1969–1972*, vol. 3 (Washington: Congressional Quarterly, 1973), pp. 6–7.

63. However, see A. James Reichley, *Conservatives in an Age of Change: The Nixon and Ford Administrations* (Brookings, 1981), chap. 15, for a review of Ford's priorities.

64. Ibid., p. 325.

65. Congressional Quarterly, *Congress and the Nation, 1973–1976*, vol. 4 (Washington: Congressional Quarterly, 1977), p. 6.

66. Congressional Quarterly, *Congress and the Nation, 1977–1980*, vol. 5 (Washington: Congressional Quarterly, 1981), p. 3.

67. Only one veto of forty-six issued during Bush's full term was overturned, that of the Cable Television Reregulation Act. For the list of vetoes see "President Bush's Vetoes," *Congressional Quarterly Weekly Report*, December 19, 1992, pp. 3925–26.

68. Beth Donovan and Congressional Quarterly staff, "Partisanship, Purse Strings Hobbled the 102nd," *Congressional Quarterly Weekly Report*, October 31, 1992, p. 3451.

Chapter Six

1. Mark A. Peterson, *Legislating Together: The White House and Capitol Hill from Eisenhower to Reagan* (Harvard University Press, 1990), pp. 273, 275.

2. George C. Edwards III, *At the Margins: Presidential Leadership of Congress* (Yale University Press, 1989), p. 220.

3. John B. Bader, "The 86th and 100th Congresses: Changing Goals and a New Definition of Success in Presidential Relations," paper prepared for the 1992 annual meeting of the American Political Science Association.

4. In a study of domestic policy formation, Steven A. Shull examines "modification" as a stage in the policy process. He finds that the president is more influential in the agenda-setting and policy initiation stages and Congress is more active in the modification stage. *Domestic Policy Formation: Presidential-Congressional Partnership?* (Westport, Conn.: Greenwood Press, 1983), chap. 4 and p. 146.

5. Two notable cases in recent years were President Carter's energy program, which moved quickly through the House and then stalled in the Senate, and President Clinton's economic stimulus package, which moved even more swiftly through the House and was then killed by a filibuster in the Senate.

6. James Willard Hurst, *The Growth of American Law: The Law Makers* (Little, Brown, 1950), pp. 23–24, 25, 26.

7. Keith Krehbiel, *Information and Legislative Organization* (University of Michigan Press, 1991), pp. 71, 76.

8. Shull, *Domestic Policy Formation*, chap. 1.

9. This characterization is not exactly what John W. Kingdon argues, but it seems consistent with his identification of various streams of "problems, policies, and politics" that are sometimes joined. *Agendas, Alternatives, and Public Policies* (Little, Brown, 1984), pp. 210–11.

10. Jon R. Bond and Richard Fleisher, *The President in the Legislative Arena* (University of Chicago Press, 1990), p. x.

11. Lawrence H. Chamberlain, *The President, Congress and Legislation* (Columbia University Press, 1946), p. 454.

12. Ibid., p. 453.

13. Ibid., p. 463.

14. Arthur M. Schlesinger, Jr., *The Imperial Presidency* (Houghton Mifflin, 1973); and James MacGregor Burns, Jr., *Presidential Government: The Crucible of Leadership* (Houghton Mifflin, 1965).

15. Samuel P. Huntington, "Congressional Responses in the Twentieth Century," in David B. Truman, ed., *The Congress and America's Future* (Prentice-Hall, 1965), pp. 7, 8. Huntington was moved to suggest that Congress's powers be changed to include a time limit on the approval or disapproval of the president's program, in recognition of the fact that "legislation has become too complex politically to be effectively handled by a representative assembly. The primary work of legislation must be done, and increasingly is being done, by the three 'houses' of the executive branch: the bureaucracy, the administration, and the President" (p. 37).

16. Ronald C. Moe and Steven C. Teel, "Congress as Policy-Maker: A Necessary Reappraisal," *Political Science Quarterly*, vol. 85 (September 1970), pp. 467-68, 469.

17. The utility of roll call votes as a data base has always been the subject of dispute. R. Douglas Arnold finds them of doubtful value for the study of constituency influence: "I am struck by how inconsequential many of these decisions really are." *The Logic of Congressional Action* (Yale University Press, 1990), p. 269. Bond and Fleisher find them of considerable use for studying presidential-congressional relations, believing that few major issues fail to reach the floor. *President in the Legislative Arena*, p. 66.

18. *Congressional Quarterly Almanac, 1989*, p. 28b.

19. Edwards, *At the Margins*, chap. 2; Peterson, *Legislating Together*, app. B; and Bond and Fleisher, *President in the Legislative Arena*, pp. 60-66. The caveats about using support scores apply as well to *Congressional Quarterly*'s "boxscore" of important legislation, which has other serious problems of reliability, mainly the fact that proposals carry over from one session, even one Congress, to the next. As Peterson points out, President Eisenhower proposed statehood for Hawaii every year from 1953 until it finally passed in 1959. Should that be calculated as five defeats and one success? Peterson found significant increases in presidential boxscores when the calendar-year constraint was eliminated. *Legislating Together*, pp. 306-07.

20. Bond and Fleisher, *President in the Legislative Arena*, p. 64. They note that as a result Republican presidential scores tend to be inflated.

21. W. H. Lawrence, "President Backs U.S. Court Order," *New York Times*, September 10, 1957, p. 29.

22. See Stephen E. Ambrose, *Eisenhower: The President* (Simon and Schuster, 1984), pp. 407, 498, and the subsequent discussion of this legislation in chapter 7 of this book.

23. Edwards, *At the Margins*, p. 20.

24. Ibid., p. 25.

25. Bond and Fleisher, *President in the Legislative Arena*, pp. 71-80.

26. Peterson, *Legislating Together*, p. 151.

27. Edwards, *At the Margins*, pp. 223, 217; and Bond and Fleisher, *President in the Legislative Arena*, pp. 225–29.

28. Woodrow Wilson, *Constitutional Government in the United States* (Columbia University Press, 1911), p. 60.

29. James L. Sundquist, "Needed: A Political Theory for the New Era of Coalition Government in the United States," *Political Science Quarterly*, vol. 103 (Winter 1988–89), pp. 629–30 (emphasis in original).

30. James MacGregor Burns, *Congress on Trial: The Legislative Process and the Administrative State* (New York: Gordian Press, 1966), p. 45; and Burns, "U. S., Model for Eastern Europe?" *New York Times*, February 8, 1990, p. A29. Unfortunately Burns did not say what could be learned from the collapsed regimes of Eastern Europe and their struggle to create viable governments.

31. James MacGregor Burns, *The Deadlock of Democracy: Four-Party Politics in America* (Prentice-Hall, 1963).

32. David R. Mayhew, *Divided We Govern: Party Control, Lawmaking, and Investigations, 1946–1990* (Yale University Press, 1991), p. 4.

33. Ibid., p. 35.

34. Ibid., chap. 3. This effort by Mayhew is of great value to scholars of national policymaking. His well-rationalized list of major legislation can now serve as a basis for analysis by others. I am much in his debt since his work spared me a similar task. Peterson (*Legislating Together*) used a very different manner to choose 299 domestic legislative proposals by the president. He drew a random sample, stratified by year, from a total set of 5,069 from 1953 to 1984 (p. 312). I find the Mayhew set more useful because he selected laws, not just proposals, and these laws include both congressional and presidential initiatives.

35. Ibid., p. 76.

36. Mayhew makes this very point in commenting on the insufficiencies of the presidential support score (ibid., p. 35).

37. Ibid., p. 122.

38. Chamberlain, *President, Congress, and Legislation*, p. 453; Kingdon, *Agendas. Alternatives, and Public Policies*, p. 210; Richard E. Neustadt, *Presidential Power: The Politics of Leadership*, (Wiley, 1960), p. 3; Baker quoted in Hedrick Smith, *The Power Game: How Washington Works* (Random House, 1988), p. 652; and Richard Rose, *The Postmodern Presidency: The White House Meets the World*, 2d ed. (Chatham, N. J.: Chatham House, 1991), pp. 175–76.

39. See Kingdon, *Agendas, Alternatives, and Public Policies*, chap. 1.

40. Quoted in Neil MacNeil, *Dirksen: Portrait of a Public Man* (New York: World Publishing, 1970), p. 238.

41. Personal interview, March 26, 1991.

42. Richard F. Fenno, Jr., *Home Style: House Members in Their Districts* (Little, Brown, 1978), pp. 249–57.

43. Mayhew, *Divided We Govern*, p. 198.

44. Neustadt, *Presidential Power*, p. 33.

45. Discussed in detail in Charles O. Jones, "The Separated Presidency—Making It Work in Contemporary Politics," in Anthony King, ed., *The New American Political System* (Washington: American Enterprise Institute, 1990), chap. 1.

Chapter Seven

1. Lawrence H. Chamberlain, *The President, Congress and Legislation* (Columbia University Press, 1946), pp. 450–52. Chamberlain also used a category of "pressure group influence preponderant," primarily to handle tariff acts. I have not found it useful to introduce this category. I use Chamberlain's term *preponderant* rather than the seemingly less awkward *dominant* because they have slightly different meanings. *Preponderant* is defined as "superior in weight, force," suggesting a balance that is tipped in favor of one side. *Dominant* is defined as "ruling or controlling."

2. It is true, of course, that if the cases of high presidential involvement among those in the joint participation category were combined with the cases of presidential preponderance, that category would then be the most numerous (eleven cases). Even so, however, these cases would constitute slightly less than 40 percent of the total.

3. David McCullough, *Truman* (Simon and Schuster, 1992), pp. 561, 562.

4. Text of Marshall speech, in Henry Steele Commager, ed., *Documents of American History*, vol. 2 (Prentice-Hall, 1973), p. 534.

5. McCullough, *Truman*, p. 565.

6. Harold F. Gosnell, *Truman's Crises: A Political Biography of Harry S. Truman* (Westport, Conn.: Greenwood Press, 1980), pp. 354, 356. In his *Memoirs* Truman confirms that he wanted "General Marshall to get full credit for his brilliant contributions to the measure which he helped formulate." Harry S. Truman, *Memoirs: Years of Trial and Hope* (Doubleday, 1956), p. 114. McCullough notes that Clark Clifford urged Truman to identify it as his plan, but "Truman dismissed the idea at once." *Truman*, p. 564.

7. For details see *Congress and the Nation, 1977–1980* (Washington: Congressional Quarterly, 1981), p. 53.

8. Truman, *Memoirs: Years of Trial and Hope*, p. 119.

9. Dwight D. Eisenhower, *Mandate for Change, 1953–1956* (Doubleday, 1963), p. 548.

10. Larry N. Gerston, Cynthia Fraleigh, and Robert Schwab, *The Deregulated Society* (Pacific Grove, Calif.: Brooks/Cole Publishing, 1988), p. 90.

11. "Congress Clears Airline Deregulation Bill," *Congressional Quarterly Almanac*, 1978, p. 496.

12. Martha Derthick and Paul J. Quirk, *The Politics of Deregulation* (Brookings, 1985), pp. 118, 121, 123.

13. Ivor P. Morgan, "Toward Deregulation," in John R. Meyer and Clinton V. Oster, Jr., eds., *Airline Deregulation: The Early Experience* (Boston: Auburn House, 1981), p. 51.

14. For background, see *Food Stamp Reform* (Washington: American Enterprise Institute, 1977), pp. 3–6; Randall B. Ripley, "Legislative Bargaining and the Food Stamp Act, 1964" in Frederic N. Cleaveland, ed., *Congress and Urban Problems* (Brookings, 1969), pp. 279–310; and Gilbert Y. Steiner, *The State of Welfare* (Brookings, 1971), chap. 6.

15. Steiner, *State of Welfare*, p. 203.

16. Ibid., p. 207.

17. Ripley, "Legislative Bargaining," p. 295.

18. Steiner, *State of Welfare*, p. 209.

19. *Congressional Quarterly Almanac*, 1964, p. 115.

20. Frank J. Munger and Richard F. Fenno, Jr., *National Politics and Federal Aid to Education* (Syracuse University Press, 1962), p. 19.

21. Hugh Douglas Price, "Race, Religion, and the Rules Committee: The Kennedy Aid-to-Education Bills," in Alan Westin, *The Uses of Power* (Harcourt, Brace and World, 1962), pp. 2–71. And this does not even account for Republican opposition, primarily based on federal control of the schools through support for teachers' salaries or curriculum management.

22. Quoted in Eugene Eidenberg and Roy D. Morey, *An Act of Congress* (Norton, 1969), p. 93.

23. Eric L. Davis, "Building Presidential Coalitions in Congress: Legislative Liaison in the Johnson White House," Ph.D. dissertation, Stanford University, 1977, p. 195.

24. Randall Strahan, *New Ways and Means: Reform and Change in a Congressional Committee* (University of North Carolina Press, 1990), p. 127.

25. Editorial examples can be found in "The Reagan Paradox," *New York Times*, August 2, 1981, p. 20E; "Democrats' Cut-and-Run Votes," *Washington Post*, July 30, 1981, p. A24; "The Experiment That Now Begins," *Washington Post*, July 31, 1981, p. A20; and "Mr. Reagan's Economy," *Washington Post*, August 2, 1981, p. C6.

26. Truman, *Memoirs: Years of Trial and Hope*, p. 29.

27. James T. Patterson, *Mr. Republican: A Biography of Robert A. Taft* (Houghton Mifflin, 1972), p. 353; and Robert J. Donovan, *Conflict and Crisis: The Presidency of Harry S. Truman, 1945–1948* (Norton, 1977), p. 299.

28. *Congressional Quarterly Almanac*, 1947, p. 280.

29. Patterson, *Mr. Republican*, p. 360. This recounting of Taft's struggle to produce an acceptable bill draws heavily on Patterson's account (pp. 353–61).

30. Donovan, *Conflict and Crisis*, p. 301.

31. "The Labor Bill," *New York Times*, June 5, 1947, p. 24; and "Slave Labor," *Washington Post*, June 6, 1947, p. 18.

32. Patterson, *Mr. Republican*, p. 365.

33. Donovan, *Conflict and Crisis*, p. 302.

34. Samuel C. Patterson, *Labor Lobbying and Labor Reform: The Passage of the Landrum-Griffin Act* (Indianapolis: Bobbs-Merrill, 1966), p. 1.

35. For details see Alan K. McAdams, *Power and Politics in Labor Legislation* (Columbia University Press, 1964), chap. 2; Patterson, *Labor Lobbying*, pp. 2–3; and *Congress and the Nation, 1945–1964*, pp. 604–07.

36. Patterson, *Labor Lobbying*, p. 13.

37. *Congressional Quarterly Almanac*, 1959, p. 162.

38. Patterson, *Labor Lobbying*, p. 18.

39. McAdams, *Power and Politics*, pp. 172–73.

40. Republican Robert Griffin of Michigan, coauthor of the substitute resolution, noted that to his knowledge Eisenhower's speech was the first use of television for generating mail. (Personal conversation, June 3, 1991.)

41. Quoted in "Meany Sees Deal Behind Labor Bill," *New York Times*, September 8, 1959, p. 41; "President Is Pleased," *New York Times*, September 6, 1959, p. 29; and Alvin Shuster, "Labor Bill Gets Mixed Reception," *New York Times*, September 3, 1959, p. 13.

42. Martha Derthick, *Policymaking for Social Security* (Brookings, 1979), p. 364.

43. Ibid., p. 365.

44. R. Kent Weaver points out that "for the president and congressional Republicans, indexing offered a way to depoliticize benefit increases and avoid costly bidding wars that could drive up benefits to unacceptably high levels." *Automatic Government: The Politics of Indexation* (Brookings, 1988), p. 71.

45. *Congressional Record*, June 30, 1972, p. 23733.

46. Weaver, *Automatic Government*, p. 77.

47. Majorie Hunter, "President Signs Bill for Increase of 20% in Old-Age Benefits," *New York Times*, July 2, 1972, pp. 1, 15.

48. Paul R. Portney, "Toxic Substance Policy and the Protection of Human Health," in Portney, ed., *Current Issues in U. S. Environmental Policy* (Johns Hopkins University Press, 1978), p. 106.

49. "Senate Action: Toxic Substances," *Congressional Quarterly Weekly Report*, April 3, 1976, p. 764; and Margaret Hornblower, "Senate Votes Toxic Controls," *Washington Post*, March 27, 1976, p. A1.

50. Mary Russell, "Ford Signs Bill on Toxic Substances," *Washington Post*, October 13, 1976, p. A3.

51. *Congress and the Nation, 1985–1988*, p. 142.

52. The House bill attracted support of nearly a third of the Republicans, who were under pressure to support a get-tough approach. But the bill was very much a Democratic bill at this point.

53. Richard J. Whalen and R. Christopher Whalen, eds., *Trade Warriors: The Guide to the Politics of Trade and Foreign Investment* (Washington: Whalen Company, 1990), pp. 27, 28.

54. Ibid., p. 26.

55. Robert A. Katzmann, "War Powers: Toward a New Accommodation," in Thomas E. Mann, ed., *A Question of Balance: The President, The Congress and Foreign Policy* (Brookings, 1990), p. 35.

56. Richard Nixon, *In the Arena: A Memoir of Victory, Defeat and Renewal* (Simon and Schuster, 1990), p. 205.

57. *Congress and the Nation, 1969–1972*, p. 856.

58. Tom Wicker, "War Power and Real Power," *New York Times*, October 7, 1973, sec. 4, p. 13; and "Foreign Policy Test," *New York Times*, October 15, 1973, p. 36.

59. "Veto Override: A Hint of Watergate, But No Trend Yet," *Congressional Quarterly Weekly Report*, November 10, 1973, p. 2943.

60. James M. Naughton, "Curb on Spending Gains in Congress," *New York Times*, April 17, 1973, p. 24.

61. *Congress and the Nation, 1973–1976*, p. 75.

62. See Richard L. Madden, "Budget Overhaul Is Voted by House," *New York Times*, June 19, 1974, p. 35; and "Budget Revolution," *New York Times*, June 7, 1974, p. 34.

63. Quoted in "Congress Gains Wide Budget Role," *New York Times*, July 13, 1974, p. 6.

64. Nixon, *In the Arena*, p. 206.

65. James L. Sundquist, *Politics and Policy: The Eisenhower, Kennedy, and Johnson Years* (Brookings, 1968), p. 297.

66. Ibid., pp. 302–08.

67. Ibid., p. 317.

68. Wilbur J. Cohen, Oral History, Lyndon B. Johnson Oral History Project, December 8, 1968, tape 2, p. 2.

69. Davis, "Building Presidential Coalitions," p. 159. Davis provides an excellent account of White House lobbying for the bill in chap. 5.

70. John F. Manley, *The Politics of Finance: The House Committee on Ways and Means* (Little, Brown, 1970), p. 150.

71. Davis, "Building Presidential Coalitions," pp. 162–63. See also the accounting in Theodore R. Marmor, *The Politics of Medicare* (Chicago: Aldine Publishing, 1973), chap. 4.

72. For his account, see Lyndon Baines Johnson, *The Vantage Point: Perspectives of the Presidency, 1963–1969* (Holt, Rinehart and Winston, 1971), p. 217.

73. Jimmy Carter, *Keeping Faith: Memoirs of a President* (Bantam Books, 1982), p. 76. See Beryl A. Rabin and Willis D. Hawley, *The Politics of Federal Reorganization: Creating the U.S. Department of Education* (New York: Pergamon Press, 1988), pp. 28–32.

74. For details, see David Stephens, "President Carter, the Congress, and NEA: Creating the Department of Education," *Political Science Quarterly*, vol. 98 (Winter 1983–84), p. 644.

75. Joseph A. Califano, Jr., *Governing America: An Insider's Report from the White House and the Cabinet* (Simon and Schuster, 1981), pp. 274–75.

76. The White House lobbied hard for the bill in the final days of 1978 but to no avail. For details, see Rabin and Hawley, *Politics of Federal Reorganization*, pp. 126–28.

77. For details, see Erwin C. Hargrove, *Jimmy Carter as President: Leadership and the Politics of the Public Good* (Louisiana State University Press, 1988), pp. 60–65.

78. Califano, *Governing America*, p. 284. Stephens notes that "the main casualty of the legislative battle of 1978 was the administration's goal of coordination." "President Carter, the Congress, and NEA," p. 650.

79. *Congress and the Nation, 1977–1980*, p. 670.

80. Stephens, "President Carter, the Congress, and NEA," p. 655.

81. Ibid., p. 656.

82. Majorie Hunter, "Congress Approves Dept. of Education; Victory for Carter," *New York Times*, September 28, 1979, p. 1.

83. Carter, *Keeping Faith*, p. 111. For a review of the early politics on this issue, see Charles O. Jones, "Congress and the Making of Energy Policy," in Robert Lawrence, ed., *New Dimensions to Energy Policy* (Lexington, Mass.: Lexington Books, 1979), chap. 14.

84. *Congressional Quarterly Almanac*, 1979, p. 47E.

85. Richard H. K. Vietor, *Energy Policy in America since 1945: A Study of Business-Government Relations* (Cambridge University Press, 1984), p. 44.

86. Walter A. Rosenbaum, *Energy, Politics, and Public Policy*, 2d ed. (Washington: Congressional Quarterly, 1987), p. 94.

87. Quoted in Adam Clymer, "Republicans Call Energy Speech Political and Vague," *New York Times*, July 16, 1979, p. A11; and Ann Pelham, "Congress 'Ahead of Game' on Energy," *Congressional Quarterly Weekly Report*, July 21, 1979, p. 1436.

88. Joseph A. Yager, "The Energy Battles of 1979," in Craufurd D. Goodwin, ed., *Energy Policy in Perspective: Today's Problems, Yesterday's Solutions* (Brookings, 1981), p. 630.

89. Ibid.

90. For an account, see M. E. Ahrari, "Congress, Public Opinion, and Synfuels Policy," *Political Science Quarterly*, vol. 102 (Winter 1987), pp. 589–606.

91. Discussed in Thomas P. O'Neill, Jr. (with William Novak), *Man of the House: The Life and Political Memoirs of Speaker Tip O'Neill* (Random House, 1987), p. 260.

92. For a review of the early analytical response to the crisis, see Martin Greenberger, *Caught Unawares: The Energy Decade in Retrospect* (Cambridge, Mass.: Ballinger, 1983), chap. 4.

93. Gerald R. Ford, *A Time to Heal: The Autobiography of Gerald R. Ford* (Harper and Row, 1979), p. 339.

94. For details, see "Extending Oil Price Controls: A Long Story," *Congressional Quarterly Almanac*, 1975, p. 221.

95. John E. Chubb, *Interest Groups and the Bureaucracy: The Politics of Energy* (Stanford University Press, 1983), p. 129.

96. James H. Quillen, Republican of Tennessee, quoted in *Congressional Quarterly Almanac*, 1975, p. 235.

97. Quoted in *Congressional Quarterly Almanac*, 1975, pp. 244–45.

98. Ford, *A Time to Heal*, p. 340.

99. Pietro S. Nivola, *The Politics of Energy Conservation* (Brookings, 1986), p. 49.

100. Ford, *A Time to Heal*, pp. 340–41; and William E. Simon, *A Time for Truth* (McGraw-Hill, 1978), p. 79.

101. *Public Papers of the President of the United States: Ronald Reagan, 1983*, bk. 1 (GPO, 1984), p. 107.

102. "The Rush to Misjudgment on Crime," *New York Times*, February 6, 1984, p. A18.

103. See "At Last, A Major Crime Bill," *Washington Post*, October 8, 1984, p. A18; and Stuart Taylor, Jr., "New Crime Act a Vast Change, Officials Assert," *New York Times*, October 15, 1984, pp. A1, B6.

104. Harry S. Truman, *Memoirs: Year of Decisions* (Doubleday, 1955), p. 512.

105. Martin Meyerson, Barbara Terrett, and William L. C. Wheaton, *Housing, People, and Cities* (McGraw-Hill, 1962), p. 287.

106. Patterson, *Mr. Republican*, p. 433.

107. Robert F. Whitney, "Congress Awaits Top Peace Budget; Tax Rise in Doubt," *New York Times*, January 10, 1949, pp. 1, 12.

108. For details, see *A History of the Committee on Rules* (Government Printing Office, 1983), pp. 158–65. The rule lasted for just the 81st Congress.

109. Robert J. Donovan, *Tumultuous Years: The Presidency of Harry S. Truman, 1949–1953* (Norton, 1982), p. 127.

110. For details see, Jacob Javits (with Rafael Steinberg), *Javits: The Autobiography of a Public Man* (Houghton Mifflin, 1981), pp. 143–47.

111. "The People Get Housing," *New York Times*, July 1, 1949, p. 18.

112. Donovan quotes a housing specialist of that time as stating that most of the time Truman "adhered to the real estate lobby's position." *Tumultuous Years*, p. 127.

113. John F. Witte, *The Politics and Development of the Federal Income Tax* (University of Wisconsin Press, 1985), p. 138.

114. Quoted in "Excess Profits Tax: Background," *Congressional Quarterly Almanac*, 1950, p. 671; and *New York Times*, December 6, 1950, p. 21.

115. Witte, *Politics and Development of Federal Income Tax*, p. 139.

116. Truman quoted in John D. Morris, "President Signs Profits-Tax Bill; Sees Much Heavier Levies Needed," *New York Times*, January 4, 1951, p. 1. For editorial comment, see, for example, "Second Defense Tax Bill," *New York Times*, December 27, 1950, p. 26; and "Excess Profits," *Washington Post*, December 26, 1950, p. 8.

117. J. W. Anderson, *Eisenhower, Brownell, and the Congress: The Tangled Origins of the Civil Rights Bill of 1956–1957* (University of Alabama Press, 1964), p. 1.

118. Eisenhower, *Mandate for Change*, pp. 235, 234.

119. Sundquist, *Politics and Policy*, pp. 227–28.

120. John D. Morris, "Congress Reacts Calmly to Speech," *New York Times*, January 11, 1957, p. 11; and John D. Morris, "Democrats Agree to Senate Test for Civil Rights," *New York Times*, January 12, 1957, p. 1.

121. Sundquist, *Politics and Policy*, p. 233 (emphasis in original). See also Howard E. Shuman, "Senate Rules and the Civil Rights Bill: A Case Study," *American Political Science Review*, vol. 51 (December 1957), pp. 955–57.

122. Sundquist, *Politics and Policy*, pp. 234–35. In addition to Sundquist's account, see that in Javits, *Javits*, chap. 18.

123. William S. White, "President Bars Ballot on Rights; Would Hear Foes," *New York Times*, July 4, 1957, pp. 1, 20.

124. Stephen E. Ambrose, *Eisenhower: The President*, vol. 2 (Simon and Schuster, 1984), p. 407.

125. See "As Congress Goes Home," *New York Times*, August 31, 1957, p. 14; and "Rights and Face-Savings," *Washington Post*, August 23, 1957, p. A16

126. Ambrose, *Eisenhower*, vol. 2, p. 410.

127. See Witte, *Politics and Development of the Federal Income Tax*, pp. 156–57.

128. Ibid., p. 157.

129. Theodore Sorenson, *Kennedy* (Harper and Row, 1965), p. 394.

130. *Congress and the Nation, 1945–1964*, p. 431.

131. John D. Morris, "Senate Approves Tax Bill in Diluted Form, 59 to 24," *New York Times*, September 7, 1962, p. 1; and *Congressional Quarterly Almanac*, 1962, p. 504.

132. Nelson W. Polsby, *Political Innovation in America: The Politics of Policy Initiation* (Yale University Press, 1984), p. 18.

133. Mark Hertsgaard, *Nuclear Inc.: The Men and Money behind Nuclear Energy* (Pantheon Books, 1983), p. 30.

134. Ibid., p. 31.

135. Eisenhower, *Mandate for Change*, p. 253.

136. Harold P. Green and Alan Rosenthal, *Government of the Atom: The Integration of Powers* (New York: Atherton Press, 1963), pp. 121–22, 125; see also Lewis L. Strauss, *Men and Decisions* (Doubleday, 1962), p. 313.

137. For details of his participation, see Richard Wayne Dyke, *Mr. Atomic Energy: Congressman Chet Holifield and Atomic Energy Affairs, 1945–1974* (New York: Greenwood Press, 1989), chap. 4.

138. Green and Rosenthal, *Government of the Atom*, p. 159.

139. *Congress and the Nation, 1945–1964*, p. 281; and Dyke, *Mr. Atomic Energy*, p. 101.

140. Eisenhower, *Mandate for Change*, p. 303. The president only mentions that it came to him for his signature along with other legislation during the month of August.

141. James T. Patterson, *America's Struggle against Poverty, 1900–1985* (Harvard University Press, 1986), p. 126.

142. *Congressional Quarterly Almanac*, 1961, p. 492.

143. Sar A. Levitan and Robert Taggart, *The Promise of Greatness* (Harvard University Press, 1976), p. 134.

144. Patterson, *America's Struggle against Poverty*, p. 127.

145. Sundquist, *Politics and Policy*, p. 87.

146. See the editorials "Jobless Tide Recedes," *New York Times*, March 9, 1962, p. 28; and "Help Wanted," *New York Times*, March 15, 1962, p. 34. See Patterson, *America's Struggle against Poverty*, pp. 128–29, for a summary of subsequent criticism.

147. Quoted in Randall B. Ripley, "Congress and Clean Air: The Issue of Enforcement, 1963," in Frederic N. Cleaveland, ed., *Congress and Urban Problems* (Brookings, 1969), p. 235. This section relies heavily on Ripley's account, along with that by Sundquist, *Politics and Policy*, pp. 351–55; and Charles O. Jones, *Clean Air: The Policies and Politics of Pollution Control* (University of Pittsburgh Press, 1975), pp. 71–76.

148. Ripley, "Congress and Clean Air," pp. 248–49.

149. Ibid., p. 251.

150. Ibid., pp. 277–78.

151. Michael D. Reagan, *Regulation: The Politics of Policy* (Little, Brown, 1987), p. 25.

152. Graham K. Wilson, *The Politics of Safety and Health: Occupational Safety and Health in the United States and Britain* (Oxford: Clarendon Press, 1985), p. 36.

153. House Republican leaders considered opposing the compromise until the secretary of labor informed them of Nixon's approval. David E. Rosenbaum, "Bill on Job Safety Sent to Nixon," *New York Times*, December 18, 1970, p. 19.

154. Martha Derthick, *Agency under Stress: The Social Security Administration in American Government* (Brookings, 1990), pp. 91–92 (emphasis in original).

155. For an overview, see Paul C. Light, *Artful Work: The Politics of Social Security Reform* (Random House, 1985), chap. 4; and Richard E. Neustadt and Ernest R. May, *Thinking in Time: The Uses of History for Decision Makers* (Free Press, 1986), pp. 17–20.

156. Light, *Artful Work*, p. 101.

157. See Lou Cannon, *President Reagan: The Role of a Lifetime* (Simon and Schuster, 1991), pp. 244–48.

158. Light, *Artful Work*, pp. 122–23.

159. Neustadt and May, *Thinking in Time*, p. 21.

160. Light, *Artful Work*, p. 124; and David A. Stockman, *The Triumph of Politics: How the Reagan Revolution Failed* (Harper and Row, 1986), p. 191.

161. Harrison Donnelly, "Senate Opposes Social Security Cuts," *Congressional Quarterly Weekly Report*, May 23, 1981, p. 895.

162. Stockman, *Triumph of Politics*, p. 192.

163. The story of how it worked and what it produced is well told in other sources, primarily Light, *Artful Work*, chaps. 12–15.

164. Ibid., p. 232.

165. *Congressional Quarterly Almanac*, 1990, p. 127.

166. Ibid., p. 128.

167. Barbara Sinclair, "Governing Unheroically (and Sometimes Unappetizingly): Bush and the 101st Congress," in Colin Campbell and Bert A. Rockman, eds., *The Bush Presidency: First Appraisals* (Chatham, N. J.: Chatham House, 1991), p. 175.

168. Ibid., p. 176.

169. The midyear review projected a $168.8 billion deficit, in part, it was said, to create a crisis atmosphere so as to get Congress to act. David E. Rosenbaum, "Estimate on Deficit Is Raised Sharply," *New York Times*, July 17, 1990, p. A14.

170. Text in *Congressional Quarterly Almanac*, 1990, p. 131.

171. Quoted in ibid., p. 134.

172. Sinclair, "Governing Unheroically," p. 181.

173. This result is consistent with Mayhew's finding that a large majority of important pieces of legislation were enacted with broad support: 186 of the 267

laws in his sample were "passed by two-thirds majorities in both houses *and* they won the backing of Democratic and Republican majorities in both houses." David R. Mayhew, *Divided We Govern: Party Control, Lawmaking, and Investigations, 1946–1990* (Yale University Press, 1991), p. 124.

174. David W. Rohde, *Parties and Leaders in the Postreform House* (University of Chicago Press, 1991), p. 175.

Chapter Eight

1. Sidney M. Milkis, *The President and the Parties: The Transformation of the American Party System since the New Deal* (Oxford University Press, 1993), pp. viii, ix. Milkis concludes that the decline of parties is the result of a "partisan project, one sponsored by the Democratic party and built on the foundation of the New Deal realignment" (p. 300).

2. David R. Mayhew, *Divided We Govern: Party Control, Lawmaking, and Investigations, 1946–1990* (Yale University Press, 1990).

3. James L. Sundquist, "Needed: A Political Theory for the New Era of Coalition Government in the United States," *Political Science Quarterly*, vol. 103 (Winter 1988-89), pp. 629–30 (emphasis in original).

4. In fact, the connections from the voters' perspective may be blurred the longer the period of split-party government continues. This is a topic that should attract greater scholarly treatment.

5. The list of bad news for Congress during the Bush presidency extended beyond the banking scandal: the resignations of Speaker Jim Wright and Majority Whip Tony Coelho, a prolonged pay raise issue, the protracted 1990 budget agreement, the "Keating five" hearings and report in the Senate, the Clarence Thomas confirmation hearings before the Senate Committee on the Judiciary, "grandfathering" the personal use of campaign funds, even the high rate of return of incumbents in 1990 at the height of the term-limitation debate. By March 1992 the public approval rating for Congress stood at 17 percent, half that of President Bush. "Public Opinion and Demographic Report: Congress, My Congressman," *American Enterprise*, vol. 3 (May–June 1992), p. 102.

6. The Committee on the Constitutional System, founded in 1981 with a distinguished membership of former government officials, exists precisely to explore and promote changes that will produce a different constitutional order. For some of what is recommended, see James L. Sundquist, *Constitutional Reform and Effective Government*, rev. ed. (Brookings, 1992).

7. They are, as well, related to the categories of reforms suggested many years ago by Roger H. Davidson, David M. Kovenock, and Michael K. O'Leary, *Congress in Crisis: Politics and Congressional Reform* (Belmont, Calif.: Wadsworth Publishing, 1966), chap. 1. See also the variations proposed in Charles O. Jones, "Congress and the Constitutional Balance of Power," in Christopher J. Deering, ed., *Congressional Politics* (Chicago: Dorsey Press, 1989), pp. 322–37.

8. Incumbent returns have been relatively high in the most recent Senate elections, but many have been by narrow margins.

9. Richard E. Neustadt, *Presidential Power: The Politics of Leadership* (Wiley, 1960), chap. 5.

10. E. E. Schattschneider, *Two Hundred Million Americans in Search of a Government* (New York: Holt, Rinehart and Winston, 1969), p. 53. Interestingly, it was Schattschneider, in his influential book, *Party Government* (Holt, Rinehart and Winston, 1942), and in his leadership of the APSA Committee on Political Parties, who was a principal promoter of the party responsibility perspective. Presumably this meant that he was certain that a political party, if not the people, could be right.

Index